JOURNAL FOR THE STUDY OF THE NEW TESTAMENT
SUPPLEMENT SERIES
1

Editors
Ernst Bammel
Anthony Hanson
David Hill
Max Wilcox

Editorial Secretary
Bruce D Chilton

Department of Biblical Studies
The University of Sheffield
Sheffield S10 2TN
England

THE BARREN TEMPLE AND THE WITHERED TREE

A redaction-critical analysis of the Cursing
of the Fig-Tree pericope in Mark's Gospel
and its relation to the Cleansing of the
Temple tradition.

WILLIAM R. TELFORD

Journal for the Study of the New Testament
Supplement Series 1

Sheffield
1980

Copyright © 1980 JSOT Press

ISSN 0143-5108
ISBN 0 905774 20 5

Published by
JSOT Press
Department of Biblical Studies
The University of Sheffield
Sheffield S10 2TN
England

Artwork by Roger Evans
Sheffield University Printing Unit

Printed by Redwood Burn Limited
Trowbridge & Esher
Printed in Great Britain
1980

British Library Cataloguing in Publication Data

Telford, William R.
   The barren temple and the withered tree.-('Journal
   for the study of the New Testament' supplement
   series; 1
   ISSN 0143-5108).
   1. Cursing of the fig tree (Miracle)
   I. Title   II. Series
   226'.7   BT367.C/

   ISBN 0-905774-20-5

To Andrena

CONTENTS

PREFACE

This investigation has as its overall aim the task of ascertaining the attitude taken to the Temple by the author of the earliest gospel, Mark, and the community to which and for which he speaks. In narrower and more concrete terms, it is concerned with one of the most curious miracle stories in the Jesus tradition, viz, his cursing of the barren fig-tree (Mk.11. 12-14, 20ff.), a story which is seen as supplying a vital clue to that attitude. The place and function of this pericope within Mark's redactional scheme, its subsequent redaction-history within the gospels, its origin, background and Sitz im Leben prior to Mark, and its particular connection with the Cleansing tradition form the basic core of the enquiry.

In this study, I have sought the answer to a twofold question. What did Mark intend this puzzling story to convey in its present context, and how in turn was it likely to have been understood by the first-century reader for whom it was intended? Investigations, therefore, have proceeded along two main lines. In the first place, literary-, form-, source- and redaction-critical work on the Synoptic gospels, and on Mark in particular, has been brought to bear on the pericope. In the second place, I have sought to trace certain related motifs pertaining to our story within background material supplied by the Old Testament, late Judaism and early Christianity. (A further chapter on the Graeco-Roman background, corroborating my findings in these three areas, has unfortunately had to be omitted, but it is hoped that it can be published separately at some future date.) In particular, the place of the tree and fig-tree within this material has been examined, and their literary, religious and symbolic usage explored. The aim has been to construct thereby a conceptual pattern or grid of related ideas and associations that will enable us to place ourselves within the interpretative frame of reference that might have been adopted by a first-century reader of the gospel.

This work was originally submitted in 1976 as a dissertation for Cambridge University, and as such is the result of my independent research into both the primary and secondary literature. For its content and conclusions, therefore, I alone am responsible. However, there are a number of people whose help I wish to acknowledge. I should like, first of all, to express my sincere thanks to Dr. Ernst Bammel, under whose supervision the dissertation was written. During that time, I benefited greatly from his seemingly inexhaustible fund of knowledge, from his high standard of scholarship, and from the continual stimulation he provided. I wish also to record my grateful thanks to Professor C.F.D. Moule for the advice and inspiration he too gave me during my period of research, and to express my appreciation of the constant interest and support I received from my former teacher and mentor at Glasgow, the late Dr. William Barclay.

In addition, I am most grateful to Professor Graham Stanton, Dr. William Horbury, Dr. David Rhoads, Professor J. Duncan M. Derrett and Professor A.T. Hanson, who have read the manuscript and have made helpful and encouraging comments on it. Thanks are also due to Oxford University Faculty of Theology for a grant towards the re-typing of the manuscript, to the University of Newcastle for a grant towards the publication of the book, to the editors of the *Journal for the Study of the New Testament*, and, in particular, to Dr. Bruce Chilton, whose help and support in connection with its publication have been invaluable. May I also express my gratitude to my former colleagues at Mansfield College, Oxford, and to my parents, parents-in-law and friends for the encouragement they have provided. But, above all, to my wife, Andrena, who in the midst of her own work, has devoted so much time and care both to her husband and to this book, my love and appreciation are offered.

The Jewish Law, declared the Rabbis, could be compared to the fig-tree. "As with the fig-tree, the more one searches it, the more figs one finds in it, so it is with the words of the Torah; the more one studies them, the more relish he finds in them" (B.'Erub. 54a-54b). Something similar might be claimed for the Cursing of the Fig-Tree pericope in Mark's gospel. The more I have searched it, the more figs I have found in it, and the more I have studied it, the greater my relish has been!

Department of Religious Studies,   William R. Telford
University of Newcastle upon Tyne,
January, 1980.

ABBREVIATIONS

AAA	Acta Academiae Aboensis
AJT	American Journal of Theology
AKG	Arbeiten zur Kirchengeschichte (ed. E. Hirsch, H. Lietzmann)
AKGW	Abhandlungen der königlichen Gesellschaft der Wissenschaften zu Göttingen
Angelos	Angelos. Archiv für neutestamentliche Zeitgeschichte und Kulturkunde
ANL	Ante-Nicene Christian Library
Ant.	Josephus, *Antiquitates Judaicae*
AO	Anecdota Oxoniensia
Ap.	Josephus, *Contra Apionem*
ASNU	Acta Seminarii Neotestamentici Upsaliensis (Uppsala)
B-B-H	G. Bornkamm, G. Barth, H.J. Held, *Tradition and Interpretation in Matthew* (1963)
B-D-F	F. Blass, A. Debrunner, *A Greek Grammar of the New Testament and Other Early Christian Literature* (transl. ed. R.W. Funk)
BEHE	Bibliothèque de l'École des Hautes Études
BETL	Bibliotheca Ephemeridum Theologicarum Lovaniensium
BFChTh	Beiträge zur Förderung christlicher Theologie
BiLeb	Bibel und Leben (ed. G.J. Botterweck, A. Vögtle)
B.J.	Josephus, *Bellum Judaicum*
BJRL	The Bulletin of the John Rylands Library
BK	Biblischer Kommentar. Altes Testament. Ed. M. Noth, 1955 ff.

BRW(Winer)	G.B. Winer, *Biblisches Realwoerterbuch* (3rd edn., 1847-8)
BS	Bollingen Series
BSt	Biblische Studien
BZ	Biblische Zeitschrift
BZNW	Beihefte zur Zeitschrift für die neutestamentliche Wissenschaft
CBC	W.K. Lowther Clarke, *Concise Bible Commentary* (London, 1952)
CBQMS	The Catholic Biblical Quarterly Monograph Series (ed. J.A. Fitzmyer et al.)
CBSC	The Cambridge Bible for Schools and Colleges
CR	The Classical Review
CThL	Crown Theological Library
DB	*Dictionary of the Bible* (ed. J. Hastings)
DB^2	*Dictionary of the Bible* (ed. F.C. Grant, H.H. Rowley), 2nd edn., 1963
DCG	*Dictionary of Christ and the Gospels* (ed. J. Hastings)
EBib	Études Bibliques (Paris)
EHPR	Études d'histoire et de philosophie religieuses (ed. R. Mehl)
EJR	*Encyclopedia of the Jewish Religion* (ed. R.J.Z. Werblowsky, G. Wigoder)
EJud	*Encyclopaedia Judaica* (ed. C. Roth, G. Wigoder)
EncBib	*Encyclopaedia Biblica* (ed. T.K. Cheyne, J.S. Black)
ET	Expository Times
ETal	*Encyclopedia Talmudica* (ed. M. Berlin)
Exp	The Expositor
ExpGT	The Expositor's Greek Testament
FRLANT	Forschungen zur Religion und Literatur des Alten und Neuen Testaments

Fs.	Festschrift
HBA(Riehm)	Handwörterbuch des biblischen Altertums (ed. E.C.A. Riehm)
HC	Hand-Commentar zum Neuen Testament (ed. H.J. Holtzmann et al.)
HeythJ	Heythrop Journal
HNT	Handbuch zum Neuen Testament (founded H. Lietzmann, ed. G. Bornkamm)
ICC	The International Critical Commentary
IDB	*Interpreter's Dictionary of the Bible* (ed. G.A. Buttrick, 1963)
ILCK	International Library of Christian Knowledge
JAAR	Journal of the American Academy of Religion
JBL	Journal of Biblical Literature
JPOS	Journal of the Palestine Oriental Society
JTS	Journal of Theological Studies
KlT	Kleine Texte für theologische und philologische Vorlesungen und Übungen (founded H. Lietzmann, ed. K. Aland)
KNT	Kommentar zum Neuen Testament (ed. T. Zahn)
LCQ	Lutheran Church Quarterly
LTT	Library of Theological Translations (ed. W. Barclay)
Meyer-Dickson	H.A.W. Meyer, *The Gospels of Mark and Luke* (MeyerK, 5th edn., transl. R.E. Wallis, ed. W.P. Dickson, 1880. Vols. I & II)
MeyerK	Kritisch exegetischer Kommentar über das Neue Testament (founded H.A.W. Meyer)
Meyer-Weiss	H.A.W. Meyer, *Die Evangelien des Markus und Lukas* (MeyerK, 8th edn., ed. B. Weiss, J. Weiss, 1892. 1st Div., Pt.2)
M-H	*A Grammar of New Testament Greek,* Vol. II, ed. J.H. Moulton, W.F. Howard (1929)
M-T	*A Grammar of New Testament Greek,* Vol III; ed. J.H. Moulton, N. Turner (1963)

NCHS	New Commentary on Holy Scripture
NLC	New London Commentary
NovTest	Novum Testamentum
NovTSup	Supplements to Novum Testamentum
NRTh	Nouvelle Revue Théologique
NTD	Das Neue Testament Deutsch (ed. P. Althaus, J. Behm)
NThS	Nieuwe Theologische Studiën
NTL	The New Testament Library (ed. A. Richardson et al.)
NThT	Nieuw Theologisch Tijdschrift
NTTS	New Testament Tools and Studies (Leiden)
NTS	New Testament Studies
NTSR	New Testament for Spiritual Reading
OCBC	Oxford Church Biblical Commentary
OTL	The Old Testament Library (ed. P. Ackroyd et al.)
Peake	*Commentary on the Bible* (ed. A.S. Peake, A.J. Grieve, 1919)
PGC	Pelican Gospel Commentaries (Harmondsworth)
PRE (Herzog-Hauck)	*Realencyklopädie für protestantische Theologie und Kirche,* 3rd edn. (ed. J.J. Herzog, A. Hauck)
RAC	*Reallexikon für Antike und Christentum* (ed. T. Klauser)
RB	Revue Biblique
RE (Hamburger)	*Real-Encyclopädie des Judentums* (ed. J. Hamburger)
RE (Pauly-Wissowa)	*Real-Encyclopädie der classischen Altertumswissenschaft* (ed. A. Pauly, G. Wissowa)
RheinMus	Rheinisches Museum für Philologie
RNT	Regensburger Neues Testament (ed. A. Wikenhauser, O. Kuss)

SBL	Society of Biblical Literature
SC	Sources chrétiennes (Paris)
SLG	Societas Litterarum Gottingensis
SNVAO	Skrifter utgitt av Den Norske Videnskaps-Akademi i Oslo
Solms-Laubach	H. Graf zu Solms-Laubach, *Die Herkunft, Domestication und Verbreitung des gewöhnlichen Feigenbaums* (1882)
SPB	Studia Post-Biblica (Leiden)
SSG	Societas Scientiarum Gottingensis
Str-B	H.L. Strack, P. Billerbeck, *Kommentar zum Neuen Testament aus Talmud und Midrasch*
SUNT	Studien zur Umwelt des Neuen Testament (ed. K.G. Kuhn)
TCL	Translations of Christian Literature (ed. W.J. Sparrow Simpson, W.K. Lowther Clarke)
ThD	Theologische Dissertationen (ed. Bo Reicke)
ThDNT	*Theological Dictionary of the New Testament* (ed. G. Kittel, transl.ed. G.W. Bromiley)
ThHK	Theologischer Handkommentar zum Neuen Testament
ThLZ	Theologische Literaturzeitung
ThStKr	Theologische Studien und Kritiken
ThTL	Theological Translation Library
UBS	United Bible Societies
UUÅ	Uppsala Universitets Årsskrift
VAA	Verhandelingen der koninklijke Akademie van Wetenschappen, Amsterdam
VAKMF	Veröffentlichungen der Alexander Kohut Memorial Foundation
VBW	Vorträge der Bibliothek Warburg (ed. F. Saxl)
v.l.	varia lectio
VT	Vetus Testamentum

YJS	Yale Judaica Series
ZNW	Zeitschrift für die neutestamentliche Wissenschaft
ZSTh	Zeitschrift für systematische Theologie
ZThK	Zeitschrift für Theologie und Kirche
ZWTh	Zeitschrift für wissenschaftliche Theologie

Book and article titles, it should be noted, are given in full when first cited but are thereafter shortened, with one or two key words of the title constituting the abbreviation. In the case of articles, the Journal reference alone is usually repeated. For our abbreviations of the Biblical books we have followed the Jerome Biblical Commentary (London: Geoffrey Chapman, 1970). For Rabbinical references, *vide infra*, p.124, n.50. For all outstanding abbreviations, see both the JBC and *Die Religion in Geschichte und Gegenwart*, 3rd edn., ed. K. Galling, Vol.I (Tübingen: J.C.B. Mohr, 1957).

Chapter I

THE CURSING OF THE FIG-TREE PERICOPE:
A HISTORY OF THE INVESTIGATION OF ITS PROBLEMS

The Variety of Hermeneutical Approaches

If the title of this chapter recalls that of Professor Kümmel's standard work on the Hermeneutics of the New Testament /1/, then this is no accident, for the variety of hermeneutical approaches taken to our passage over the last one hundred and fifty years reflects, in microcosm, the approaches that have been taken to the problems of New Testament exegesis overall during this period. The past century and a half has witnessed the development of a bewildering array of methodological tools which have been employed, sometimes in opposition to one another, to 'open up' the New Testament and its world to the contemporary reader. From the 'grammatico-historical' method advanced by K.A.G. Keil in 1788 and taken up in H.A.W. Meyer's *Critical and Exegetical Commentary on the New Testament* (1829), we have seen the 'consistently historical' approach of the Tübingen school (cf. D.F. Strauss, F.C. Baur), the idealistic, liberal view of the Life-of-Jesus school (e.g. H.J. Holtzmann), the 'religionsgeschichtlich' approach taken by the History-of-Religions school (e.g. H. Gunkel, G. Dalman, W. Bousset), the emphasis placed on 'consistent eschatology' (cf. J. Weiss, A. Schweitzer), the 'radical historical' view (e.g. W. Wrede, A. Loisy), the rationalist, historical and mainly conservative approach taken by the majority of English-speaking scholars (e.g. R.C. Trench, E.P. Gould, H.B. Swete, F.C. Burkitt, T.W. Manson), the literary-critical approach taken by the majority of German scholars (e.g. J. Wellhausen, E. Klostermann, E. Wendling), Formgeschichte (e.g. H. Gunkel, K.L. Schmidt, M. Dibelius, R. Bultmann), Redaktionsgeschichte (e.g. G. Bornkamm, W. Grundmann, J. Schniewind, N. Perrin), and, of late, a considerable interest in the value of the background provided by the Old Testament, Rabbinical literature and midrashic studies.

The task before us, then, will be to summarize the contributions made by German, French and English-speaking commentators to the exegesis of the Cursing of the Fig-tree story over these last one hundred and fifty years, and thus, in the light of these developments in Hermeneutics, to ascertain the present state of the enquiry.

The Nineteenth Century

In 1829, H.A.W. Meyer wrote:

The area of dogmatics and philosophy is to remain off limits
for a commentary. For to ascertain the meaning the author
intended to convey by his words, impartially and historico-
grammatically - that is the duty of the exegete. How the
meaning so ascertained stands in relation to the teachings
of philosophy, to what extent it agrees with the dogmas of
the church or with the views of its theologians, in what way
the dogmatician is to make use of it in the interest of his
science - to the exegete as an exegete, all that is a matter
of no concern./2/

Despite these bold words, Meyer himself shared with other
nineteenth-century commentators on the Markan story a common
concern, viz, to remove the *moral* difficulties of the story and
to offset the impression of 'unreasonableness' on Jesus' part
that the story appears to convey. For these exegetes, Jesus was
a moral hero, an ethical giant cast in an essentially nineteenth-
century heroic mould, the proclaimer of the Kingdom of God as a
lofty, universal, spiritual 'idea', and above all - a gentleman!
Regarded as an actual historical occurrence taking place at the
Passover season, this incident, and especially the words of 11.13d,
seemed to cast doubt on Jesus' reasonableness in expecting fruit
from the tree when "it was not the season for figs" /3/.

In general four main solutions were advanced. In the first
place, emendations to the text were made and different nuances for
the words were suggested /4/. A second approach was to ascribe the
words to a glossator /5/. In the third place, evidence was adduced
to show that some form of edible figs could be found at this time
of year, neglected figs of last season's crop that had remained on
the tree over the *winter* /6/, or immature first-ripe figs, or
green knops (פגים), which, though not ripe until May or June, may
have been digestible /7/, or even *first-ripe figs* themselves
(בכורים), whose maturation had been hastened by exceptionally
clement weather /8/. Other commentators, however, accepting the
text as it stood, read the enigmatic and seemingly contradictory
nature of this datum as a sign that the incident was to be
regarded in a symbolic light /9/.

Later scholarship has, in the main, forsworn the nineteenth-
century scholar's exaggerated recourse to textual emendation but

the 'gloss' theory has been championed by certain scholars, most
notably Adalbert Merx, who published his important text-critical
work, *Die vier kanonischen Evangelien*, in the period 1897-1911.   On
the strength of the evidence from the recently discovered Codex
Syriacus (in which the γάρ of 11.13d is lacking) and from the
considerable variation in word-order evidenced by the Greek
manuscripts, Merx argued that 11.13d had originally been a marginal
comment which had been incorporated into the Markan text and
subsequently attached more closely to the context with the
connective γάρ /10/.

A popular explanation for the gloss has been, in turn, the
suggestion that the pericope has been chronologically misplaced.
Originally associated with a different period of the year (e.g.
Tabernacles), the pericope came to be connected with the Passover
season. A comment to that effect has therefore been added, either
by a post-Markan scribe /11/, or even perhaps in the pre-Markan
tradition /12/. Other scholars, however, have been of the opinion
that the explanatory but awkward comment linking the pericope to
the Passover season might equally be ascribed to Mark himself /13/.

The debate over Jesus' expectation of figs has likewise
carried over into the twentieth century. The 'winter figs' theory
(a theory at least as old as Ephrem /14/) was espoused by Strack-
Billerbeck and followed by Hauck, Hirsch and Grundmann /15/.
Jesus, Billerbeck maintained, could not have hoped to find first-
ripe figs at the Passover season. He could have expected to find
figs from the previous year, however, which had not ripened then,
but, remaining over the winter, had come to maturity in the spring
(in clement conditions) when the tree regained new life. In an
article in the *Expository Times* of 1909-10, J. Boehmer argued, a
trifle confusingly, that what he called the 'early' or 'first figs',
growing from buds of the previous year, would ripen in spring but
were only half-ripe at Passover season. Such unripe fruit, however,
he stated, was eaten in the East and, indeed, with special relish
/16/. E.F.F. Bishop told of an unripe fig plucked on April 16, 1936,
which was fit to be eaten by 'hungry Palestinians' /17/. A.H.
McNeile also states that this early fruit, even if not mature in
April, is preferred by natives to the summer figs ripening in
August and September /18/. G. Dalman, on the other hand, was of
the opinion that with a late Passover and favourable weather
conditions, even early first-ripe figs might have been found by
Jesus. Only these, he claimed, could here be in view /19/.
Carrington appealed indeed to a photograph he had seen of branches
loaded with figs at Passover time /20/, and C.H. Turner for his

part concluded that "something more or less edible might be anticipated on the tree"/21/.

The majority of scholars have not been convinced, nevertheless, by this 'special pleading'. The winter figs theory has been almost unanimously rejected /22/ on various grounds. The Roman Catholic scholar, M.-J. Lagrange, for example, who himself had lived in Palestine for many years, declared, "il est tout à fait sans exemple dans le pays que les figues demeurent sur les arbres pendant tout l'hiver" /23/. G.E. Post, while conceding the possibility of finding one or two such figs, nevertheless confessed that during a residence of thirty-three years in Syria he had searched and enquired in vain for them /24/. B.W. Bacon remarked facetiously that "the statement of Edersheim (*Life and Times*, V. ii, p.374) that such left-over fruit about April 1 'would of course be edible' becomes admissible only by inserting a 'not' after 'of course'" /25/. It has frequently been pointed out, moreover, that the presence of such figs (unlike the 'first-ripe' figs) would in no way be signalled by the presence of leaves such as the Markan story indicates (so Meyer, Weiss, Holtzmann) /26/. The offence of the tree would consist, in addition, "of not having what must have been a very exceptional relic of a former harvest" (so Post) /27/.

The 'green knops' theory has encountered a similar scepticism /28/. Bacon has also questioned, for example, the evidence drawn from the Talmud by Edersheim that the unripe figs or paggîm were edible /29/. Such evidence only suggests that unripe figs were used *at a later season* and only as a condiment with bread. This, however, was after the paggîm had begun to assume a red colour and not when the foliage had only just begun to cover the developing fruit-bud. Lagrange, too, stated in no uncertain terms that such unripe figs were inedible /30/. All explanations, moreover, that have attempted to prove that *in the normal course of events* Jesus could have expected edible figs "shatter", in R.C. Trench's words, "upon that οὐ γὰρ ἦν καιρὸς σύκων of St. Mark" /31/.

It was for this reason that Trench in England and Meyer in Germany made their classic statement of what Merx was to call the 'trügerische Blätterschmuck' interpretation /32/. What had drawn Jesus to the tree was the *abnormal* foliage. Since fruit precedes leaves on the fig-tree, they maintained, the tree offered promise of *precocious* figs. Since it had none, it proved to be pretentious, and for such *hypocrisy*, and not for its lack of fruit per se, the tree was cursed.

This view has proved to be a popular one and has been adopted by a number of scholars in the twentieth century, most notably by English-speaking commentators taking a strictly historical and rationalist approach to the story /33/. Three difficulties, however, present themselves. In the first place, while it is true to say that the fruit-bud of the fig develops prior to the leaf-bud, it cannot be inferred that the presence of leaves signals the presence of *fruit*. The presence of leaves signals only that the fig-tree ought by now to have *fruit-buds in a developing state* but not necessarily ripe or edible figs /34/. In the second place, if it could be held that the leaves led Jesus to expect precocious figs, then it still remains incredible that the tree should be condemned for failing to produce the *extraordinary* /35/. In the third place, if the fig-tree was to be regarded as culpable, then we still have the difficulty of explaining Mk.11.13d, the words of which appear to exonerate the tree.

Commentators following Bishop Trench in England and Bernhard Weiss in Germany have generally argued that the incident, therefore, has to be seen in a symbolic light, Jesus' action against the 'braggart' fig-tree (so Plummer) being an object lesson directed against religious hypocrisy in general /36/ or against the Jewish people /37/ (perhaps even Jerusalem, or the Temple) /38/ in particular. It has not always been clear, however, whether this symbolism is to be viewed as a function of Markan redaction, as adhering to the pre-Markan tradition, or as the ingredient of an 'acted parable' historically performed by Jesus himself. Bernhard Weiss, who followed Meyer's 'trügerische Blätterschmuck' theory, took this latter view (as have most older exegetes) and argued that in the tree Jesus himself had seen a symbol of Israel, appearing to offer the fruit of faith to its Messiah but in reality displaying nothing but leaves. He maintained, moreover, that Jesus had only intended his cursing of the tree to be taken symbolically /39/. God, however, had taken him at his word and withered the tree, a view Wellhausen sardonically dismissed by commenting, "er (Weiss) hat Jesum verstanden und Gott hat ihn misverstanden" /40/.

Objections have since been raised against the 'symbolische Handlung' theory, the principal one being that the story itself as presented by Mark does not actually read as an acted parable /41/. Hunger, combined with a real expectation of fruit, is given as the motivation for Jesus' approaching the tree /42/. The sequel, moreover, appears to interpret the story purely as a display of power on Jesus' part and as an object lesson in the efficacy

of faith, prayer and forgiveness /43/. More recently, Norman Beck,
in a dissertation for Princeton University on the symbolic acts of
Jesus (1967), pointed out that symbolic acts in the prophetic
tradition were not themselves supernatural phenomena /44/. The
nature miracle described here would therefore be superfluous, if
this were a symbolic act. The tenor of the sequel, he too claimed,
rendered the acted parable interpretation extremely doubtful. The
work of G. Stählin, has served to show that the overwhelming number
of Jesus' symbolic actions were eschatological in import /45/, or,
as Heinz Schürmann has recently called them, 'eschatologische
Erfüllungszeichen' /46/. It was in the light of this fact that
J. Jeremias doubted whether the cursing of the fig-tree should be
considered in this context /47/, although a gathering weight of
scholarly opinion has begun to challenge this view /48/.

    The 'acted parable' view which looks on the fig-tree story as
essentially an historical incident in the life of Jesus (and has a
pedigree stretching back to the Church Fathers) has been taken up
most notably by a majority of English-speaking commentators who
might be described loosely as belonging to the 'historical,
rationalist' school. The hallmarks of this approach may, in
general terms, be described as follows. The gospels are taken to
be fairly accurate accounts of the events and chronology of Jesus'
ministry /49/. The gospel of Mark, it is alleged, draws its data
directly from Peter or the Petrine tradition /50/. Colourful
details are taken as the mark of eye-witness report rather than as
the importation of late tradition in the course of development (as
form-critics aver). The gospels have the tenor of 'reminiscence
journals', faithful in the main to the historical situation they
reflect. They are taken, in many cases, as mirrors of Jesus' own
self-consciousness, rather than that of the evangelist or early
church community that produced them. Discrepancies, ambiguities
and awkwardness in the text are explained, not in literary-, form-,
source- or redaction-critical terms but by appeal to an historical
scenario constructed by the liberal imagination. Doublets of
events and sayings are seen as distinct and independent accounts
of things said and done by Jesus at repeated times during his
ministry. The chronology of that ministry itself is often
constructed by conflating details drawn indiscriminately from all
four gospels. The total picture of Jesus that emerges is of One who
acts with reason, dignity and high-mindedness, a picture that
portrays and betrays the moral fervour and reverent christology of
the nineteenth-century liberal Life-of-Jesus school.
    Taking up the cudgels against W. Wrede's radical attack on the
historicity of Mark's gospel /51/, F.C. Burkitt, in 1911, appealed

to the fig-tree story as exhibiting "the evangelist as a transmitter of reminiscence, rather than as a dogmatic historian".

"I cannot but suppose," declared the Norrisian Professor of Divinity at Cambridge, "that the story in Mark, so odd, so unmoral, so unlike conventional ideas of what Jesus ought to have done and said, does really rest upon reminiscence, however inaccurate, of an actual occurrence." The final verse 11.25, for example, is "quite unlike what a mere compiler would have added", and hence suggests to him "a genuine Saying, corresponding to a change in mood in Jesus himself" /52/.

Approached in this light, the allegedly *historical* details of the account, the *moral* difficulties pertaining to Jesus' behaviour and the *literary* problem of the sequel all called for an answer. The Scottish exegete, A.B. Bruce, for example, remarked on the surprising fact that Jesus was hungry after spending the night with friends. "Had the sights in the temple killed sleep and appetite, so that He left Bethany without taking any food?" /53/ G. Wohlenberg speculated that Jesus may have spent the best part of the night in prayer (cf. Mk.1.35; 6.46) before meeting his disciples who had already breakfasted /54/. Plummer, borrowing from Luke (21.37) claimed that Jesus had not spent the night with friends at Bethany, but had passed the night on the slopes of the Mount of Olives /55/.

Others, however, have claimed that Jesus had only simulated hunger in order to draw a lesson from the tree /56/, a performance enacted before the disciples which Loisy described cynically as "une sorte de comédie". /57/ More recently, C.E.B. Cranfield has suggested that Jesus may have been *both* hungry *and* eager to teach his disciples a lesson, even though no figs could have been expected from the tree /58/.

The 'hunger' motif has also been viewed as a secondary feature of the story. It was invented, some scholars claim (so, for example, Bradley, Bartlet, Tonkin and Robin), to supply a motive for Jesus' approach to the tree, when his original motivation had been misunderstood. Indeed, the *misunderstanding* theory has been a popular explanation for this enigmatic story, and has appeared to many to offer a way out of the *moral* difficulties arising from Jesus' conduct. The original event, it is claimed, was misunderstood by the disciples (so, for example, Swete, Menzies, Lagrange, Tonkin, T.W. Manson, Robin), perverted by Mark (so Bacon, Bradley), or distorted in the course of transmission (so Bartlet, Cranfield, Hatch, Violet). In an article published in 1923, and most conspicuous for its concern to remove the blemish ("um das Bild des Heilandes von diesem Flecken zu reinigen") from Jesus' character, Bruno Violet proposed that Jesus' original words to the tree, uttered in Galilean Aramaic, had been a cry of disappointment and grief in view of his impending death: *The Son of Man will* never again eat fruit from you!" /59/. Similar theories have subsequently been offered by T.W. Manson /60/ and H.-W. Bartsch /61/.

Further highly rationalistic hypotheses claiming to reconstruct this elusive 'original event' or 'kernel' were offered by W.P. Bradley and S. Tonkin. The former claimed that Jesus, noting the abnormal features of the tree, observed that it had an illness and was going to die. "No one will ever again eat fruit from you," he said, but in the course of the story's transmission this utterance was taken to have been a curse and the death of the tree interpreted as the effect of his words /62/.

Tonkin's version was similar. Jesus, a lover of 'bird and beast and the wild, open countryside', noticed (as the disciples did not) that this tree was one of those that had sprouted on rocky ground, had no depth of soil, and was fated, therefore, to wither very soon under the scorching heat of the sun. Jesus saw the tree as a symbol of the fated city of Jerusalem. His words to the tree, uttered with a mixture of vehemence and grief, were, in fact, uttered to the city. Next day, the tree had withered, and the disciples, with Peter as their spokesman, had jumped to the conclusion that his words had been a curse and had brought about this effect. In his reply to Peter, Jesus made no attempt to correct this impression. Perhaps, suggested Tonkin, Jesus, under the stress of these fateful days, was too exhausted to try! Instead, verses 22ff. are in the nature of a soliloquy prompted by Peter's words, in which Jesus rallies his own faith, and despite the doom projected for the city, expresses his confidence in the power of God /63/.

In two more recent articles appearing in 1961-62, A. de Q. Robin /64/ and J.N. Birdsall /65/ both, apparently in ignorance of each other, likewise suggest that the fate of Jerusalem was uppermost in Jesus' mind when he approached the fig-tree. Prompted by the barrenness it displayed, he had quoted the opening words of Micah, chapter 7: "My soul desireth the first-ripe fig." These words were taken to mean, however, that he was simply approaching the tree because he was hungry

Certain objections can be made against these theories which
are based on the assumption of an *historical misunderstanding* of
what took place. Whether the 'original event' that is claimed to
have been distorted was a simple 'acted parable' or 'object
lesson', as Swete, Menzies, Lagrange, Plummer and Bartlet, for
example, would have us believe, or a scenario such as the highly
inventive and fanciful theories of Bradley, Tonkin, Manson, Violet,
Robin and Birdsall would suggest, a satisfactory account of Mark's
datum that the tree *withered* must be given.

To dismiss the miraculous element, as Manson does, by
postulating "some combination of circumstances" which "hastened
the shedding of the leaves, so that by the next day the tree was
bare", is surely too glib, as are the other naturalistic hypotheses
of Bradley and Tonkin /66/. Carrington, echoing a view advanced
earlier by B. Weiss that the πρωΐ of Mark 11.20 could read "in the
morning" or "at dawn", though not necessarily the next day (although
this is suggested), proposed that the fig-tree may in actuality
have withered later, that the curse form developed in the tradition
and that the interval was subsequently shortened /67/. Bartlet,
Violet and Hunter /68/ have posited legendary accretion, which may
come nearer to the truth, but overall the actual *withering* element
in Mark's account has not been satisfactorily explained by those
of the liberal historical school.

Apart from the objection that it should not be the province
of the scholarly exegete, qua scholar, "das Bild des Heilandes von
diesem Flecken zu reinigen" /69/, it is surely optimistic to think
that we can ascertain what Jesus' actual words were (far less the
tenses of his verbs!) on this occasion. The very diversity of
views regarding the nature of the 'original historical event'
furnishes ample warning against the unfettered imagination of the
liberal historical school. One can in principle imagine a
limitless number of historical scenarios, the significance of
which the disciples, the tradition or Mark have distorted or
misunderstood. The *reductio ad absurdum* of this approach indeed
is seen in the opinion offered by C.G. Montefiore (representing
Liberal Judaism) that since "the story must have been greatly
perverted from what actually took place", it was "needless to
discuss these very hypothetical questions. The story has, in any
case, no moral or religious value for us to-day" /70/.

In this respect the application of literary-criticism has
provided a necessary check to the supposed reconstructions of the
liberal historical imagination. By focusing attention on the text

itself, it has sought to explain the discrepancies, ambiguities
and awkwardness often adhering to the gospel accounts in terms of
the form, source and redaction of the literary or oral material
drawn upon by the evangelists. It has asked after the *origin*,
Sitz im Leben and *function* of this material, rather than pre-
occupying itself solely with the question of *historicity*. With
regard to the fig-tree story, such an approach has served better
to explain the awkward connection of the sequel to the body of
the story itself where the historical, rationalist school has
attempted, unconvincingly, to account for this lack of organic
unity by a direct appeal to a putative historical context.

The Turn of the Century to the First World War

The influence of this Higher Criticism began to make itself
felt in the opening years of the present century. In 1903 the
distinguished Old Testament scholar Julius Wellhausen, having
transferred his attention to the New Testament, published the
first edition of his *Das Evangelium Marci*. Wellhausen was
concerned first and foremost with the literary composition of the
gospel, with its sources, its structure, with the function and
dogmatic motivation of its individual components. The fig-tree
story, he argued, was an intrusion into the complex of traditional
material contained in chapter eleven. The story itself broke the
connection between the Entry and Cleansing accounts, and the sequel
in turn the link between the Cleansing and the Questioning of
Jesus' Authority, or Vollmachtsfrage, pericopes. The story was
employed, moreover, as a vehicle for the attachment of dominical
sayings which certainly did not belong to it /71/.

This judgement was expressed likewise by Johannes Weiss, the
son of Bernhard Weiss and a more radical critic than his father.
While Professor of New Testament at Göttingen, J. Weiss had
published, in 1892, his epoch-making *Die Predigt Jesu vom Reiche
Gottes,* a book which issued a profound challenge to the portrait of
Jesus painted by the liberal school. Weiss had maintained that the
life of Jesus was to be seen against the background of contemporary
Judaism, and that he, himself, and the early church (unlike modern
liberal exegetes) had shared with Jews of the time an *eschatological*
orientation. This view, an offshoot of the History-of-Religions
approach to the gospels, was to flower in the yet more radical
'consistent eschatology' position taken by Albert Schweitzer /72/.
In *Das älteste Evangelium* (1903), Weiss held that Mark had inserted
the fig-tree story at this point in his redactional scheme because

in the pre-Markan tradition the story had been connected with the
road from Bethany to Jerusalem /73/. This view was further
developed in *Die Schriften des Neuen Testaments,* first published
in 1906, in which he suggested that the story itself was a legend
that had developed from Luke's parable (Lk.13.6-9) when it had
been seen, especially after 70 CE, that Israel, the fig-tree,
had not repented and borne fruit but was in fact cursed. The
belief may then have arisen that Jesus had actually cursed a
fig-tree, and, indeed, suggested Weiss, popular fantasy
(Volksphantasie) may have attached this legend to a specific
withered fig-tree on the road from Bethany to Jerusalem /74/.

This latter view was not entirely new. In 1897, Eberhard
Nestle had theorized that the story may have developed out of
popular etymological speculation surrounding the place-name
Bethphage, as the 'place of unripe figs' /75/. In 1904, barely
two years before *Die Schriften des Neuen Testaments,* Eduard
Schwartz had given classic expression, moreover, to the hypothesis
that in the Markan story we have the vestige of *an aetiological
legend* /76/. Schwartz drew attention to what he regarded as a
connection between the cursing story and Mark's parable of the
fig-tree in 13.28-32. He suggested, like Weiss, that there had
been an actual withered fig-tree on the Bethany-Jerusalem road,
and that the eschatological imagination of the Urgemeinde had
transferred itself to this local landmark. A legend had arisen
that it was withered because Jesus had been refused fruit by it.
He had declared that henceforth *until he returned* (11.14) it
would be barren. However, when it did begin to blossom, the
faithful would know that the eschatological judgement was about
to come (13.28-32).

This hypothesis has received a mixed following. Although
Wellhausen himself was antagonistic towards a purely
'religionsgeschichtlich' approach to the New Testament, and in
particular to the consistently eschatological viewpoint /77/,
he eagerly embraced Schwartz's theory in the second edition of
his commentary /78/. The French scholar Goguel, too, favoured
Schwartz's idea, although he disinclined from that of J. Weiss
regarding the legend's derivation from the Lukan parable /79/.
B.W. Bacon, on the contrary, was guarded about the Markan fig-tree's
identification with "some sun-bleached skeleton from the orchards
of Bethphage", but reviewed with apparent favour the evidence
supporting the Lukan parable view /80/. Others have accepted the
theory as a possibility but have expressed themselves with
varying degrees of caution (so Wood, Blunt, Schniewind, Nineham

and Bartsch).

Criticism, however, has come from different quarters, though principally from the historical school. M.-J. Lagrange objected that a withered fig-tree was too ordinary a sight to give rise to a legend /81/, and, echoing this view, A. Plummer stated that it was only extraordinary objects which excited curiosity and led to folklore /82/. A. de Q. Robin thinks that what he regards as the eye-witness details of the Markan account speak for an historical rather than a legendary origin /83/. E. Meyer felt that the Schwartz-Wellhausen hypothesis laboured under the disadvantage of being quite unprovable /84/, and Münderlein, more recently, has echoed Meyer's criticism and called for stronger evidence from the text of a legendary Gattung /85/. C.W.F. Smith, too, feels that it is unnecessary to invent such an unusual dessicated tree to provide an origin for the story, since symbolical trees are much more common in religious literature /86/. It should also be pointed out that if Mark has taken pains to insert such a legend into his Vorlage at this particular point then a satisfactory account must be given of his reasons. The topographical link is surely too weak a motive for this procedure. Was he so short of material that he had to employ a distorted legend merely as a vehicle for the attachment of inappropriate sayings, a better setting for which could surely have been found?

In this respect, the contribution of the radical German scholar, Emil Wendling, was more satisfactory. In two scholarly works, *Ur-Marcus*, published in 1905, and *Die Entstehung des Marcus-Evangeliums*, published in 1908, Wendling sought to separate, on the basis of painstaking literary analysis, source material in the gospel from later redactional work performed on it. In so doing, he laid more emphasis than had earlier scholars on the *creative* theological work of the Markan redactor. In the second of these works, he showed convincingly that the three-day chronological scheme in chapter eleven (das Dreitagewerk) was secondary and a function purely of the insertion of the fig-tree story /87/. The redactor of the gospel (Ev), he claimed, had got his story from Luke's parable, in a source known to both. The 'show of leaves' motif (11.13) was taken simply from the parable of 13.28-32. The parable of the vineyard had suggested the Lukan parable to him, and he had inserted it therefore at this point (though clumsily), in an historicized form, to act as a prelude to the Cleansing account, which was thus to be interpreted symbolically as a curse on Israel. This approach had the advantage of doing justice at a literary level to the symbolic dimension discernible in the Markan account, without

at the same time appealing to an historical, distorted or
misunderstood 'Ur-Ereignis'. Its disadvantage was, however, that
it was allied to an 'Ur-Markus' hypothesis which has since been
generally rejected by scholars /88/.

This literary-critical approach in Germany was paralleled at
about the same time in France by the Catholic theologian, Alfred
Loisy, who, in 1893, had been removed from his teaching post
because of his views on biblical criticism. In *Les Évangiles
Synoptiques* (1907-8) and *L'Évangile selon Marc* (1912), Loisy
issued what was the bitterest attack to date on historical,
rationalist approaches to the problems of the fig-tree pericope.
Mark's chronological scheme in chapter eleven, he likewise claimed,
was artificial, as could be seen from the liberties that Matthew
had taken with it. The story itself appears freely conceived and is
adventitious. Though it does not belong with the Entry and
Cleansing traditions, it has at the same time "l'air d'un symbole",
with suggestive details that appear to link the story with these
traditions, so hinting at its allegorical significance /89/.
Mark's story was based on Luke's parable, Loisy stated, and
although this idea had been suggested by scholars before him (by
Strauss, Weisse, de Wette and Holtzmann in the nineteenth century,
and by J. Weiss, J.E. Carpenter and A. Merx shortly before), Loisy
gave it great prominence. The Lukan parable could easily have been
understood in early Christian tradition as an allegory of the fate
of Israel, he suggested, and then subsequently connected with Jesus'
visit to Jerusalem. The owner of the vineyard comes to his fig-tree
looking for fruit. From here it was but a short step to the
'matérialisation' of the parable-allegory into a symbolic act in
Old Testament prophetic style. This historicization, while it may
have occurred in the pre-Markan tradition, was probably the work
of Mark himself, Loisy thought. To make the story nothing short
of historical, Mark added by way of a sequel a dominical discourse
consisting of sayings on faith, prayer and forgiveness. Though
rendered freely, perhaps from memory, these had come from the
sayings source ("le recueil de discours") known to Matthew and
Luke, and were in this source already connected. The apparent
inappropriateness of these sayings in regard to the story itself
led Loisy to conclude that for Mark the moral lessons to be drawn
from the story were uppermost and the symbolic, allegorical
significance of the story of secondary interest.

Loisy's radical historico-critical views led him to be
described as strongly 'modernist' (Rawlinson), and he encountered
fierce opposition, particularly, as was to be expected, from the

historical rationalist school. Lagrange and Burkitt rejected the
Lukan parable theory outright, claiming that Mark's direct
dependence on Peter's eye-witness testimony made such an origin
inconceivable /90/. The style, content and details of the Lukan
parable are quite different, it has also been claimed /91/. Luke's
fig-tree is threatened with being cut down, not withered (so
Branscomb). Judgement is merely threatened, not executed, and a
period of grace is promised (so Meyer-Weiss, Jülicher, Goguel,
Plummer, Hatch). Would the story, furthermore, have been quite so
chaotic if it had been freely conceived from Luke's parable (so
Bradley)? How is it that Mark is pictured using Lukan material,
when the borrowing is generally believed to have occurred in
reverse, it is asked (so R.M. Grant, C.W.F. Smith) /92/. Is it
really possible, moreover, in form-critical terms, that a miracle
story could have grown in the pre-Markan tradition out of a parable?
Bultmann, in referring to this theory, commented that such an
origin was hardly possible with any other miracle stories /93/.
In short, while reasons can be given - a number of scholars have
concluded - why Luke should lack Mark's fig-tree *story* while
presenting at the same time his own fig-tree *parable*,it is quite
a different thing to say that the story and the parable have a
common origin (so, for example, Robin).

Despite such objections and reservations, the approach taken
by Loisy, and before him by J. Weiss, has gained a respectable
measure of acceptance. In addition to the scholars already
mentioned, the Lukan parable theory has been actively espoused,
for example, by E. Klostermann /94/, W.L. Knox /95/, and S.E.
Johnson /96/. J. Schniewind, likewise, in his commentary /97/
considered this a possible genesis for the story, and a number of
English-speaking commentators have given a favourable judgement
to this view (so, for example, Bacon, Wood, Rawlinson, Taylor,
Nineham). Others, less committed, have not, however, ruled it out
of court (so, for example, Blunt).

Where doubts continue to exist with regard to the origin of
the story, there has been (following J. Weiss, Wellhausen and
Loisy) a growing recognition that Mark's chronological scheme is
suspect and that the fig-tree story is indeed adventitious /98/.
While he doubted the Lukan parable view, Loisy's fellow-countryman,
Maurice Goguel, was even convinced that the division into days,
the cursing of the fig-tree, the sleeping at Bethany and the
'anointing' pericope were all secondary additions to Mark, known
to Matthew but not to Luke /99/. The primitive tradition, he
argued, gave no precise indications about the stay of Jesus in

Jerusalem. The Holy Week pattern is a product of the evangelist's
redactional activity and we are obliged, therefore, in respect of
his account of Jesus' words and deeds, to expand the chronological
framework within which these traditions are to be located.

This latter viewpoint was strongly affirmed in the 'misplaced
chronology' hypotheses of Hatch, Manson and Smith referred to
above /100/. While Hatch speculated that the connection of the
fig-tree story with Passover week had been made prior to Mark,
Manson wished even to question whether Mark himself had intended
his material to occupy the space of a week. The specific
connection of the traditions in chapter eleven with the Passover
season, he claimed, was made later, with 11.13d being a gloss by a
post-Markan scribe who had operated with this assumption. Smith,
in turn, was content to regard the Passover connection as *either*
the work of the evangelist, an editor or a later glossator. Philip
Carrington suggested that Mark's chronological references were "an
ingenious method of presenting material from more than one source",
and seemed "to link together certain sequences of lections" which,
he held, were originally associated with the Feast of Tabernacles
/101/.

Attention has also been focused subsequently on Mark's
practice, in general, of 'dovetailing' his sources. E. von Dobschütz,
in 1928, drew attention to Mark's fondness for *intercalation* or
chiasmus and this redactional device has been commented upon by
succeeding scholars /102/. It has only been relatively recently,
however, when more redaction-critical work has been done, that the
precise significance of this procedure has begun to be realized /103/.

General agreement has, in addition, been reached in respect of
the secondary nature of the sequel, though few would accept the
specific insistence of Wellhausen, Loisy, Goguel and E. Hirsch
that the mountain-moving saying of 11.23 shows its alien context, in
that it could only have been spoken in the vicinity of the Sea of
Galilee /104/. Nor have most scholars been prepared to accept
Loisy's view that the sayings of the sequel existed in a cluster
before Mark /105/. The majority adhere to the view that what we
have here is a series of *stray logia* which originally circulated
independently, but were attached loosely by Mark by a process of
catchword association (so Bacon, Bultmann, Montefiore, Klostermann,
Hatch, Lohmeyer, Blunt, Rawlinson, Knox, Johnson, Nineham, Dowda).
However, with Loisy, they have generally held that Mark's
compositional motives were guided by *moral*, *apologetic* and
catechetical concerns, and that any *symbolic* function for the story

was either of secondary interest to him, or adhered only in the
pre-Markan tradition /106/. The disadvantage of this opinion (which
persists to the present day) is that it, too, fails adequately to
explain why Mark should have gone to all the trouble of inserting
at this point such a puzzling story merely to offset what earlier
significance it might have had by drawing from it untimely and
inappropriate lessons with the use of previously disconnected logia.

Between the Wars

The period between the Wars saw relatively little in the way
of new departures and fresh solutions. It was characterized, in
general, by the gradual acceptance of a literary- and form-critical
perspective and the growing influence of the Religionsgeschichte
approach. Attempts were made to absorb the results and methods of
this Higher Criticism into what had been hitherto a basically
historical approach, and this can be seen, for example, in the
commentaries and articles of English-speaking scholars such as
H.G. Wood (Peake), W.H.P. Hatch, A.E.J. Rawlinson (Westminster),
A.W.F. Blunt (Clarendon Bible) and B.H. Branscomb (Moffatt), though
less so in the commentaries of J.V. Bartlet (Century Bible) and
C.H. Turner (NCHS). In 1920-21, J.E. Roberts published an article
in which he sought to establish, though unconvincingly, that there
was a tradition-connection between John, chapters 15 and 16 (and
particularly the parable of the Vine) and the Markan discourse on
the fig-tree /107/. These Johannine chapters, he suggested,
constituted a summary (perhaps originally in document form) of
Jesus' teaching to his disciples (dimly remembered) on his daily
walks from Jerusalem to Bethany. The parable of the Vine and the
importance of fruit-bearing had been, in fact, the original teaching
given by Jesus in connection with his withering of the barren fig-
tree. This wayside teaching, undated, had been inserted by John
within the framework of the Last Supper discourse and in
connection with Jesus' 'table-talk' on this latter occasion. A
similar 'displaced pericope' theory was propounded also by Selma
Hirsch in 1938, although in this case a tradition-connection
between Mk.11.12-14, 20ff., Lk.13.1-9 and Jn.9.1-3 was proposed
/108/.

In 1922, with the commencement in publication of Paul
Billerbeck's prodigious *Kommentar zum Neuen Testament aus Talmud
und Midrasch* a new impetus was given to the search for an
understanding of early Christianity in the light of the literature
of Rabbinical Judaism. While scholars such as John Lightfoot,

Gustaf Dalman and Adolf Schlatter had earlier pressed for such a
study, their evidence had for the most part been neglected /109/.
Billerbeck's contribution to what was a new phase in the History-
of-Religions approach helped stimulate the increasingly revised
estimation of Jesus. As time went on, he came to be viewed less
as a nineteenth-century gentleman, and more as a Jew, in a first-
century Jewish environment. Billerbeck, for example, drew attention to a number of Jewish stories in which the power of a Rabbi's
curse to effect the miraculous was both described and assumed /110/.
Against English-speaking and German exegetes alike, the Jewish
scholar C.G. Montefiore, indeed, in commenting on Mk.11.23,24,
exclaimed vehemently:

> "A Jew of the first century who had not the slightest idea
> of any law of nature and knew nothing of science, who had
> no difficulty whatever in conceiving God working any
> miracle if He chose, must necessarily have thought about
> petitionary prayer very differently from ourselves. Why
> should we wish to make him think as we think, or to conceal
> the gulf that lies between us! We, at least, who have no
> apologetic purposes to serve, like Mr. Rawlinson and J.
> Weiss, can be more historic." (!) /111/

The influence of this renewed emphasis on Religionsgeschichte,
and of Jewish Studies in particular, showed itself, however, more
in the search for an *origin* for the story, and less in the construction of an authentic background against which the story would
have had meaning and significance for *Mark and his readers*. This
was due, no doubt, to the growing value attached to form-criticism,
particularly after Bultmann's *Die Geschichte der synoptischen
Tradition*. Bultmann's method, by prising apart the traditional
'building blocks' of Synoptic material from their redactional
framework, had served to focus attention on the former. Taken in
isolation from its context, the fig-tree story was for Bultmann a
miracle story (with a Jewish provenance) /112/, whose original
significance was uncertain, and which had been employed as a
setting for an apophthegm (11.20-25) /113/. The separation of
this miracle story into two parts was due to editorial activity
/114/ which broke up the admittedly unoriginal connection between
the Entry pericope (a Messianic legend) /115/, the Cleansing
account (an historical datum with a secondary interpretative
logion) /116/ and the Vollmachtsfrage (a Palestinian apophthegm
with a transformed setting) /117/, the latter two pericopes being,
however, connected prior to Mark /118/. The appended logia /119/,
which were probably Gemeindebildungen /120/, were attached in

degrees, a process which has continued in the history of the text
(cp. 11.26 at least) /121/.

Investigation after the story's *origin before* Mark rather than
after its *function in* Mark, produced relatively inconclusive
results, nevertheless, and this state of affairs has continued
more or less to the present day. E. Meyer regarded the story as
a 'Strafwunder', similar to those recounted of the prophets in the
Book of Kings and subsequently in the apocryphal gospels and
hagiographies. Mark employed it, he claimed, to demonstrate
Jesus' miraculous power and to illustrate the efficacy of faith /122/.
Rawlinson thought it approximated "more closely than any other
episode in Mk to the type of 'unreasonable' miracle characteristic
of the non-canonical Gospel literature"/123/.   Derivation from
the Lukan parable or the aetiological legend hypothesis described
above, was the genesis most frequently mentioned, nonetheless,
despite the drawbacks that have been discussed.

In 1937, Ernst Lohmeyer's *Das Evangelium des Markus,* the
tenth edition of Meyer's commentary, was published, and this
proved, as with the edition of B. Weiss and J. Weiss, yet another
departure in the long history of that commentary. Lohmeyer held
that the story was "eine fromme personale Legende" whose original
import was no longer discernible. Showing features common to
Semitic stories in general, and to Rabbinic miracle stories in
particular, the legend may have been given its impetus by a
withered fig-tree which Christian imagination said Jesus (a Rabbi
par excellence) could and did make wither (cf. Schwartz, J. Weiss,
et al.). Lohmeyer made two further suggestions, however, which
may be taken as examples of two exegetical trends which one can
trace emerging with greater force in the post-war period. In the
first place, he noted in passing that the presupposition of the
story was that Jesus was the Lord of Nature and that nature should
automatically have succoured him. In the second place, he ventured
the opinion that the story did not have, originally, a symbolic
import but that it may have been placed in its present context by
Mark precisely to give it one. The allegorical lesson intended may
have been either general – the Lord punishes that which does not
serve him – or concrete – the Lord punishes the Jewish people who
refuse to respond to him /124/.

The first of these suggestions, which echoes that of Albert
Schweitzer /125/, was not developed by Lohmeyer at this time and
had to await the posthumous publication of his commentary on
Matthew (1956). In this latter work, the eschatological background

of the story was more strongly affirmed. Hauck, in 1931, had
also cautiously sided with Albert Schweitzer's position, and was
inclined to view Jesus' words to the tree as being "ein
messianisches Machtwort" pronounced within a climate of
expectancy regarding the marvellous productivity of the Messianic
Age /126/. Samuel J. Cohon, too, in an article for the *JBL* in
1929, had in similar terms proposed that the miracle be viewed as
a Messianic sign based on Ct.2.13 /127/ but there was no evidence,
it was claimed, that Jesus had harboured such expectations as
Schweitzer, Hauck and Cohon had predicated of him /128/. The
second of Lohmeyer's suggestions, while echoed in the comments of
certain other exegetes with a redaction-critical perspective (so,
for example, R.H. Lightfoot /129/ and J. Schniewind /130/, also
remained to be developed more closely in the post-war period.

The Immediate Post-War Period

     Scholarly opinion, as we have already noted, had, in the main,
long rejected Albert Schweitzer's 'consistent' or 'thoroughgoing
eschatology' as the key to the understanding of Jesus' life and
mission. After the War this situation began to change. In 1948,
R.M. Grant, in an article in the *JBL* /131/ gave a spirited defence
of Schweitzer's position and drew attention to certain central
passages in Mark's Gospel (e.g. 1.15; 8.12; 9.1; 10.30; etc.)
which had not been discussed by Schweitzer or his opponents, but
which indicated, Grant maintained, that Jesus had indeed expected
the imminent coming of the Kingdom in the earlier period of his
ministry. He had, nevertheless, modified this expectation (in the
light of Jer.31.31-34 and Zech.9.11) when the reign of God had,
after his arrival in Jerusalem, failed to materialize. Between
Mk.11.1-23 and the apocalyptic section of Zechariah (chaps.9-14)
and other apocalyptic writings there are so many parallels, Grant
claims, that a literary relationship between them is certain /132/.
Since the evangelist appeared to be unaware of this relationship
(cf. Mk.11.23 with the following verses connected *ad vocem*), Grant
concludes, "Jesus himself and/or the disciples around him must have
believed that he was fulfilling the prophecies." Citing numerous
parallels between this chapter and Old Testament passages, he
suggested that the fig-tree story in particular was to be viewed
in the light of the miraculous fruitfulness that was a prominent
feature of the eschatological hope (cf. especially Ez.47.12 and
also Zech.14.8 Ap.22.1-3 Enoch 24.4; 25.4-6 4 Ezra 8.52 etc.). The
cursing of the fig-tree reflects, therefore, Jesus' subsequent
belief that there would be a period of tribulation or "messianic

woes" before the New Age itself would dawn.

    With the publication, in turn, of E. Lohmeyer's *Das Evangelium des Matthäus* (first edition 1956) a further stimulus was given to the emerging school of those /133/ who hold that Mark's story should be seen against an *eschatological* background. The fig-tree was condemned because, in failing to produce fruit for Jesus 'out of season', it had thereby failed to recognize the advent of the Messiah and of the Messianic Age. In the End-time, trees would bear fruit for the righteous all the year round and mountains would be made low before them /134/. In thus suggesting an eschatological Sitz im Leben for the mountain-moving saying too, Lohmeyer helped forge a closer contextual link between this logion and the story itself, an original link which, he claimed, had gone unrecognized or been misunderstood (in Matthew's *independent* account) when the story was turned into a "Paradigma für die Macht des Glaubens". /135/ Lohmeyer hence recognized the different hermeneutical strata that are to be discerned within the fig-tree story, although his account of the relation between the story's original meaning and Sitz im Leben and Matthew and Mark's subsequent redactional work upon it tends to be somewhat imprecise and confusing. Few would agree, moreover, that Matthew's version of the story was not derived from Mark, as he maintained /136/.

    It was in the fifties that certain further emphases and approaches could be seen emerging. Breaking with the historical, rationalist tenet that Mark was a somewhat crude collector and 'scissors and paste' editor of historical reminiscences, C.H. Bird, in company with a growing number of other scholars /137/, insisted that Mark should be seen as a *theologian,* the *creative* author of a symbolic and highly allusive gospel. Profounder meanings lie behind the arrangement and redaction of his material. In particular, Mark's frequent and enigmatic γάρ clauses (usually omitted by Matthew and Luke) are indicators, Bird suggests, of his 'allusive' method. Clouding rather than explaining the meaning of the passages in which they occur, these intentionally striking clauses function such as to draw the reader's attention to the significance of what he is reading. This significance is to be perceived in the light of external data, the Old Testament in particular. Ezekiel Chap.47, suggests Bird, provides the clue to the interpretation of Mk.11.13d, "for it was not the season of figs". The 'ideal' and therefore 'faithful' tree according to Ez.47.12 (cf. also Ps.1.3 Jer.17.7,8 Ap.22.2) would bear fruit unceasingly. The fig-tree (as also the vineyard in the Old Testament) is a symbol for Judaism or for the

people of Israel /138/ and a tree's barrenness a figure for
religious sterility or for the punishment of unfaithfulness or
hypocrisy. The incident of the fig-tree and the parable of the
vineyard are hence mutually interpretative, and both in turn
serve to elucidate the significance of the Cleansing pericope.
Bird suggests further that the mountain of 11.23, no less than the
fig-tree, stands for the people of God, or even, following Dodd,
the Temple. Judaism, indicted "for worldliness, prayerlessness,
and hypocrisy" and "contaminated at its source", must, like the
fig-tree, according to Mark, "be destroyed by a mighty act of
power in order that it may be replaced /139/".

     In sharp contrast to Bird's approach was that of J.W. Doeve
in an article in *NTS* for 1954-5 /140/. Doeve drew attention to
the important point that gospel research could not seek to account
for the Christian gospels merely in terms of the original Sitz im
Leben of their component units of tradition, as form-criticism had
attempted to do, but had also to illuminate the process whereby
this pre-Synoptic material had come to evince the arrangement,
order and structure that it does within the gospels, and to suggest
reasons for the often apparently arbitrary differences in order
existing between the gospels. Such was to be seen in the diverse
arrangement of the material in Mk.11.1 - 12.12 and parallels.
Doeve claimed, however, that the ordering of material here in the
respective gospels was not a function of the redaction of literary
sources and hence of a certain amount of creative redactional
activity on the part of the individual evangelists. It was rather
the product of *the midrashic technique*, whereby diverse units of
pre-Synoptic tradition became attached to specific Old Testament
passages upon which this material functioned as a commentary.
These Old Testament proof-texts or passages hence acted as a kind
of 'template' which first 'guided' diverse material into more
fixed orders, and served as the catalyst for the subsequent
connection of this material. Since different schools may have
preserved such pre-Synoptic tradition in connection with different
Old Testament passages, different arrangements of common material
would arise and would appear arbitrary when their original link
with the Old Testament had receded into the background. It is
upon these separate 'schools', Doeve suggests, that Mark, Matthew
and Luke each drew. According to one school, there had been
preserved, in connection with Jeremiah 7, the Cleansing (cf.7.11),
Fig-tree (cf. 7.20) and Vollmachtsfrage (cf. 7.25) traditions and
these, via the link of Jer.7.26, had been intercalated into the
Entry and Parable of the Vineyard pericopes, traditions which had
themselves been preserved in connection with Ps.118.22-26.

Matthew and Mark, drawing upon this common midrashic tradition,
hence show a greater degree of uniformity in material and
arrangement than Luke does, because Luke's tradition had lacked
the fig-tree's attachment to Jer.7.20 but had conserved the
prophecy of Jerusalem's destruction in connection with Jer.6.6,14,
15,21.

This ingenious but complicated theory has undeservedly received
little attention and even less endorsement, despite its suggestive
insights /141/. On the negative side it can be said that since
Mk.11.1 - 12.12 contains echoes of so many Old Testament passages
other than those cited by Doeve, it would appear arbitrary to give
significance to the specific complex of passages from which he
wishes to draw a pattern. His position also seriously weakens the
solution advanced by literary source theory and redaction-criticism,
an approach which, while it does not solve all the problems of
Synoptic comparison, has the virtue of being, in essence, simpler.
Doeve's thesis, in particular, fails adequately to account, indeed,
for the principal differences to be discerned in the Markan and
Matthean fig-tree story accounts, viz, Mark's chronological scheme
and the division of his story into two parts.

On the positive side, Doeve, nevertheless, like Bird, has not
only continued that trend of exegesis which wishes to interpret the
story against a Jewish background - Doeve, too, regards the cursing
of the tree in an eschatological light /142/ - but he has drawn
legitimate attention to *the place of the Old Testament* in the
formation and interpretation of gospel tradition and of the cursing
of the fig-tree in particular.

Some Recent Trends

When we now consider, lastly, the work that has appeared on
the exegesis of our passage over the last fifteen years or so, a
number of observations can be made. In the first place, it is to
be remarked that an increasing emphasis has come to be placed on
studies of *late Judaism*. Resemblances noted between the details of
the Entry and Cleansing accounts and features adhering to the
Jewish Feast of Tabernacles have contributed, as we have seen, to
the continuing popularity of the 'misplaced chronology' theory and
the view that Mk.11.13d is a compensatory gloss or Markan addition
(so Carrington, Smith, Johnson and van Goudoever). The growing
stress on late Jewish and early Christian eschatology has led
equally, on the other hand, to the view that 11.13d is genuine,

indeed crucial, for these words, it is alleged, are a pointer to
the eschatological dimension within which the story was conceived
(so, for example, Hiers, Derrett, Bartsch, Münderlein /143/).

Since 1965, the emerging popularity of *midrashic studies* in
particular has been evident. In that year, John Bowman's *The
Gospel of Mark. The New Christian Jewish Passover Haggadah*
appeared. Bowman suggests that the fig-tree story is either a
midrashic development of the Lukan parable or an actual occurrence
that Luke treated parabolically because by this time the basic
symbolism would have been incomprehensible to Gentile readers. By
blasting the fig-tree, Jesus was blasting the Messianic hopes of
the Jews of his time. As evidence for this he adduces Cant.2.11-13.
This passage was the starting-point of a midrash on the Second
Deliverance to usher in the Messianic Age (cf. Shir.R.II.13). The
New Exodus would occur, as the first had done, in springtime, and
would be signalled by the blossoming of the fig-tree. In symbolic
commentary upon this Jewish expectation, Jesus withers the tree,
so indicating that the Jewish view of the New Exodus and Messianic
Age is not to be /144/.

But such evidence, it has been claimed, is late, scanty, and
gives the midrashic scholar no licence, as W. Grundmann had
earlier pointed out, to presume that Jesus would have held this form
of apocalyptic expectation /145/. Since Grundmann's opinion was
expressed, however, evidence for a more widespread expectation
regarding the marvellous productivity of the Messianic Age has been
accumulating and much of this material (from the Old Testament, the
New Testament, the Apocrypha and Pseudepigrapha, the Rabbinic
literature, etc.) is presented in the article by R.H. Hiers, which
appeared in 1968 /146/. Hiers' emphasis on the *haggadic background*
to the story has, in turn, been followed more recently still by J.
Duncan M. Derrett in a stimulating article appearing in 1973 /147/.
Derrett claims that Jesus, in approaching the tree, was deliberately
miming Is.28.4 and Mi.7.1 and doing so with a Messianic import
and upon a principle analogous to sympathetic magic. He was "in
biblical terms, looking for a 'first-ripe fig' at a time when no
one could expect an eatable fig, ripe or unripe" /148/. In
refusing him fruit at this time, the fig-tree proved that *it* was
wrong, not Jesus, for it failed to recognize the advent of the
Messianic Age and was thus rightfully condemned. J.G. Kahn too
has highlighted the haggadic features of the story, though
primarily against a background of cosmological rather than
eschatological belief /149/.

While these background studies have proved enormously
valuable in placing Mark's gospel within its proper setting in
the literature of late Judaism and early Christianity and hence
within the context of a first-century Weltanschauung, it must be
said that there has been, at the same time, a tendency on the part
of such studies to bypass Mark and to assume, too readily, that
we are dealing with an actual historical event in the life of
Jesus. The otherwise excellent articles of Hiers and Derrett give
virtually no form-, source- or redaction-critical analysis of the
fig-tree pericope, nor do they, in common with Kahn, attempt to
relate the story to the Cleansing pericope. Where a literary-
critical perspective is adopted no clear consensus has emerged
with regard to the question whether the alleged historical kernel
of the story - an acted parable in the nature of a Messianic sign
(so Bowman), an "eschatologisches Drohwort" (so Münderlein) or an
apocalyptic prediction (so Bartsch) - was eschatological, or
whether Mark himself took material with a different Sitz im Leben
and gave it an eschatological import (so Gaston). Much confusion
exists.

This is to be seen, too, in the growing trend to illuminate
the passage with the light of the *Old Testament*. The hypothesis
advanced by A. de Q. Robin and J.N. Birdsall, described above /150/,
is essentially 'historical, rationalist' in approach. The
'misplaced chronology' hypotheses of Smith and Carrington /151/,
too, while reflecting the influence of modern trends in exegesis and
pointing to an Old Testament background, present nevertheless a
similar approach. Carrington, in particular, who advances a
'lectionary' theory for the formulation of Mark, presents an
exegesis of the fig-tree story which is complex and confused, a
situation largely due, in our opinion, to the different approaches
he appears to be combining. While Holtzmann, for example, had
earlier suggested that the Old Testament had influenced the actual
formation of the story *in the tradition* (rather than directly in
respect of an historical action performed by Jesus), this view has
been mentioned by subsequent scholars but, with the exception of
J.W. Doeve, little developed /152/.

Our discussion hitherto of the diversity of views expressed,
approaches taken and tools employed by scholars with regard to the
understanding of Mk.11.12-14,20 ff., clearly indicates that the
passage even today defies adequate exegesis. A clear overall
account of the redaction-history of the periocope requires still,
in our opinion, to be given, with a key emphasis being directed to
Mark's place in that history. A method must be adopted which will

seek to draw together the results of scholarly work in the
different fields described in this chapter. For some years now,
Mark's gospel has been subjected overall to detailed literary
analysis. Investigation of Markan style and vocabulary has been
conducted by scholars such as C.H. Turner /153/ and M. Zerwick /154/.
More recent studies have concentrated on the source-redactional
analysis of specific passages, such as the Trial narrative (J.R.
Donahue) /155/, or of themes, such as the Kingdom of God (A.M.
Ambrozic /156/, W. Kelber /157/) or have sought to isolate
specific collections of pre-Markan material (H.-W. Kuhn) /158/.
Since W. Wrede's epoch-making *Das Messiasgeheimnis in den Evangelien*
(1901), redaction-critical enquiries have been focused in pursuit
of the overall purpose and intention of the gospel and its
christology in particular (cf. e.g. J. Schreiber) /159/. As a
result of these studies, there has emerged a new regard for Mark's
creativity as an evangelist and of his role as a theologian (cf.
e.g. W. Marxsen) /160/. The gospel has been increasingly
described, indeed, in terms of 'drama', its material, it is
believed, being arranged and presented for symbolic and dramatic
effect (cf. e.g. N. Perrin /161/, T.J. Weeden /162/).

     It is this redaction-critical approach, then, that we suggest
can supply the key to the understanding of this difficult passage,
and which can, we believe, subsume within itself many of the
diverse areas and results of scholarly concern already described.
Earlier exegesis has focused, we believe, too much on the
historicity of the story. It has been guided over-much by the
dogmatic concern to remove the story's apparent blot on Jesus'
character. Form-critical studies, on the other hand, have placed
undue emphasis on the story's *origin*. While not avoiding this
question, our study will seek primarily to examine the pericope's
function within Mark's redactional scheme. Our fundamental
question will be a twofold one: What did Mark intend his story
to convey in its present context, and how in turn was it likely
to have been understood by the first-century reader for whom it
was intended? The first part of our thesis, therefore, will focus
on Mark's redactional procedure and literary-critical studies on
the gospel as a whole will be brought to bear on the passage.
Background supplied by the Old Testament, late Judaism and early
Christianity will subsequently be adduced in order to suggest an
answer to the second part of the question. To think Mark's
thoughts over again or, to borrow the words of H.A.W. Meyer with
which this chapter commenced, "to ascertain the meaning the author
intended to convey by his words, impartially and historico-
grammatically" - that is the task before us.

NOTES

/1/   *The New Testament: The History of the Investigation of its Problems* (1970). Henceforth, *History of the Investigation.*

/2/   *Das Neue Testament Griechisch nach den besten Hülfsmitteln kritisch revidiert mit einer neuen deutschen Übersetzung und einem kritischen und exegetischen Kommentar,* div.1, pt.1, xxxi, cited Kümmel, *op.cit.,* p.111.

/3/   De Wette, Bleek, Baur, Strauss and Schenkel, for example, found these words incomprehensible for they seem to imply that the tree's fruitlessness was altogether natural at this time and that Jesus' curse was hence unjustifiable. See H.A.W. Meyer, *Die Evangelien des Markus und Lukas* (MeyerK, 8th edn., ed. B. Weiss, J. Weiss, henceforth *Meyer-Weiss*),I,p.192, fn.1; H.A.W. Meyer, *The Gospels of Mark and Luke* (MeyerK, transl. R.E. Wallis, ed. W.P. Dickson, fr. 5th edn., henceforth *Meyer-Dickson),* p.178.

/4/   Among such, the following highly ingenious readings may be noted: 'for it was *not yet* (οὐ = οὔπω) the time for the gathering of the fruit' (Kuinoel, Deyling, Dahme, Wetstein, Baumgarten-Crusius); 'for *where* (οὗ rather than οὐ) he was, it was the season of figs' (Heinsius, Knatchbull, Gataker); the interrogative view, 'for was it not the time of figs?' (Majus); 'for it was not a *good year* (καιρός = καιρὸς εὔφορος) for figs' (Hammond, Clericus, Homberg, Paulus, Lange, D'Outrein); 'for it was not a *place suitable for* figs' (Abresch, Triller); 'for it was not *favourable weather* (καιρός = *tempus opportunum*) for figs' (Olshausen, Bornemann). See *Meyer-Dickson*,I, pp.179-80; *Meyer-Weiss, ibid.;* R.C. Trench, *Notes on the Miracles of our Lord,* pp.479-80, fn.1; B. Weiss,*Das Marcusevangelium und seine synoptischen Parallelen,* p.370.

Some commentators have even suggested emendations in respect of an original Hebrew source e.g. Chajes, *Markusstudien,* p.62, who surmised that the translator of the original Hebrew had read לא היה עת 'it was not the season (for figs)' instead of לא היה עדי 'there were no more (figs)', cited M. Goguel, *L'Évangile de Marc,* p.216, fn.3.

/5/   So Toup, Tittmann, Wassenbergh, Wittichen. See *Meyer-Dickson ibid; Meyer-Weiss, ibid.*

        T.K. Cheyne, *EncBib.,* II, 'Fig Tree' ad loc., p.1522, following Toup, also regarded the words as "a comment of an early reader which has made its way into the text".

/6/   So, for example, O. Holtzmann (*Leben Jesu,* p.324, cited W.H.P. Hatch, "The Cursing of the Fig Tree", *JPOS,* 3 (1923), p.8, fn.4).

/7/   So, for example, A. Edersheim (*The Life and Times of Jesus the Messiah* (1886), Vol.II, p.374). Edersheim also suggests that the finding of winter figs by Jesus was equally possible.
/8/   So, for example, B. Weiss (*Marcusevangelium*, p.370; *Meyer-Weiss*, I, pp.191-2).
    Other appeals to special-case instances were also made. As early as the seventeenth century, J. Lightfoot (*Horae Hebraicae et Talmudicae*, Vol.II, pp.279 ff., 432) had suggested that the tree approached by Jesus was, in fact, a special kind of fig-tree, the בנת שוח, or white fig, which never lacked leaves or fruit, but whose figs did not mature until its third year.
    Other commentators have pointed to B.J.III.519 where Josephus records that in the Galilean region of Gennesaret figs could purportedly be found for some ten months of the year (cf., for example, A.B. Bruce, *The Synoptic Gospels* (ExpGT, Vol.I), Mt.21.19 ad loc.; cf. also the note in Whiston's Josephus, p.673, *gratia* Hatch, *op.cit.*, p.8, fn.4). Were this true, the situation would scarcely apply to Judaea; cf. H.J. Holtzmann, *Die Synoptiker* (Hand-Commentar zum Neuen Testament, henceforth *HC*, Vol.I), p.232, who commented: "Von dorther aber brachte Jesus seine Erfahrungen in das keineswegs gleich paradiesische Judäa mit."
/9/   So, for example, Volkmann and Weizsäcker (see B. Weiss, *Marcusevangelium*, p.370, and *Meyer-Weiss*,I,p.192, fn.1) and, in the twentieth century, Schlatter, Lagrange, Loisy, Wohlenberg and Grundmann.
/10/   *Die Evangelien des Markus und Lukas*, p.133. So also K.L. Schmidt, *Der Rahmen der Geschichte Jesu*, p.299. Later scholars have generally been more guarded, stating the gloss merely as a possibility, cf. E. Klostermann, *Das Markusevangelium*, p.116; F. Hauck, *Das Evangelium des Markus*, p.133; E. Lohmeyer, *Das Evangelium des Markus*, p.234; C.W.F. Smith, "No Time for Figs", *JBL*, 79 (1960), pp. 316-7, 325-7; D.E. Nineham, *The Gospel of St. Mark*, p.303. Philip Carrington, in his *The Primitive Christian Calendar*, p.194, originally accepted the gloss theory, but suggested he was less happy with it in his later commentary. See *According to Mark*, p.237. For many scholars it has seemed too easy a way out.
    Cf. *Meyer-Dickson*,I, pp.179-80; Hatch, *op.cit.*, p.8, fn.2; R.H. Hiers, "Not the Season for Figs", *JBL*, 87 (1968), p.394; J.D.M. Derrett, "Figtrees in the New Testament", *HeythJ*, 14 (1973), p.252.
    For the view that 11.13d is characteristically Markan, see, for example, V. Taylor, *The Gospel according to St. Mark*, p.460, and C.H. Bird, "Some γαρ Clauses in St. Mark's Gospel", *JTS*(NS), 4 (1953), pp.177-9.
/11/   Although this view was suggested in the nineteenth century by Bleek (cf. *Meyer-Dickson*,I,p.180, fn.1), it was stated classically

by T.W. Manson ("The Cleansing of the Temple", *BJRL*, 33 (1950-1),
pp.271-82). See also J. van Goudoever, *Biblical Calendars*, p.264;
S.E. Johnson, *The Gospel according to St. Mark*, p.188 (following
Carrington, *Calendar*, p.194) and cf. Cranfield, *The Gospel according to Saint Mark*, pp.354-7.
/12/   G. Münderlein, "Die Verfluchung des Feigenbaumes", *NTS*, 10
(1963-4), pp.89-104, esp.91-2, 99 (*infra*, p.37, n.143).
/13/   So, for example, Lohmeyer, Smith, Carrington and Nineham.
Zahn, *Einleitung in das Neue Testament*, Vol.II, p.250, thought
that Mark's explanatory note was for the benefit of Roman readers
not acquainted with the fruit-bearing season of Palestinian figs.
See also Rawlinson, *St. Mark*, p.155, and Hatch, *op. cit.*, p.8.
/14/   Cf. H.B. Swete, *The Gospel according to St. Mark*, p.254.
/15/   H.L. Strack, P. Billerbeck, *Kommentar zum Neuen Testament
aus Talmud und Midrasch*, Vol.I, p.857 (henceforth *Str-B*); F. Hauck,
Markus, p.134; E. Hirsch, *Frühgeschichte des Evangeliums*, I, p.125;
W. Grundmann, *Das Evangelium nach Markus*, p.229.
/16/   "The Cursing of the Fig-Tree", *ET*, 21 (1909-10), pp.328-9.
Some confusion exists among commentators over the precise number
of crops produced by the fig-tree. I. Löw (*Die Flora der Juden*,
I (VAKMF, Vol.4), p.238) and Lohmeyer (*Das Evangelium des Matthäus*,
p.303, fn.1), for example, give *three* annual crops, while B.W.
Bacon (*DCG*, Vol.1, 'Fig-Tree' ad loc., p.592) states categorically
that "the fig-tree has *two* (not three) successive crops of fruit
each year."
         In reality, figs are usually gathered in one main harvest
from the middle of August to well on in October. These are the
'summer figs' or תאנים, and have developed from buds sprouting on
the new wood of the tree. The 'first-ripe' fig, or בכורה, is produced, however, from buds sprouting on the old wood of the previous
year. These buds, remaining undeveloped throughout the winter,
swell into little green knops or פגים in March-April, followed
shortly thereafter by the development of the leaf-bud. Leaves are
usually to be found on the tree in April, therefore. The 'paggîm'
or unripe, green figs mature in June and the 'first-ripe' figs,
the 'bikkûrîm', are considered a delicacy. Many 'paggîm' do not
ripen, however, and simply drop off. The so-called 'winter figs',
which many commentators suggest are both rare and, if found,
inedible, are basically neglected or immature 'summer' figs which
have survived the winter and ripened with clement conditions in the
springtime. They are 'chance finds', then, and unlike the 'paggîm'
have no organic connection with the tree's sprouting of leaves.
         Cf. e.g. C.-H. Hunzinger, *Theological Dictionary of the New
Testament* (henceforth *ThDNT*), Vol.7, συκῆ ad loc., p.753. For
general works on figs and fig-trees, *vide infra*, p.165, n.17. A

comprehensive Bibliography of general works can also be found at
the end of this book.
/17/   *Jesus of Palestine*, p.217, *gratia* Derrett, *op.cit.*, p.253,
fn.3. See also Taylor, *Mark*, p.460, fn.1.
/18/   *The Gospel according to St. Matthew*, p.302.
/19/   *Arbeit und Sitte in Palästina*, Vol.I, pp.380-1.
/20/   *Mark*, p.237.
/21/   *The Gospel according to St. Mark*, p.94.
/22/   So Meyer, B. Weiss, Trench, H.J. Holtzmann, Swete, Post,
Bacon, Loisy, Lagrange, Klostermann, Hatch, Lohmeyer, Branscomb,
Taylor, Hiers.
/23/   *Évangile selon Saint Marc*, p.293.
/24/   *DB*, Vol.2, 'Figs' ad loc., p.6.
/25/   *DCG*,1,p.593.
/26/   "Also nicht überwinterte Feigen (Kermusen) erwartete er zu
finden (Keil, Schegg u.A.), da deren Vorhandensein mit der
Belaubtheit in keinem Zusammenhange steht..." *Meyer-Weiss*,I,p.191;
see also *Meyer-Dickson*,I,pp.178-9; B. Weiss, *Marcusevangelium*,
p.370; H.J. Holtzmann, *HC*, Vol.I, p.232.
/27/   *Ibid*.
/28/   Cf. e.g. Bacon, Lagrange, Hatch, Rawlinson, Manson, Taylor,
Smith.
/29/   *DCG*, 1, p.593, citing Edersheim, *Life and Times*, v.ii,
p.375.
/30/   "La figue verte n'a rien d'agréable, et si l'on a vu quelque
enfant en manger, ce n'est pas un fait normal." - M.-J. Lagrange,
Marc, p.293.
/31/   *Miracles*, p.479, fn.1.
/32/   R.C. Trench, *Miracles*, pp.479-81; *Meyer-Dickson*,I,pp.178-9;
Meyer-Weiss,I,pp.191-2.   Cf. A. Merx, *Markus und Lukas*, p.133,
fn.1.
/33/   So, for example, Gould, Swete, Post, Wohlenberg, Bartlet,
Turner, Plummer.
/34/   "Not, indeed, as used to be assumed and as one still hears
too often asserted, that the fig-tree bears fruit *before* leaves.
Such is not the case, for then the name 'fruit' would be given to
fruit-buds the size of a pea, or, at most, of a bean." - Boehmer,
op. cit., p.329.
        There is some doubt, too, as to whether the presence of
leaves at this time would have been quite as *extraordinary* as
Meyer and Trench maintained.   Talmudic evidence suggests that trees
began to leaf in the month of Nisan, hence about the time of
Passover. See J. Lightfoot, *Horae*, II, p.277, though cf. p.281;
and Holtzmann, *HC*, Vol.I, p.232, who states: "An sich war der Anblick
nicht auffallend, da die Feigenbäume in Syrien, wo sie übrigens zu
Hause sind, im April allgemein ihren Laubschmuck anlegen."

/35/   So Post, *op.cit.*, p.6, who argued therefore that the tree was condemned for having *no fruit at all*, not even unripe fruit, the presence of which would not have provoked the curse. See Bacon's criticism of this view, however, *DCG*, 1, p.594.
/36/   So Post, Lagrange, Turner. See also P. Charles, "Non enim erat tempus ficorum (Marc, 11, 13)", *NRTh*, 61 (1934), pp.514-6.
/37/   So J. Lightfoot, Edersheim, H.J. Holtzmann, Gould, Bruce, Swete, Menzies, Wendling, Loisy, Allen, Hatch, Blunt, Schniewind, Lohmeyer, Hunter, W.L. Knox, Carrington, Robin, Birdsall, Nineham, Gaston, Schweizer, Giesen.
        In a recent article, J.G. Kahn decried what he regarded as the anti-Semitic tenor of this exegesis! Cf. "La parabole du figuier stérile et les arbres récalcitrants de la Genèse",*NovTest*, 13 (1971), pp.38-45, esp. p.45.
/38/   So Zahn, Wohlenberg, Plummer, Schlatter, Bartlet, Tonkin, R.H. Lightfoot, Bird, Cranfield, Grundmann, Smith, Johnson, Münderlein.
        "Der Feigenbaum ist das Bild nicht Israels, sondern Jerusalems, und der Fluch Jesu über ihn eine Ankündigung des schon durch v.13 angedeuteten Gerichts der Zerstörung der Stadt und des Tempels." -T.Zahn, *Das Evangelium des Matthäus*, p.616.
/39/   *Meyer-Weiss*,I,p.195.
/40/   *Das Evangelium Marci* (1909), p.89.
/41/   So, for example, H.G. Wood, "Mark" (*Peake*, 1919), p.694.
/42/   So V. Taylor, *Mark*, p.459.
/43/   Cf. J. Weiss, *Das älteste Evangelium*, p.268; *Die Schriften des Neuen Testaments*, Vol.I, pp.178-9; Lagrange, *Marc*, pp.298-9; Bacon, *DCG*, 1, pp.593-4; Taylor, *Mark*, pp.458-9; E. Haenchen, *Der Weg Jesu*, pp.381-2; J. Schmid, *Das Evangelium nach Markus*,pp.209-10.
/44/   *Efficacious Symbolic Acts of Jesus Christ during his Public Ministry*, pp.125-6.
/45/   "The overwhelming number of Jesus' symbolic actions serve to proclaim the fulfilment of the ἔσχατα," Stählin, 'Die Gleichnishandlungen Jesu' in *Kosmos und Ekklesia*,Fs. for W. Stählin, (1953), p.20; cited J. Jeremias, *The Parables of Jesus*, p.228.
/46/   "Die Symbolhandlungen Jesu als eschatologische Erfüllungszeichen. Eine Rückfrage nach dem historischen Jesu", *BiLeb*, 11 (1970), pp.29-41, 73-8.
/47/   *Parables*, p.228, fn.2.
/48/   *Vide infra*, pp.10 (and n.72), 19ff.
/49/   Cf. e.g. E.P. Gould's words in the Preface (p.vi) to his commentary published in 1896, *The Gospel according to St. Mark:* "An important part of the critical question is the historicity of the miracles. This doubt - for the question has grown into a widespread doubt - I have attempted to meet on the general ground

of the credibility of the narrative as contemporaneous history,
and of the verisimilitude of the miracles."
/50/   So, for example, Gould, Swete, Zahn, Bartlet, Robin.
/51/   *Das Messiasgeheimnis in den Evangelien* (1901).
/52/   "The historical character of the Gospel of Mark", *AJT*, 15
(1911), pp.169-93, esp. 179-80.
/53/   *Synoptic Gospels*, p.417.
/54/   *Das Evangelium des Markus*, p.298.
/55/   *The Gospel according to St. Mark*, pp.135-6. See also Bruce,
Synoptic Gospels, p.264 (Mt.21.18 ad loc.). Against such
speculation, the words of J. Duncan M. Derrett are apt: "Several
scholars have thought it absurd that Jesus should be hungry soon
after leaving his lodging: one cannot take this seriously, for,
apart from the relationship between the story and actual chronology
(which is unknown), no one knows what arrangements were made for
breakfast!" (op.cit., p.252).
/56/   This view was held by a number of the Church Fathers, e.g.
Victor Antiochenus, Euthymius Zigabenus and Chrysostom. Cf.
Meyer-Dickson, I,p.179; Lagrange, *Marc,* pp.293-4. It was followed
by Mill, Hofmann, Trench and, closer to our own time, by Menzies
(The Earliest Gospel) and Lagrange.
        For a critique, see Loisy, *Les Évangiles Synoptiques,* Vol.II,
pp.284 ff., and Taylor, *Mark,* pp.459-60. Zahn *(Matthäus,* p.616),
Wohlenberg *(Markus,* p.298) and Plummer *(An Exegetical Commentary on
the Gospel According to St. Matthew,* p.290) likewise repudiate the
notion that Jesus could have staged this event for pedagogical
reasons.
/57/   *Op.cit.,* p.285.
/58/   *Mark,* pp.356-7. See Bruce, *op.cit.,* p.417, and Post,
op.cit., p.6, for further 'compromise' views of this sort.
/59/   "Die„ Verfluchung" des Feigenbaums" in *EYXAPIΣTHPION: Studien
zur Religion und Literatur des Alten und Neuen Testaments für
Hermann Gunkel,* pp.135-40. Violet argued that, in the Aramaic
original, the verb may have expressed a *future* tense, rather than
an optative, and that ברנשא meaning either 'man' or 'the Son of Man',
rather than אנש (man) was used.
/60/   T.W. Manson, *op.cit.,* p.280, argued that while Jesus had
meant *either* "No one shall ever eat fruit from you again" (i.e.
that the Day of the Lord, or the destruction of Jerusalem would
occur before the next fig-harvest) *or* "One will never eat fruit
from you again" (i.e. that he himself would die before the next
fig-harvest), his disciples had understood him to say, *"Let* no
one ever eat fruit from you again" (i.e. as a curse).
        W.H.P. Hatch, *op.cit.,* pp.10-12, thinking similarly with
Manson that the event had taken place at a different time of the

year, and that the original utterance in Aramaic had been
misunderstood, claimed that Jesus had merely stated that the
tree would never again bear figs. His words, however, were
interpreted as a curse that had caused the subsequent withering
of the tree.
/61/   H.-W. Bartsch, "Die „Verfluchung" des Feigenbaums" *ZNW*, 53
(1962) pp.256-60, has claimed that the pre-Markan kernel of the
story, Mk.11.13-14a, was an apocalyptic saying or Chria in which
Jesus' words had stated that his Parousia = Resurrection would
occur in less than eight weeks, viz, before the fig season came.
Later tradition, no longer regarding the Resurrection as Jesus'
Parousia, interpreted the words as a curse which Jesus had
effected.
/62/   "The "Cursing" of the Fig Tree", *LCQ*, 9 (1936), pp.184-96.
This view was held also by older exegetes such as Paulus,
Baumgarten-Crusius and Bleek. See *Meyer-Weiss*, I, p.192, fn.2.
/63/   "The Withered Fig-tree", *ET*, 34 (1922-3), pp.323-6.
/64/   "The Cursing of the Fig Tree in Mark XI. A Hypothesis",
NTS, 8 (1961-2), pp.276-81.
/65/   "The Withering of the Fig-tree", *ET*, 73 (1961-2), p.191.
/66/   T.W. Manson, *op.cit.*, p.280. See Derrett, *op.cit.*, p.254,
who argues, rightly, that such rationalization "destroys the
story as St. Mark conceived it."
/67/   *Mark*, pp.240-2. Cf. B. Weiss, *Marcusevangelium*, p.375;
Meyer-Weiss,I, p.195; Bruce, *Synoptic Gospels*, p.418.
/68/   Bartlet, *St. Mark*, p.317; Violet, *op.cit.*, p.139; A.M.
Hunter, *The Gospel according to Saint Mark*, p.110.
/69/   B. Violet, *op.cit.*, p.136.
        It has frequently been asserted that the cursing of the
fig-tree story should not allow us to pass moral judgement on
Jesus' action. The spiritual lesson for which the tree is alleged
to have been 'sacrificed' is, this view would argue, a reflection
of Jesus' concern for man over nature. The φιλανθρωπία indeed, of
this miracle was alleged by Theophylact: ξηραίνει οὖν τὸ δένδρον,
ἵνα σωφρονίσῃ ἀνθρώπους (cf. Trench, *Miracles*, p.477 and fn.1).
Man is 'of more value than many sparrows' and the animal and
vegetable creation exists for his use (so Turner, *Mark*, p.94).
Withering the tree, declared Gould (*Mark*, pp.211-12), enabled
Jesus to condemn hypocrisy without hurting anyone. See also J.E.
Roberts, "The Parable of the Vine. Its place in the Fourth
Gospel", *ET*, 32 (1920-1), p.74; Lagrange, *Marc*, p.299; and, more
recently, J.W. Wenham, *The Goodness of God*, pp.117-8.
/70/   *The Synoptic Gospels*, Vol.I, pp.265-6. A similar judgement
was passed by B.H. Branscomb, *The Gospel of Mark*, p.201: "It is
wise in such a situation to confess our inability to discover from

the fragmentary evidence what the original facts in the case were."
/71/   *Marci* (1903), p.97.
/72/   See Albert Schweitzer, *Von Reimarus zu Wrede* (1906), a
second edition of which appeared in 1913 as *Geschichte der Leben-
Jesu-Forschung*. On pp.310-11 of the latter, Schweitzer made the
pregnant suggestion that the fig-tree story be viewed against a
background of eschatological expectation in which the Coming Age
would be a period of marvellous productivity, and nature would be
responsive to man. Jesus, he claimed, shared this view, and
because this fig-tree had failed to offer the Son of Man its fruit
while he walked on earth, it would henceforth be barren when the
Kingdom came, so suffering a fate similar to that of the city of
Jerusalem. This approach was not taken up until considerably later
(although cf. Lagrange, *Marc*, p.294).
/73/   *Op.cit.*, pp.267-70.
/74/   *Op.cit.*, I, pp.178-9.
/75/   Nestle himself was not entirely convinced of this etymology,
however. In his *Philologica Sacra* (1896), pp.16-17, and in an
article, "Zwei Varianten in der Gadarener-Geschichte", *ThStKr*, 3
(1896), p.324, fn.1, he had suggested that the name derived from
בית פגעא meaning "place of meeting" or "at the crossroads" (bivium
Lat.; ἐπὶ τοῦ ἀμφόδου Gk.; cf. Mk.11.4). A year later he was less
sure, and in an article, "Etymologische Legenden?" *ZWTh*, 5 (1897),
p.148, confessed that, although he preferred his earlier view, it
was possible that the etymology "place of unripe figs" suggested
by Arnold Meyer had been a popular explanation for the place-name,
and had given rise, in turn, to the fig-tree story. See also
EncBib., I, 'Bethphage' ad loc., ed. T.K. Cheyne.
/76/   "Der verfluchte Feigenbaum", *ZNW*, 5 (1904), pp.80-4.
/77/   Cf. Kümmel, *History of the Investigation*, p.309.
/78/   *Marci* (1909), p.106.
/79/   *Marc*, pp.217-18; cf. also E. Hirsch, *Frühgeschichte*, Vol.I,
pp.123-4.
/80/   *DCG*, 1, pp.593-4.
/81/   *Marc*, p.299.
/82/   *Mark*, p.137.
/83/   *Op.cit.*, pp.276-7.
/84/   *Ursprung und Anfänge des Christentums*, Vol.I, p.115, fn.3.
/85/   See Münderlein, *op.cit.*, pp.92-3, where a detailed critique
of the Schwartz theory is given.
/86/   *Op.cit.*, p.324; cf. R.E. Dowda, *The Cleansing of the Temple
in the Synoptic Gospels*, Dissertation for Duke University, 1972,
p.219.
/87/   *Entstehung*, pp.144-51.
/88/   See, for example, V. Taylor, *Mark*, Introd. Chap.VII, pp.67-72.

/89/   The enigmatic and contradictory 11.13d points the reader,
claims Loisy, to the spiritual meaning of the story. The tree's
luxuriant foliage represents the Jewish enthusiasm for their
Messiah; the tree's barrenness, their lack of faith; its withering,
the fate that was in store for them. The visit to the tree
corresponds to the first visit to the Temple (11.11), the words
to the tree to Jesus' reproach of the Jews in the person of the
Temple tradesmen. In Mark's story there is a delay between the
judgement expressed on the tree and its subsequent death. In
Luke's parable there is a period of forbearance (the divine ἀνοχή)
during which the Jews are given time to repent before judgement
falls. See Loisy, Marc, p.327; cf. also G. Münderlein, op.cit.,
p.103, fn.2.
/90/   Lagrange, Marc, p.298; Burkitt, op.cit., pp.179-80; cf.
also Robin, op.cit.,pp.277-8.
/91/   . Cf. e.g. Carrington, Mark, p.242, and, for a more detailed
critique, Robin, ibid.; Münderlein, op.cit., pp.93-4.
/92/   Some commentators have therefore suggested that the parable
of Luke may be, conversely, a correction of Mark's story. Cf.
e.g. van Goudoever, Calendars, p.266; J. Bowman, The Gospel of
Mark. The New Christian Jewish Passover Haggadah, p.221.
/93/   The History of the Synoptic Tradition, pp.230-1, 425; cf.
J.D.M. Derrett, op.cit., p.254, fn.1.
/94/   Markusevangelium, p.116.
/95/   The Sources of the Synoptic Gospels, Vol.I, p.82.
/96/   Mark, p.188.
/97/   Das Evangelium nach Markus, p.149; cf. also W. Grundmann,
Markus, p.229.
/98/   Cf. e.g. Rawlinson, Mark, p.157.
        The 'insertion' theory of J. Weiss and Wellhausen was also
taken up and developed in an article by W.H. van de Sande Bakhuyzen
("De vervloeking van den vijgenboom", NThT, 7 (1918), pp.330-8).
Sande Bakhuyzen claimed, however, that the fig-tree pericope was in
fact a pre-Markan insertion into an earlier Aramaic Ur-Markus that
had been translated into Greek. The insertion has broken the
original connection between Entry, Cleansing and Vollmachtsfrage
pericopes, so leaving the ταῦτα of 11.28 without its previous
referent, viz, Jesus' action in the Temple. Mark and Matthew had
access to this expanded version (in Greek) while Luke possessed a
version lacking the insertion. Cf. Hirsch, Frühgeschichte, I,
pp.121 ff.
/99/   Marc, pp.215-18; The Life of Jesus, pp.238-41; cf. also
Montefiore, Synoptic Gospels, I, p.265.
/100/   Supra, p.3.
/101/   Mark, p.236; cf. also Johnson, Mark, p.188.

/102/ *ZNW*, 27 (1928), pp.193-8, esp. 197-8; cf. L. Gaston, *No Stone on Another*, p.83, fn.1. See also Hauck, *Markus*, p.134; Schniewind, *Markus*, p.148; Smith, *op.cit.*, p.317 and fn.12; Nineham, *Mark*, pp.298-9; H.-W. Kuhn, *Ältere Sammlungen im Markusevangelium*, pp.200-1; Dowda, *Cleansing*, p.218.

/103/ In a recent dissertation published in the SBL Dissertation Series (No.10), J.R. Donahue (*Are You the Christ?*, pp.42, 58-63) argues that these intercalations may be an index of Mark's theological concerns. "There is," he claims, "a dialectical relationship between the inserted material and its framework whereby the stories serve to interpret each other" (p.42).

/104/ "The objection that the saying must have been uttered in Galilee is unsound, for the Dead Sea can be seen from the Mount of Olives." - Taylor, *Mark*, p.466 (so also Lagrange, Rawlinson, Lohmeyer, Hauck, Klostermann; contr., however, Haenchen, *Weg*, p.390).

/105/ See, however, Cranfield, *Mark*, p.360, and Münderlein, *op.cit.*, p.102.

/106/ See, for example, Bacon, *op.cit.*, pp.593-4; Klostermann, *Markusevangelium*, pp.118-19; Goguel, *Marc*, p.218; E. Meyer, *Ursprung*, I, pp.115-16; Rawlinson, *Mark*, pp.158-9; Branscomb, *Mark*, p.202; Taylor, *Mark*, pp.465-7; W.L. Knox, *Sources*, I, pp.82-3; Johnson, *Mark*, pp.191-2; Nineham, *Mark*, pp.298-300.

A number of more recent scholars, however, would credit Mark with an equal and, in some cases, a predominant concern for the symbolic dimension of the story. The attached logia, they suggest, were intended by Mark to relate specifically to the passing away of the old Israel and its replacement by the new, the Christian community of faith, prayer and forgiveness. Cf. e.g. Gaston, *No Stone*, pp.83-4; H. Cousin, "Le figuier désséché. Un exemple de l'actualisation de la geste évangélique", in Fs. S. de Dietrich, *Foi et Vie*, Cahiers Bibliques - special edition, May, 1971, pp.82-93; E. Schweizer, *The Good News according to Mark*, pp.234-6; Dowda, *Cleansing*, pp.239-51; H. Giesen, "Der verdorrte Feigenbaum - Eine symbolische Aussage?", *BZ*, 20 (1976), pp.95-111, esp.110-11.

/107/ "The Parable of the Vine. Its place in the Fourth Gospel", *ET*, 32 (1920-1), pp.73-5.

/108/ "Die Verfluchung des Feigenbaumes", *NThT*, 27 (1938), pp.140-151. Hirsch's link between these pericopes is made by a number of (in our view) slender threads. By emending Mk.11.21, for example, to read, "Rabbi, was the fig-tree cursed when it withered (as it did)?", the sequel becomes an exact parallel, claims Hirsch, to Jn.9.1-3 where a similar question is asked regarding the blind man. The theodicy of suffering also links the latter

passage with Lk.13.1-9 (cf. vv.1-5).
/109/ See Kümmel,*History of the Investigation*, pp.342-3.
/110/ *Str-B*, I, pp.858-9.
/111/ *Synoptic Gospels*, Vol.I, p.270.
/112/ *History*, pp.230-1, 235.
/113/ *Op.cit.*, pp.54-5, 57.
/114/ *Op.cit.*, p.218.
/115/ *Op.cit.*, pp.261-2, 305.
/116/ *Op.cit.*, pp.36, 56, 389.
/117/ *Op.cit.*, pp.19-20.
/118/ *Op.cit.*, pp.19-20, 36, 218.
/119/ *Op.cit.*, pp.77, 81, 91, 93-4, 132, 146, 147.
/120/ *Op.cit.*, pp.54-5.
/121/ *Op.cit.*, pp.25,61.
/122/ *Ursprung*, I, pp.115-16; cf. also Schmid, *Markus*, pp.209-10;
Branscomb, *Mark*, p.202; contr., however, L. Brun, *Segen und Fluch
im Urchristentum*, pp.74-6, who claims that the story's redactional
position suggests that it was understood by Mark as a symbolic
prediction of judgement upon the Jewish people and especially on
the city and Temple cultus.
/123/ *Mark*, p.154; cf. also Johnson, *Mark*, p.188.
/124/ *Op.cit.*, pp.234-5.
/125/ *Supra*, p.10 and n.72.
/126/ *Markus*, p.134.
/127/ "Thus the miracle of the drying up of the fig tree (Mark
11^{12-14} ; Matt.21^{18-19}), which astounded the disciples and has
perplexed the commentators, becomes intelligible when viewed as
a Messianic sign. It is based on the Song of Songs 2^{13}, התאנה
חנטה פגיה   literally 'the fig-tree spiceth her figs'. The
word חנטה was evidently understood by the Evangelists as meaning
'embalmeth'. As the entire Song of Songs was considered an
allegory in which the Messianic drama is the main theme, the
drying up or 'embalming' of the fig-tree was naturally taken as
one of the portents that had to be fulfilled. Cf. Song of Songs
Rabba ad loc., Pesikta Rabb. XVII." - "The place of Jesus in the
religious life of his day", *JBL*, 48 (1929), p.85, fn.11. Contr.
Löw, *Flora*, I, p.229, fn.2.
/128/ See, for example, W. Grundmann's critique of A. Schweitzer
in *Das Evangelium nach Markus*, pp.228-9.
/129/ *History and Interpretation in the Gospels*, pp.86, fn.2,
123-4.
/130/ *Markus*, pp.148-51.
/131/ "The Coming of the Kingdom", *JBL*, 67 (1948), pp.297-303.
/132/ For a similar view, see C. Roth, "The Cleansing of the
Temple and Zechariah xiv 21", *NovTest*, 4 (1960), pp.174-81.

/133/   So, for example, C.H. Bird, H.-W. Bartsch, G. Münderlein,
J. Bowman, R.H. Hiers, R.E. Dowda, J.D.M. Derrett.
/134/   Cf. e.g. Derrett, *op.cit.*, p.253.
/135/   *Matthäus*, pp.302-4 (cf. also pp.271-4).
/136/   Though cf. Bartlet, *Mark*, p.321.
/137/   "Some γαρ Clauses in St. Mark's Gospel", *JTS*(NS), 4 (1953),
pp.171-87. See also R.H. Lightfoot, *The Gospel Message of St.
Mark*, esp. pp.78-9, and W.G. Kümmel, *Introduction to the New
Testament*, p.64.
/138/   This view of Bird's was challenged by J.W. Wenham. For a
review of the Old Testament fig and fig-tree passages, see his
"The Fig Tree in the Old Testament", *JTS*(NS), 5 (1954), pp.206-7.
/139/   *Op.cit.*, p.178.
/140/   "Purification du Temple et desséchement du figuier", *NTS*, 1
(1954-5), pp.297-308.
/141/   Though cf. Dowda, *Cleansing*, p.340, fn.1, and Derrett,
op.cit., p.250, fn.2.
/142/   "La malédiction du figuier est ainsi un fait eschatologique"
(*op.cit.*, p.304).
/143/   Münderlein's article, "Die Verfluchung des Feigenbaumes",
appearing in *NTS*, 10 (1963-4), pp.89-104, gives an excellent form-
and redaction-critical analysis of the Markan story and concludes
that 11.12b-14 was the original pre-Markan kernel, with all else
being secondary. In origin, the story was an "eschatologisches
Drohwort" on the part of Jesus, directed to the people of Israel,
but uttered at a different time. By placing it here Mark makes it
refer more specifically to the Temple. 11.13d is a gloss, although
perhaps a pre-Markan one, containing the vestige of an original
"Deutwort" associated with the story. This "Deutwort" or
interpretative saying has been suppressed, perhaps by Judaeo-
Christians, because it presented Jesus as declaring a fate similar
to that of the tree upon Israel and Jerusalem. Mark, too,
understood the story symbolically, as did his source, and hence,
Münderlein claims, allowed the gloss to stand, despite its
difficulties.
/144/   *Op.cit.*, pp.221-2 (*vide supra*, pp.34 (n.92), 19 and n.127).
/145/   Cf., for example, Dowda, *Cleansing*, pp.225-6, and *supra*,
p.19 and n.128.
/146/   "Not the Season for Figs", *JBL*, 87 (1968), pp.394-400.
/147/   "Figtrees in the New Testament", *HeythJ*, 14 (1973),
pp.249-65.
/148/   *Op.cit.*, p.253, fn.3.
/149/   The clue to the story, whose dramatic features and
cosmological echoes derive from Mark, is to be seen in terms of
cosmological belief prevalent in the first-century world. It was

held, says Kahn, that not only men were subject to the Fall but
nature, too, and trees in particular were cursed for disobeying
God. He draws attention to Ber.R.V.9 where, although it had been
decreed that all trees (and all the individual parts of trees)
were to be edible as fruit (Rabbinic exegesis claimed), the
trees, nevertheless, had produced non-fruitbearing kinds. Hence
trees reveal a resistance to the Divine Will which will be
reversed in the New Age, when trees will bear fruit all the year
round, and every part will be edible, even the wood! Jesus'
cursing of the tree, then, is to be understood as indicating that
no such sterile trees would henceforth share in the New World.
See "La parabole du figuier stérile et les arbres récalcitrants
de la Genèse", *NovTest*, 13 (1971), pp.38-45, and *supra*, p.30, n.37.

/150/ *Supra*, p.8.

/151/ *Supra*, pp.3, 15.

/152/ The story, Holtzmann suggested, was an "Umsetzung des
Gleichnisses Lc 13$^{6-9}$ in Geschichte, nach Anleitung von Mch 7^1,
Hos 9^{10} (Gott sucht und findet Israel wie Frühfeigen)." - *HC*, I,
p.232. Cf. also J.E. Carpenter, *The First Three Gospels*, pp.156-8,
and E. Klostermann, *Markusevangelium*, p.116.

/153/ "Marcan Usage", *JTS*, 25 (1923-4), pp.377-86; 26 (1924-5),
pp.12-20, 145-56, 225-40; 27 (1925-6), pp.58-62; 28 (1926-7),
pp.9-30, 349-62; 29 (1927-8), pp.275-89, 346-61.

/154/ *Untersuchungen zum Markus-Stil* (1937).

/155/ *Are You the Christ?* (1973).   *Supra*, p.35, n.103.

/156/ *The Hidden Kingdom* (1972).

/157/ *The Kingdom in Mark. A New Place and a New Time* (1974).

/158/ *Ältere Sammlungen im Markusevangelium* (1971).

/159/ "Die Christologie des Markusevangeliums", *ZThK*, 58 (1961),
pp.154-83.

/160/ *Mark the Evangelist* (1969).

/161/ *The New Testament. An Introduction* (1974), pp.143-67, esp.
144-5.

/162/ *Mark - Traditions in Conflict* (1971); cf. also Carrington,
Mark, p.238.

Chapter II

SOURCE AND REDACTION IN MARK CHAPTER 11

"And he entered Jerusalem": The Three-Day Scheme

In commencing our study of Mark's redactional procedure /1/, we should first remark on the wider context within which our passage stands. The integrity, at the redactional level, of the section 11.1 - 13.37 has been widely noted /2/. Though diverse in nature, the material in this section of the gospel shows itself to have been subject to a certain editorial organization. Its total context is that of the Temple. The action begins in the vicinity of the Mount of Olives, prior to Jesus' entry into Jerusalem and his cleansing of the Temple (11.1). It ends likewise on the Mount of Olives, after Jesus has left the Temple, having pronounced its destruction (13.1,2). The intermediate material is almost entirely concerned with Jesus' action and teaching in the Temple, and with his confrontation with representatives of the Jewish nation.

Following Jesus' departure from the Temple in 13.1,2 there is no further mention of any subsequent dealings with this famous institution. His break with it is complete. He has announced its imminent destruction and further references to it are for the most part confined to this theme. Chapter 14 commences a new section. In 14.49 Jesus is made to refer back to this period of teaching in the Temple. In 14.58 and 15.29, the charge that he would himself destroy the Temple is levelled against him and in 15.38 his death is accompanied by the rending of the καταπέτασμα leading to the Holy of Holies. Where further mention of dealings with the Temple may have been appropriate (at the Passover meal, for example - 14.12 ff. - where the lamb vital to such a meal is left unmentioned), there is only silence.

In short, then, the arrangement of the material in 11.1 - 13.37 is such as to present Jesus' visit to the Temple as an historic occasion, the climactic event of his ministry in which he criticizes the Temple cultus, is challenged by the nation's leaders, confronts and bests in argument their chief representatives and finally pronounces the Temple's destruction. In this light, the inclusion of the cursing of the fig-tree story within this particular complex of material appears all the more curious.

When we turn to chapter 11 specifically, we note the following sequence of events. The chapter begins with the story of the Triumphal Entry into Jerusalem. It recounts Jesus' despatching of two disciples to find an ass which will bear him into the city. It further relates how Jesus, seated upon the ass, is fêted by his disciples and the crowd as he makes his way into the city. Though hailed in the words of Ps.118.25,26, a greeting originally addressed to pilgrims coming to the Temple /3/, the additional reference to the coming Kingdom of David (11.10a) seems to suggest that a Messianic ovation is here in view /4/. The scene ends abruptly, however, in verse 11 with the notice that "he *[Jesus]* came into Jerusalem into the Temple" and, in what amounts to a startling anticlimax, merely "looked around at everything and, *since it was already late, went out to Bethany with the Twelve.*"

It is on *the following day* (τῇ ἐπαύριον) as they go out *from Bethany,* that the cursing of the fig-tree occurs (11.12-14). Jesus condemns the tree to future barrenness. Curiously, his words on this occasion are said explicitly to have been heard by the disciples: καὶ ἤκουον οἱ μαθηταὶ αὐτοῦ.

Immediately thereafter, the second arrival in Jerusalem is announced, at which time Jesus drives out those who are buying and selling in the Temple. In defense of his action, he is made to cite the words of Is.56.7 and Jer.7.11. His words on this occasion too are said explicitly to have been heard by the chief priests and the scribes: καὶ ἤκουσαν οἱ ἀρχιερεῖς καὶ οἱ γραμματεῖς (11.18). Again in verse 19, there is a chronological reference, which abruptly ends the scene: "and when*[ever]* /5/ it got late, they /6/ went out of the city."

The sequel to the cursing of the fig-tree takes place as they are passing by *in the morning* or *at dawn (...* παραπορευόμενοι πρωΐ). The tree is now observed to have withered to its roots, and Peter, 'remembering' (καὶ ἀναμνησθεὶς ὁ Πέτρος...), draws Jesus' attention to the fact. Jesus thereupon delivers a series of sayings which serve to interpret the cursing episode as an object lesson in the efficacy of faith (11.22,23), prayer (11.24), and the need for a forgiving spirit (11.25,26).

Following this conglomerate of sayings is the third arrival in Jerusalem, where at once Jesus is found walking around in the

Temple (11.27). He is approached by the chief priests, the
scribes and the elders, who ask him by what authority he does
"these things" (11.28). The ταῦτα is a 'floating' pronoun which
appears to have no immediate referent /7/. Jesus meets this
challenge with a counter-question which defeats his opponents.
Thereafter, in chapter 12, we are presented with a series of
controversy and doctrinal discourses, the story of the Widow's
Mite (12.41-44), and finally, in chapter 13, with Jesus' departure
from the Temple, followed by the Apocalyptic Discourse on the
Mount of Olives. In 14.1, the commencement of a new section, there
is a further chronological reference to the effect that it was the
Passover and the Feast of Unleavened Bread in two days time (Ἦν δὲ
τὸ πάσχα καὶ τὰ ἄζυμα μετὰ δύο ἡμέρας).

It can be seen, therefore, from this brief summary of the
sequence of events that *at least* three separate days form the
chronological structure within which material is presented. Much
has been made of this three-day structure in Mark. A number of
commentators have viewed the Markan time-scheme in strictly
historical terms, the chronological references in 11 - 13
corresponding, in their opinion, to events that actually took place
during a final (and climactic) week spent by Jesus in Jerusalem /8/.
R. Thiel saw in the three successive visits to the Temple evidence
for the compilation of three separate literary sources /9/. Hirsch
too maintained that the three-day structure was not the artificial
creation of a redactor but adhered to an older tradition contained
in an earlier version of the gospel /10/. K.L. Schmidt, on the
other hand, presented a case that the chronological unity of
chapters 11 - 13 was purely artificial /11/, and, following in his
footsteps, scholars such as Dibelius and Bultmann have claimed
that Mark himself was responsible for dividing up disparate
traditional material into a definite number of days /12/.
Following Bultmann, J. Schreiber has in turn argued that the
Markan chronological structure serves a theological function.
Jesus' stay in Jerusalem and the events leading up to his
crucifixion have been made to occupy a period of seven days, such
that his death on the seventh day corresponds to the account of
the Transfiguration earlier (9.2-8) - which also occurs, he notes,
on the seventh day. Thus Jesus' crucifixion is to be understood
as his exaltation as the Redeemer Son of God, in line with the
kerygma of the Hellenistic church /13/.

On closer examination, however, the three-day structure,
while it may be a function of redaction, seems unlikely to carry
the additional theological weight that Bultmann and Schreiber

attach to it. Wendling points out, with justice, that there is a
great disproportion in the three days and the three visits /14/.
The third day, deemed to commence at 11.20, is disproportionately
fuller than the other two. Of the three chapters, it comprises
two and a half, or 95 verses, whereas the first covers 11 verses,
the second 8 verses. A similar disproportion exists in the three
Temple visits. The third (11.27 - 12.44) has eight scenes (58
verses), the second (11.15-19) one scene (4 verses) and the first
(11.11) merely περιβλεψάμενος πάντα.

However, in addition to this observation by Wendling, we
may note that it remains only a matter of speculation that the
material in 11.20 - 13.37 has been placed within a chronological
framework comprising a period of *only* one day. In fact, after
11.19,20, there is no precise chronological reference until 14.1.
While stating that the Passover and the Feast of Unleavened Bread
were now two days away, this datum gives, however, no indication
of precisely *how many* days have elapsed since Jesus' third visit
to Jerusalem in 11.27. While the two successive days of 11.1-19
are framed by 'evening/morning' notices (11.11 ὀψὲ ἤδη οὔσης τῆς
ὥρας, 11.12 καὶ τῇ ἐπαύριον, 11.19 ὅταν ὀψὲ ἐγένετο, 11.20
παραπορευόμενοι πρωΐ)/15/, the third day commencing at 11.20 has
no corresponding terminal 'evening' reference. It is open-ended.
This fact, combined with the undue length that such a third day
would occupy relative to the material, would seem to militate
against the view that a three-day structure has been intentionally
devised in order to provide the framework for *all* of the material
that is to be found in 11 - 13.

In support of this view we may refer to 14.49: καθ᾽ ἡμέραν
ἤμην πρὸς ὑμᾶς ἐν τῷ ἱερῷ διδάσκων, καὶ οὐκ ἐκρατήσατέ με.
Referring back to Jesus' period of teaching in the Temple, this
verse conveys, by its use of the term 'day by day', 'daily' or
'every day', the distinct impression that Jesus' teaching was not
understood to have been confined to either one or at most two
specific days.

From this it follows that the three-day structure is
principally related to the material in chapter 11, viz, the
Triumphal Entry (first day), the Cursing of the Fig-tree and the
Cleansing of the Temple (second day), and the Lesson from the
Fig-tree and the Question about Jesus' Authority or Vollmachtsfrage
(third day). If this is so, then we may go on to explore two
alternatives which present themselves for discussion:

1. *The three-day structure belongs to a pre-Markan tradition* which associated the cursing of the fig-tree with the cleansing of the Temple and disassociated, on the other hand, the story of the triumphant entry as also the Vollmachtsfrage immediately from that event. This is the position adopted by Emanuel Hirsch, for example /16/.

2. *The three-day structure is a function of redaction.* Its effect has been to connect the cursing of the fig-tree with the Entry, the Cleansing (in particular) and the Vollmachtsfrage. This association is, therefore, artificial, the fig-tree pericope having had no earlier connection with these traditions prior to our edited version of Mark. This is the position adopted by Wellhausen, J. Weiss, Wendling, Loisy, Dibelius and Bultmann, as we have seen /17/, and by Jeremias /18/ and Sundwall /19/ also. Disagreements occur principally over the question of the connection of Entry, Cleansing and Vollmachtsfrage to each other in the earliest recoverable tradition /20/.

The case for the two possibilities that we are exploring, then, depends very largely on our evaluation of the crucial verses 11, 12, 15, 19, 20 and 27 of chapter 11. Are these to be regarded as belonging to material that predates our version of Mark or are they attributable to the redactor of our gospel? Hirsch has no difficulty with verses 11, 12, 15 and 19, which he assigns to an earlier version of the gospel, an Ur-Markus, Mk I. This version, representing the earliest recoverable tradition, recounted the entry as occurring on the first day, the cursing of the fig-tree and the cleansing of the Temple on the second, and the Vollmachtsfrage on the third. The structure is clear and transparent. Only verses 19/20 and 27 sound a disharmonious note and are to be regarded as redactional seams between which later hands have added the verses of the sequel by way of commentary on the puzzling fig-tree story. The first of these hands, a redactor of Mk I, R, was responsible for verses 20-24, and it was his version of Mark that Matthew used. Verses 25 and 26 are, however, late glosses. In addition, Hirsch posits a second redaction of Mark that occurred before R's version adding verses 20-24 to Mk I. This version, Mk II, omitted the first visit to the Temple and the fig-tree story (verses 11-14) and brought together for the first time thereby the Entry and Cleansing pericopes. This was the version that Luke used and accounts therefore for that evangelist's association of these two traditions and his corresponding lack of the fig-tree pericope /21/.

This rather complicated reconstruction can, be summarized as follows:

Text history

Mk I   an Ur-Markus representing earliest recoverable
               tradition; contained 11.1-14,15-19,27-33 (vv.20-26
               absent)

Mk II   a revision of Mk I; contained 11.1-10,15-19,27-33
               (omitted vv.11-14; vv.20-26 also absent)

Lk   based on Mk II (no knowledge, therefore, of vv.
               11-14,20-26).

R(Mk I)   an expanded version of Mk I; contained 11.1-14,
               15-19,20-24,27-33 (added vv.20-24)

Mt   based on R(Mk I) (absence of vv.25,26 in his text
               of Mk)

late scribe(s) - glosses vv.25-26

While admitting that seams occur at verses 19 and 20 and at verses 24, 25, 26 and 27, Hirsch regards 11.1-19, nevertheless, as a seamless garment of four traditions (Entry; first Temple visit; Cursing of the Fig-tree; second Temple visit - Cleansing) that are connected together harmoniously. This is doubtful. The first Temple visit conveys almost nothing of substance. Jesus is said merely to have looked around at everything and then departed to Bethany with the Twelve. A sense of anticlimax after the triumphant entry scene is felt. One wonders why such a tradition persisted if so little is predicated of it /22/. Indeed, Hirsch himself suggests that it was the anticlimactic nature of these two traditions (first Temple visit and fig-tree story) that led Mk II to omit verses 11-14 from his version of the original. Following on the triumphant entry, they merely suggested that Jesus was an ordinary pilgrim-tourist.

On the other hand, he wishes to find historical significance in περιβλεψάμενος πάντα . Jesus is seeing the Temple for the first time, according to Mark. He looks around just like an ordinary pilgrim, although he sees and judges differently. Indeed, says Hirsch, the fact that he waits until the following day before acting to cleanse the Temple shows up certain ethnic features that may be learned of Jesus. He acts out of considered thought and decisive resolution and not out of a passion which follows his

immediate impressions. This behaviour, he declares, is not
oriental or semitic!

If this is, indeed, the significance to be attached to
verse 11 (and we seriously doubt it), one wonders why Jesus
appears to revert to more 'typically oriental or semitic'
behaviour in the following scene when he is said to curse an
innocent tree. Hirsch, however, allows for this action, which
he interprets as the result of stress!

Explanations that attempt to give historical, traditional or
even theological substance to the datum in verse 11 appear, in
our opinion, to be less plausible than the supposition that this
verse is redactional. On historical or traditional grounds alone,
its content is questionable. The verse conveys the impression
that Jesus was a stranger to the city and its Temple (so H.J.
Holtzmann, C.G. Montefiore) /23/, a presumption that Matthew makes
even more explicit when editing his Vorlage at this point (Τίς
ἐστιν οὗτος; Mt.21.10). The gospels furnish material, however,
that conveys a different impression /24/. In presenting Jesus as
lodging overnight in Bethany, moreover, the verse contradicts the
datum given by Luke that he 'bivouacked' (ηὐλίζετο) every night
on the Mount of Olives (21.37) /25/.

On literary-critical grounds, on the other hand, there is much
to suggest that it is purely a Markan connecting link /26/. The
reference to Jesus' disciples as οἱ δώδεκα is typically Markan, it
is generally held /27/, and not the product of a special 'Twelve-
Source' (so E. Meyer, K.L. Knox) /28/. The loose linkage of
separate pericopes with the use of καί with the verb of motion
ἔρχεσθαι or its compounds (καὶ εἰσῆλθεν ... καὶ ... ἐξῆλθεν) /29/ as
well as by the temporal (ὀψὲ ἤδη οὔσης τῆς ὥρας) /30/ and the
topographical datum (εἰς Ἱεροσόλυμα ... εἰς Βηθανίαν) /31/, the
repetition of the preposition first in the compound verb and then
independently before the following noun (εἰσῆλθεν εἰς Ἱεροσόλυμα)
/32/, and even the verb περιβλέπειν /33/ have all likewise been
identified as characteristic of his redactional procedure, style
and vocabulary.

There is an awkwardness, moreover, about verses 11 and 15
which suggests the possibility that they are seams between which
the cursing of the fig-tree story has been inserted. Verse 11a
recounts Jesus' entry into Jerusalem and into the Temple. Verse
15b repeats this datum. Two references to the Temple, indeed,
occur in the space of this one half-verse: καὶ εἰσελθὼν εἰς τὸ ἱερον

ἤρξατο ἐκβάλλειν τοὺς ... ἐν τῷ ἱερῷ ...   If verses 11b-15a, along
with this repeated datum καὶ εἰσελθὼν εἰς τὸ ἱερόν, were removed,
the Cleansing account would follow on more or less smoothly from
the account of the Triumphal Entry. The final indication,
therefore, that 11.11 is an editorial connecting link lacking any
historical substance may rest in the fact that both Matthew and
Luke *have* in fact simply omitted it, and apparently with impunity
(Mt.21.10-12 Lk.19.41-45).

A similar concentration of specifically Markan features is
likewise to be discerned in verses 12, 15, 19, 20 and 27. Apart
from the temporal /34/ and topographical notices that appear in
each, καί with Mark's favourite verbs of motion ἔρχεσθαι and
πορεύεσθαι and their compounds are present. The auxiliary verb
ἄρχεσθαι (ἤρξατο ἐκβάλλειν) in 11.15 /35/, the redundant
preposition (ἐξεπορεύοντο ἔξω) in 11.19, the "and passing by -
they saw" construction (καί plus participle plus aorist verb) in
11.20 /36/ and πάλιν /37/ in 11.27 are all common Markan usages.

In short, then, verses 11, 12, 15 and 19, as well as 20 and
27, are more likely to be redactional than integral components of
an earlier united block of material covering verses 1-19 and 27-33.

Hirsch claims, however, that while verse 27 follows smoothly
on from verse 19 ("they left the city ... they come again to
Jerusalem") there is not the same smooth correspondence between 19
and 20 ("they left the city" - no mention of Bethany as in verse
11; "and passing by in the morning", i.e. from Bethany to the
city, cf. verse 12). Hence, verses 20 ff. are secondary
developments of the fig-tree story, verse 20 itself looking to
verse 12. The variant reading ὅταν of verse 19 has replaced the
more original ὅτε as an attempt to disguise this obvious seam.
Verse 19, he believes, was originally intended to inform the reader
that Jesus spent one night in Bethany, but the second night
elsewhere outside the city, perhaps as a precautionary measure.

While there is an undoubted awkwardness in verses 19 and 20,
Hirsch's view that the entire sequel is post-Markan is subject to
doubt. If this were so, then his Ur-Markus would have related a
story of the cursing of the fig-tree which failed to say anything
regarding the effect of Jesus' curse. Verse 20, at least, then,
belongs with verses 12-14. How much more of this section (verses
21-26) can be attributed to the original redactor responsible for
connecting the fig-tree story with the Cleansing of the Temple, is
a question to which we will return shortly. Before doing so,

however, let us sum up our impressions thus far of the redactional organization that may be discovered in the passage.

The three-day structure providing the chronological framework for the material in chapter 11 is artificial. It results merely from redactional activity which has attempted rather awkwardly to insert into an earlier complex of tradition (comprising the Triumphal Entry, the Cleansing of the Temple and the Vollmachtsfrage) the story of the cursing of the fig-tree. Seams occur at verses 11, 12, 15, 19, 20 and 27. The effect of this insertion of the fig-tree story such as to sandwich the Cleansing of the Temple account has been in turn, therefore, to split up the more original connection between these three events. When the story (verses 12-14, 20-26) together with the redactional verses is removed, a smoother and more plausible sequence of events is recovered.

In order to insert the first half of the story at a point following on verse 10, the redactor has deliberately suspended the action for a period of one day, employing a popular "Now it was already late" redactional device, borrowed from earlier stories perhaps a characteristic action of Jesus (περιβλεψάμενος πάντα) to supply the minimum of detail concerning the *first* visit which he has now, thereby, created, and made Jesus withdraw to Bethany with the Twelve, so providing both space and time the following morning for his story. In doing so, however, he has at the same time created within his narrative sequence a sense of anticlimax, as well as giving to Jesus an air of provincial naivety /38/.

In order to insert the sequel after the Cleansing account, he has carried out the same process between verses 17/18 and 27, employing the same devices, though more awkwardly.

The components of the chapter, therefore, consist of a Messianic legend /39/ possibly connected prior to this redactor with the Cleansing of the Temple account and the Vollmachtsfrage, the connection between all three having been broken in turn by the insertion of this story and its sequel /40/. The effect of Jesus' curse, viz, the withering of the fig-tree, is more likely, moreover, to have been originally the culmination of the story than its sequel.

In support of this analysis, we may cite three further pieces of evidence. In verse 28, Jesus is challenged to disclose the authority whereby he does "these things". A number of exegetes have surmised that the reference is to Jesus' whole career, his

provocative words and deeds, his teaching and healing /41/. No
special authority, however, was needed for healing and teaching,
and it is unlikely, in any case, that the reference would be so
wide. The immediate context intimates only that Jesus was
walking about in the Temple (verse 27). Yet can we really believe,
with Thiel /42/, for example, that they were challenging him for
trespassing illegally upon the Temple precincts? In the Lukan
(and perhaps the Matthean) /43/ account of this story, Jesus is
specifically said to be *teaching* when the challenge is presented
to him. The ταῦτα in this case most naturally refers to this
activity (cf. Lk.20.1,2). In Mark, however, the most likely
antecedent for the ταῦτα is Jesus' actions and words in verses
15-17, some ten verses away! This observation strengthens,
we think, the case for an insertion of material between 15-17 and
27ff.

     In addition to the literary connection (between Cleansing
and Vollmachtsfrage accounts) that appears to have been severed
by the insertion of this material, the logical connection between
them appears equally to have been disrupted. One would have
expected that a tradition claiming that Jesus acted as
provocatively as he did in the Temple would have been accompanied
by an account of his *immediate* challenge by the Temple authorities.
Instead, a full day's delay occurs before a response is given.
When we examine John's account of the Cleansing episode, we find
that while the content and interpretation of the event are
different, Cleansing and challenge to Jesus' authority are
immediately connected (2.13-17,18-22). This sequence appears
more plausible. That such may have been felt even by the redactor
may be indicated by verse 18. Awkward in syntax /44/, summary
in content /45/, and announcing some familiar Markan motifs /46/,
this verse too is almost certainly redactional and serves to bridge
this severed gap between Cleansing and Vollmachtsfrage accounts.

     A final consideration is that the "dovetailed" or "sandwiched
narrative" is a phenomenon that can be observed elsewhere in the
gospel /47/, and is now generally held to be attributable to the
evangelist himself /48/. These intercalations, moreover, may not
simply be a device, in the manner of the skilled raconteur, to
fill up a space of time in the ongoing narrative (so von Dobschütz)
but may be intended in certain cases to point the reader to a
significant parallel between both pericopes. Both accounts, in
other words, are mutually interpretative /49/.

This, we believe, is the case here /50/. Mark has not filled
up a space of time with the Cursing pericope. He has deliberately,
and with much awkwardness, created a space of time for it! In
light of this, it would be reasonable, then, to suppose that the
pericope was intended to provide, by virtue of its odd position,
his commentary on these traditions of chapter 11 (and in
particular the Cleansing). It would have had a *symbolic* function,
in other words. Its connection with the material in 11.1 - 13.37
would naturally be understood in the light of his overall intent
to bring each of the pericopes of this section into relation with
the Temple and Jesus' action at the seat of Jewish religious life.
This is the position that we wish to adopt and defend, and whose
significance for Mark's estimation of the Temple we wish to
explore. Supporting evidence for it will be adduced as our
investigations proceed.

"And passing by in the morning": The Sequel

In claiming that Mark's story was intended to have a symbolic
function, we are at once confronted with a serious objection. It
has been frequently pointed out /51/, with justice, that vv.22-26
of the sequel do not appear to interpret the fig-tree story in a
symbolic or allegorical light. These logia are undoubtedly
secondary, a view now widely recognized. 'Uprooted and
transplanted' here, they serve to interpret the story as an object
lesson in the efficacy of faith, prayer and forgiveness. These
lessons, moreover, are quite inappropriate. At best this story
would seem to illustrate the *destructive* power of a Rabbi's curse.
Implications for Christian faith and subsequently Christian prayer
derive only awkwardly from it. The story itself mentions neither.
Its tenor is quite alien to the loving and forgiving spirit that is
urged on the believer in 11.25,26.

This much is clear. The crux of the problem, however, lies
in the reflection that if Mark himself either found these sayings
already attached to the story and did not remove them /52/, or,
conversely, himself connected them to the story /53/, then it is
hard to see how he himself could have intended that the story be
understood as a specific commentary on the Cleansing account. At
most this redactional concern would seem to have been secondary,
for the appended logia do not appear to bring out the significance
of this juxtaposition. Taken together, they serve rather to
weaken its effect. The symbolic interpretation suggested by the
story's attachment to the Cleansing account could apparently only

be preserved, therefore, by attributing this attachment to an
earlier tradition, with the sayings of vv.22 ff. having been
added later in pre-Markan tradition, or by Mark himself. Since
we have expressed ourselves in favour of the view that the redactor
of Mark is responsible for the fig-tree story's curious position,
and hence its symbolic function, then we are pressed ipso facto
towards the view that the sequel to the story has been to some
extent subject to a developing hermeneutical process conducted
subsequently upon the Markan text. We must now consider the
evidence which may be adduced for this position.

     In the first place, it should be remarked that the
authenticity of v.26 is very much in question. While a number
of important textual witnesses do transmit it /54/, the major
editions of the Greek text of Mark's gospel include only vv.20-25
of the sequel as part of the original Markan text /55/.

     It is worth observing, moreover, that M and some twenty other
minuscules, as well as several lectionaries /56/, have yet another
verse following 26:

λέγω δὲ ὑμῖν· αἰτεῖτε καὶ δοθήσεται ὑμῖν, ζητεῖτε
καὶ εὑρήσετε, κρούετε καὶ ἀνοιγήσεται ὑμῖν· πᾶς
γὰρ ὁ αἰτῶν λαμβάνει καὶ ὁ ζητῶν εὑρίσκει καὶ
τῷ κρούοντι ἀνοιγήσεται.

This latter verse should be compared with Mt.7.7,8.

     Despite the not inconsiderable weight of external attestation
for v.26, the majority of textual critics have rightly judged both
v.26 and the following verse cited above to be corruptions of the
Markan text which have crept in from Matthew's gospel /57/. The
gloss from Mt.7.7,8 is identical in wording with the Matthean
version /58/ while the earlier gloss from Mt.6.15 appears to have
been shaped somewhat to v.26 /59/.

     This much is certain, and such evidence confirms that the
sequel to the fig-tree story in Mark had a developing textual
history. But where did the process begin? How much of the sequel
can be ascribed to Mark and how much to the hand of later scribes?

     When we turn our attention to v.25, a number of curious,
almost striking features meet the eye. In the first place, we
should note the very loose connection that this verse has with what
precedes. This is characteristic, indeed, of the structure of the

sequel as a whole. Vv.22 ff., it would seem, have been built up
progressively by the peripheral association of a number of
catchwords /60/. The content here of v.25 appears to have been
suggested by the mention of prayer in v.24, and the effect of its
insertion is such as to define more precisely the appropriate
attitude to be adopted in Christian prayer, viz, a forgiving
spirit. Such an emphasis in turn serves to qualify what may have
been regarded as too thaumaturgic an emphasis in the preceding
verses, by introducing the notion of the proper attitude to be
observed when God is asked to produce miracles for the intercessor
/61/. We should note also that v.26, which has been shown to be a
gloss, is closely modelled in structure and content upon v.25. It
is, in fact, the corollary of v.25. In terms of content both verses
belong together (cf. Mt.6.14-15). If v.26 has been shown to be the
insertion of a scribe, should not v.25 be considered in this light
also?

        A second feature of this verse is its language and grammar
which is distinctly non-Markan. The ὅταν στήκετε phrase, to begin
with, is odd for two reasons. Where we should expect the subjunctive
here after ὅταν, we have the present indicative /62/. This usage is
rare and virtually unique in the New Testament /63/. The nearest
parallels to it are either in variant readings which are
insufficiently attested /64/, or ones which give ὅταν with the
future indicative /65/ or with the past tense indicating a past
definite action /66/, or which involve ἐάν with the present
indicative /67/. The construction appears several times in the
LXX but is more common with writers of the Koinē. In the papyri it
appears only in the post-Christian period. It is common with
Byzantine writers, however, and is also a feature of modern
Greek /68/.

        What is of especial note, however, is that ὅταν with the
present indicative occurs nowhere else in Mark's gospel. Mark's
usage of this conjunction is strictly grammatical, with 11.19 being
a possible exception if a definite action in the past, rather than
an iterative one, were here in view /69/. In 3.11 he uses the
imperfect indicative correctly of a past repeated action. Elsewhere
he consistently uses the subjunctive /70/. In every case, without
exception, where a possible future action is considered, or a
general action in present or future is envisaged, he uses ὅταν
strictly with the subjunctive. The construction here, therefore,
is inconsistent with Mark's style, or with that of his sources.

        This phrase is odd, too, in that it employs the verb στήκειν,
which is a late Hellenistic formation derived from the perfect of

ἵστημι viz, ἕστηκα /71/. The form is otherwise virtually confined
to Paul, and when it occurs, is mostly in the imperative, with the
sense "stand firm", "hold one's ground" /72/. In the present
indicative form στήκετε it appears only here and in 1 Thes.3.8 and
Phil.1.27. Where Mark uses the verb "to stand" in the sense of
"standing firm", "holding one's ground", as in 3.24,25,26, σταθῆναι
and στῆναι (forms of the commoner ἵστημι) are employed. Where he
uses the verb "to stand" in the sense of bodily position, as in
11.5; 13.9,14; 14.47,69-70; 15.35,39, he uses the commoner ἵστημι
again, with the weak participle form ἑστηκώς being more frequent
than the stronger ἑστώς form favoured by other writers /73/.

A further non-Markan item of vocabulary is the noun παράπτωμα
which is a hapax legomenon in the gospel. It occurs in Matthew,
however /74/, and is frequent in Paul /75/. Where Mark elsewhere
uses the word 'sin' or 'transgression', the noun ἁμάρτημα is
employed /76/.

By far the most striking non-Markan expression, however, is
the phrase ὁ πατὴρ ὑμῶν ὁ ἐν τοῖς οὐρανοῖς. Nowhere else in Mark
is God referred to in this way. He is addressed as 'the Father'
in 13.32 and 14.36 (cf. also 8.38) but the designation 'heavenly
(οὐράνιος) Father' or 'Father who (is) in the heavens' is a
circumlocution that is characteristically Matthean. The two
formulae, which are both translations of a common Jewish-Aramaic
expression /77/, appear in Matthew some twenty times. Of these
occurrences, the ὁ ἐν τοῖς οὐρανοῖς formula is the more frequent,
being found on seven occasions in material peculiar to Matthew /78/,
and on six occasions where the Synoptic parallel lacks it /79/.
On one occasion, Luke has ὁ πατὴρ ὁ ἐξ οὐρανοῦ (11.13) where
Matthew has ὁ πατὴρ ὑμῶν ὁ ἐν τοῖς οὐρανοῖς, but Luke's second ὁ
may be a gloss /80/. Earlier in this same passage a scribe has
introduced the Matthean formula into the Lukan text of the Lord's
Prayer (11.2; cf. Mt.6.9). The formula, on the other hand, does
not appear in Paul or John. The problem, then, is to account for
the presence in this sole verse in Mark of an expression that
properly belongs to Matthew.

The most common explanation is that in Mk.11.25 we have a
reminiscence of the Lord's Prayer in the form in which it was
deemed to have been employed by Christians when Mark was writing
(so e.g. Rawlinson). Apart from the fact that Mark nowhere else
quotes this prayer, this view presumes too much, for what we have
here is not, strictly speaking, a reminiscence of the Lord's
Prayer as such, but a reminiscence of the Lord's Prayer as we have
it in Matthew's gospel. The ὁ ἐν τοῖς οὐρανοῖς formula is peculiar

to Mt.6.9. The Lukan version of the Lord's Prayer lacks it (cf.
11.2). Mk.11.25, moreover, is clearly related to Mt.6.14, the
verse whose corollary (6.15) was later introduced into the Markan
text (11.26). Yet the position (if not also the content) of both
these verses (Mt.6.14,15) is in all probability the product of
Matthew's redactional activity. They were unlikely, therefore,
to have circulated originally in connection with the prayer.

Further echoes of Mt.6, and, indeed, of Matthew's Sermon on
the Mount as a whole, may also be discerned. "When you stand
praying" recalls to mind Mt.5.23,24 and 6.5,7. Where Matthew
gives a sense of locality to the "standing" in prayer at the altar,
in the synagogue or at the street corner, the στήκετε here appears
abruptly and without any such referent. The ἔχειν τι κατά τινος
construction /81/ also recalls to mind Mt.5.23,24, where the
notion of reconciliation (διαλλάγηθι) is also present. The turning
around of this phrase from the Matthean μνησθῆς ὅτι ὁ ἀδελφός σου
ἔχει τι κατὰ σοῦ may reflect the predominant influence of 6.14,15,
where, as here, the notion is of forgiving men their trespasses
(cf. also Mt.18.35) /82/.

In many respects, therefore, this verse reminds one of those
numerous quotations of the Church Fathers where in quoting a
scriptural verse,presumably from memory, the author confuses
several scriptural passages which have a common theme, and so
produces unintentionally a hybrid citation. A different
explanation for these observed parallels, however, has normally
been proferred by scholars. Matthew, it is argued, has himself
fashioned the logia of 5.23-24 and 6.14-15 directly from or under
the influence of Mk.11.25 /83/. M.D. Goulder has even claimed
that the Lord's Prayer in its entirety is a Matthean composition
created out of such elements (inter alia) as Mk.9.1, 11.25 and
14.36,38 /84/. Such a borrowing is, in the words of John Chapman,
"possible, like so many improbable things" /85/. The saying of
Mt.5.23-24 which presupposes the existence of the sacrificial
system in Jerusalem, is clearly more primitive than Mk.11.25, /86/
which, in any case, seems to be a pastiche of elements from related
prayer and forgiveness logia. On the other hand, the obvious
priority of the Matthean sayings here, in respect of Mk.11.25, is
hardly a case for abandoning the priority of Mark's gospel as a
whole, as both Chapman and Butler have claimed /87/. The simplest
solution is to hold that 11.25 did not belong to the original Markan
text.

This view is, on the whole, the most reasonable one. Taken
singly, each of the above considerations does not possess in itself

overwhelming force, but taken together they suggest the strong
probability that v.25, like v.26 (and 27 of M et al.) should be
assigned not to the redactor of Mark but to a later scribe (or
scribes) /88/. Familiar with Matthew's gospel, the latter has
expanded this Markan passage with the insertion (from memory) of
devotional material from Matthew which further develops the thought
of v.24 /89/. Having alluded to the first half of Mt.6.14, he has
in turn opened the way for a later scribe to supply in v.26 the
corollary to that verse from Mt.6.15. A further scribe at an even
later date inserted a gloss from Mt.7.7,8, thus supplying another
'efficacy of faith and prayer' saying to the number previously
appended here. The total effect of this process, however, has
been to obscure the purpose of Mark's original redactional activity.

The final piece of corroborative evidence is the fact that
in the Matthean parallel passage of 21.18-22, this verse does not
appear. If Matthew were following Mark, then it is curious that
he would have omitted this verse if it had in fact appeared in his
text of Mark. There is simply no reason for such an omission had
it occurred. The verse is entirely at one with Matthew's spirit.
It echoes, indeed, his language. Although its sentiments are
otherwise expressed in his own gospel in 5.23-24; 6.5,7,9,12,14-15;
18.35, he would scarcely have omitted it in order to avoid
duplication, as some have argued /90/. He shows no such
punctiliousness elsewhere, as, for example, when he includes the
mountain-moving saying of Mk.11.22,23 in two separate contexts
(Mt.17.20; Mt.21.21). Such doublets are frequent /91/. On the
contrary, it appears more reasonable to assume that, had he used
Mark, this verse was absent from the Markan text.

We may now turn to v.24. The internal evidence that this
verse is the work of someone other than Mark is less compelling
than it is for v.25, but in favour of this view we may draw attention to the following. As with vv.25,26 and (27), v.24 develops
the preceding verse peripherally and by catchword association /92/.
If vv.25,26 and (27) have been built up in this way, then, and
there are compelling grounds for believing that they are secondary
to the Markan text, might this not be the case also with v.24?

V.24 draws a generalizing lesson concerning the efficacy of
faith when exercised through the medium of *prayer*. It commends
itself to Christian piety. Its link with the preceding story is
tenuous. While appearing to be addressed to the disciples, it
addresses itself, in fact, to the Christian community at large.
Some have viewed it, indeed, as a purely homiletic expansion of the

preceding logion /93/. Its function, as with 11.25, is possibly
to offset too strictly thaumaturgic an interpretation of the
preceding verses and to locate faith-inspired activity more
specifically within the proper sphere of Christian prayer. V.25,
as we have seen, insists that such faith-inspired prayer, in turn,
be exercised in the proper forgiving spirit.

The connection with what precedes is made with the rather
vague conjunctive term διὰ τοῦτο. To what precisely does the
τοῦτο refer? The expression is used only twice elsewhere in Mark
(6.14; 12.24), but not for the purpose of coupling stray logia or
dominical sayings. On the other hand, διὰ τοῦτο or διὰ τοῦτο λέγω
ὑμῖν appears frequently in Matthew /94/, does introduce such logia
and, in certain cases, is employed to connect a logion to a passage
in the Markan Vorlage in order, as here, to bring out or extend
its meaning (cf. e.g. 21.43). The ἔσται ὑμῖν construction (which
appears too in v.23) might also be compared with Mt.19.27, where
Matthew adds this particular construction to his source (τί ἄρα
ἔσται ἡμῖν; cf. Mk.10.28).

In terms of vocabulary and style, it should also be remarked
that Mark, with few exceptions /95/, uses πιστεύειν or its cognate
πίστις absolutely /96/, and very often with christological
overtones /97/. Here in v.24, however, the verb is followed, as
in v.23, by ὅτι and an object clause, and has the simple meaning
of 'believing that ...' without such overtones. The use, moreover,
of προσεύχεσθαι with the accusative of the things requested (πάντα
ὅσα προσεύχεσθε) is rare in the New Testament /98/. The verb is
normally used absolutely, or followed by ἵνα or ὅπως with a clause
expressing the desire (cf. Jas.5.16) or by τοῦ with the infinitive
(cf. Jas.5.17) /99/. Where Mark elsewhere employs this verb, he
follows the normal usage (cf. e.g. 1.35; 14.38).

The syntax and grammar, too, are awkward and there are a
number of correctional variants. The doubling of the two verbs
προσεύχεσθε καὶ αἰτεῖσθε is a trifle clumsy /100/, and it has, in
some textual witnesses, been altered to correspond more closely with
the smoother Greek of the Matthean version (cf. Mt.21.22). The
surprising aorist tense of πιστεύετε ὅτι ἐλάβετε has likewise
occasioned difficulty and been replaced by λαμβάνετε or λήμφεσθε
in many prominent authorities /101/.

While Mark's syntax and grammar often show a characteristic
awkwardness /102/, especially when combining disparate sources,
the possibility also lies open, on the other hand, that we have

here, as in v.25, the work of a scribe making an insertion from
memory and doing it rather clumsily. As in v.25, the content of
the verse echoes a number of prayer-faith passages to be found
elsewhere in the New Testament, and particularly in Matthew (Mt.7.
7,8; 18.19; 21.22   Lk.11.9,10 Jn.14.13,14; 15.7,16; 16.23,24
1 Jn.5.14,15 Jas.1.5,6). Apart from the Matthean parallel in
21.22, the strongest echo is of Mt.7.7,8 /103/, a verse connected,
as we have seen, in more recognizable form with vv.22-26 by the
gloss present in M and other witnesses. The implication that
faith presumes that, in the act of prayer, prayer requests *have
been* realized (ἐλάβετε) may also be an echo of 1 Jn.5.14,15.

These observations are indicative, although, as we have said,
they are less compelling than the evidence for the secondary nature
of vv.25 and following. Matthew's text, it must be conceded, does
have the equivalent of v.24 (cf. Mt.21.22) and in a form that is
much smoother than its Markan parallel. The simpler conclusion, on
the surface, would be to assume that this verse was present in
Matthew's copy of Mark, although he has improved the syntax and
grammar when taking it over. On the other hand, the possibility
does exist that Matthew did not read this verse in Mark but was the
first to attach it to the sequel when attempting to interpret Mark's
puzzling fig-tree story. In this case, v.24 in Mark would be an
early scribal insertion from Mt.21.22, echoing Mt.7.7,8 and even
perhaps 1 Jn.5.14,15. It would, therefore, be part of the
developing hermeneutical process to which the Markan pericope was
subject and which had, in fact, begun with Matthew, as we shall
see in chapter III.

We must now consider the mountain-moving saying of vv.22b,23
and at this point our difficulties have become even more acute.
If we were to regard this saying as secondary to the Markan text,
then we are obliged also to discard the verses which introduce it,
viz, vv.21 and 22a. However, these verses show no positive signs
of *not* having been written by the author of the gospel, unlike
v.25 and possibly v.24. The 'remembering' motif which serves to
link the sequel with vv.12-14 is employed in 14.72 (cf. also 8.18).
Peter also figures frequently elsewhere, particularly as the
spokesman for the disciples /104/. Jesus, too, is elsewhere
addressed as ῾Ραββί or ῾Ραββουνί /105/ and the use of ἴδε or ἰδού
to draw attention to something is common /106/.

In addition the twin clauses καὶ ἀναμνησθεὶς ὁ Πέτρος λέγει
αὐτῷ and καὶ ἀποκριθεὶς ὁ Ἰησοῦς λέγει αὐτοῖς in 21 and 22a are
examples of a construction employed twelve times in Mark and yet
not in other gospels (exc. Jn.5.6; 21.19) /107/. The pleonastic

participle (ἀποκριθείς), too, is a feature of the gospel /108/.
Mark also uses λέγει, as well as εἶπεν (with no apparent distinction)
to introduce various sayings of Jesus (cf. 10.42). More formal
teaching discourses tend to be constructed with ἔλεγεν /109/.

The vocabulary and diction of 11.20 indicate likewise that
this narrative verse was almost certainly composed by Mark /110/,
although it is difficult to say whether it was the evangelist who
was responsible for the datum that the tree had actually withered.
This effect of Jesus' curse may have been described in his source,
although, if so, it would have been the culmination of the story,
we believe, rather than its sequel /111/.

In short, then, the substance of the mountain-moving saying
of verses 22b,23, by virtue of its apparently authentic framework,
is more likely to have belonged to the original Markan text than to
have been a later insertion /112/. We say the 'substance' of the
logion advisedly, for there is some doubt as to the actual form of
the logion in his original text as well as in the pre-Markan
tradition /113/. The syntax of vv.22b,23 is very awkward /114/.
The passage has undergone considerable revision in the manuscript
tradition, as a glance at the numerous variant readings clearly
shows /115/. Many of these variants appear to stem from the
attempt by scribes to harmonize Mark's text with that of Matthew
and Luke. The objective genitive θεοῦ after πίστις is uncharacter-
istic of Mark /116/ and may be a gloss /117/. The long and
unwieldy καὶ μὴ διακριθῇ κτλ. clause is pleonastic. Taylor
suggests it may be a homiletic expansion of the logion, since the
parallel Q form lacks it (cf. Mt.17.20: Lk.17.6) /118/. The
οὐ/μή ... ἀλλά construction /119/ suggests that Mark himself was
responsible for the clause, however, although the use of πιστεύειν
here is, as we have said, unusual /120/.

The mountain-moving saying may best be understood, therefore,
as a secondary interpretative logion which did not belong originally
with the fig-tree story but was later attached to it. This
attachment was made by the redactor of Mark who was also responsible
for connecting the story with the Cleansing of the Temple account.
Appended by means of the 'remembering' motif (cf. Jn.2.17,22),
which looks back to 11.14c, the saying was intended to draw a
lesson from the story. What this lesson was we shall suggest in a
moment but at this point we should now draw together the
conclusions that result from our investigations.

In the first place we may say that the sequel to the fig-tree
story in Mark has been subject to a developing textual history.

It incorporates various levels of redactional activity with correspondingly different hermeneutical concerns. It has been built up in stages, each successive addition serving to cloud the original significance of the Markan redaction. Part of this material is secondary to the Markan text, and has been inserted by later scribes, who may have been puzzled, dissatisfied or embarrassed by the theological import of the passage before them, or who wished to add further comments by affixing additional 'faith and prayer' sayings to it. Matthean material in particular has been a strong influence on them.

With regard to the Mt.7.7,8 saying appearing in M and some 20 other minuscules, both internal and external attestation combine to make it absolutely certain that we have here a gloss. With regard to v.26, we may say confidently that it too is almost certain to be a later gloss, although here the external attestation for its inclusion is considerably greater. It is also highly probable that v.25 is a later scribal insertion, although here a considerable weight of internal evidence for its omission runs in the face of the external attestation for its inclusion.

With v.24, the situation is less clear. External attestation for its inclusion, as with v.25, is overwhelming, but internal attestation suggests that it is non-Markan. Since this evidence, though indicative, is not as considerable as for 25, we may only say that it is a reasonable possibility that it comes from the hand of a later scribe.

With regard to vv.20, 21 and 22a, on the other hand, it may safely be said that Mark's hand is very much in evidence. We are led, therefore, to view the substance of the mountain-moving saying of 22b and 23 as having originally belonged to the sequel and to conclude that he himself has attached it to the story. But if this is so, then we must return to the question that was raised earlier. Can he have intended the fig-tree story to have conveyed a symbolic meaning with respect to the Cleansing account when he has added a logion that appears to express his understanding of that story as an object lesson in the efficacy of faith (and perhaps also of prayer)?

It is our view that a symbolic intent for the story can still clearly be recognized and that *by virtue of,* and not *despite,* this appended logion. The disciples, it is to be observed, are summoned to believe that "this mountain" can and will be uprooted and cast into the sea. This saying, we suggest, may have been intended, along

with the curious positioning of the story, to be read as a comment
on the specific action of Jesus in the Temple. The "this mountain",
in other words, was to be seen (and could quite naturally be taken)
as the Temple Mount /121/, whose removal is even more explicitly
promised in 13.2.

According to this view, Mark has Jesus connect both events.
Jesus' power, or perhaps rather his faith in God's power to act in
judgement against a tree which failed to live up to its promise,
has been vindicated, to the surprise of his disciples. Similarly,
his disciples are invited to understand that the removal of the
Temple Mount, which in like manner has failed to fulfil its raison
d'être (cf. 11.17), can and will be accomplished as easily in
response to such faith. Vv.22b and 23, therefore, may be
considered in the same light as 13.1,2; 14.58 and 15.29, viz, as
'destruction of the Temple' prophecies. The fact that the
disciples show surprise at the withering of the tree and appear,
perhaps, to be admonished by Jesus for lack of faith, may also
be significant. Despite the Cleansing scene and despite his words
here following the withering of the tree, they continue apparently
to maintain a reverential attitude towards the Temple ἴδε ποταποὶ
λίθοι καὶ ποταπαὶ οἰκοδομαί 13.1). Mark, it is to be noted, places
Jesus' more explicit prophecy of destruction directly in contrast
with this expressed attitude of worshipful admiration.

If this redaction-critical position is to be sustained, then
it becomes necessary to ascertain more precisely what the original
form, context and Sitz im Leben of the mountain-moving saying was,
so that, in turn, we may determine the nature and significance of
Mark's redactional work on it. This we shall do in chapter IV.
Since we have also claimed that the Markan pericope has been
subject to a post-Markan hermeneutical expansion that was inspired
by the first gospel, we must first turn our attention to the
intermediate stage in that process. We shall go on immediately,
therefore, to consider Matthew's account of the story.

NOTES

/1/   In the course of our discussion, we shall be referring to
the author of the gospel as 'Mark', 'the Markan redactor', 'the
redactor of the gospel', 'the second evangelist' and so on. The
use of these terms is purely formal, and does not of itself
presuppose a specific identification of this author with the
John Mark of Acts. References to the Greek text, moreover, are
to the British and Foreign Bible Society edition (London, 1958,
ed. E. Nestle, G.D. Kilpatrick), unless otherwise indicated.
/2/   See E. Trocmé, *La Formation de l'Évangile selon Marc,* pp.
63-9, esp. 64,66,67-8; N. Perrin, *Introduction,* pp.147,158-9; C.K.
Barrett, "The House of Prayer and the Den of Thieves" in *Jesus und
Paulus,* Fs. W.G. Kümmel, p.13.
/3/   Ambrozic, *Hidden Kingdom,* p.38.
/4/   Cf. Jeremias, *The Eucharistic Words of Jesus,* pp.256 ff.
/5/   Most commentators take verse 19 in an iterative sense, an
interpretation that is borne out by the use of ὅταν here with the
indicative (cf. 3.11) combined with the imperfect ἐξεπορεύοντο.
Some, however, view it as a statement of fact rather than of custom,
claiming that such a sense is demanded by the context, despite the
improper use of ὅταν for a definite past action (cf. e.g. W.C. Allen
The Gospel according to Saint Mark, pp.144-5; Taylor, *Mark,* p.465).
Lagrange suggested that the distinction (classical) between ὅτε and
ὅταν may have been dropped in common speech (cf. also Turner, *Mark,*
p.95) but consistent Markan usage is against this (*vide infra,*p.51).
The Byzantine witnesses, it is to be noted, as well as A D Γ Φ
157. 700 pm, actually read ὅτε here.
/6/   ἐξεπορεύετο (v.l.).
/7/   Such demonstratives, left in mid-air like this, are said by
Wendling to be a sign of redaction (*Entstehung,* p.145). So also
Bultmann, who conjectured that the ταῦτα may originally have
referred to Jesus' (or the Church's) practice of baptism. The
apophthegm has been transformed by its manipulation (possible prior
to Mark) into the context of chapter eleven (*History,* pp.19,20 and
fn.1).
/8/   For this Holy Week pattern, see, for example, Swete and
Turner ad loc. Cf., however, the attack made on this position by
T.W. Manson (*BJRL,* 33 (1950-1), pp.271-82) who argued that Mark
himself furnished indications that the period covered by these
events was not one week but something more like six months.
/9/   *Drei Markus-Evangelien* (AKG 26), pp.53-9, 114, 170-5.
/10/   *Frühgeschichte,* I, pp.121-6.
/11/   *Rahmen,* pp.274-303.

/12/ Dibelius, *Formgeschichte*[5], p.225, fn.1; Bultmann, *History*, pp.340-1; cf. also G. Strecker, *Der Weg der Gerechtigkeit*, p.93.

/13/ *ZThK*, 58 (1961), pp.161-2.

/14/ *Entstehung*, pp.144 ff.; cf. also Goguel, *Jesus*, p.239.

/15/ The two latter references, it is worth remarking, have not even been framed with any great precision. Verse 19 can be read as a customary action on the part of Jesus and his disciples (*supra*, p.60, n.5). The use in 11.20 of the word πρωΐ = 'in the morning', 'in the early morning light', 'at dawn', rather than a more definite expression for 'on the next day', again weakens the case for a precise three-day chronology (*vide supra*, p.9). There is no exact indication, moreover, that the third visit to Jerusalem in 11.27 terminates the journey begun in 11.20. The use of πάλιν may even serve, it has been said, to disconnect these two journeys (so Menzies, *Earliest Gospel*, p.213).

/16/ *Frühgeschichte*, I, pp.121-6.

/17/ *Supra*, pp.10 ff.

/18/ *Eucharistic Words*, pp.90-1; *Jesus als Weltvollender*, pp.35-44.

/19/ *Die Zusammensetzung des Markusevangeliums*, pp.70-1.

/20/ Jeremias holds, for example, that Entry, Cleansing and Vollmachtsfrage form an indivisible whole (*ibid.*). While he, too, regarded Cleansing and Vollmachtsfrage pericopes as forming a single unit in pre-Markan tradition, J. Weiss stated that Entry and Cleansing accounts were not so linked (*Ält.Evang.*, pp.267-8). Dibelius, however, was of the opinion that Mark had brought the Vollmachtsfrage (which may originally have been handed down as a saying of Jesus and not in narrative form) into connection with the Cleansing account (*Formgeschichte*[5], p.42, fn.1, and *The Message of Jesus*, pp.28, 139-40). Bultmann thought that the Vollmachtsfrage may have been connected with the Cleansing in an earlier edition of Mark, but again not originally, since the Cleansing of the Temple would not have been an appropriate cause for a Rabbinic debate like this (*History*, pp.19-20). Sundwall linked 11.27b with 11.15 and 16 and (like Bultmann) regarded 11.17 as a secondary interpretation which was, however, pre-Markan (*Zusammensetzung*, pp.71-2).

/21/ See Hirsch, *Frühgeschichte*,I, pp.121-6.

/22/ Cf. J. Schmid, *Matthäus und Lukas*, p.30 and fn.2.

/23/ Not all scholars have accepted, of course, that this is the significance of Jesus' 'looking around at all things' (contr. e.g. Meyer-Weiss, Loisy, Rawlinson, Hauck, Taylor ad loc.). J. Lightfoot claimed that it was "a beholding with reproof and correction" (*Horae*, II, p.431) and Meyer that it was "deeply serious, sorrowful, judicial" (cf. 3.5,34 and *Meyer-Dickson*, I, p.178). Many have regarded it as a preliminary reconnoitre on Jesus' part before the morrow (so e.g. Menzies, *Earliest Gospel*, p.207).

/24/ Cf. e.g. Mt.4.5; 5.23-24; 12.6; 23.16 ff. Mk.3.8; 15.43.
Lk.2.41 ff. Jn.7.1 ff. and see Wellhausen, *Marci*[2], p.88; J.
Schniewind, *Das Evangelium nach Matthäus*, p.215.
/25/ Cf. J. Weiss, *Ält.Evang.*, p.268; contr. Taylor, *Mark*, p.458.
/26/ Cf. Jeremias, *Eucharistic Words*, p.91; Ambrozic, *Hidden Kingdom*, p.34.
/27/ See Bultmann, *History*, p.345; Kuhn, *Sammlungen*, pp.137,159;
Jeremias, *ibid*.
/28/ It is to be noted, in addition, that Meyer in fact exempted
Mk.11.1-11 from the influence of this alleged source in view of
δύο τῶν μαθητῶν αὐτοῦ in 11.1 (*Ursprung*, I, pp.145-6; cf. Taylor,
Mark, p.458).

In the pre-Markan tradition μαθηταί may originally have
referred to an unspecified number of followers, and not the Twelve,
hence Mark's addition of σὺν τοῖς δώδεκα to the words of his source
in 4.10 (ἠρώτων αὐτὸν οἱ περὶ αὐτόν). Later copyists have written
simply οἱ μαθηταὶ αὐτοῦ since this identification was by now self-
evident (Bultmann,*History*, p.67).
/29/ Cf. e.g. 1.39,40; 3.20; 5,1,22; 6.1; 8.22; 9.33; 10.46; 11.15,
27; 12.18; 14.32 (ἔρχεσθαι) 2.1; 3.1; 11.15 (εἰσέρχεσθαι) 1.35;
2.13; 6.1; 8.11,27; 14.26 (ἐξέρχεσθαι) 3.20; 14.53 (συνέρχεσθαι)
12.28 (προσέρχεσθαι).
/30/ Cf. e.g. 1.32,35; 4.35; 6.35,47; 9.2; 11.12,19,20; 14.17;
15.42.
/31/ See Bultmann, *History*, pp.339-40; Kümmel, *Introduction*, p.63.
/32/ See Allen, *Mark*, pp.14-15.
/33/ Jeremias, *Eucharistic Words*, p.91, fn.1. A note of caution
should be sounded, however. The verb is used six times in Mark and
in five out of six cases it describes a characteristic action of
Jesus (cf. 3.5,34; 5.32; (9.8); 10.23; 11.11). It may be
arbitrary, therefore, to assume this is a characteristic Markan
word. It may equally belong to Mark's traditional material, as
H.-W. Kuhn has argued *(Sammlungen, p.149)*. Even so, doubt does
exist whether this is the case here.
/34/ For τῇ ἐπαύριον (11.12) cf. Jn.1.29,35,43; 12.12 and see
Schmidt, *Rahmen*, p.300.
/35/ Cf. e.g. 1.45; 4.1; 5.20; 6.2,7,34,55; 8.31,32; 10.28,32,41,
47; 12.1; 13.5; 14.19,33,65,69,71; 15.8,18 and Allen, *Mark*, p.18;
Turner, *JTS*, 28 (1926-7), pp.352-3; Donahue, *Are You the Christ?*,
p.56.
/36/ Cf. e.g. 1.16,19,20,31,35; 2.1,4,14 etc. and Allen, *Mark*, p.17.
/37/ Cf. e.g. 2.1,13; 3.1,20; 4.1; 5.21; 7.14,31; 8.1,13; 10.1,10,
32 etc. and Allen, *Mark*, p.19; Turner, *JTS*, 29 (1927-8), pp.283-7;
Donahue, *op.cit.*, pp.57,88.
/38/ See Trocmé, *Formation*, p.182, fn.30.

/39/ So Bultmann, who thinks that the story of the entry into
Jerusalem is a Messianic legend influenced by Zech.9.9 which had
perhaps already grown up in Palestinian Christianity (*History*,
pp.261-2,305). Dibelius regarded it as a cultic legend, similar
in form to Mk.14.12-16, which developed within the context of the
church's worship and preaching, although there was no reason to
doubt its inherent historicity (*Formgeschichte*[5], pp.118-19, 128-9;
Message, pp.184-5). For a review of scholarly opinions regarding
this pericope, see Ambrozic, *Hidden Kingdom*, pp.36-7.

/40/ The story itself, while showing a certain degree of Markan
influence in its narration (cf. e.g. the γάρ clause 11.13d; the
double negative μηκέτι ... μηδείς 11.14b; the use of the imperfect
ἤκουον 11.14c) is unlikely to have been freely composed (so Loisy)
or invented. The very incongruity of its parts and the awkwardness
revealed in the effort to insert it, militate against such a view.

/41/ For a review and a critique of these opinions, see the
Sande Bakhuyzen article referred to above (*supra*, p.34, n.98).

/42/ *Markus-Evangelien*, pp.55-6.

/43/ The authenticity of διδάσκοντι in Mt.21.23 is debatable. A
number of witnesses such as the Old Latin and Sy[s.c] omit it. See
Sande Bakhuyzen, *op.cit.*, p.331, fn.1.

/44/ Note the awkward γάρ clauses and cf. e.g. 1.22; 6.20,50; 9.6;
12.12; 14.2; 15.10; 16.8.

/45/ The mention here, not of the one high priest who presided
over the nation's religion nor of the captain of the Temple who
alone maintained order (Menzies, *Earliest Gospel*, p.210) but rather
of a large group of "chief priests and scribes" reveals a wider
perspective than the context in fact warrants. In 11.27, the entire
Sanhedrin is in view.

/46/ Viz, *the plot to kill Jesus* cf. 3.6; 8.31; 9.31; 10.32-34;
12.12; 14.1-2,10-11; *the 'fear' motif* cf. 4.41; 5.15,33,36; 6.50;
9.6,32; 10.32; 11.32; 12.12,34; 16.8; *the 'amazement' motif* cf.
1.22,27,28; 2.12; 5.20,42; 6.2,51; 7.37; 9.15; 10.24,26,32; 12.17;
15.5,44.

/47/ Cf. 1.23-26 in 1.21-22,27; 3.22-30 in 3.21,31-35; 5.25-34 in
5.21-24, 35-43; 6.14-29 in 6.6-13,30-31; 14.3-9 in 14.1-2,10-11;
14.54,66-72 in 14.53,55-65.

/48/ *Vide supra*, p.15.

/49/ On 1.21-27, see, for example, E. Schweizer, "Anmerkungen zur
Theologie des Markus" in Fs. O. Cullmann, *Neotestamentica et
Patristica*, p.39, fn.1, *gratia* Giesen, *BZ*, 20 (1976), p.102; on
3.21-35, Dowda, *Cleansing*, p.218; on 5.21-43, Bird, *JTS*, 4 (1953),
pp.179-82; see also Gaston, *No Stone*, p.83, fn.1, and *supra* p.15
and n.103.

/50/   Note, for example, the parallelism of 'And his disciples
heard' (11.14c) and 'And the chief priests and scribes heard'
(11.18a). Both statements are redactional.
/51/   *Supra,* pp.5-6,15-16.
/52/   So, E. Best, "Mark's Preservation of the Tradition", in
L'Évangile selon Marc. Tradition et rédaction (BETL, 34), ed.
M. Sabbe, p.30.
/53/   So e.g. Nineham, *Mark,* p.298.
/54/   Some Alexandrian witnesses (e.g. C 33.1241.579 and several
Bohairic manuscripts), a number of Western witnesses (e.g. D a aur
b c d f ff^2 (i) q r^1 vg - except one manuscript; Diatessaron Cyp
Aug), most of the Caesarean witnesses (except W 700.565), as well
as the majority of the Byzantine witnesses (e.g. A E F G H K M Γ V
Π Y), most minuscules, sy$^{p.h}$ goth eth and the lectionaries, in the
Synaxarion and in the Menologion.
/55/   Tischendorf, Westcott and Hort, Nestle-Aland, Nestle-
Kilpatrick, Souter, H. von Soden, Vogels, Merk, Legg. Bernhard
Weiss includes v.26 as part of his text, however, and so does
Bover. Meyer claimed that its omission was explained from the
homoeoteleuton of vv.25 and 26 (*Meyer-Dickson,* I, p.175).
/56/   For the precise list, see Hermann Freiherr von Soden,
Die Schriften des Neuen Testaments, Vol.II, and S.C.E. Legg,
Novum Testamentum Graece, Mk.11.26 ad loc.
/57/   C.S.C. Williams, for example, cites Mk.11.26 as a prime
example of a scribal insertion made by someone familiar with
the Matthean text. Cf. *Alterations to the Text of the Synoptic
Gospels and Acts,* p.1.
/58/   579, however, omits ζητεῖτε καὶ εὑρήσετε; cf. Legg, ad loc.
Was this an oversight, or was it omitted because the scribe
realized how inappropriate it was in the light of the original
story? Jesus sought but did *not* find (Mk.11.13)? One wonders!
/59/   As it stands, in the apparatus of the Nestle-Kilpatrick
text, the gloss differs from Mt.6.15 and is correspondingly closer
to Mark 11.25 in respect of the following details of wording:
    a) the initial protasis is introduced by εἰ plus the
        indicative (cf. v.25 and v.1. of 22b εἰ ἔχετε) rather
        than ἐάν plus the subjunctive (cf. Mt.6.15 and
        Mt.21.21).
    b) the general plural τοῖς ἀνθρώποις of Mt.6.15 is
        omitted in light of the singular κατά τινος of v.25.
    c) ὁ ἐν τοῖς οὐρανοῖς is added in parallel with v.25
        where it does not appear in Mt.6.15; cf. Mt.6.14
        ὁ οὐράνιος.
/60/   *Vide supra,* p.15.
/61/   Cf. e.g. Wood, *Peake,*(1919), p.695.

/62/   Several variant readings have στήκητε and στῆτε but are
less well attested. They appear, therefore, to be correctional
emendations.
/63/   Cf. F. Blass, A. Debrunner, *A Greek Grammar of the New
Testament and Other Early Christian Literature,* ed. R.W. Funk, §
382 (henceforward *B-D-F*); J.H. Moulton, *A Grammar of New Testament
Greek,* Vol.II, ed. J.H. Moulton, W.F. Howard, p.73 (henceforward
M-H); A.T. Robertson, *A Grammar of the Greek New Testament in the
light of historical Research,* pp.958, 972-3; C.F.D. Moule, *An
Idiom Book of New Testament Greek,* p.133.
/64/   *B-D-F,* §382(4)
/65/   Cf. Mt.10.19 (v.l.) Lk.13.28(v.l.) 1 Tm.5.11 (v.l.) Ap.4.9
B-D-F § 382; Robertson, *Grammar,* pp.972-3.
/66/   Cf. Ap.8.1; *B-D-F,ibid.;* Robertson, *ibid.*
/67/   Cf. Lk.6.34 (v.l.).Rom.14.8(v.l.) 1 Thes.3.8 1 Jn.5.15;
Robertson, *Grammar,* p.1010.
/68/   *B-D-F,* §382(4); Robertson, *Grammar,* pp.972-3.
/69/   See, however, p.60, n.5.
/70/   Cf. e.g. 4.15,16,29,31,32; 13.4,7,11,14,28,29; 14.7.
/71/   *B-D-F,* §73; *M-H,* p.241; Robertson, *Grammar,* pp.65-6, 150.
/72/   Cf. e.g. 1 Cor.16.13 Gal.5.1 Phil.4.1 2 Thes.2.15.
/73/   Cf. *M-H,* p.222.. One note of caution, however, must be
advanced. In 3.31 the more strongly attested reading gives
στήκοντες (contr. v.l. στάντες, ἑστηκότες, ἑστῶτες) and if we
accept this reading then it always remains possible that Mark could
have employed στήκειν in 11.25.
        Codex W, dating from the fifth century, interestingly,
however, replaces the ἑστηκότα of 13.14 with a form of the later
verb στήκειν and in 3.32 inserts it where it did not stand
originally.
/74/   Cf. Mt.6.14,15; 18.35 (v.l.).
/75/   Cf. Rom.4.25; 5.15^2,16,17,18,20; 11.11,12 2 Cor.5.19
Gal.6.1 Eph.1.7; 2.1,5 Col.2.13^2.
/76/   Cf. 3.28,29.
/77/   See H. Traub, *ThDNT,* 5, οὐρανός ad loc., p.538; J. Chapman,
Matthew, Mark and Luke, p.190.
/78/   Cf. 5.16; 6.1; 7.21; 16.17; 18.10,14,19.
/79/   Cf. 5.45; 6.9; 7.11; 10.32,33; 12.50.
/80/   See Schmid, *Matthäus und Lukas,* p.233, fn.1.
/81/   Found only (apart from here and in Mt.5.23) in Jn.19.11 and
Ap.2.4,14,20.
/82/   Cf. Wendling, *Entstehung,* pp.147-8.
/83/   See e.g. Bultmann, *History,* p.132, although contr. pp.25,61;
G.D. Kilpatrick, *The Origins of the Gospel according to St.Matthew,*
p.97.

/84/   See "The Composition of the Lord's Prayer", *JTS*, 14 (1963), pp.32-45; *Midrash and Lection in Matthew*, pp.110, 287, 296-301 (cf. also pp.41, 65, 402-4).

/85/   *Matthew, Mark and Luke*, p.190, fn.3.

/86/   Bultmann himself admits this (*History*, p.132). Contr. Goulder, *Midrash*, pp.258, 287.

/87/   See Chapman, *op.cit.*, pp.64, 76-7, 190, fn.3; B.C. Butler, *The Originality of St. Matthew*, pp.120, 134-6, 161 .

/88/   This possibility is in fact entertained by Bultmann (*History*, pp.25, 61). Cf. also Lagrange, *Évangile selon Saint Matthieu*, p.407; Montefiore, *Synoptic Gospels*, I, p.270; Bartlet, *Mark*, p.323; Nineham, *Mark*, p.305; Kuhn, *Sammlungen*, p.149, fn.21. More certain are Klostermann, *Markusevangelium*, p.119; Strecker, *Weg*, p.18, fn.2. More recently,· M.-É. Boismard has argued that Matthean influences upon the final redaction of Mark can be traced not only here but elsewhere in the gospel. See "Influences matthéennes sur l'ultime rédaction de l'évangile de Marc" in *L'Évangile selon Marc*, ed. M. Sabbe, pp.93-101.

/89/   That scribal harmonization of the text of Mark to that of Matthew was a common feature of textual transmission is generally recognized. (See Williams, *Alterations*, pp.1-2; Hauck, *Markus*, p.8; cf. also Swete on 11.3; Merx on 11.8; Allen on 11.15; Cranfield on 11.22). Von Soden saw the influence of Tatian's Diatessaron (c.172-173 CE) as the overriding one contributing to the harmonization of Synoptic parallels, but, as Williams has pointed out, "scribes did not always need Tatian's Harmony before them to make them harmonize, as von Soden should have realized" (*op.cit.*, p.1). The process, then, was undoubtedly early, only receiving an additional impetus from Harmonies such as the Diatessaron. This goes also for the doctrinal modifications that also took place and for which, therefore, little manuscript evidence is available. (See Lake, Inaugural Lecture before the University of Leyden, 1904, 10; cited Williams, *op.cit.*, pp.5-6). In turn, there can be little reason to doubt that the insertion of secondary material, drawn from Matthew and elsewhere, and attached in the interests of hermeneutics, would likewise have occurred at an early period. (One should also note how ready scholars have been to dismiss 11.13d as a post-Markan gloss, *supra*, pp.2-3, despite the weight of manuscript evidence for it. Yet 11.25 shows more signs of being non-Markan than 11.13d does.)

/90/   So, for example, Wellhausen, *Das Evangelium Matthaei*, p.105; Allen, *Mark*, pp.145-6.

/91/   *Vide infra*, p.72 and n.11.

/92/   The mention of *speech* (ἀλλὰ πιστεύῃ ὅτι ὁ λαλεῖ γίνεται 11.23) in connection with the expression of faith, appears to lead to the more specific notion of faith expressed in *prayer*. The appended logion, therefore, goes on to relate this *faith* specifically to *prayer*. Attached by means of the conjunctive διὰ τοῦτο, it is also closely modelled on the preceding verse (cf. 11.23 ἀμὴν λέγω ὑμῖν ... 11.24 διὰ τοῦτο λέγω ὑμῖν; 11.23 πιστεύῃ ὅτι ... 11.24 πιστεύετε ὅτι; 11.23 ἔσται αὐτῷ ... 11.24 ἔσται ὑμῖν). See Lohmeyer, *Markus*, p.239 and fn.3; Sundwall, *Zusammensetzung*, p.71; Taylor, *Mark*, p.467.

/93/   Cf. e.g. Knox, *Sources*, I, p.83.

/94/   Cf. Mt.6.25; 12.27,31; 13.13,52; 18.23; 21.43; 24.44.

/95/   Cf., however, 1.15; 9.42; 11.22 (the θεοῦ may be a gloss), 23,31. The εἰς ἐμέ of 9.42, it should be noted, may also be a gloss (cf. Mt.18.6 to which the verse may have been assimilated). A number of important textual witnesses omit it.

/96/   Cf. 2.5; 4.40; 5.34,36; 9.23,24; 10.52; 13.21; 15.32.

/97/   *Vide infra*, p.82.

/98/   Cf., however, Lk.18.11 Rom.8.26.

/99/   See Swete, *Mark*, p.260.

/100/   Contr., however, A. Pallis (*Notes on St Mark and St Matthew*, p.41), who remarks that the construction is used in modern Greek, and Lagrange (*Marc*, p.300), who thinks it is Semitic. Merx recognized here the hand of a glossator, the two verbs being originally alternatives which were later conflated (*Markus und Lukas*, p.135).

/101/   See Tischendorf, Mk.11.24 ad loc.

/102/   He also shows, it must be admitted, a fondness for catchword composition, particularly in respect of the 'Sayings conglomerates' that appear at certain points in his gospel (cf. e.g. 9.33-50 and see Bultmann, *History*, p.325; Taylor, *Mark*, pp.408-10; Donahue, *Are You the Christ?*, pp.77-8).

/103/   See Wendling, *Entstehung*, p.147; Holtzmann, *HC*, I, p.235; Klostermann, *Markusevangelium*, p.119.

/104/   Cf. 3.16 where his name appears first; 5.37; 8.29 ff.; 9.2 ff; 10.28 ἰδοὺ ἡμεῖς ... 13.3; 14.29 ff.,54,66-72; 16.7.

/105/   Cf. 9.5; 10.51; 14.45.

/106/   E.g. 2.24; 3.32,34; 4.3; 10.28; 13.1,21; 14.41,42; 15.4,35; 16.6.

/107/   The construction, coming before direct speech, has in essence the following sequence: καί plus a participle in the aorist, followed by the subject, then the verb λέγειν in the present indicative, followed in turn by the object in the dative cf. 2.5,8,17; 3.5; 5.39,41; 8.17; 9.5; 10.23,42; 11.21,22. It is frequently found in Mark's traditional material, although it occurs also in redactional verses. See Kuhn, *Sammlungen*, pp.149-50.

/108/   See Taylor, *Mark*, p.63.

/109/   Zerwick, *Untersuchungen*, pp.60-9.

/110/   See Taylor, *Mark*, pp.465-6.

/111/   On form-critical grounds, it is more likely that the fig-tree story was originally a single literary unit. The division into two parts is manifestly the result of a conscious literary decision. See W.R. Farmer, *The Synoptic Problem*, p.259.

/112/   This conclusion is strengthened by the observation that the saying appears not only in the parallel Matthean account, but also again in an earlier passage (Mt.17.14-20). The twin contexts for the one apophthegm may best be explained by the suggestion that Matthew favoured the earlier context as being more appropriate. Encountering it, however, in his source material in connection with the fig-tree story, he has decided, nonetheless, to retain it. We shall presently be considering the nature and significance of his redactional activity. (*Infra*, chap.III.)

/113/   *Infra*, chap.IV.

/114/   This is even more so if we read εἰ ἔχετε κτλ. in 22b along with the UBS translators' edn. (1966, ed. K. Aland et al.).

/115/   See Merx, *Markus und Lukas*, p.134, and cf. Tischendorf, Legg and von Soden ad loc.

/116/   *Vide supra*, p.55. Bultmann notes that πίστις employed in connection with God appears only here and in Rom.3.3. It is not an Old Testament Jewish expression, he claims, but derives from the missionary usages (*History*, p.395). Taylor, however, (*Mark*, p.466) denies that even Rom.3.3 is a parallel, but invites a comparison with 1 Thes.1.8 (πρὸς τὸν θεόν) Heb.6.1 (ἐπὶ θεόν) Jn.14.1 (εἰς τὸν θεόν) as well as Rom.3.22 (χριστοῦ) and 26 ('Ιησοῦ).

/117/   So, for example, Lohmeyer, (Nineham). It is lacking in 28 a c k r^1 r^2 bo^{ms}. It is possible, too, that the αὐτῷ after ἔσται was also added. Sy^s, for example, lacks it. Cf. also Mt.21.22 which merely has γενήσεται.

/118/   *Mark*, p.466.

/119/   Cf. 1.45; 3.26,29; 4.17,22; 6.8-9,52; 7.5,15,19; 8.33; 9.37; 10.8,40,45.

/120/   For διακρίνω also cf. Acts 10.20 Rom.4.20 Jas.1.6; 2.4 and see Taylor ad loc. For ἐν τῇ καρδίᾳ αὐτοῦ cf. Mk.2.6 Mt.5.28.

/121/   Both in the Old Testament and the Talmud, the Temple is commonly referred to as "the mountain of the house" or even simply as "this mountain" (cf. e.g. Is.2.2 Mi.4.1 and *vide infra*, p.170, n.65).

The suggestion, moreover, that this identification is here implicit is not a new one; cf. e.g. C.H. Dodd, *The Parables of the Kingdom*, p.63, fn.1; R.H. Lightfoot, *Mark*, p.78; C.H. Bird, *JTS*, 4 (1953), pp.177-8; Gaston, *No Stone*, pp.83-4; Dowda, *Cleansing*, pp.250-1; Carrington, *Mark*, pp.242-3.

Chapter III

THE FIG TREE PERICOPE IN MATTHEW'S GOSPEL

"And Jesus entered the Temple": The Two-Day Scheme

In considering the part played by Matthew in the redaction-history of the fig-tree pericope, we should first remark on the place occupied by this pericope in his redactional scheme. The arrangement of material in both gospels (Mk.10.46 - 13.37 Mt.20.29 - 25.46) is as follows /1/:

		Mark	Matthew
(XII.264)	The Healing of the Blind Men (Bartimaeus)	10.46-52	20.29-34
(XIII.269)	The Triumphal Entry	11.1-10	21.1-9
(271)	Jesus' first Visit to the Temple and the Return to Bethany	11.11	——
	Jesus' Arrival in Jerusalem and the Reaction of the City	——	21.10-11
(271/273)	*The Cleansing of the Temple*	——	21.12-13
(271)	Jesus' Healings in the Temple and the Challenge from the Authorities	——	21.14-16
	The Return to Bethany	——	21.17
(272)	The Cursing of the Fig-Tree	11.12-14	21.18-19
(271/273)	*The Cleansing of the Temple*	11.15-17	——
(274)	The Chief Priests and Scribes conspire against Jesus; the Withdrawal from the City	11.18-19	——
(275)	The Fig-Tree is withered	11.20-26	21.20-22
(276)	The Question about Authority	11.27-33	21.23-27
(277)	The Parable of the Two Sons	——	21.28-32
(278)	The Parable of the Wicked Husbandman	12.1-12	21.33-46
(279)	The Parable of the Great Supper	——	22.1-14
(280)	On Paying Tribute to Caesar	12.13-17	22.15-22

	Mark	Matthew
(281) The Question about the Resurrection	12.18-27	22.23-33
(282) The Great Commandment	12.28-31	22.34-40
	12.32-34	——
(283) The Question about David's Son	12.35-37a	22.41-46
(284) Woe to the Scribes and Pharisees	12.37b-40	23.1-36
(285) Jesus' Lament over Jerusalem	——	23.37-39
(286) The Widow's Mite	12.41-44	——
(XIV.287-293) The Eschatological Discourse	13.1-32	24.1-36
(294) Conclusion: Take Heed, Watch!	13.33-37	24.42
		25.13-15
(XV.296-300) Parables about Coming which Supplement the Eschatological Discourse	——	24.37-25.46

From this it can be seen that the order of material in both evangelists is virtually identical from paragraph 275 onwards. Matthew has more material than Mark (paragraphs 277, 279, 285, 296-300), though Mark also has the Widow's Mite story (286) and the additional 12.32-34, which Matthew does not have. The order of the common material, nevertheless, remains the same.

The arrangement in Mk.11.1-26 = Mt.21.1-22 (paragraphs 269-274) is different. In Matthew, the Cleansing of the Temple follows *immediately* upon the Triumphal Entry with the Cursing of the Fig-Tree and its consequent withering occurring *in one scene* before the Vollmachtsfrage and *on the day following* the Temple visit. This contrasts with the Markan arrangement of Entry (first day) – Cursing-Cleansing (second day) – Withering-Vollmachtsfrage (third day), as we have seen. Instead of Mark's first (anticlimactic) Temple visit (11.11) Matthew brings the Triumphal Entry to a more emphatic climax with a datum regarding the city's reaction to Jesus (21.10-11). In addition, he presents a shorter version of Mark's expulsion scene (Mk.11.16, for example, is lacking) but records healings by Jesus within the Temple precincts amid a Messianic fervour that provokes a challenge from the chief priests and scribes (21.14-16). Mark lacks this material /2/ but has the redactional notice about the conspiracy against Jesus and his withdrawal from the city (11.18-19).

Matthew, then, it would appear, has deliberately rearranged
Mark's material by placing it within a *two-day scheme* /3/: Entry-
Cleansing (first day) - Cursing-Withering-Vollmachtsfrage (second
day). In so doing, he has brought the Entry and Cleansing into
their more logical (and perhaps also their traditional)
relationship /4/. His redaction, however, has produced certain
curious effects. Matthew's second day has now become inordinately
long (21.18 - 25.46) /5/. By introducing, moreover, what amounts
to a second Vollmachtsfrage (21.15-16) he may be seen to be
bending the account to the more natural and original Entry-Cleansing-
Vollmachtsfrage sequence interrupted by Mark. However, his
redactional work has not proceeded entirely smoothly. The challenge
issued in 21.15-16 appears to be against Jesus' healings and/or
his acceptance of Messianic acclaim and not against his interference
with the sacrifices. This latter challenge comes the following
day (as in Mark) and is even more awkward and unlikely as a result
/6/. It should further be noted that, by having the Cleansing
pericope follow immediately upon the Triumphal Entry, Matthew has
produced an order of events that here *and nowhere else* agrees with
Luke over against Mark /7/. Luke, for his own reasons, has omitted
Mark's story altogether, so passing naturally from Mk.11.10 to
11.15, with Lk.20.1 indicating his departure from Mark's
chronological scheme. The separate redactional policies of both
evangelists, therefore, have resulted in a similar order of events.
It is this easy abandonment of Mark's chronological framework and
the reversion of both evangelists to an order of events that was
perhaps, at the same time, the traditional one /8/, which once
again highlights the artificiality of Mark's arrangement.

In passing these judgements on the Synoptic accounts of these
traditions we have, of course, been presupposing that solution of
the Synoptic problem which is favoured by most scholars, viz, that
Mark's gospel is prior and that Matthew has used it in general as
a source for his own gospel. Other solutions in respect of the
fig-tree pericope have been advanced, viz, that Matthew's account
is here prior and Mark was dependent upon him (so, for example,
Baur, Butler, Chapman, Farmer), or that both drew on an independent
source (so, for example, Lagrange, Bartlet, Lohmeyer, Doeve).
Space does not permit a detailed treatment of this vexing problem.
The standard theory, one must admit, cannot always be rigidly
adhered to without certain modifications (as we shall see in
Chapter IV) but the following points nonetheless in defence of
Markan priority here can be made.

In the first place, it should be said that if Matthew's
account of the fig-tree story were here prior /9/, then we are

still obliged to account for the curious presence of this
pericope at this point in *the first evangelist's* redactional
scheme. Matthew's miracle stories are otherwise largely confined
to chapters 8 and 9, are arranged there in a well-ordered cycle,
and appear to have been intentionally grouped and edited in line
with a firm christological purpose /10/. What the redactional
purpose could have been within the context of chapter 21, however,
is difficult to discern, for there the fig-tree story appears
without any obvious relation to the surrounding material. With
Mark's account, on the other hand, we can discern obvious signs
of the story's 'intrusion', with indications of a redactional
intention to connect it *specifically* with the Entry and Cleansing
accounts.

     While the presence of doublets in Matthew's gospel need not
always indicate an overlapping of sources /11/, it is not
unreasonable to suppose furthermore that the twin contexts for
the mountain-moving saying supplied by Matthew here (21.21) and in
17.20 indicate that Matthew was following Mark (and not vice versa)
when repeating the saying in chapter 21 /12/.

     In the third place, it is more likely that the additional
Matthean material in chapters 21-25 was added to a Markan Vorlage
than omitted from a Matthean one. Scholars have commented, for
example, on the elaborate details supplied by Mark in respect of
the finding of the ass (cf. Mk.11.4-6). Even were a motivation to
be suggested for such /13/, is it likely that he would have omitted
the Zechariah proof-text of 21.5 from a Matthean Vorlage merely
in order to supply such details?   Would he have had any reason,
moreover, to suppress a datum that Jesus was regarded as a prophet
by the people (21.10-11; 21.46) /14/ or to omit a verse that spoke
of the Kingdom being given to the Gentiles (21.43)? Additional
material such as 21.5, 21.10-11 and 21.14-16, on the other hand,
shows characteristic Matthean emphases and typical features of the
first evangelist's language and style /15/.

     Conversely, it is more likely that the smaller amount of
additional material appearing in Mark was omitted by Matthew from
a Markan Vorlage than added by Mark to a Matthean one. In this
category belong the description of the finding of the ass as before
(Mk.11.4-6), the Widow's Mite story (12.41-44) and possibly the
answer of the scribe in 12.32-34 /16/. Mark's account of the
Cleansing (cf. esp. 11.16) may also have been abbreviated to make
room for Jesus' Healings in the Temple (21.14-16).

Finally, it should be noted that Matthew's narrative shows itself frequently to be smoother in syntax /17/, more concise in form /18/, and clearer in meaning /19/ than its Markan parallel. Matthew lacks Mark's repetitious and frequently superfluous details and phrases /20/. In general his account is stylistically superior /21/. Surely, therefore, it is more reasonable to accept that Matthew has improved a Markan Vorlage than that Mark has adulterated a Matthean one.

But it is Matthew's specific treatment of Mark's fig-tree story that we are concerned with, and having defended the priority of the Markan account, we must now examine the treatment in detail.

The Nature of Matthew's Redaction

It is a standard presupposition of present-day Redaktionsgeschichte that Matthew, like Mark before him, was not just a mere collector or redactor of Christian tradition, but an active interpreter (or re-interpreter) of it /22/. To ascertain what that interpretation was in this case we must examine the similarities and differences existing between the two accounts. Having described these in detail, we shall then be in a position to draw conclusions regarding Matthew's contribution to the hermeneutical development of the story.

The similarities between the two accounts are very obvious. Mark tells the story in approximately 132 words /23/ if we leave out v.25, in approximately 156 words if we include it. Matthew recounts it in approximately 98 words. Given Matthew's shorter version of the story, the word order within each verse is remarkably similar /24/. In addition, Matthew reproduces most of Mark's vocabulary with only a handful of words which do not appear in the Markan text /25/. There are several phrases which are not in Mark /26/ but these, like a number of the words, may proceed largely from the process of abbreviation Matthew has conducted upon Mark's story. Both accounts also agree very largely in content, although in the sequel, as we have previously noted, Matthew lacks Mk.11.25,26.

The differences between Matthew and Mark may be recognized and discussed in terms of the following:

a)   the chronological scheme
b)   the instantaneousness of the miracle
c)   the general abbreviation of the content

d)   the minor expansions
e)   the form of the curse
f)   the question posed
g)   the mountain-moving saying
h)   verse 22.

In the first place, then, as we remarked earlier, Matthew has
curtailed Mark's chronological scheme. The two morning journeys of
Mark (11.12,20) have been compressed into one. Mark's three-day
scheme (11.11,12,19,20) has been reduced to a two-day scheme
(21.17,18).

The content of vv.17 and 18 largely represents a combination
of data /27/ drawn from Mk.11.11,12,19 and 20. Where Mark records
a withdrawal to Bethany in 11.11, but leaves the destination
unspecified in 11.19, Matthew offers the datum that Jesus /28/
went to Bethany specifically after the Cleansing incident "and
lodged there" /29/. Moreover he links this datum more closely
with the Cleansing incident by his introductory καὶ καταλιπὼν
αὐτούς (cf.16.4) and by his use of the aorist (ἐξῆλθεν) instead
of the imperfect (ἐξεπορεύοντο).

This illustrates a characteristic feature of Matthean
redaction, which is to bring the vaguer chronological and
topographical references in Mark into sharper focus and to make
Mark's looser connections between pericopes stronger /30/. Indeed,
if Mk.11.19 is read iteratively /31/ then Matthew has turned what
in Mark was a recurring practice into a precise and concrete event
at the conclusion of the Cleansing scene.

Allied with this curtailment of Mark's chronological scheme
is Matthew's emphasis on the fact that *the miracle occurred
instantaneously*. Some scholars think that no difference exists
here between both accounts and that Mark's interval conveys no more
than that the tree's withering (stated explicitly by Matthew) was
only seen to have happened the following day. Hence the effect of
the curse may have been immediate even in Mark, although he does not
specifically say so /32/.

This harmonizing view, however, fails to give sufficient weight
to the reiterated and hence emphatic use by Matthew of the word
παραχρῆμα ('immediately'), an adverb never used elsewhere by him
/33/. The term emphasizes the immediacy of the response in a way
that a more ambiguous term like εὐθύς would not. Παραχρῆμα is a
word that is always employed in the New Testament in connection with
the sudden happening of a miraculous or striking event, and almost

exclusively by Luke, who utilizes it in the gospel and Acts'some
sixteen times (cf. esp. Lk.18.43 and parallels) /34/. Matthew's
unique use here of this stronger term, therefore, is surely
significant /35/. The introduction of the 'amazement' motif also
heightens the miraculous element. The useof θαυμάζειν here (21.20)
is striking since Matthew seldom uses this verb of the disciples
/36/.

It is Matthew's practice elsewhere, moreover, to magnify Mark's
miracle stories /37/. This he does frequently by stressing either
the instantaneousness of their effect /38/ or the breadth of their
effect /39/. It is significant, indeed,that where two Markan
miracle stories (7.31-37; 8.22-26) show Jesus labouring over the
process of healing, Matthew has omitted them /40/, while amply
compensating for their omission with a generalizing Healings
summary (15.29-31) /41/. In 13.58 he alters Mark's "he *could* not
perform any miracle there" to "he *did* not perform many miracles
there".

For these reasons, then, the distinction between Matthew's
stress on the instantaneousness of the miracle as opposed to
Mark's unusual interval should not be minimised, as some scholars
have argued. Matthew was not "moins préoccupé de grossir le
miracle que d'unifier la narration" (so Loisy), nor did he
introduce this motif merely to meet compositional requirements (so
Grundmann), to conform to the characteristic manner of presenting
apophthegms (so Lagrange), for reasons of space (so Box) or for
liturgical convenience (so Kilpatrick, Goulder). The magnification
of the miracle serves in itself the additional function of focusing
attention on the *miraculous power* which effects the withering
(21.20 π̲ω̲ς̲ παραχρῆμα ἐξηράνθη ἡ συκῆ) whereas in Mark significance
is attached more to the tree itself, Jesus' cursing of it and its
subsequent withering (11.21 ἴδε ἡ συκῆ ἣν κατηράσω ἐξήρανται).

A third feature of Matthew's treatment already touched upon is
the considerable *abbreviation* conducted upon Mark's story. Mark's
description of the tree (11.13) seen from afar with its show of
leaves (ἀπὸ μακρόθεν ἔχουσαν φύλλα), Jesus' hopeful approach as a
result (εἰ ἄρα τι εὑρήσει) and the problematic explanation for its
detected lack of fruit (ὁ γὰρ καιρὸς οὐκ ἦν σύκων) have all been
eliminated. So too has Mark's curious ἀποκριθείς (11.14a) /42/.
The suggestive 'hearing-seeing-remembering' notices in Mark
linking action and sequel /43/ have been curtailed and replaced by
Matthew's succinct καὶ ἰδόντες οἱ μαθηταὶ ἐθαύμασαν λέγοντες (21.20).
Mark's long and cumbrous καὶ μὴ διακριθῇ ἐν τῇ καρδίᾳ αὐτοῦ ἀλλὰ

πιστεύῃ ὅτι ὃ λαλεῖ γίνεται, ἔσται (αὐτῷ) in v.23b is replaced by
the equally succinct ἐὰν ἔχητε πίστιν καὶ μὴ διακριθῆτε of 21.21.
Finally, Mark's διὰ τοῦτο λέγω ὑμῖν (11.24a) is lacking, with the
remainder of that verse appearing in a smoother form in Matthew.
Mk.11.25,26 are absent altogether.

In condensing Mark in this way, Matthew has given only what
is necessary for the drawing of the lesson from Jesus' action and
nothing more /44/. The abridgment of Mark's details removes
attention from the tree and the action surrounding it, and centres
it on Jesus' *power* and the lesson that such power may be exercised
likewise by the disciples.

Matthew does have some *minor expansions*, however /45/. These
have led Lagrange to doubt that Matthew is in fact abbreviating
the Markan text and to suggest that his version is based on an
Aramaic Ur-Matthäus whose primitive conclusion alone has been
replaced by a conclusion borrowed from Mark /46/. Lohmeyer, too,
has claimed that Matthew is here independent of Mark and points
to Matthew's Aramaisms (e.g. συκῆν μίαν) and "Biblizismen" (e.g.
the unusual subjunctive of the curse) as evidence for this view
/47/.

While συκῆν μίαν may mean a 'solitary' tree, a single tree
standing by itself /48/, most scholars are agreed that here it
does mean a 'certain' fig-tree and is a synonym with a Semitic
origin for the Greek τινά /49/. Matthew elsewhere shows his
preference for this usage /50/, particularly, as here, in the yet
more Semitic adjectival form /51/, but this need reflect no more
than the sometimes deliberate /52/, sometimes unconscious
linguistic proclivities of a writer of Greek who is, at the same
time, thoroughly immersed in a Semitic culture. The minor
linguistic differences frequently exhibited by the evangelists
are often puzzling but their number, nature, distribution and
pattern are not enough, in our view, to allow one to say that they
in all cases represent independent translation variants.

Another construction with an Aramaic flavour /53/ is the
οὐ ... εἰ μή construction appearing here in the form οὐδέν ... εἰ
μὴ φύλλα in Mk.11.13c but in the form οὐδέν ... εἰ μὴ φύλλα μόνον
in Mt.21.19. On the whole the construction appears more frequently
in Matthew and Mark than in Luke who often in parallel passages
renders the verse differently /54/. Matthew himself sometimes
uses it where Mark has something different /55/ or lacks a parallel
/56/. Here some scholars suggest that Matthew, while abbreviating

Mark, has added μόνον to preserve Mark's emphasis on the
fruitlessness of the tree despite the promise offered by the
leaves /57/. Elsewhere Matthew has the stronger μόνον where
the word is lacking in parallel passages /58/. In Mt.24.36 =
Mk.13.32, Matthew has strengthened his Vorlage by adding the
adjective μόνος to Mark's οὐδεὶς οἶδεν ... εἰ μὴ ὁ πατήρ (cf. also
Mt.12.4 and parallels).

    In the case of both μίαν and μόνον, therefore, it is likely
that we are dealing not with translation variants but with minor
stylistic preferences on the part of Matthew the redactor. This
can be seen also from 21.21 where Matthew's supplementary
οὐ μόνον τὸ τῆς συκῆς ποιήσετε ἀλλὰ κἂν ... has the function of
connecting the mountain-moving saying (loosely attached in Mark)
more closely with the context, a procedure that is characteristic
of the first evangelist, as we have seen /59/. With the τὸ τῆς
συκῆς expression we may compare 8.33 and parallels, and the μόνον
with what has been said immediately above. The ποιήσετε further
strengthens the case for the redactional nature of this clause,
for it is a dominant theme in Matthew that the disciples themselves
actively participate in the authority and miraculous power wielded
by Jesus /60/. This leaves only the ἐπὶ τῆς ὁδοῦ phrase (21.19)
which appears as a simple and natural compensatory datum in the
light of the drastic abbreviation of Mark's story /61/.

    A further difference between the two accounts is *the form of
the curse*. While Mark uses an optative, "Never again may anyone
eat (φάγοι) fruit from you", to express what is undoubtedly a
curse /62/, Matthew uses a subjunctive tense (γένηται) instead.
If μηκέτι ἐκ σοῦ καρπὸς γένηται κτλ.is read /63/, then Matthew's
version likewise expresses a strong wish on the part of Jesus,
amounting virtually to a prohibition: "Never *may* fruit come from
you again." If οὐ is read before μηκέτι, however /64/, then
Jesus' words are transformed, according to a number of scholars,
from a strong wish, imprecation or curse to a solemn prediction of
doom (eine Drohweissagung) /65/, a prophecy /66/, or even a
"Machtwort" (Grundmann) in the style of the Old Testament /67/.
"Never again *shall* fruit come from you" /68/. J. Weiss and H.J.
Holtzmann think furthermore that this change in Matthew serves
to make even clearer the symbolic connection of the story with
Israel and Jerusalem /69/.

    Such attempts to draw significance from the Matthean version
of Jesus' words may be too subtle, however. Matthew, it is true,
does omit Mark's explicit reference to the curse (11.21) but both

versions leave it in no doubt that the withering of the tree was
still, nonetheless, a consequence of Jesus' words, and Matthew's
choice of a subjunctive rather than an optative tense may reflect
again merely a stylistic preference. The presence of οὐ before
μηκέτι in the Matthean text is not sufficiently certain to allow
meaningful distinctions to be drawn from these linguistic
differences, but even were it certain, and were the "οὐ μή ...
γένηται" construction an echo of Old Testament prophetic usage,
this need again reflect no more than that Matthew's style was
consciously or unconsciously influenced by the style of the Old
Testament. All other indications serve to show that Matthew has
removed, either deliberately or unintentionally, those features of
Mark's version which have symbolic undertones.

How Matthew *did* understand the story, on the other hand, can
be seen from the method he employs to introduce and treat Mark's
interpretative (and symbolical) mountain-moving saying. Instead
of the withered tree being pointed out by Peter, as in Mk.11.21,
the reaction of the disciples as a whole is described.   This
reaction is placed in *the form of a question:* πῶς παραχρῆμα
ἐξηράνθη ἡ συκῆ;(21.20). What is of prime concern is the *means*
whereby the tree has withered /70/, the *modus operandi* of the
miracle, in other words, and not what the tree's withering
signifies to the reader in its Markan context. Matthew's hand is
clearly at work here. The question is modelled exactly on what
precedes (καὶ ἐξηράνθη παραχρῆμα ἡ συκῆ). Catchword connections
of this type are characteristic of him /71/. H.J. Held points out
the frequency with which Matthew employs direct speech where Mark
has indirect speech, and how often in miracle stories dialogue
(often introduced) serves as a vehicle for highlighting the role
played by faith in miracle-working /72/.

Here the question appears unusual on the lips of the disciples.
Had they not after all witnessed countless other miracles of Jesus?
Why question this one? "How did the fig-tree wither so quickly?",
then, reveals in essence how Matthew interpreted Mark's story /73/.
The question, though artificially conceived, points forward to and
highlights the answer given by Jesus.

A central place is accorded, therefore, to *the mountain-moving
saying* which in Mark performs only a secondary interpretative role.
Matthew's desire "to get to the point", indeed, has led him to
forgo his usual interest in Peter /74/. As elsewhere in his
treatment of Mark's miracle stories, strictly unnecessary details
concerning people and actions are reduced or eliminated in order

that Jesus' miracle-working saying be given prominence /75/.
Throughout vv.21 and 22, the disciples as a group are addressed
directly and consistently in the second person (contr. Mk.11.20 ff.).
The saying is reproduced in a smoother form, the ἔχετε πίστιν of
Mark introduced as a conditional clause /76/. Mark's καὶ μὴ
διακριθῆ clause is abbreviated and placed earlier. Small,
characteristic stylistic changes are introduced /77/, and the
whole is anchored more firmly to the context. The addition of
οὐ μόνον τὸ τῆς συκῆς ποιήσετε, as we saw, specifically relates
Jesus' power in making the tree wither to that of the disciples,
whose promised share in that power, by virtue of faith, now becomes
the point of the saying. The mountain of the saying is no longer
suggestive, then, of the Temple Mount, as it is in Mark. The
saying has reverted to its more general, hyperbolic and proverbial
character.

Matthew's smoother connection between action and sequel has
not made his account entirely convincing, however. It has been
commented that Jesus' answer in terms of the mountain-moving
saying does not appear to be a direct reply to the disciples'
enquiry as to the source of Jesus' power /78/. But since it was
he who formulated the question, then Matthew himself must have
understood it from the very beginning as a question about the
miraculous power that was available through faith to the disciples
/79/. Moreover, as McNeile points out /80/, the sense would have
been much clearer here had it been a contrast between the *removing*
of a tree (as in Lk.17.6) and the removing of a mountain. Matthew's
reinterpretation, therefore, still reflects here the awkwardness
apparent in his Markan Vorlage.

The presence of v.22 does, nevertheless, reflect the
consistency of the Matthean treatment. Continuing in the second
person plural and expressed in smooth Greek style /81/, this
culminating verse addresses itself not only to the miraculous
power available to the disciples through faith but available to
them through *supplicating* faith /82/. Hence the story, which
nowhere speaks of Jesus either exercising faith in his cursing
of the tree nor of *praying* for its withering, is taken as a
paradigm for the power of supplicating faith, a power available
to the disciples, and thereby to Christian believers in general.

Verse 22, therefore, smoothly rounds off Matthew's account
of the fig-tree story and is to be contrasted with its Markan
parallel (11.24), which appears as something of an afterthought.
While Matthew may certainly have taken this verse over from Mark,
the possibility earlier suggested that Mk.11.24 is itself a scribal

gloss based on Matthew should also be considered. If this were
so, then this culminating verse would represent hermeneutically
a significant Matthean contribution to the fig-tree story. By
viewing the story as an object lesson in the efficacy of faith
and *prayer,* Matthew could have provided later scribes with the
basis for that further development of the story in a didactic
direction which we have seen reflected in the Markan sequel.

The Significance of Matthew's Redaction

We have now examined the similarities and differences between
the two accounts in considerable detail. R.C. Trench, we confess,
has denounced those who magnify such differences as "the true
Pharisees of history, straining at gnats and swallowing camels" /83/.
Bearing in mind the good bishop's warning, we must now go on to
state in general terms what the effect of Matthew's redactional
work has been.

In the first place, Matthew's treatment, whether intentionally
or otherwise, has removed practically all of those elements in
Mark's account which suggest that it was originally intended to be
seen primarily in a symbolic light. With Jesus' miracles of
healing in the Temple (21.14), the cursing of the fig-tree no
longer stands out as it does in Mark as the *only* miracle performed
by Jesus in Jerusalem. Abbreviation of the story has removed or
altered suggestive details such as Jesus' survey of the Temple
(11.11), his disappointed search for fruit, the show of leaves, the
curious "for it was not the season for figs" /84/, the delay in the
effect of the curse. The Markan hearing-seeing-remembering motif
which invites the reader to ponder the significance of Jesus'
action is eliminated. The strange position of the story before
and after the Cleansing episode has been altered, and the signs of
the story's intrusion into the Entry-Cleansing-Vollmachtsfrage
cycle are less apparent. The position of the story in Mt.21, while
derivative of Mark, appears logically unrelated to the surrounding
material, despite Matthew's attempt to provide closer contextual
links. The story has been removed from the sphere of judgement
and eschatology, and is treated as if it were a normal miracle
story /85/.

In dealing with Mark's story as a normal miracle story,
Matthew has made it, in turn, a vehicle for instruction on the
efficacy of prayer and faith. In Ernst Lohmeyer's words, it has
become a "Paradigma für die Macht des Glaubens" /86/. In Walter

Grundmann's words, Mark's "Symbolhandlung" has been transformed
into a "Glaubensbelehrung" /87/.

This transformation, it can be said, is characteristic of
Matthew's treatment of Mark's miracle stories /88/. Consistently
these have been abbreviated in order that the essentials be reached
more quickly. The stories are important not for their own sake but
for the message, teaching or admonition they convey. Concern is
focused throughout on what the story illustrates about christology,
faith or the nature of discipleship.

In consequence of this, we should further note that Matthew,
in giving a central place to the mountain-moving saying, has
created thereby a kind of *apophthegm*. Emphasis rests on the
saying and not on the action, while in Mark the action is uppermost
and the interpretative saying is a secondary attachment. This
approximation of the Markan miracle stories to the style of an
apophthegm (or paradigm, in Dibelius' terminology) can be observed
elsewhere /89/.

In thus turning Mark's miracle stories into "illustrative
didactic stories" (Marxsen) Matthew betrays his ecclesiastical bias
/90/. The stories are re-narrated principally for the instruction
of the Church. The disciples who witness Jesus' deeds and receive
Jesus' teaching do so as representatives of the Church, as types of
the Christian believer /91/. "The result is," as H.J. Held has it,
"that for a number of miraculous healings in Matthew's Gospel the
Christological theme is united with the question how the believer
comes to share in Christ and his benefits"/92/.

This underlying concern on the part of Matthew is seen most
clearly in his understanding and use of the concept πίστις. It is
frequently pointed out that Matthew tends to idealize the disciples,
removing from Mark's account features that show the disciples in a
bad light /93/. On the other hand, Jesus is frequently shown
rebuking the disciples for their little faith (ὀλιγοπιστία) and for
their disobedience /94/. The solution to such an apparent contradiction lies in the differing connotations given by Matthew and
Mark to the notion of faith.

Πίστις, for Matthew, primarily designates *trust*. It is a
trust directed in particular to the divine power resident in
Jesus, and a trust, moreover, that Jesus' power is available to
the one who believes /95/. The corollary of such faith is
ὀλιγοπιστία, 'little faith', the reluctance on the part of the

disciple to seek the divine support, to cast himself wholly upon
the one who has revealed himself as the Christ, the Son of God
(cf. 14.28-33). But πίστις and ὀλιγοπιστία apply equally *to the
believer* /96/. There is no suggestion in Matthew that the
disciples lack *understanding*, although they may lack faith. From
the beginning such understanding is granted them /97/, a Matthean
emphasis which is to be contrasted with Mark's presentation. In
Matthew, the disciple who may be called ὀλιγόπιστος cannot be
considered ἄπιστος.

In Mark, however, an additional intellectual element is
strongly reflected in the word πίστις. Faith involves *understanding*
who Jesus is, *perceiving* the true significance of his words and
deeds, *recognizing* his divine nature. Its corollary is
unbelief, failure to recognize and acknowledge Jesus as the Son
of God. Such an understanding is not predicated of the disciples
during Jesus' lifetime, despite Jesus' efforts to enlighten them
/98/. It is not surprising, then, that Matthew should choose to
alter this characteristically Markan emphasis.

Mark's interest frequently devolves upon the disciples'
inability to discern the true nature of Jesus' person, words and
deeds. The christological motif is primary. Matthew's interest,
on the other hand, is both christological and *ecclesiastical*. The
disciples, who do recognize Jesus' true nature, are nevertheless
types of Christian believers, always in a position of 'little
faith', requiring to be upheld, strengthened, taught and nurtured
in faith.

The import of Mark's fig-tree story, then, is seen in the
invitation to the disciples (and hence the readers) to understand
the significance of what has happened in the light of Jesus'
action on the Temple Mount. Mark's Ἔχετε πίστιν (11.22) /99/
here may almost mean Συνίετε - 'understand this!' /100/ In
Matthew's account, on the contrary, the connection with the
Cleansing is severed, and the story, which could as easily appear
elsewhere in the Matthean redactional scheme, functions purely as
a paradigm for Christian faith and prayer.

These latter comments on Matthew's redactional work prompt
one final question concerning the motivation behind these changes.
Has Matthew altered Mark because he took exception to what the
Markan account implied? Did he disapprove of the suggestion here
that Jesus, in cursing the fig-tree, had, *mutatis mutandis*, cursed
either his own people, or more specifically their most precious

institution, the Temple?

A positive answer might seem to be indicated by the following observations. By recording Jesus' miracles in the Temple (21.14) Matthew implies that the Temple was *reconsecrated* by Jesus after the Entry rather than cursed /101/. He omits Mk.11.16, a datum which, we believe, refers to Jesus' interference with the course of the sacrifices /102/. He omits Mk.12.32-34 which, although it shows a Matthean opponent in a good light /103/, also disparages the Temple cultus. While he retains the Temple charge against Jesus (26.61 = Mk.14.58) he does alter Mark's intentional "I *shall* destroy this sanctuary" (καταλύσω) to the potential "I *am able to* destroy God's sanctuary" (δύναμαι καταλῦσαι). While, too, he retains the prophecy concerning the Temple's destruction (24.1-2 = Mk.13.1-2), he does precede it by the Lament over Jerusalem (23.37-39), which shows Jesus' attitude to be one of regret over the imminent demise of the city and its Temple. In general, moreover, "there is no gospel which seeks to conserve the place of the Jews in the purpose and the plan of God as Matthew does" /104/. For Matthew (5.17), Jesus is the one who has come to fulfil (πληρῶσαι) rather than to destroy (καταλῦσαι).

On the other hand, it must be admitted, "there is no gospel which so unsparingly condemns the Jews, and especially the Pharisees"/105/, as the first gospel does. It is Matthew, one must note, who has the Jews accept responsibility for the death of Jesus (27.25). A number of passages in his gospel elsewhere convey approximately, though perhaps not so strongly, the substance of what Mark symbolizes in his fig-tree story (cf. e.g. 3.7-10; 15.13; 21.43). Matthew also retains the rending of the veil incident (27.51 = Mk.15.38) and it is in his gospel too that one finds the words "I tell you someone (or something) greater than the Temple is here" (12.6).

It was on the basis of this latter evidence that Lohmeyer claimed that a deep opposition to the Temple and priesthood could be detected in Matthew /106/. But this view clearly runs against the tenor of the evidence submitted above. Matthew's attack on the Jews is directed principally against their orthodox leaders and not so much against their institutions /107/. The Temple Tax pericope (17.24-27), for example, while showing Jesus and his disciples to be free from Temple obligations and cultic laws, instructs Peter nevertheless to pay the tax in order not to give offence. The 5.23-24 logion clearly also upholds the sacrificial system. Matthew's attitude, therefore, is perhaps best represented

as one emphasizing the sovereignty of Jesus over the Temple rather
than one reflecting an antagonism towards it /108/.

It is not unlikely, in conclusion, then, that Matthew's
redaction of the fig-tree story was prompted by his disapproval of
what he saw were the symbolic undertones in Mark's account. This
conclusion, however, must be stated cautiously, given the discordant
nature of the evidence reviewed above /109/. Instead of omitting
the pericope altogether, as Luke has done, Matthew has nevertheless
found in the story a natural point of departure for a characteristic
didactic theme. In this respect, the parallel with Mk.7.31-37 and
8.22-26 is instructive, for there, too, Mark has included within
his redactional scheme two miracle stories, both having an
independent Sitz im Leben, but each doubtless intended in their
context to convey a symbolic meaning. Both are meant, it would
seem, to be viewed in the light of the disciples' lack of
understanding /110/. Since they do not possess, however, the
same symbolic meaning for Matthew, but, at the same time, do *not*
provide him with a point of departure for his own characteristic
emphasis, they are omitted as unimportant.

NOTES

/1/   Paragraph headings and enumeration follow, for the most part,
those in Kurt Aland's *Synopsis Quattuor Evangeliorum,* 8th edn.
(Stuttgart, 1973).
/2/   It is curious, however, that Luke too has a scene similar to
Matthew's, although his 'rebuke your disciples' episode occurs
prior to the Temple visit (cf. 19.39-40). A tradition-connection
between both accounts has been suggested (so, for example, H.J.
Holtzmann, A.H. McNeile) and this is not unlikely, although one
would assume, in view of the absence of verbal links, that the
connection lay fairly far back in the tradition.
/3/   Klostermann thinks that Matthew wishes to distinguish one
day as a day of *acting,* the other day a day of *teaching (Das
Matthäusevangelium,* p.167).
/4/   See Jeremias, *Eucharistic Words,* p.91; *Weltvollender,*
pp.35-44.
/5/   It is possible, perhaps, that he intends a caesura at 22.46
but the verse is chronologically vague.
/6/   Cf. Montefiore, *Synoptic Gospels,* II, p.281. A number of
witnesses read διδάσκοντι in Mt.21.23, hence implying that the

challenge here was to Jesus' *teaching*. This reading, however, may be a gloss from Lk.20.1. *Vide supra*, p.48 and n.43.

/7/   Their consensus *on this one occasion* cannot, therefore, be taken as an argument for Matthean priority, as W.R. Farmer argues (*Synoptic Problem*, p.260). Contr. Schmid, *Matthäus und Lukas*, pp.30-1.

/8/   See Montefiore, *Synoptic Gospels*, II, pp.280-1; Perrin, *Introduction*, p.187; Dowda, *Cleansing*, p.293.

/9/   See, for example, the arguments of Farmer, *Synoptic Problem*, pp.168, 258-62. For a succinct summary of the arguments for Matthean priority in general, see W. Barclay, *The First Three Gospels* pp.228-44.

/10/   See G. Bornkamm, G. Barth, H.J. Held, *Tradition and Interpretation in Matthew*, pp.246-7. Henceforth *B-B-H*.

/11/   For a discussion on the Matthean doublets, see Kilpatrick, *Origins*, pp.84-92, esp. 87-8; Goulder, *Midrash*, pp.36-8; Butler, *Originality*, pp.138-46.

/12/   See B. Weiss, *Das Matthäusevangelium und seine Lucas-Parallelen,* p.457.

/13/   Cf. *infra*, p.266, n.30.

/14/   Cf. Mk.6.3-4,14-16; 8.27-28. Is it possible that Mt.21.10-11, 46 were suggested by Mk.6.14-16, which Matthew has omitted? Careful redaction and compensation for omitted material is a characteristic of Matthew *(vide infra*, p.75 and n.41).

/15/   For the Matthean *"formula quotations"* and his use of *Messianic proof-texts* (present here in 21.5 and 21.16) see, for example, R.H. Gundry, *The Use of the Old Testament in St. Matthew's Gospel*; F.C. Grant, *IDB*, 'Matthew, Gospel of', pp.307-11, and the New Testament Introductions of Kümmel, Marxsen, Fuller and Perrin ad loc.

Note also Matthew's common reference to ἡ πόλις (21.10), his characteristic οἱ ὄχλοι (21.11, cf. 21.9), his favourite verb προσέρχομαι (21.14, cf. 21.23), his emphasis on healing (καὶ ἐθεράπευσεν αὐτούς, cf. 14.14; 19.2 and parallels), his frequently recurring οὐδέποτε ἀνέγνωτε (21.16, cf. 12.3,5; 19.4; 21.42) and his ναί (21.16, cf. 13.51; 17.25). Cf. Kilpatrick, *Origins*, p.51; B. Weiss, *Matthäusevangelium*, pp.455-6.

The use of direct speech in 21.10-11 and 21.15-16 and the emphasis on *the Son of David* in 21.15-16 are not un-Matthean either, and the conjunctive διὰ τοῦτο (21.43), too, appears frequently elsewhere (*vide supra*, p.55 and *infra*, pp.78, 265, n.17)

/16/   In Mk.12.28-34 Jesus receives "a genuine enquiry from a scribe". In Mt.22.34-40 he faces "a hostile question from a Pharisee" (H.A. Guy, *The Gospel of Matthew*, p.121). Many commentators therefore suggest that Matthew has carefully omitted

Mark's sympathetic exchange between Jesus and the scribe because
it showed Matthew's opponents in a good light (so, for example,
Perrin, *Introduction*, p.187). An additional motivation, however,
may lie in the anticultic note sounded in this passage, an
attitude that Matthew may have disapproved of (cf. 5.23-24 where
he appears to recognize the validity of sacrifices).

/17/   Cf. e.g. Mt.21.8,9,21,22,24 and 26 and their Markan
parallels.

/18/   Cf. e.g. Mt.21.6,19,21 and 22 and their Markan parallels.

/19/   Cf. e.g. Mt.21.3,25,45 and 46 and their Markan parallels.

/20/   Cf. e.g. Mk.10.49; 11.2 (εἰσπορευόμενοι εἰς αὐτήν), 4-6,
13,28 (ἵνα ταῦτα ποιῇς) and their Matthean parallels.

/21/   Note, for example, Mark's use of parataxis, where Matthew
employs the more stylish δέ (cf. 21.3,6,8,9,18,21,25 and parallels).

/22/   See, for example, G. Bornkamm, "Matthäus als Interpret der
Herrenworte", *ThLZ*, 79 (1954), pp.341-6; W. Marxsen, *Introduction
to the New Testament*, pp.146-54.

/23/   Taking the text as it is in Aland and commencing at 11.12.

/24/   Apart from Matthew's preference for δέ in second place,
rather than καί in first place (*vide supra*, n.21), what changes
in word order there are stem from an observable process of
abbreviation, cf. the transposition of ἐν αὐτῇ in 21.19b = 11.13b
or the rearrangement and smoother syntax of 21.21,22 = 11.22,23,24.
Only in 21.19d = 11.14b does εἰς τὸν αἰῶνα appear in a different
position.

/25/   Cf. 21.17 ηὐλίσθη; 21.18 ἐπαναγαγών; 21.19 συκῆν μίαν ...
εἰ μὴ φύλλα μόνον ... γένηται; 21.19,20 παραχρῆμα; 21.20 ἐθαύμασαν;
21.21 γενήσεται.

/26/   Cf. 21.18 εἰς τὴν πόλιν; 21.19 ἐπὶ τῆς ὁδοῦ; 21.21 οὐ μόνον
τὸ τῆς συκῆς ποιήσετε, ἀλλὰ κἄν...

/27/   From Mk.11.19, Matthew has taken ἔξω τῆς πόλεως (ἔξω is a
characteristically Markan word; cf. B. Weiss, *Marcusevangelium*,
p.375), from 11.11 ἐξῆλθεν εἰς Βηθανίαν, from 11.20 πρωΐ (hence
removing the need for τῇ ἐπαύριον 11.12). In place of ἐξελθόντων
αὐτῶν ἀπὸ Βηθανίας (11.12) and παραπορευόμενοι (11.20), Matthew
has the hapax legomenon ἐπαναγαγὼν εἰς τὴν πόλιν (see Lohmeyer,
Matthäus, p.303, fn.1, although cf. Lk.5.3,4).

/28/   Mark, it should be observed, has the group depart and
return (11.11,19,20), while Matthew focuses on Jesus alone
(ἐξῆλθεν ... ἐπαναγαγών).

/29/   Some commentators have suggested that αὐλίζεσθαι here has
its proper meaning 'to bivouac' or 'camp in the open air' (so
Wetstein, Grotius), a fact that would hence explain Jesus' hunger
the following morning (*vide supra*, pp.7 0). See, however,
Lagrange, *Matthieu*, p.404; McNeile, *Matthew*, pp.301-2; Bruce,

Synoptic Gospels, p.264. Curiously, Luke uses the same verb when describing Jesus' nightly sleeping arrangements (cf. Lk.21.37).
/30/ See Kümmel, *Introduction,* p.76. Plummer (*Matthew,* p.290, fn.1) draws attention to the insertion here of Matthew's characteristic ἐκεῖ (cf. 14.23; 15.29; 19.2; 26.36,71; 27.47).
In more general terms, Strecker points out how Matthew in his gospel 'historicizes' the traditional material he has taken over by adding a genealogy, amplifying temporal references, turning Mark's topographical references into geographical ones, relating Jesus' life to the Old Testament, etc. (*JAAR,* 35 (1967), pp.219-30).
/31/ *Vide supra,* p.60, n.5, and cf. also Lk.21.37-38; 22.39.
/32/ So Zahn, Plummer. For a critique of this view, see Klostermann, *Matthäusevangelium,* p.169.
/33/ Matthew's favourite expression is ἀπὸ τῆς ὥρας ἐκείνης (cf. e.g. 9.22; 15.28; 17.18) or ἐν τῇ ὥρᾳ ἐκείνῃ (cf. e.g. 8.13). Otherwise he follows Mark who has a predilection for εὐθύς, a word variously meaning 'at once', 'immediately', 'accordingly', 'duly', 'in due course'. See D. Daube, *The Sudden in the Scriptures,* pp.46-62.
/34/ Daube points out that παραχρῆμα = 'straightway', 'forthwith' has a very special meaning for Luke. He frequently replaces the εὐθύς of his source with it (*op.cit.,* pp.38-46).
/35/ So Daube (*op.cit.,* pp.39, 62).
/36/ Lohmeyer, *Matthäus,* p.303, fn.1; Grundmann, *Das Evangelium nach Matthäus,* p.453. Both Lohmeyer and Grundmann state that Matthew *nowhere* else uses this verb of the disciples but cf. 8.27. For the use of θαυμάζειν elsewhere cf. 8.10; 15.31; 22.22; 27.14.
/37/ See Strecker, *Weg,* p.121; M.S. Enslin, *Christian Beginnings,* III, pp.395-6.
/38/ Cf. ἐν τῇ ὥρᾳ ἐκείνῃ 8.13; ἀπὸ τῆς ὥρας ἐκείνης 9.22; 15.28; 17.18.
/39/ Cf. πάντας (contr. Mark's πολλούς) in Mt.8.16; 12.15, and θεραπεύων πᾶσαν νόσον καὶ πᾶσαν μαλακίαν in 4.23; 9.35. Note also the addition to Mark's text of πάντας/πάντες in 14.35; 15.37 (cf. 14.20) and the qualification χωρὶς γυναικῶν καὶ παιδίων in 14.21; 15.38.
/40/ H.J. Held argues that these stories were omitted not because Matthew disapproved of the realistic or irreverent nature of their content but rather because he found in them no point of departure for his own doctrinal interests (*B-H-H,* pp.207-11). While Held is probably right in what he affirms, he may be mistaken in what he denies. Part of Matthew's doctrinal interest is to heighten the sense of the miraculous, so stressing "the awesome nature of Jesus and his ministry" (Perrin, *Introduction,* p.191). These stories present Jesus healing by stages and using techniques reminiscent

of a normal thaumaturge. Hence they may have been deemed
inappropriate by Matthew.

/41/   Where Matthew omits material, he frequently compensates for
it. The mention of *two* blind men in 20.29-34 where Mark has one
(Mk.10.46-52) may be by way of compensation for the omission of
Mk.8.22-26 (cf. also Mt.9.27-31). Compare, for example, Mt.20.34
and 9.29 with Mk.8.23,25.

        The reference to *two* demoniacs in 8.28-34 where again Mark
has one (Mk.5.1-20) may be by way of compensation for the omission
of the exorcism of Mk.1.21-28. Cf. F.W. Green, *The Gospel according
to Saint Matthew*, p.11; F.V. Filson, *The Gospel according to Saint
Matthew*, p.219.

/42/   For the use of the pleonastic participle in Mark's gospel,
vide supra, pp.56-7. Some commentators have expressed
surprise that Jesus should address the tree as if it were a person
(so Wohlenberg, Haenchen) or 'answer', for that matter, when
nothing apparently has been said. A number had claimed that he
was answering "the deceptive profession of the tree" (so Plummer;
cf. also Swete, Bartlet ad loc.). Lagrange points out, however,
that a typical Hebraism is here in view (ויאמר...ויען; *Marc*, p.294).
Ambrozic also remarks that ἀποκριθείς in Mark does not always imply
a previous question (cf. 9.5; 10.24; 12.35; 14.48; *Hidden Kingdom*,
p.164, fn.145). Talking to trees, however, is nothing unusual
in the Jewish Haggadah, a fact that supplies a clue perhaps to the
story's background. *Vide infra*, pp.186 ff.

/43/   11.14c καὶ ἤκουον οἱ μαθηταὶ αὐτοῦ cf. 18a; 11.20 καὶ
παραπορευόμενοι πρωῒ εἶδον τὴν συκῆν ἐξηραμμένην ἐκ ῥιζῶν; 11.21
καὶ ἀναμνησθεὶς ὁ Πέτρος λέγει αὐτῷ ...

/44/   Plummer, *Matthew*, p.290.

/45/   Cf. 21.19 συκῆν μίαν ἐπὶ τῆς ὁδοῦ ... εἰ μὴ φύλλα μόνον;
21.21 τὸ τῆς συκῆς ποιήσετε ἀλλὰ κἂν ...

/46/   *Matthieu*, p.405.

/47/   *Matthäus*, p.302.

/48/   So, for example, B. Weiss, Edersheim, Bruce, Plummer,
Grundmann, Wohlenberg.

/49/   The use of εἷς for τις is evidenced in Hellenistic Greek
and in the papyri, but Blass-Debrunner think that for the New
Testament a Semitic 'Vorbild' lies behind the usage. The word is
used either as a pronominal adjective or as a full pronoun with the
genitive (sometimes also with ἐκ). See M. Black, *An Aramaic
Approach to the Gospels and Acts*, pp.104-6; Goulder, *Midrash*, p.120.

/50/   Cf. e.g. 8.19; 9.18; 13.46; 18.24; 19.16; 26.69 and
parallels.

/51/   Cf. 8.19; 9.18; 26.69 and parallels; 13.46 and 18.24
without parallel, and see Chapman, *Matthew, Mark and Luke*, p.198.

/52/   Cf. Matthew's use of ἡ βασιλεία τῶν οὐρανῶν, ὁ πατὴρ ὁ ἐν τοῖς οὐρανοῖς, τότε, ἰδού etc.
/53/   K. Beyer, *Semitische Syntax im Neuen Testament,* pp.104-5; McNeile, *Matthew,* p.174.
/54/   Cf. Mt.5.13; 12.24; 13.57; 14.17; 17.8 and parallels; but cf. Mt.11.27 and Lk.10.22; Mt.12.4 and parallels; Mt.16.4 and Lk.11.29.
/55/   Cf. Mt.12.24; 14.17; 16.4; 17.8 and parallels.
/56/   Cf. Mt.5.13; 11.27; 15.24. Mark, it should be noted, sometimes uses the construction where Matthew lacks it (cf. Mk.5.37; 6.5,8; 8.14; 9.9,29; 10.18). In a number of these cases, however, Matthew fails to reproduce it simply because he has altered Mark on other grounds. He omits 5.37 altogether, for example, presumably for the sake of brevity. In other cases he has turned Mark's indirect speech into more stylish direct speech (cf. 6.8; 9.9; and parallels). In 6.5; 9.29 and 10.18, the Markan Vorlage may have been altered for theological or doctrinal reasons.
/57/   So, for example, B. Weiss, Loisy, Grundmann.
/58/   Cf. 5.47; 9.21; 10.42; 14.36 (but contr. also Mk.9.2,8 and parallels). The addition of μόνον to this basically Semitic construction is a function of Greek influence (Beyer, *Semitische Syntax,* p.126 and fns.3,4).
/59/   *Supra,* p.74. Οὐ (μὴ) μόνον - ἀλλὰ καί, Beyer points out, is a classical Greek and Koinē construction which has no commonly used Semitic equivalent (*Semitische Syntax,* p.126, fn.4).
/60/   See *B-B-H,* pp.253, 270 ff., 288 ff.
/61/   For a variety of opinions, however, on the precise meaning and significance of ἐπὶ τῆς ὁδοῦ, see J. Lightfoot, *Horae,* II, p.277; B. Weiss, *Matthäusevangelium,* p.456, fn.1; Bruce, *Synoptic Gospels,* p.264; Klostermann, *Matthäusevangelium,* p.168.
/62/   Some scholars have denied that the words can properly be called a curse (so e.g. Lagrange, Swete). Apart altogether from 11.21 (ἡ συκῆ ἣν κατηράσω), the use of an optative for an imprecation is exactly paralleled in Acts 8.20 (*Meyer-Dickson,* I, p.180; Münderlein, *NTS,* 10 (1963-4), p.91, fn.4; cf. also Taylor, *Mark,* p.460). It has also been suggested that the words only came to be understood as a curse as a result of a translation error from the original Aramaic. So, for example, Violet, Hatch, T.W. Manson, Bartsch, T.H. Robinson (*The Gospel of Matthew,* p.174). *Vide supra,* pp.7-8.
/63/   With most authorities except B L O. This text is transmitted by von Soden, Souter, Vogels and the UBS edn. (London, 1966; ed. Aland, Black, Metzger and Wikgren). It is accepted by commentators on the gospel such as Lagrange and Bruce.
/64/   This text is transmitted by Tischendorf, Westcott and Hort,

Nestle-Kilpatrick, Merk and Aland (*Synopsis*) and is accepted by
commentators such as B. Weiss, Loisy, McNeile and Holtzmann.

/65/   So Holtzmann and B. Weiss (cf. also McNeile, *Matthew*, p.302).
Allen thinks that Matthew "modifies the imprecation or wish,
Mk^{14b}, into a solemn prophecy of fact" (*A Critical and Exegetical
Commentary on the Gospel according to S. Matthew*, p.224).

/66/   So Klostermann.

/67/   Cf. Jl.2.26-27 Is.14.20; 25.2; 45.17 Hos.14.9, and see
also Lohmeyer, *Matthäus*, p.303, fn.1.

/68/   Οὐ μή plus the subjunctive is equivalent to *an emphatic
negative future* (cf. Mk.9.1; 13.2,19,30; 14.25,(31) and parallels).

/69/   See J. Weiss, *Schriften*, I, p.350; Holtzmann, *HC*, I, p.232;
cf. Klostermann, *Matthäusevangelium*, p.168.

/70/   Πῶς = 'how, in what way, for what reason, by what means?'
It is also possible for πῶς to introduce an exclamation: "(See) how
suddenly the fig-tree withered!" The AV and most early English
versions translate it as such, but most commentators take it more
naturally as a question here. Cf. McNeile, *Matthew*, p.303;
Lagrange, *Matthieu*, p.406.

/71/   See *B-B-H*, pp.188-9, 201-2, 205, 216-17, 225, 237 ff., 285,
289.

/72/   See *B-B-H*, pp.198-9, 203-4, 214-15, 216-17, 222, 224, 233 ff,
266. Cf.21.10-11, 14-16, 26, 28-32, 41.

/73/   The question and answer format here introduced by Matthew
may be a pointer furthermore to the *catechetical* interest that
motivated his redaction. See H. Cousin, *Foi et Vie* (May, 1971),
p.90 and fn.20.

/74/   While Peter is even more prominent in Matthew's gospel than
he is in Mark (McNeile, *Matthew*, p.131, Mt.10.2 ad loc.), there
are places where he prefers naming the disciples as a group rather
than as individuals. In most cases this has apparently been for
the sake of brevity (cf. e.g. Mk.5.37 and parallels). The specific
naming of Peter in Mk.11.21 (vis-à-vis Matthew's reference to the
group) is not therefore of necessity an indication that Mark's
account is secondary (*pace* Farmer, *Synoptic Problem*, p.134 and
fn.11; cf. Bultmann, *History*, pp.67 ff.).

/75/   See *B-B-H*, pp.165 ff., 210-11, 213-25, 239-40, 242, and
Kümmel, *Introduction*, p.76.

/76/   Matthew is here probably influenced by the wording of 17.20,
although it is also suggested (so Klostermann) that he had εἰ
before him in Mark. *Vide infra*, p.120, n.4.

/77/   Note change from καὶ ἀποκριθείς to ἀποκριθεὶς δέ, εἶπεν for
λέγει and the omission of Mark's ὅτι as often. See Allen, *Matthew*,
p.224.

/78/   So B. Weiss, Lagrange, Holtzmann.

/79/ See *B-B-H*, pp.289-90.
/80/ *Matthew,* p.303.
/81/ In contrast to its awkward parallel in the Markan text, one
should here note the use of ἄν with the subjunctive, the stylish
verb and participial phrase (αἰτήσητε ἐν τῇ προσευχῇ) and the
future λήμψεσθε with the subordinate participle πιστεύοντες. Allen
points out that Matthew in general prefers subordinate clauses to
co-ordinate ones (cf. e.g. 8.3,25; 9.14; 14.27; 20.30; 21.1-2,23,
46; 26.67-68; and parallels; *Matthew*, p.75, 8.3 ad loc.).
/82/ See *B-B-H*, pp.281 ff., 290-1.
/83/ *Miracles*, p.474.
/84/ On the whole, we are unconvinced by the arguments of those
who hold that this comment is a post-Markan gloss (*vide supra,* p.2
and n.5, p.3 and n.10). C.H. Bird has clearly shown that such
γάρ clauses are characteristic of Mark (*supra*, pp.20-1 and 27 (n.10);
cf. also p.63, n.44). We doubt, too, if the function of this
statement is to smooth over the chronological misplacement allegedly
suffered by the pericope by virtue of its secondary attachment to
the Passover season (*supra*, pp.3,22-3). Even without this comment
it would have been obvious from the general Passover context that
Jesus was seeking figs 'out of season'. Moreover, as Lagrange
points out, Mark would scarcely have entertained the thought that
Jesus was less instructed on this score than he himself was. Such
rationalistic theories fail furthermore to recognize or acknowledge
the kind of story we are dealing with. The address to the tree,
the belief that the tree should respond, the curse, the withering
have all to be taken into account and these features suggest that
the story has a folklorish background rather than a strictly
historical one (*infra*, chap.VI). The 'out of season' request may
indeed have been the essential element of the original story
(*supra,* pp.22 ff.). Mark's deliberate addition or (if it is
pre-Markan) retention of this striking and enigmatic datum has,
therefore, we hold, a symbolic function (cf. *supra*, pp.2,13 and
n.89).
/85/ See Dowda, *Cleansing*, p.300. Matthew, it should be
remarked, may hence have produced a version of the miracle story
which approximates more closely to the form it earlier had before
Mark put it to unusual use as an eschatological sign. Both the
instantaneousness of the miracle and the expression of amazement
by the disciples conform to the style of normal miracle stories.
Cf. Bultmann, *History*, p.218; Knox, *Sources*, I, p.80, fn.2. This
fact has led Farmer to argue on form-critical grounds for the
priority of Matthew's account (*Synoptic Problem*, pp.168, 258-62,
and *supra,* p.57 and n.111) but it should be noted that the Markan
account of miracle stories as a general rule appears elsewhere to

be more primitive (*B-B-H*, p.211).

/86/   *Matthäus*, p.302.

/87/   *Matthäus*, p.452.

/88/   See Strecker, *Weg*, p.176 ("Paränetische Bedeutung gewinnen die Wundertaten, indem sie die Macht des Glaubens demonstrieren"); Marxsen, *Introduction*, p.150.

/89/   See *B-B-H*, pp.241-6.

/90/   For Matthew as the 'ecclesiastical' gospel, see Barclay, *Three Gospels*, pp.223 ff.; Grant, *IDB*, 'Matthew, Gospel of', pp.311-12; Strecker, *JAAR*, 35 (1967), pp.219-30.

/91/   See Marxsen, *Introduction*, p.150; *B-B-H*, pp.110-11, 266 ff.

/92/   *B-B-H*, p.275.

/93/   Cf. e.g. Mk.4.13, 40-41; 6.52; 8.17-18; 9.6a,32,33-34,38-39; 10.13-14,24,32,35 and parallels, and see Kümmel, *Introduction*, pp.76-7.

/94/   Cf. e.g. 8.26; 14.28-33; 16.8,23; 17.20, and see *B-B-H*, pp.118-21.

/95/   See Bornkamm, *ThLZ*, 79 (1954), p.343; Allen, *Matthew*,p.224; *B-B-H*, pp.112-16, 275-96.

/96/   "Matthew is not concerned with the question of becoming a Christian (unbelief-belief) but with the building up of the Christian life (belief-little belief)", Marxsen, *Introduction*, p.150.

/97/   Cf. 13.14-17,19,23,51; 14.31-33; 16.9,12; 17.9,13,23.

/98/   Cf. 4.13; 6.51-52; 7.18; 8.17-21; 9.6,10,32; 10.32.

/99/   "In God" (θεοῦ) may be a scribal gloss, *Vide supra,* p.57.

/100/   For Mark's stress on *understanding* cf. 4.9 (v.l.), 4.12; 6.52; 7.14,18; 8.17,21, but note esp. 4.39-41 and 6.50-52.

/101/   Matthew emphasizes 'healing' more than 'teaching' at this point. The healing of the blind and lame was a sign of the Messianic Age (cf. Mt.11.5 Mk.2.9 ff.) and the reconsecration of the Temple at the End-time a function of the Messiah. See B. Weiss, *Matthäusevangelium*, p.455; Schniewind, *Matthäus*, pp.139-40; 215; P.A. Micklem, *St.Matthew*, p.203; W. Trilling, *The Gospel according to St. Matthew*, 2, p.133; Jeremias, *Weltvollender*, pp.35-44.

/102/   The standard interpretation of this verse (following J. Lightfoot) is that Jesus was reinforcing a standing rule (then a dead letter) prohibiting the profane use of the Temple as a common thoroughfare much like Old St. Paul's, London. The σκεῦος here named would refer then to any variety of domestic utensils or goods whose transport from one part of the city to the other was made more convenient by using the Temple as a shortcut. The Mishnah (M.Ber.9.5) and even Josephus (Ap.II.106) have been cited in support of this view. This explanation, in our opinion, is scarcely convincing. The Mishnah passage makes no mention of the

carrying of vessels, while the Josephus passage refers only to a
prohibition against the carrying of any vessel (presumably by the
priests) *into the inner sanctuary itself* (ναός) whose complement of
sacred furniture was prescribed by law (see Lagrange, *Marc,* p.295;
Gaston, *No Stone,* p.85; Farmer, *Synoptic Problem,* p.261, fn.10).
Interpreting the incident in a Messianic and eschatological light,
C. Roth has claimed that Jesus, in fulfilment of Zech.14.21, was
commandeering for sacred purposes all vessels *brought into* the
Temple, but this interpretation strains the meaning of διὰ τοῦ
ἱεροῦ here (cf. *NovTest,* 4 (1960), pp.177-8). Others have taken
the σκεῦος as a commercial or trading vessel (so Kuinoel,
Olshausen; contr. B. Weiss ad loc.) but its most natural meaning
here within the context of the Temple is surely that of a sacred
cult vessel (so Volkmann, cited B. Weiss ad loc.; H.-W. Bartsch,
"Early Christian Eschatology in the Synoptic Gospels", *NTS,* 11
(1964-5), p.394; Kelber, *Kingdom,* pp.100-1). More than one-third
of the references to σκεῦος in the LXX are to the sacred cult
objects of the tabernacle, altar or Temple (C. Maurer, *ThDNT,* 7,
σκεῦος ad loc., p.359, cited Kelber, *ibid.*) and this use is common
also in Josephus (cf. e.g. Ant.XVIII.85 B.J.I.39; II.321; V.562).
Jesus' action then, according to Mark, was aimed directly against
the sacrificial cultus, there being no more effective means of
stopping the flow of sacrifices than by seizing the vessels in
which gifts and offerings were received and carried by the priests
(on behalf of the worshippers) *through* the various Temple courts
to the altar (cf. Ap.II.103-9 B.J.V.562). In Mark's view, the
Cleansing was not the act of a passionate reformer indignant at
the fleecing of the people and the secularization of the Temple
precincts (*pace* Lagrange, Taylor). The fact that *buyers* as well as
sellers were expelled bears this out (Luke, it should be noted, and
at least one Markan witness, W, have omitted all reference to the
buyers). The term 'Cleansing' as applied to Mark's account (though
perhaps not to Matthew's or even to that of the pre-Markan
tradition, *infra,* chap.VIII) is hence a misnomer, although for
convenience we shall continue to use it (cf. Gaston, *No Stone,*
pp.81-2; C.K. Barrett, "The House of Prayer and the Den of Thieves"
in *Jesus und Paulus,* Fs. W.G. Kümmel, p.14).

/103/ *Supra,* p.85, n.16.
/104/ W. Barclay, *Three Gospels,* p.218. Cf. e.g. 5.17-18; 10.5-6;
13.52; 15.24-26; 23.3.
/105/ W. Barclay, *op.cit.,* p.219. Cf. e.g. 8.12; 13.11-17;
21.40-43; 22.1-10; 23.1 ff.
/106/ See *Matthäus,* p.184; *Lord of the Temple,* pp.52-61.
/107/ Cf. e.g. 3.7; 5.20; 7.29; 9.11,14,34; 12.2,14,24; 15.1; 16.6,
11-12; 19.3 ff.; 21.45-46; 22.15; 23; 27.62.

/108/ See R.S. McConnell, *Law and Prophecy in Matthew's Gospel* (Dissertation, Basel, 1964), pp.72-5, and esp. p.75.
/109/ Contr. Cousin, *Foi et Vie* (May, 1971), p.92, who asserts that Matthew failed altogether to recognize the symbolic thrust of the Markan story.
/110/ See *B-B-H*, pp.207-11, 296-9, and *supra*, p.75 and n.40.

Chapter IV

"WHOEVER SAYS TO THIS MOUNTAIN": THE MOUNTAIN-MOVING SAYING

Introduction

The Talmud records that prominent Rabbis such as Resh Lakish, R. Meir, Ben Azzai and Rabbah were known as 'uprooters of mountains' because of the great skill they exercised in solving difficult problems of exegesis within the Law /1/. These distinguished men would certainly have needed all their ingenuity to solve the puzzle of the interrelationship of the mountain-moving sayings within the gospel tradition.

The saying occurs in different contexts and with different wording in the gospels of Matthew, Mark and Luke. It appears also in Paul and in the gospel of Thomas. A synopsis of these passages is given overleaf /2/. While our chief concern is to determine the form of the saying as it was known to Mark, and hence to evaluate the extent, function and significance of the redaction he carried out on it, a full appraisal of such cannot be made until we have examined the saying elsewhere, in the variety of forms and contexts in which it appears.

Our view up to this time has been that Mark has attached this logion to the story of the fig-tree as a secondary interpretative saying, whose function it was to alert Mark's readers to the parallel that existed between the withering of the fig-tree (after a suitable interval) and the removal of the Temple Mount (likewise after a suitable interval). Matthew, in turn, has wedded the saying even more closely to the fig-tree story, thus creating a kind of apophthegm, but failed, however, to bring out its *symbolic* significance. He chose rather to interpret the saying purely in terms of the *thaumaturgy* displayed in the miracle, and its subsequent lesson for the nature of faith and prayer. Can this view be supported from a closer analysis of the saying as it is employed elsewhere?

An examination of these differing forms and contexts raises certain key questions which it will now be our purpose to explore. These questions are:

Mark 11.22-23.	Matthew 21.21.
Καὶ ἀποκριθεὶς ὁ ᾽Ιησοῦς λέγει αὐτοῖς·	᾽Αποκριθεὶς δὲ ὁ ᾽Ιησοῦς εἶπεν αὐτοῖς·
[t]ἔχετε πίστιν[o](θεοῦ) 23. ἀμὴν λέγω ὑμῖν ὅτι	ἀμὴν λέγω ὑμῖν, ἐὰν ἔχητε πίστιν[t]
	καὶ μὴ διακριθῆτε, οὐ μόνον τὸ τῆς συκῆς ποιήσετε, ἀλλὰ
ὃς ἂν εἴπῃ τῷ ὄρει τούτῳ·	κἂν τῷ ὄρει τούτῳ εἴπητε·
ἄρθητι καὶ βλήθητι εἰς τὴν θάλασσαν, καὶ μὴ διακριθῇ ἐν τῇ καρδίᾳ αὐτοῦ ἀλλὰ πιστεύῃ ὅτι ὃ λαλεῖ γίνεται, ἔσται (αὐτῷ).	ἄρθητι καὶ βλήθητι εἰς τὴν θάλασσαν, γενήσεται·
[t]εἰ א D θ φ 33.[c] 565. 700 pc it sy[s] [o] 28. a c k r[1] r[2] bo[ms]	[t]ὡς κόκκον σινάπεως φ 474

Mark 9.28-29.	1 Corinthians 13.2.
Καὶ ... οἱ μαθηταὶ ... ἐπηρώτων αὐτόν· ὅτι ἡμεῖς οὐκ ἠδυνήθημεν ἐκβαλεῖν αὐτό; [29.] καὶ εἶπεν αὐτοῖς· τοῦτο τὸ γένος ἐν οὐδενὶ δύναται ἐξελθεῖν εἰ μὴ ἐν προσευχῇ.[t]	... κἂν ἔχω πᾶσαν τὴν πίστιν ὥστε ὄρη μεθιστάναι, ἀγάπην δὲ μὴ ἔχω, οὐδέν εἰμι.
[t]καὶ νηστείᾳ rell(sy[s.p]) txt B א* K geo[nt]; Cl	

Matthew 17.19-20.	Luke 17.5-6.
Τότε...οἱ μαθηταὶ...εἶπον· δια τί ἡμεῖς οὐκ ἠδυνήθημεν ἐκβαλεῖν αὐτό; 20. ὁ δὲ λέγει αὐτοῖς·	Καὶ εἶπαν οἱ ἀπόστολοι τῷ κυρίῳ· πρόσθες ἡμῖν πίστιν. 6. εἶπεν δὲ ὁ κύριος·
δια τὴν ⌐ὀλιγοπιστίαν ὑμῶν· ἀμὴν γὰρ λέγω ὑμῖν, ἐὰν ⌐ἔχητε πίστιν	εἰ ⌐ἔχετε πίστιν
ὡς κόκκον σινάπεως,	ὡς κόκκον σινάπεως,
⌐ἐρεῖτε τῷ ὄρει τούτῳ·	ἐλέγετε ἂν τῇ συκαμίνῳ °ταύτῃ·
μετάβα ἔνθεν ἐκεῖ,	ἐκριζώθητι καὶ φυτεύθητι ἐν τῇ θαλάσσῃ·
καὶ ⌐μεταβήσεται, καὶ οὐδὲν ἀδυνατήσει ἡμῖν.ᴛ	καὶ ὑπήκουσεν ἂν ὑμῖν.
⌐ἀπιστίαν C 𝕬 D W pm latt syˢ·ᵖ ⌐εἴχετε sy_sˢ(Merx) ⌐εἴπατε/ἐλέγετε sy_sˢ(Merx) ⌐μετεβαίνεν syˢ(Merx) ᴛ21. τοῦτο δὲ τὸ γένος οὐκ ἐκπορεύεται (ἐκβάλλεται ℵᶜᵒʳʳ) εἰ μὴ ἐν προσευχῇ καὶ νηστείᾳ ℵᶜᵒʳʳ C 𝕬 D W λ φ pl lat syᵖ boᵖᵗ txt B ℵ* θ pc e ffˡ syˢ·ᶜ sa boᵖᵗ	⌐εἴχετε syˢ D E G H al lat ° p⁷⁵ ℵ D pc syᶜ
Gospel of Thomas 106.	Gospel of Thomas 48.
When (ὅταν) you make the two one, you shall become sons of Man, and when you say: "Mountain, be moved," it will be moved.	Jesus said: If two make peace (εἰρήνη) with each other in this one house, they shall say to the mountain: "Be moved," and it shall be moved.

1. What was the earliest and most primitive *form* of the saying in the Christian tradition?

2. What is its earliest discernible *context* within the gospels?

3. Is this context the original one, or was this saying 'free-floating' in the pre-Synoptic tradition?

4. What is the origin and *Sitz im Leben* of the saying?

   a. Does it go back to Jesus himself, or was it a Gemeindebildung?

   b. Are there similar sayings in Rabbinic Judaism? If so, in what contexts were they used? What was their meaning and import? What light do they shed on the Christian mountain-moving saying?

   c. How might the mountain-moving saying have been understood in primitive Christian tradition? Was it originally a saying specifically about the power of Christian faith to produce a display of thaumaturgy? Did it have an eschatological significance, or was it understood and transmitted simply as a vivid metaphor for the doing of the impossible? Is there any possibility that it might have referred, even in the pre-Markan tradition, to the specific removal of the Temple Mount?

5. How was the saying used, interpreted and understood by the Synoptists, Paul and Thomas? In particular, what was its meaning and function in Markan redaction?

The Saying's most primitive Form

Our first task, then, is to determine what might have been the most primitive form of the saying. From a comparison of the passages set out in the synopsis, the following points of similarity and difference may be noted.

1. In all four Synoptic versions, and in Paul, the saying is spoken in connection with *faith* as the precondition for the removal of a mountain. This is to be contrasted with the Thomas versions where faith is not mentioned /3/. While the Matthean and Lukan versions introduce the faith motif by a conditional clause ἐὰν ἔχητε or εἰ ἔχετε πίστιν (cf. Paul κἂν ἔχω πᾶσαν τὴν πίστιν), Mark, by contrast, introduces this motif in the form of a solemn and separate exhortation (or question) /4/, perhaps gives θεοῦ as the object of πίστιν /5/,

and renders the saying in the third person singular. The
faith motif is, however, repeated once again in the long,
tautologous καὶ μὴ διακριθῇ ... clause placed after the
saying.

2. While the Markan, Matthean, Pauline and Thomean versions
    describe the object to be removed as a *mountain*, Luke refers
    to the uprooting of a *tree*, the συκάμινος, which may mean
    either the sycamore fig or the mulberry /6/. Paul, it is to
    be noted, refers to "mountains" in the plural, while the
    Thomas logia drop the demonstrative adjective "this" /7/.
    Matthew alone, in 21.21, gives the clause "not only that of
    the fig-tree (τὸ τῆς συκῆς) will you do but ..."

3. Both Matthew (17.20) and Luke concur in describing the amount
    of faith necessary as that of a *mustard seed,* ὡς κόκκον σινάπεως.
    Paul refers simply to "all faith", πᾶσαν τὴν πίστιν. Mark
    lacks this mustard seed phrase but has the long *doubt* clause
    (and perhaps also the objective genitive θεοῦ after πίστιν)
    as mentioned above. He elsewhere refers to a grain of mustard
    seed, it should be remarked (cf. 4.31 and parallels). Matthew,
    in 21.21, likewise lacks this phrase and also has the doubt
    motif. It is more succinctly expressed, however, ("and do not
    doubt") and is placed after "if you have faith", so forming
    a tautology. The phrase is lacking in the Thomas versions.

4. The *tenses* in the various versions are different. For the
    address, both Mark and Matthew, in 21.21, have the subjunctive
    "whoever says" (ὃς ἂν εἴπῃ) or "if you should say" (κἂν εἴπητε),
    despite the difference in person. Mt.17.20 has the future "you
    will say" (ἐρεῖτε); cf. Gosp. Thomas logion 48 "they shall
    say". Luke has most unusual tenses: "If you have faith ...
    you would have said (ἐλέγετε) ... and it would have obeyed you
    (ὑπήκουσεν ἂν ὑμῖν)."

5. The *command* given differs in its wording. Both Mark and
    Matthew, in 21.21, have "Be lifted up and cast into the sea"
    (ἄρθητι καὶ βλήθητι εἰς τὴν θάλασσαν). Luke's version,
    likewise, though different in content, has basically the same
    form, "Be uprooted and planted [curiously!] in the sea"
    (ἐκριζώθητι καὶ φυτεύθητι ἐν τῇ θαλάσσῃ). In contrast, Mt.17.20
    has merely "Be removed from hence yonder" (μετάβα ἔνθεν ἐκεῖ) and
    this may be the form reflected also in Paul and Thomas.

6. Finally, the *result* of these words of command is expressed

differently in each version. Mark has "it will be to him"
(ἔσται αὐτῷ) /8/. Matthew, in 21.21, has "it will happen"
(γενήσεται), but in 17.20 has "it will move" (καὶ μεταβήσεται)
and this appears to be the Thomas version also. In addition,
17.20 has "and nothing will be impossible to you". Luke has
"and it would have obeyed you".

From these similarities and differences, the following
conclusions may be drawn.

From the fact that all five New Testament passages connect the
saying with faith it may be inferred that the saying in its most
primitive Christian form was prefaced by the condition that the
power to uproot "this mountain" or "this tree" was dependent upon
the exercise of *faith*. The concurrence of Mt.21.21; 17.20 and
Lk.17.6 indicates that this preface took the form ἐὰν ἔχητε (or
εἰ ἔχετε)πίστιν rather than the form taken by Mark's version. Paul's
version, although clearly less accurate and structured than the
Synoptic versions /9/, may be seen, perhaps, to confirm this.

Secondly, the form of the saying in Mt.17.20 shows itself to
be sufficiently dissimilar from the Markan version and its
doublet in 21.21 as to suggest that it came from a different
source /10/. Moreover, the concurrence of Mt.17.20 and Lk.17.6 in
the phrase ὡς κόκκον σινάπεως (as well as in the conditional
introduction) also suggests that the third evangelist knew this
source. Luke's version, however, of what was probably then a Q
saying may have been modified to some extent by his reminiscence
of Mark's version.

What Mark appears to have done is to have altered the initial
protasis of the saying, viz, "if you have faith as a grain of
mustard seed". He has dropped the mustard seed reference and
turned "if you have faith" into a separate, formal introduction in
the form of a solemn exhortation. By way of compensation for this,
perhaps, he has then appended the clumsy and tautologous "and does
not doubt" clause at the conclusion of the saying /11/. Mark's
version, therefore, offers the kernel of the mountain-moving saying
as a centre-piece, framed by the repetitious faith motif. The
solemn character of the reference to "this mountain" is emphasized,
in addition, by the characteristic 'whoever' form adopted by Mark
for the saying /12/, as well as by the introductory ἀμὴν λέγω ὑμῖν
formula /13/.

While Matthew got the 17.20 version from Q, he has taken the
21.21 version substantially from Mark, although the Q version has

had some influence. Mt.21.21 begins as the Q version did, "if you have faith", but drops the mustard seed reference, taking up Mark's καὶ μὴ διακριθῇ clause instead. This has been abbreviated and placed immediately after ἐὰν ἔχητε πίστιν. The saying is rendered completely in the second person plural, consistent with good style, and Mark's "Be lifted up and cast into the sea", has been followed (contr. 17.20). Mark's more formal ἔσται αὐτῷ has been replaced by γενήσεται, suggested perhaps by γίνεται (Mk.11.23e), and οὐ μόνον κτλ. has been added to provide better linkage with the story /14/.

From this it can be seen that both Mk.11.22-23 and Mt.21.21 belong together, the latter being modelled substantially on the former with only a little influence from Q. Mt.17.20 and Lk.17.6 also belong together by virtue of the ὡς κόκκον σινάπεως phrase which is unlikely to be due to the influence of the Mustard Seed parable as Butler and Goulder suggest /15/.

But how do we account for the difference which exists between Mt.17.20 and Lk.17.6? If we can assume that neither knew the other /16/, and both drew here from a source independent from Mk.11.22-23, a source which presumably is Q, why do they differ so sharply from one another? Indeed, there is more in which they differ in form and content, than in what unites them.

There are three possibilities:

(i) *Mt.17.20 represents the original pre-Synoptic Q saying*, while Lk.17.6 barely reflects it, having been grossly modified as a result of its association with the fig-tree story. This view is held by scholars such as Schanz, B. Weiss, Holtzmann, Wellhausen, Loisy, Harnack, Taylor and Schweizer /17/.

(ii) *Lk.17.6 represents the original pre-Synoptic Q saying*, while Mt.17.20 has been so influenced by the Markan version that the sycamine tree has been replaced by the mountain. This view is held, for example, by Schmid, Streeter and Kilpatrick /18/.

(iii) *Two sayings existed in Q*, which were parallel in form, the one referring to the uprooting of a mountain, the other to the uprooting of a tree. This view is held, for example, by T.W. Manson, Lagrange, Wendling, Lohmeyer and Branscomb /19/.

To each of these positions, however, there are some objections. To (i) it can be said with reason that the tree of

Mark's story is a fig-tree (συκῆ), while that of Luke's saying is
either a mulberry or a sycamore fig. Why should Luke have
referred to a συκάμινος when Mark's story talked of a συκῆ? When
the third evangelist wishes to refer elsewhere to a fig-tree he
uses the proper term (cf. 13.6; 21.29). Elsewhere, too, when he
refers to a sycamore fig he uses συκομορέα (19.4), the proper
Greek word for it. This might suggest then that in 17.6 a
reference to the mulberry was in fact intended and, if this is
so, the hypothesis that Lk.17.6 harbours a reminiscence of or
tradition-connection with the fig-tree story becomes even more
strained.

Luke's version is odd indeed, for here the image is not
purely 'destructive', as is the case with the wholesale removal of
a mountain and its subsequent 'disposal' under the sea. In Luke,
the tree image has a suggestion of regeneration. It will be
transplanted (φυτεύθητι) and presumably will take root under what
must be the most impossible of circumstances (ἐν τῇ θαλάσσῃ).
In some respects, too, this horticultural image harmonizes better
with the notion of faith "as a grain of mustard seed", which also
takes root and grows prodigiously despite adverse conditions (cf.
Mk.4.30-32 and parallels) /20/.

Nevertheless, against view (ii) that Lk.17.6 reflects the more
primitive Q saying is the weighty objection that every other
version of the saying figures a mountain (cf. Mk.11.23 Mt.17.20;
21.21 1 Cor.13.2 Gosp.Thomas 48,106). The mountain image,
therefore, has every right to be considered primitive. While we
can go some way to explaining Luke's substitution of a tree image
for a mountain image in the light of Mark, the reverse procedure
on the part of Mark, Matthew, Paul and Thomas is one that is more
difficult to account for.

These observations might appear to lend support, therefore to
option (iii). T.W. Manson, in fact, argues that the ambiguity
over Luke's use of συκάμινος (= mulberry or sycamore fig) in 17.6
and συκομορέα (= sycamore fig) in 19.4 may stem from Luke's
employment of different sources in these passages. In 17.6, he
maintains, Luke has faithfully copied Q which had mistranslated
an Aramaic shikma (or sycamore fig) as a συκάμινος. The uprooting
of a tree (and more particularly the sycamore fig, carob or cedar,
which were especially deep-rooted) as well as the uprooting of a
mountain were both images popular in Jewish circles, as we shall
see /21/, and it would certainly not be surprising if both images
were involved in Q sayings preserved by the Jewish Christian

community. If such were the case, and could we assume that Mark
did know the tree form as well as the mountain form, it would be
significant that he chose the mountain form when the tree form
was at first sight more appropriate. This might again be support
for the view that he wanted the *mountain* of the saying to allude
to the Temple Mount.

However, despite its attractiveness, hypothesis (iii), too,
is subject to question. Attention has already been drawn to the
correspondence existing between Mark's version and Lk.17.6, and
this correspondence must cast doubt on the autonomy of the Lukan
saying. Mark's context does after all mention a tree, albeit a
fig-tree, and Luke's form of command, ἐκριζώθητι καὶ φυτεύθητι,
corresponds to Mark's ἄρθητι καὶ βλήθητι (contr. Mt.17.20 μετάβα),
while being suitably altered in respect of a tree. An echo of
Mark's ἐκ ῥιζῶν (11.20) might conceivably be heard in Luke's
ἐκριζώθητι. The sea reference is common to both and is, perhaps,
more appropriate in Mark's version than in Luke's, where it
produces a less natural image. Moreover, the context given here
by Luke does not appear to be original, as we shall presently
suggest. The Lukan version appears to reflect a knowledge of both
the Markan context for the saying and also one in which the
disciples' lack of faith had been exposed, viz, that of Mt.17.14-20
(cf. Lk.17.5 Πρόσθες ἡμῖν πίστιν and the awkward tenses). In short,
there are sufficient grounds for regarding Lk.17.5,6 as inferior to
Mt.17.20.

The conclusion to be drawn, on the whole, then, is that the
Mt.17.20 version appears to correspond more closely in literary
form to the pre-Synoptic saying than do any of the other versions.
Its claim to be considered more primitive may be seen, in addition,
to be supported by Paul, and, possibly, by the Gospel of Thomas,
if Thomas can be regarded as witnessing to forms of putatively
dominical sayings that derive not from the gospels themselves but
from traditions lying behind them /22/.

The Lukan version, while possibly original, is in the final
analysis best regarded, in our view, as a conflation and hence as
secondary. The problem of Luke's choice of συκάμινος rather than
συκῆ still remains, it must be admitted, but is less acute if
συκάμινος here is read as the sycamore fig, the fig-tree's distant
relative. The term, a hapax legomenon in the New Testament, does
refer primarily in Greek to the mulberry, but it is noteworthy that
the LXX on some six occasions translates the Hebrew שׁקמה = sycamore
fig (Ficus sycomorus) by συκάμινος /23/. This may well be the

meaning here, notwithstanding 19.4, for συκάμινρς and συκομορέα
were often interchanged in ordinary usage, according to Dioscorides
/24/. Could it be, then, that Luke, having chosen to speak of a
fig-tree in reminiscence of Mark's story, opted in turn for the
sycamore fig since the latter was particularly deep-rooted, was
hence more appropriate for a tree-uprooting saying and was, indeed,
prominently employed in this capacity in Jewish folklore and
imagery /25/?

The earliest discernible Context

Having suggested that Mt.17.20 reflects the most primitive
literary form of the saying, we should now consider what might
have been the earliest context within which the saying appeared.
This is not to say that the saying may not have been free-floating
at a very early period in Christian tradition. We believe that it
was, but the divergence of contexts, particularly within the
Synoptic tradition, prompts the question as to their priority.

Mark, as we have seen, has the saying within the context
of the Cursing of the Fig-tree story and the Cleansing of the
Temple. Matthew reproduces this in 21.21. Earlier, however, he
gives the saying in connection with the healing of the boy
possessed by a spirit. Luke does not give his version of the
saying within the context of a miracle story, but rather introduces
it, in his Reisebericht section, within a block of miscellaneous
Sayings material. There are signs, too, that the short quasi-
historical introduction he gives to it (καὶ εἶπαν οἱ ἀπόστολοι τῷ
κυρίῳ· πρόσθες ἡμῖν πίστιν. εἶπεν δὲ ὁ κύριος...) has been composed
by himself. Both the use of ἀπόστολοι for the disciples and
ὁ κύριος for Jesus are characteristic of him /26/.

The demand "Increase our faith!" (πρόσθες ἡμῖν πίστιν),
however, may not be a creatio ex nihilo, but may derive from the
tradition /27/. Luke reveals here perhaps an acquaintance with a
prior context for the saying in which the disciples' lack of faith
had been exposed and in which instruction on the nature of faith
had been given. The awkward tenses in his version may also point
to this conclusion. At once, the Puer Lunaticus pericope springs
to mind (Mt.17.14-20 = Mk.9.14-29 = Lk.9.37-43a), for there, too,
in the Matthean version, the disciples are shown to possess 'little
faith' (ὀλιγοπιστία) or even, perhaps, 'no faith' (ἀπιστία) /28/,
and are therefore given a lesson on the efficacy of faith.

When we turn to the pericope as it is presented by our three evangelists, the following main features may be observed /29/.

1.   Both Matthew and Luke present the story in a form drastically
      shorter than the Markan one. Mark's version covers 16 verses,
      while those of Matthew and Luke cover 7 verses.

2.   While such abbreviation is characteristic of Matthew's
      procedure, it is thoroughly untypical of Luke. H.J. Held
      considers it, in fact, "remarkable" for "in all other miracle
      narratives the third evangelist preserves the longer Markan
      text over against the Matthaean abbreviations" /30/.

3.   Both Matthew and Luke concur over against Mark in respect of
      the scene between Jesus and the father of the boy (Mk.9.21-24).
      It is absent in both.

4.   Luke also lacks the epilogue in which instruction regarding
      the miracle is given.

5.   On the other hand, while both Mark and Matthew report such an
      epilogue, the content of each is entirely different. When
      asked by the disciples why they had been unable to perform
      the miracle, Jesus, in Matthew's version, gives ὀλιγοπιστία
      ('little faith') as the reason, and then proceeds to give the
      mountain-moving saying. In the Markan text, however, we are
      told that the exorcism required, not faith, but *prayer* and,
      perhaps, *fasting* to make it effective: τοῦτο τὸ γένος ἐν οὐδενὶ
      δύναται ἐξελθεῖν εἰ μὴ ἐν προσευχῇ (καὶ νηστείᾳ) /31/.

A number of considerations make it likely that, as with the
form of the mountain-moving saying, Matthew here in chapter 17 gives
us the more primitive (though not necessarily original) context
for the saying. While there are signs of Matthean style and
vocabulary in 17.18 ff./32/, and hence of Matthean redactional
influence, the evidence above from Luke would appear to argue in
favour of a pre-Synoptic, and hence a pre-Matthean, *attachment* of
the saying to the Puer Lunaticus story /33/.

This attachment is unlikely to have been made by Matthew
himself, as is often argued. Goulder, for example, thinks the
Matthean epilogue was designed by Matthew to replace Mark's
unsatisfactory one /34/. But would Matthew have replaced a Markan
epilogue which exonerated the disciples with one which accused
them explicitly of ὀλιγοπιστία or even ἀπιστία?

The Mt.17 context for the saying is a natural one and the

saying fits in easily here. In the first place, the episode is
said to have taken place specifically within the vicinity of a
mountain (17.1-9) /35/. In the second place, the question posed
by the disciples about their inability to perform the exorcism,
and the content of the answer given by Jesus to that question, have
a logical connection with what is reported in the story itself
(cf. 17.16,17).

On the other hand, the Markan epilogue bears little, if any,
connection to what is reported in the story. If "this kind" went
out only by *prayer*, then Jesus is clearly not represented as having
prayed. Far less so did he *fast*, if the longer version is to be
read. Indeed, according to Mk.2.18 ff., this was not considered
by Mark to have been a practice of his!

Mk.9.18,19 suggests that it was a lack of *faith* on the part
of both scribes (peculiar to Mark here) and disciples (cf. 9.14)
that made them unable to perform the exorcism. Such a situation,
in fact, had prompted Jesus to exclaim impatiently, "O *faithless*
(ἄπιστος) generation, how long am I to be with you? How long am
I to bear with you?" (9.19). Mk.9.23,24 suggests clearly, on the
other hand, that by contrast with the scribes and disciples the
father of the boy *did possess the necessary faith*, or at least
confessed to a certain degree of faith, but asked for it to be
increased: Πιστεύω· βοήθει μου τῇ ἀπιστίᾳ.

In view of these clear features of the story, the Markan
epilogue is certainly an enigma, for the import of Jesus' words is
there to suggest that it was *not* lack of faith that defeated the
disciples. Instead, it was the especially difficult nature of the
case that did so. It was a case requiring a special technique -
prayer (and fasting) instead of a direct display of thaumaturgic
power. The effect of this 'qualifier' is hence to spare the
disciples, a motive not elsewhere characteristic of Mark /36/.
When we consider, in addition, the very loose connection (contr. Mt.)
that 9.28,29 has with the preceding story, the 'house' that
mysteriously appears from nowhere /37/, the relationship of this
epilogue to the story, and indeed to the Markan text, calls for
explanation.

We have observed already that the Markan scene between Jesus
and the believing father is peculiar to the second evangelist, and
we have noted that the absence of this scene in Luke is especially
significant, since Luke elsewhere always preserves the longer Markan
text over against the Matthean abbreviations. When we consider

that the words spoken by Jesus in 9.23 ("If you can! All things
are possible to him who has faith") and by the father in 9.24
("I do believe; help my lack of faith!") bear a very close
resemblance to the Lukan introduction ("Increase our faith!" 17.5)
and to the Matthean epilogue ("Because of your lack of faith",
17.20) then an intriguing possibility emerges. Could it be that
all three evangelists knew a version of the Puer Lunaticus
pericope to which in the pre-Synoptic tradition the mountain-
moving saying had been attached? The function of this attachment
would have been to provide instructional material on how the
disciples were to overcome their failure to produce a miracle.

The existence of such a primitive version lying behind all
three Synoptic accounts would further serve to explain the
concurrence that exists in some points between Matthew and Luke
over against Mark, which is puzzling if both Matthew and Luke were
independently employing Mark as their sole source here. Both, as
we have said, lack the scene involving the father of the boy.
Both have καὶ διεστραμμένη after Mark's ὦ γενεὰ ἄπιστος in 9.19
(cf. also ὧδε in that same verse). Both have the reference to the
παῖς in the parallels to 9.27. Both employ the verb ἀδυνάτειν,
where Mark uses ἰσχύειν in 9.18 and parallels. Curiously, all
three refer to the man from the crowd in different ways. He is an
ἄνθρωπος in Matthew (17.14), εἷς ἐκ τοῦ ὄχλου in Mark (9.17), an
ἀνὴρ ἀπὸ τοῦ ὄχλου in Luke (9.38). Could these be independent
translation variants /38/?

If this view is sound, then the following might be said in
respect of the way each evangelist has handled this pericope.
Matthew, in the first place, would appear to preserve it better
than do Mark or Luke. In his account, the attachment of the
saying to the story remains, although, as has been pointed out,
the epilogue itself has been subject to Matthean redactional
influence /39/. Luke, however, chose to omit the epilogue
reflected in Mt.17.19,20, perhaps because he was unhappy with the
ascription of ὀλιγοπιστία, or even ἀπιστία, to the disciples /40/.
Elsewhere, nevertheless, he has re-introduced it, devoid of its
previous narrative context and provided with a refashioned,
suitably respectful, quasi-historical introduction. The mountain-
moving saying has also been reproduced in a form influenced by the
Markan version, as we have argued. In thus separating this
epilogue from its prior connection with the Puer Lunaticus pericope,
Luke has not succeeded in disguising his knowledge of this prior
context. The content of the introduction and the awkward tenses
reveal this. Moreover, it may be of significance that Luke places

his version of the epilogue within the context of *offence* (17.1-2)
and *forgiveness* sayings (17.3-4) which in Matthew follow *in the
same order after the Puer Lunaticus story* (Mt.18.6-7,15,21-22).
While the offence saying likewise occurs in Mark in Sayings
material following this story (9.42), the concurrence in order
between Matthew and Luke cannot be because each is independently
following Mark, for the forgiveness saying (Mt.18.15,21-22 =
Lk.17.3-4) does not here occur in Mark. The order may therefore
reflect that obtaining in the pre-Synoptic tradition, and hence,
possibly, goes back to Q /41/.

   What Mark may have done, on his part, is to have removed the
mountain-moving saying from its location here in the exorcism
story, and transferred it to what was for him a more pregnant
context, viz, that of the Cleansing of the Temple /42/. In turn
he may then have expanded the body of the exorcism narrative /43/
by creating the scene between Jesus and the believing man from the
crowd, hence transferring to the latter the instruction on faith,
that, in that epilogue, had been associated with the disciples.
The father is shown to be *weak in faith* (cf. τὸ εἰ δύνῃ Mk.9.23b
with διὰ τὴν ὀλιγοπιστίαν v.1. ἀπιστίαν Mt.17.20). He asks for an
increase in faith (cf. πιστεύω· βοήθει μου τῇ ἀπιστίᾳ Mk.9.24b with
πρόσθες ἡμῖν πίστιν Lk.17.5). He is told that *nothing is impossible
for genuine faith* (cf. πάντα δυνατὰ τῷ πιστεύοντι Mk.9. 23c with
ἐὰν ἔχητε πίστιν ὡς κόκκον σινάπεως ἐρεῖτε κτλ. Mt.17.20 = Lk.17.6)
/44/. In Mark's account, therefore, the disciples stand together
with the scribes, in their relation to Jesus' person and power, as
part of the γενεὰ ἄπιστος (9.19). The man in the crowd, by
contrast, reveals an attitude appropriate to the true believer /45/.

   In thus detaching the mountain-moving saying from its context
here and transferring it to chapter 11, Mark would thereby have
created a lacuna. How then may we explain the puzzling 9.28-29?

   To begin with, we note that the saying here is a *prayer* saying
which exudes something of the atmosphere of early church piety and
religious practice. It qualifies the display of thaumaturgy
described in the miracle story, by drawing the notion of prayer
(and perhaps fasting) into connection with the exorcism. In this
respect, it has a certain resemblance to Mk.11.24 which is also a
prayer saying serving to qualify, perhaps, too excessively
thaumaturgic an emphasis in the fig-tree miracle story and
particularly in its attached mountain-moving saying /46/. Both
sayings also have no integral relation to the miracle story to which
they are attached. Mk.11.24 also bears a striking resemblance to

Mk.9.23. When we note further that the prayer (and fasting)
saying of Mk.9.29 is also given as part of the Matthean text
of chapter 17 (17.21) by a great many textual witnesses, then
the following two possibilities suggest themselves.

Could it be that in the early tradition there had become
attached to the mountain-moving saying within its primitive
Puer Lunaticus context a prayer (and fasting) saying which
functioned as a qualifier to a purely thaumaturgic interpretation
of the exorcism and its attached logion? If so, then both
Mt.17.21 and Mk.9.29 may reflect this. In transferring material
from this context to its new Fig-tree and Temple Cleansing
context, Mark may have left this residual prayer saying, in a
sense, 'high and dry', lacking its prior connection with the
displaced material. In 11.23,24, however, the prayer motif may
have been carried over to act again as a qualifier to a purely
thaumaturgic interpretation of 11.23.

Or could it be, as we suspect, that 9.28-29 is again the work
of a later scribe or scribes, who, having added the prayer and
forgiveness sayings of 11.24 ff. to the Markan text, similarly
added a prayer saying here where Matthew or tradition suggested a
lacuna? Mt.17.21 may not then be a gloss that has come from the
Markan text. The influence may be in reverse. Such a view
would certainly explain the enigmatic features of this Markan
epilogue pointed out above, and would harmonize with what we have
suggested so far with regard to the Cursing of the Fig-tree
sequel.

In making these early additions to the Markan text, a post-
Markan redactor or glossator would probably have had two aims in
mind. He may have been unhappy with the Markan portrayal of the
disciples as lacking faith and may have wished to spare them the
ignominy of powerlessness in the face of an evil spirit. He may
also have been unhappy with the notion of charismatic miracle-
working per se, described without reference to the limits imposed
by Christian piety and church practice. In this respect, he would
reflect a Pauline emphasis: "I may have all the faith necessary
to move mountains, but if I have no love, I am nothing(1 Cor.13.2)."

Origin, Meaning and Sitz im Leben

Thus far, then, we have concluded that Mt.17.20 preserves the
more primitive form of the saying, and that the Puer Lunaticus

story was its earliest context. Mark, we suggest, may have found
the mountain-moving saying himself within this context, a context
to which possibly a series of church piety and practice sayings
(prayer, offence, forgiveness, greatness, etc.) had been already
attracted, but transferred the saying (and possibly an associated
prayer logion 11.24) to its present context in chapter 11.

However, in light of the 'fluidity' of context shown by the
saying in the Synoptic gospels, and in view of the Pauline evidence
(1 Cor.13.2), it appears likely that at the very earliest period of
Christian tradition the saying was a free-floating one. We have
seen that the saying is connected with the exercise of faith -
fides mirifica - in all of the five New Testament logia. In the
Thomas logia, however, this is not the case, and this raises the
question whether the saying, or a similar one, had a currency
outside of Christian circles, before it was brought into connection
with the specific exercise of Christian faith, and subsequently
attached to the Puer Lunaticus story.

It is our view that Mark intends the 'mountain' of the mountain-
moving saying to allude to the Temple Mount. This has not been the
usual interpretation of this verse. The standard view is that the
reference here is entirely figurative /47/, or that "this mountain"
refers in this context to the Mount of Olives, but again with
purely metaphorical intent /48/. In support of this popular
position, it has been customary to refer to the datum that the
'uprooting of mountains' was a common Rabbinic hyperbole for the
doing of the impossible or the incredible /49/. Since this parallel
is obviously important, we should examine more closely the examples
that have been cited.

In *B.Sanh.24a* /50/ we read:

"Ulla /51/ said: One who saw Resh Laḳish /52/ in the
Beth-Hamidrash (engaged in debate) would think he was
uprooting mountains (כאילו עוקר הרים) and grinding them
against each other! (וטוחנן זה בזה) - Rabina /53/ said:
But did not he who saw R. Meir /54/ in the Beth-Hamidrash
feel that he was uprooting yet greater mountains
(כאילו עוקר הרי הרים) and grinding them against each other?"

The term עוקר הרים, therefore, was applied to a Rabbi with an
exceptional dialectic skill. The 'uprooter of mountains' was able
to resolve by his wits and ingenuity extremely difficult
hermeneutical problems within the Law. Here R. Meir's superiority

in this regard even over the formidable Resh Lakish is being
attested.

Again in *B.'Erub.29a* we read:

"Raba /55/ (once) said: I am (today) in the condition of
Ben Azzai /56/ in the markets of Tiberias."

Ben Azzai was the most prominent dialectician of his day
(cf. B.Bek.58a) and his discourses were usually delivered in the
market-place of Tiberias, as a gloss to that effect states:

"Like Ben Azzai, who taught profoundly in the streets of
Tiberias; nor was there in his day עוקר הרים כמותו such
another *rooter up of mountains* as he" /57/.

The term עוקר הרים was not simply a picturesque compliment
paid to a gifted Rabbi, however. In the Talmud, it approaches the
character of a technical term. It is, for example, contrasted with
another epithet, applied to a learned teacher of the Law, viz, the
'Sinai' (סיני). This can be seen from *B.Hor.14a* (= *B.Ber.64a)*
which reads:

"R. Johanan /58/ said: (On the following point) there is a
difference of opinion between R. Simeon b. Gamaliel /59/ and
the Rabbis. One view is that a well-read scholar (lit. a
'Sinai' סיני) is superior (to the keen dialectician) and the
other view is that the keen dialectician (lit. 'the uprooter
of mountains' עוקר הרים) is superior. R. Joseph /60/ was a
well-read scholar (סיני); Rabbah /61/ was a keen dialectician
(עוקר הרים). An enquiry was sent up to Palestine: Who of
these should take precedence (i.e. in being appointed as head
of the Rabbinic school of Pumbeditha)? They sent them word in
reply: 'A well-read scholar (סיני) is to take precedence';
for the Master said, 'All are dependent on the owner of the
wheat' (i.e. all need the one who possesses a widespread
knowledge of the authentic traditions)."

The 'Sinai', therefore, was a scholar with an encyclopaedic
knowledge of the Law, which was believed to have been communicated
in its entirety to Moses on Sinai. By virtue of being thus well-
read, he could give reliable decisions based on a sound knowledge
of these halakic traditions. The 'uprooter of mountains', by
contrast, was a skilled dialectician whose acuteness of intellect
(rather than simply his appeal to authority) enabled him to resolve

the most difficult of legal problems.

Viewed in this light, the Christian mountain-moving saying might seem to suggest that the disciple of Jesus is promised that he too can be as much an 'uprooter of mountains', a עוקר הרים, as the most gifted Rabbi, except that it is not his command over the intricacies of the *Law* that counts within the circle of Jesus' followers, but his capacity to exercise *faith*.

However, the figure 'uprooter of mountains' was not one reserved exclusively for gifted legal scholars. In *B.B.B.3b*, there is a discussion upon the rule that a synagogue should not be pulled down before another is built to take its place. Reference is made to the tradition that Baba b. Buta /62/ had advised Herod to pull down the Temple (cf. B.B.B.4a) and rebuild it. Had the rule then been broken on this occasion, it was asked, for the new Temple had not been built before the old was pulled down? The answer given is:

"... if you like I can say that the rule does not apply to Royalty, since a king does not go back on his word. For so said Samuel /63/: If Royalty says, *I will uproot mountains*, it will uproot them and not go back on its word."

This passage is very interesting. Not only does it employ the figure in respect of the ability of kings to issue irrevocable decrees that brook no resistance, and that are to be obeyed, however impossible they may be to fulfil, but it brings Samuel's dictum into specific connection with king Herod and the Temple. The dictum is being employed because of its capacity to suggest a *double entendre*. If kings can uproot *mountains*, and cannot be gainsaid, then king Herod can pull down the *Temple Mount*, without exception being made to his illegal procedure. The double entendre here, then, is a suggestive parallel to our Markan passage, for there too Mark has employed the mountain-moving image in its capacity to suggest in its context the removal of the Temple Mount.

A further reference in the Talmud to the uprooting of mountains is given in *B.Soṭ.9b (= Vay.R.VIII.2)*. The Talmud passage is a commentary on the Judges text of the story of Samson. Jgs.13.25 reads:

"And the Spirit of the Lord began to stir him in Mahaneh-dan between Zorah and Eshtaol." (RSV)

B.Soṭ.9b gives this commentary on the words "between Zorah and Eshtaol":

> "R. Assi /64/ said: Zorah and Eshtaol are two great mountains, and Samson uprooted them and ground one against the other."

In the Midrash Rabbah passage, a similar piece of exegesis is ascribed to R. Samuel b. Nahman /65/:

> "R. Samuel b. Naḥman said: When the Holy Spirit began to ring in Samson, it began in three places, as it is said, 'And the spirit of the Lord began to ring within him in Mahaneh-Dan, between Zorah and Eshtaol.' R. Samuel b. Naḥman said: Scripture here informs us that he took two mountains and knocked them one against the other, just as a man takes two stones and knocks them one against the other."

In this passage, it should be noted, the image of mountain-moving elsewhere expressed as a metaphor, is employed *literally*. It appears in a legendary form, describing the thaumaturgy displayed by the charismatic Samson, acting under the influence of the Spirit of God. Here we might compare, for example, those legends in later Christian tradition where the mountain-moving saying in the gospels was likewise given a literal application. One such is the legend of Gregory Thaumaturgus: Gregory, it was said, managed to get a mountain to move aside, so leaving him sufficient room for the church he wished to build /66/! Charismatic power, then, in both these cases, achieved the literal moving of a mountain.

The thaumaturgic application of the image is particularly interesting, for here we have links with yet another Talmud passage where not the uprooting of a mountain but the uprooting of a tree is described as evidence of divine approbation. This passage is found in *B.B.M.59a-59b (= P.M.Ḳ.III.1*, Schwab, pp.321-2) /67/ and concerns the celebrated R. Eliezer b. Hyrcanus /68/. Eliezer, a first century conservative Tanna, and a follower of the school of Shammai, was excommunicated in the year 96 CE for not accepting a ruling on a point of law made by the majority of his more liberal colleagues (of the Hillel school). Eliezer is said to have used every argument to persuade them that his ruling was correct.

> "If the halachah agrees with me, let this carob-tree prove it (חרוב זה יוכיח)! Thereupon the carob-tree was torn

(lit. 'uprooted' נעקר) a hundred cubits out of its place -
others affirm, four hundred cubits. 'No proof can be
brought from a carob-tree,' they retorted."

The *P.M.Ḳ.III.1* version is even more elaborate. There Eliezer
orders the tree to uproot itself if the halakah agreed with his
opponents. It fails to do so Then he orders it to uproot itself
if the halakah agreed with him. Thereupon it uproots itself. In
turn, he invites it to return to its former position if the
halakah agreed with his opponents. It fails to do so. When
bidden to do so if the halakah agreed with him, however, it again
returns to its place.

R. Eliezer's opponents were not convinced, despite other
prominent displays of thaumaturgic power: a stream of water flowing
backwards, the walls of a schoolhouse bending over, and finally a
voice from heaven, a Bath-Qôl, which declared itself in favour of
Eliezer's judgement. Witnessing in a most remarkable way to the
sovereignty of human reason, the assembled Rabbis declared that
not even a Bath-Qôl could contradict the ruling given in the Law
at Sinai that the majority voice must be heeded (Ex.23.2) /69/.
Eliezer was over-ruled, therefore, and excommunicated, and both
Talmuds give vivid descriptions of the calamities that resulted
thereafter, and that befell, in particular, anything upon which
the formidable Rabbi cast his eye.

This passage has a striking affinity with the Lukan saying
(17.6). The carob-tree (חרוב) here mentioned is linked together
closely in the Rabbinical literature with the sycamore fig (שקמה)
/70/ which the LXX, as we have seen, translates on six occasions
as συκάμινος. The sycamore fig, it was said, could stand for 600
years /71/. Both trees have especially deep roots and hence were
natural candidates for an uprooting of a tree metaphor, image or
legend. Their aptness in this regard, and their connection with
such images and legends might possibly then have been a factor
influencing Luke to substitute the συκάμινος for its more distant
cousin the Markan συκῆ, when reproducing the saying in isolation
from its prior contexts. In the Lukan passage, it is to be noted,
however, the uprooting of the συκάμινος is confidently promised
in response to an act of faith. In the Talmud legend, the carob
is said to have uprooted itself to prove, not Eliezer's faith, but
the correctness of his halakic teaching /72/.

Another tree with strong roots and a celebrated reputation for
firmness and endurance was, of course, the cedar of Lebanon, and

it is not surprising that it, too, figures in another tree-
uprooting tradition. This tradition is to be found in *Ekah R.II.*
*2.4 (= P.Ta'an.IV.5,*Schwab, p.189). Here it is said that as a
test of courage, Bar Kochba /73/, leader of the Jewish revolt
against Rome in 132-135 CE, had ordered each recruit to cut off a
finger. When challenged by the doctors of the Law on how long he
would continue to make the men of Israel blemished, he in turn
asked them how else he could test his army's courage. "Let anyone,"
they answered, *"who cannot uproot (עוקר) a cedar from Lebanon*
(P.Ta'an. adds 'on horseback') be refused enrolment in your army."
Bar Kochba, we are told, thereupon had 200,000 men of each class,
those with an amputated finger, and those who had uprooted a cedar,
and with this force of formidable soldiers, he went to war, his men
crying, "O God, neither help us nor discourage us!" The battle,
however, went against him, and he was killed at Bethar in 135 CE.

In all these examples from the Rabbinical tradition, therefore,
what stands out is the variety of ways in which the mountain-moving
image, and its correlative tree-uprooting image, were employed in
Jewish circles for feats of an exceptional, extraordinary or
impossible nature. We have seen that it was not simply used in a
figurative sense, as a vivid metaphor for the doing of the
impossible. It could be used in the Talmud in something of a
technical sense, applied to a Rabbi with an acumen that enabled
him, in contrast to another (the 'Sinai') to solve perplexing
hermeneutical problems within the Law. It could be applied to
kings, and employed in relation to the seemingly irrevocable and
irresistible nature of royal decrees. It could even be used in a
kind of double entendre, the 'mountain' of the image suggesting
the Temple Mount, in order to bolster an argument. It could
appear, moreover, in a legendary context, being applied *literally*
to the feats of heroes like the charismatic Samson, acting under
the influence of the Spirit of God. Its service, indeed, as a
popular element in descriptions of thaumaturgy was recognized in
all of the three latter passages quoted above, and it is in the
climate of these passages, we suggest, that the Christian
mountain-moving saying may have its particular Sitz im Leben.

Indeed, in the Bar Kochba passage above, we are confronted
not only by an act of thaumaturgy, but one deemed to have been
accomplished within an *eschatological* context. Bar Kochba had been
acknowledged by no less than R. Akiba as the Jewish Messiah, the
precursor of the New Age. His committed disciples, therefore, in
following him into eschatological battle with the Romans, are
deemed capable of doing the impossible, of uprooting cedar trees,
and this even on horseback! Likewise, the followers of Messiah

Jesus are promised that they too will be able to remove a
mountain or uproot a sycamine. In the case of Bar Kochba, this
gift must be demonstrated before enrolment in his Messianic
movement is permitted. Courage must be shown by the willingness
to dispense with a finger. In the case of Jesus' followers, this
gift is *promised* on the condition that *faith* is exercised,
although the disciple of Jesus must also be willing to dispense
with his entire hand, foot or eye, if these prove a 'scandalon'
(Mk.9.43 ff.). In both cases, powers of an extraordinary nature
are predicated of the disciples within the context of the Messianic
Age, the coming Kingdom of God.

It is this *eschatological* background that gives to the image
something more than the force of a simple metaphor, that makes it
more than a figure signifying, in the vivid imagery of the
oriental mind, that men can do the impossible if only they try
hard enough. What is in view is *actual* thaumaturgy, the belief
that men *will* do the impossible, and will do it *in the New Age*.
Wonder-working, indeed, is the visible sign of the Kingdom's
advent and presence in the gospel tradition (cf. Mt.11.2 ff. and
parallels). In the Messianic Age, the impossible becomes possible,
the metaphor becomes reality, men themselves in that beatific time
will find nature respond to them in undreamt-of ways!

This theme prevails in a whole panoply of Jewish and Christian
sources /74/ and will be explored in the following chapters. The
Messianic Age, it was believed, would be a time of marvellous
productivity and fruitfulness. "In the Messianic Age the children
of Israel, returning to their Home, with the Messiah at their head,
will find a constant supply of fruit along the way, and shade
also, for the trees will bend forward to give them shade, just as
the low places will fill up, rough places will become smooth, hills
will be levelled and the sea will become dry land over which the
redeemed will pass (Isai 40:4-5; 45:2; 49:11; 51:10; 54:10;
Ps.Sol.11:4; 1 Bar 5:7)." /75/

It is this eschatological context, then, that provides a
fitting background for the gospel mountain-moving saying /76/.
The removal of mountains is an image that is employed as early as
the Old Testament to describe what will happen when the New Age
comes (as the examples above illustrate). "Every valley shall be
lifted up, and every mountain and hill be made low" (Is.40.4, RSV).
Indeed, the advent of the Messiah himself will cause such an event.

"On that day his feet shall stand on the Mount of Olives
which lies before Jerusalem on the east; and the Mount of
Olives shall be split in two from east to west by a very
wide valley; so that one half of the Mount shall withdraw
northward and the other half southward." (Zech.14.4).

Summation: The Saying in Markan Redaction

How, then, are we to sum up what has been said so far? What
are the answers to the questions we raised at the beginning of
this chapter? What has this analysis of the form, context and
Sitz im Leben of the mountain-moving saying, both in the Christian
and Jewish tradition, achieved? In conclusion, we might say the
following:

1.   The most primitive literary form of the saying discernible
      within the New Testament passages quoted (and supported
      perhaps by Thomas) is Mt.17.20. Its wording probably went
      something like:

      ἐὰν ἔχητε (perhaps εἴχετε) πίστιν ὡς κόκκον σινάπεως,
      ἐρεῖτε (perhaps ἐλέγετε) τῷ ὄρει τούτῳ· μετάβα ἔνθεν
      ἐκεῖ, καὶ μεταβήσεται (perhaps μετεβαῖνεν) /77/.

      If Merx's evidence can be upheld, then the original pre-
      Matthean form in its context (although not, possibly, the
      Matthean text itself) may have implied a sharper rebuke of
      the disciples than is here apparent. Luke's version is a
      less primitive form of the Q saying, showing, we think,
      influence from Mark and possibly also from tree-uprooting
      sayings and legends (especially concerning the sycamore fig,
      carob and cedar) current in Jewish circles.

2.   The most primitive context is again that of Mt.17.14-20(21),
      the Puer Lunaticus story. The attachment of the saying here
      is probably pre-Matthean, and was possibly known to both Mark
      and Luke as well. Mark, however, may have transferred it
      from this context to that of the fig-tree story and the
      Cleansing of the Temple. Luke also may have detached it from
      this context and given it as an isolated dominical saying
      within his Reisebericht section. He has not been able to
      disguise his knowledge of this attachment, we think, for his
      awkward tenses and his quasi-historical introduction appear
      to reveal his awareness of the *two* contexts given by Matthew
      and Mark.

3.   Although the context of Mt.17 may have been the earliest one
     discernible within the gospels, at the very earliest period
     we think the saying was free-floating. The evidence of Paul
     and Thomas may confirm this.

4.   There is no apparent reason to doubt that this free-floating
     logion goes back to Jesus. Its imagery has a home in Jewish
     usage, and Jesus himself was a Jew. Mountain-moving and
     tree-uprooting images appear in a variety of forms and
     contexts, although they are not attached specifically to the
     notion of faith. Such a connection may have been a Christian,
     even a dominical, development. (So too might be the mustard
     seed reference, otherwise a common image in Jewish circles
     for a very small quantity). In Jewish circles, the correlative
     mountain- and tree-uprooting images were found in legal,
     legendary, thaumaturgic and eschatological contexts, and
     employed in connection with the Rabbi, the king, the hero,
     the thaumaturge or the Messianic follower. In a legal
     context, the term 'uprooter of mountains' was found to have
     a *technical* meaning. Applied to the king (and to Herod in
     particular), it could be employed as a *double entendre,*
     bolstering a legal argument for the exceptional nature of
     Herod's pulling down of the Temple. In the three latter
     contexts, it was found to have a *literal* application, and in
     its *thaumaturgic* and particularly its *eschatological* Sitz im
     Leben, we suggest, is to be found its closest parallel with
     the saying in its Christian setting.

5.   In the course of its transmission a certain "embarrassment"
     over the thaumaturgic emphasis of the original saying may be
     discerned. Paul, for example, felt the need to qualify the
     saying by insisting that such wonder-working faith was of no
     value to the disciple if it was not governed by ἀγάπη
     (1 Cor.13.2). Similarly, in Mk.9.29; 11.24 ff. and in
     Mt.17.21, the Christian practice of prayer, (fasting) and
     forgiveness has been brought into connection with the saying
     to moderate its effect. In the R. Eliezer story a similar
     opposition to the unfettered display of thaumaturgic power
     was expressed, and an appeal to the ongoing, regular,
     democratic process of Rabbinic tradition and practice was
     made. In Thomas, the power to move mountains appears also
     to have been interpreted in a non-eschatological light. Here
     the power will be granted, it seems, when the Gnostic has
     achieved the hoped-for inner state (in this one house?) of
     archetypal unity /78/.

In Mark, however, the eschatological import of the saying may
have been preserved. We have seen that he has himself attached
the saying to its fig-tree and Temple setting. As a result of
his redaction, the kernel of the saying, viz, *the removal of
the mountain,* stands as a centre-piece framed by the
repetitious *faith* motif /79/. The more primitive μετάβα ἔνθεν
ἐκεῖ has been expanded to include not only the mountain's
removal to another site, but *its complete disappearance* (εἰς
τὴν θάλασσαν). The promise that this will be the case is
given in the more general 'whoever' form, and the solemn,
introductory ἀμὴν λέγω ὑμῖν formula, introducing an important
saying, is retained.

The function of this redaction is therefore to announce, we
believe, that 'the moving of mountains' expected in the last
days was now taking place. Indeed, about to be removed was
the mountain *par excellence,* the Temple Mount. The Temple,
known to the Jewish people as 'the mountain of the house' or
'this mountain' was not to be elevated, as expected, but cast
down! As R.E. Dowda states: "The temple is the mountainous
obstacle which is to vanish before the faith of the gospel
movement. The temple system, with its corrupt clericalism
and vested interests, is to be removed in the eschatological
era, which is now being experienced." /80/.

This, then, is the import of the mountain-moving saying in
its Markan function and redaction. It is a bold and indeed
startling claim /81/, but one that Mark puts on the lips of
Jesus even more explicitly before he leaves the Temple for
the last time (13.2). It is a fitting supplement, therefore,
to the equally surprising, if not shocking, story of Jesus'
cursing of the fig-tree, to whose meaning it thereby gives
the clue. The Temple was to be removed in the lifetime of
the Markan community and Mark prepares his readers for it.
Its demise is suggested proleptically in the rending of the
veil following Jesus' death (15.38). "Whoever says to *this
mountain,* Be uprooted and cast into the sea ... it shall be
(to him)."

NOTES

/1/   See J. Lightfoot, *Horae*, II, p.283; *Str-B*, I, p.759.
/2/   The Greek passages from the gospels are taken from Aland,
Synopsis; Paul (1 Cor.13.2) from Nestle-Kilpatrick, and the
Thomas logia from *The Gospel according to Thomas* (ed. A.
Guillaumont et al.).
/3/   Logion 48, however, does introduce the saying with a
conditional clause, the curious "If two make peace (εἰρήνη) with
each other in this one house ..." (cf. Mt.18.19; 12.25 = Mk.3.25).
For a discussion of this saying, see W. Schrage, *Das Verhältnis
des Thomas-Evangeliums zur synoptischen Tradition*, pp.116-18.
/4/   A number of important witnesses read εἰ ἔχετε κτλ. here
(*vide* synopsis). Most commentators, however, regard this as an
assimilation to Lk.17.6, although it should be noted that the
harmonizers have thereby produced a very long and unwieldy
conditional sentence with what amounts to four protases combined
with an abrupt change of person in midstream! It is just
conceivable that εἰ is original but is not conditional. We may
have here an example of *aposiopesis* (see Robertson, *Grammar*, p.1203)
expressing in this case either *a strong wish or unfulfilled desire*
("If only you had faith!" cf. Lk.19.42 and J.H. Moulton, *A Grammar
of New Testament Greek*, Vol.III, ed. N. Turner, p.91; henceforth
M-T) or even *an emphatic denial* ("You have no faith at all!" cf.
Mk.8.12 and Moule, *Idiom Book*, p.179; *M-H*, pp.468-9; *M-T*, pp.319,
333). Εἰ may also introduce indirect or even direct questions
(see Moule, *Idiom Book*, pp.151, 154; *M-T*, p.333, and Wohlenberg,
Markus, pp.303-4).
/5/   "In God", however, may be a scribal gloss. *Vide supra*, p.57.
/6/   See C.-H. Hunzinger, *ThDNT*, 7, p.758.
/7/   Logion 48 has merely "the mountain", while Logion 106 has
the vocative. A variant reading of Lk.17.6 also omits ταύτῃ after
συκαμίνῳ (p^{75} ℵ D pc sy^c).
/8/   "To him", however, may perhaps be a gloss. *Vide supra*, p.68,
n.117.
/9/   See Goulder, *Midrash*, pp.147-8.
/10/   *Pace* Butler, *Originality*, pp.142-3, and Goulder, *Midrash*,
pp.36-38, 395, who hold that Matthew in 17.20 has simply borrowed
forward (21.21) from his own material, with the ὡς κόκκον σινάπεως
a reminiscence of the Mustard Seed parable (cf. Mk.4.31 and
parallels).
/11/   *Vide supra*, p.57.
/12/   Cf. 3.29,35; 4.25; 8.35,38; 9.37,40,41,42; 10.11,15,43,44.
Note that the Thomas logia have both second person and third
person plural forms.

/13/ "The solemn preface which prepares for a specially important
saying (iii.28, viii.12, ix.1,41, x.15,29)." - Swete, *Mark,* p.259.
Cf. also Lagrange, *Marc,* p.299, and Lohmeyer, *Matthäus,* pp.108-9.
/14/ *Supra,* pp.77, 79.
/15/ Loisy thinks, for example, that the rhythm of the verse
itself demands that ὡς κόκκον σινάπεως be original (*Évangiles
Synoptiques,* II, p.288, fn.2). Cf. also Schmid, *Matthäus und
Lukas,* p.304, fn.2.
        Note: the description "as a grain of mustard seed" was used
by the Rabbis to refer to a very small quantity. See J. Lightfoot,
Horae, II, Mt.13.32 ad loc. Most commentators, therefore, give the
phrase a 'quantitative' interpretation. For a contrasting
'qualitative' view, viz, faith like the mustard seed's prodigious
growth demonstrates, see E. Omar Pearson, "Matthew xvii.20.",
ET, 25 (1913-14), p.378; D.W. Simon, "Faith as a grain of mustard
seed", *Exp,* 9 (1879), pp.307-16; A. Peloni, "Faith as a grain of
mustard seed", *Exp* (2nd Series), 8 (1884), pp.207-15.
/16/ This assumption is challenged, of course, by the opponents
of Q. Cf. e.g. Goulder, *Midrash,* chap.21; Butler, *Originality,*
pp.28-9. Butler thinks that Lk.17.6 is a conflation of both
Matthean passages with the συκάμινος replacing the 'mountain'
because Luke either shrank from the idea of removing something as
big as a mountain (?) or because he had not placed the story in
the vicinity of a mountain (?). Had he placed it in the vicinity
of a tree?
/17/ See, for example, B. Weiss, *Marcusevangelium,* p.376, fn.1;
Matthäusevangelium, pp.457-8; Holtzmann, *HC,* I, p.203; Loisy,
Évangiles Synoptiques, II, pp.288-9; A.Harnack, *The Sayings of
Jesus,* pp.91, 145, 225; Taylor, *Mark,* pp.466-7.
/18/ Schmid, *Matthäus und Lukas,* p.304; B.H. Streeter, *The Four
Gospels,* pp.284-5; Kilpatrick, *Origins,* pp.87-8.
/19/ See T.W. Manson, *The Sayings of Jesus,* pp.140-1; Lagrange,
Matthieu, p.405; Wendling, *Entstehung,* pp.148-9; Lohmeyer, *Markus,*
p.239; *Matthäus,* pp.271-4; Branscomb, *Mark,* pp.206-7.
/20/ I am grateful to Dr. Ernst Bammel for this observation.
/21/ *Infra,* pp.113 ff.
/22/ For a discussion of this issue, see Schrage, *Verhältnis,*
pp.1-27. Schrage himself thinks Thomas is dependent upon the
Synoptic gospels, but through the medium of the Coptic translations
of the latter.
/23/ See Hunzinger, *ThDNT,* 7, p.758.
/24/ See Zahn, *Introduction,* III, p.162.
/25/ *Infra,* p.114.
/26/ See W. Grundmann, *Das Evangelium nach Lukas,* p.332; M.-J.
Lagrange, *Évangile selon Saint Luc,* pp.453-4.

/27/   So Lagrange, *ibid.*; Loisy, *Évangiles Synoptiques*, II, p.289.
/28/   *Infra*, n.39.
/29/   For the synopsis of these passages, see Aland, *Synopsis*,
pp.240-2. For a full analysis of the pericope, see Schmid,
Matthäus und Lukas, pp.123-5; *B-B-H*, pp.187-92.
/30/   *B-B-H*, p.189. See also Chapman, *Matthew, Mark and Luke*,
p.137.
/31/   Opinions are divided over the question of the inclusion of
the fasting datum within the text of Mark 9.29. All textual
witnesses but ℵ* B k geo[pt] and Clement have either ἐν νηστείᾳ καὶ
προσευχῇ or ἐν προσευχῇ καὶ νηστείᾳ. See Merx, *Markus und Lukas*,
pp.103-4, who prefers the longer version. Cf. also 1 Cor.7.5 (v.l).
/32/   Cf. 17.18 καὶ ἐθεραπεύθη ... ἀπὸ τῆς ὥρας ἐκείνης (*vide supra*,
p.85, n.15 and p.87, n.33); 17.19 τότε προσελθόντες (*supra*, p.89,
n.52 and p.85, n.15); 17.20 διὰ τὴν ὀλιγοπιστίαν ὑμῶν (*supra*,
pp.81-2) and the use of direct speech (*supra*, p.78) with the
question modelled by catchword connection on what precedes (cf.
17.16 and *supra*, p.78). See also Goulder, *Midrash*, p.395.
/33/   It is noteworthy, in respect of the disciples' question, that
instead of διὰ τί ἡμεῖς οὐκ ἠδυνήθημεν θεραπεῦσαι αὐτόν which
would be strictly modelled on 17.16, Matthew has ἐκβαλεῖν αὐτό
(17.19). A comparison with Mk.9.18, but more especially with
Lk.9.40, indicates that these words may reflect the more primitive
form of the pericope here. While Matthew has altered the words in
17.18, his reversion to this form in 17.19 may be a further tiny
pointer to the pre-Matthean connection of this epilogue with the
Puer Lunaticus story. The catchword connection is completed by
Matthew, however, in his own interpretative addendum καὶ οὐδὲν
ἀδυνατήσει ὑμῖν (17.20).
/34/   *Midrash*, p.395.
/35/   See Lagrange, *Matthieu*, p.405.
/36/   *Infra*, pp.258-9.
/37/   Reference to the 'house' (οἶκος/οἰκία) occurs frequently
elsewhere in Mark's gospel; cf. 2.1,(15); 3.20; 7.17,24; 9.33;
10.10. Cf. also 1.29; 2.11; 5.38; 6.4,10; 7.30; 8.3,26; 10.29,30;
(11.17);(12.40); 13.15,34,35; 14.3,14.
/38/   See, for example, J.C. O'Neill's article, "The Synoptic
Problem", *NTS*, 21 (1974-5), pp.273-85, esp. p.281. For a contrary
view, see Schmid, *Matthäus und Lukas*, pp.123-5; *B-B-H*, pp.187-92.
/39/   Adalbert Merx has argued on the basis of the Old Syriac (sy[s])
that the original Matthean text gave ἀπιστία as the reading in 17.20,
rather than ὀλιγοπιστία, and that the tenses originally read εἴχετε
... εἴπατε ... μετεβαίνεν viz, "Because of your lack of faith ... if
you had had faith (which you didn't) ... you would/could have said
(which you didn't) ... and it would have removed." A similar form

lies behind Lk.17.6 and has even better attestation. The text of
the mountain-moving saying in its Mt.17 context, therefore, might
originally have entailed an even harsher rebuke of the disciples,
a state of affairs that has subsequently been softened in the
textual tradition by a change in the tenses and the substitution
of ὀλιγοπιστία for ἀπιστία. It is certainly hard to see why an
original ὀλιγοπιστία might have been changed to the harsher ἀπιστία
in the Matthean text and the term 'little faith', indeed, does
appear to create a contradiction with what follows. If faith even
as small as a grain of mustard seed could move a mountain, the
disciples' 'little faith' must have been infinitesimal!

The presence of the 'little faith' motif elsewhere in Matthew,
however, (supra, pp.81-2) does militate against Merx's view that
the Matthean text originally read ἀπιστία rather than ὀλιγοπιστία.
One might have expected Matthew to have written ὀλιγοπιστία, despite
its disharmony with what follows. How then are we to account for
the formidable array of witnesses that preserve the harsher
reading? Some commentators suggest that the occurrence of ἄπιστος
earlier in 17.17 has influenced the change away from this less
familiar expression, but this is weak. Could it be that these
witnesses preserve a tradition regarding the state of the text of
this pericope prior to Matthew's redaction of it? Has Matthew
himself altered an original ἀπιστία to his favourite ὀλιγοπιστία,
a word and a motif that he has elsewhere introduced into his
Markan Vorlage (cf. 8.26; 14.28-33; 16.8 and parallels; cf. also
6.30 = Lk.12.28)? If this were so, then he would be seen once
again characteristically softening a harsher treatment of the
disciples handed down by the tradition. See Merx, Das Evangelium
Matthaeus, pp.255-60; Markus und Lukas, pp.340-1; Lagrange,
Matthieu, pp.339-40; McNeile, Matthew, pp.255-6; Lohmeyer,Matthäus,
p.271.

/40/ See, for example, Chapman, Matthew, Mark and Luke, p.136.
/41/ One should here compare Loisy's view that a series of such
offence, faith, prayer and forgiveness logia were all connected in
Q and that Mark's fig-tree sequel, therefore, was not constructed
in random fashion from previously unconnected logia (Évangiles
Synoptiques, II, pp.289-91, and supra, pp.13,15-16). Curiously,
too, the Thomas logion 48 gives the mountain-moving saying in
connection with a saying which appears to parallel one standing in
Matthew in this same context (18.19)!
/42/ If the offence saying (Mk.9.42 = Mt.18.6-7 = Lk.17.1-2) did
occur in the pre-Synoptic tradition in close proximity to the
mountain-moving saying and the Puer Lunaticus pericope, is it
possible that Mark has taken his reference to the 'sea' from here?
In this logion, a large millstone is cast into the sea (βέβληται
εἰς τὴν θάλασσαν). Mark, it appears, has expanded the kernel of

the primitive mountain-moving saying by such a reference ἄρθητι
καὶ βλήθητι εἰς τὴν θάλασσαν, Mk.11.23; contr. μετάβα ἔνθεν ἐκεῖ
Mt.17.20), a procedure that is unusual for him. Hyperbole, as
Goulder points out, (*Midrash*, p.397) is rare in the second
evangelist. If this is so, it might reflect once again his
desire to give prominence to the kernel of the saying, viz, the
removal of "this mountain" *and its permanent disposal* (cf.
Ez.27.27; 28.8).

/43/ See J. Weiss, *Ält. Evang.*, pp.249-50; W. Bussmann, *Synoptische
Studien*, I, *Zur Geschichtsquelle* (1925), pp.81-3, cited *B-B-H*,
p.190, fn.1.

/44/ The resemblances between Mk.9.23,24, indeed, and Mt.17.20 =
Lk.17.5,6 have been noted by some commentators; cf. e.g. Swete,
Mark, p.260; Loisy, *Évangiles Synoptiques*, II, p.289.

/45/ It is often pointed out that in Mark the crowd (ὄχλος) plays
a prominent role; cf. 2.4,13; 3.9,20,32; 4.1,36; 5.21,24,27,30,31;
6.34,45; 7.14,17,33; 8.1,2,6,34; 9.14,15,17; 10.1,46; 11.18,32;
12.12,37,41; 14.43; 15.8,11,15 (cf. also 1.22,27,32,45; 2.12; 5.20;
11.32; 14.2). T.J. Weeden (*Mark*, pp.22-3) is of the opinion
(despite 5.17; 6.2 ff.; 14.43 and 15.11) that the role of the crowd
is to dramatize, by contrast with the religious leaders, the
positive response to Jesus. Cf. also Trocmé, *Formation*, pp.146-7.

/46/ Cf. e.g. Wendling, *Entstehung*, p.147.

/47/ So, for example, Allen, Wood, Rawlinson, Montefiore, Taylor,
Nineham.

/48/ So, for example, Gould, Swete, Plummer (*Matthew*, ad loc.),
Lagrange, Bartlet, Hauck, Grundmann, Turner, Cranfield. R.M. Grant,
who gives a detailed review of the logion's interpretation by the
Church Fathers, thinks, however, that the original meaning is to
be sought through Zechariah and apocalyptic (cf. Zech.14.4 and
JBL, 67 (1948), pp.301-2).

/49/ Cf. Edersheim, *Life and Times*, II, p.376 and fn.1, and *supra*,
p.95 and n.1.   1 Cor.13.2 may also suggest that the saying had a
proverbial or figurative currency, especially if Paul were not
alluding to the saying in the Synoptic tradition (cf. Plummer,
Mark, p.140).

/50/ For the text of all Rabbinic passages, we have used the
following (unless otherwise stated). For the *Babylonian Talmud*,
the editions published by the Soncino Press, London (Hebrew-English
edn. in selected tractates, 1960-74; English transl. edn.
throughout, 1935-52; ed. I. Epstein) or otherwise the Hebrew-
German edn. by L. Goldschmidt (Berlin, 1897-1935). For the *Mishnah*,
the English transl. edn. of H. Danby (Oxford, 1933). For the
Palestinian Talmud, the French edition of M. Schwab (Paris, 1871-
90). For *Midrash Rabbah*, again the Soncino Press edition (London,

1939; ed. H. Freedman, M. Simon). For *abbreviations* of the
Talmud tractates, those given in the Index volume of the Soncino
Press English edition (J. Slotki, 1952) and otherwise as in
J. Bowker's *The Targums and Rabbinic Literature*. For *general
background* we have used *Encyclopaedia Judaica* (Jerusalem, 1971;
ed. C. Roth, G. Wigoder; henceforth *EJud*); *Encyclopedia of the
Jewish Religion* (London, 1967; ed. R.J.Z.'Werblowsky, G. Wigoder;
henceforth *EJR*); *Encyclopedia Talmudica* (Jerusalem, 1969; ed.
M. Berlin; henceforth *ETal*); A.J. Kolatch, *Who's Who in the Talmud*.
/51/ Ulla Ben Ishmael. A Palestinian Amora of the last half of the
third and beginning of the fourth century. An outstanding scholar,
he was often invited to come to Babylonia to lecture on matters of
halakah.
/52/ Simon Ben Lakish. One of the outstanding Palestinian Amoraim
of his generation. He was born about 200 CE and spent most of his
years in Sepphoris. Legends abound with regard to his enormous
physical strength as well as to his scholarship and integrity. He
died in 275 CE.
/53/ Either Rabina I, a Babylonian Amora of the fourth and fifth
centuries, who died in 420 CE, or Rabina II (Ben Huna), his nephew,
the last principal of the Sura academy, who died in 500 CE. Both
men played an important role in the editing of the Talmud after
Ashi.
/54/ An eminent Tanna of the second century, Meir was one of the
seven disciples of Akiba who fled to Babylonia after the latter's
martyrdom during the Hadrianic persecutions. He was one of the
chief authorities involved in the editing of the Mishnah.
/55/ The third/fourth century Babylonian Amora, Raba b.Joseph b.Hama,
a pupil of Rabbah b. Nahmani and R. Joseph b.Hiya (*infra*, ns.60,61).
/56/ Simon Ben Azzai. A lifelong bachelor scholar who was a
younger companion and disciple of Akiba, as well as a pupil of
Joshua ben Hananiah.
/57/ See Lightfoot, *Horae*, II, p.283.
/58/ Johanan Ben (Bar) Nappaha. A Palestinian Amora, born in
Sepphoris at the end of the second century. Simon ben Lakish was
his brother-in-law and friend. His academy in Tiberias was a
renowned seat of learning and attracted scholars from Babylonia.
He died in 279 CE.
/59/ Gamaliel II, the son of Simon II, grandson of Gamaliel I
and brother-in-law of Eliezer ben Hyrcanus (*infra*, pp.113-14), who
took over from Johanan ben Zakkai in 90 CE the leadership of the
Sanhedrin. He continued Johanan's work at Jabneh despite
differences with his colleagues. He died in 110 CE.
/60/ Joseph Bar Hiya. A Babylonian Amora (270-333) with a great
memory for the Mishnayot and Beraitot. Known as "Sinai" or

"Possessor of Storehouses" consequently. He was a contender for
the post of principal of the academy at Pumbeditha which was
offered to Rabbah, however. Joseph succeeded the latter as
principal in 330.
/61/ Rabbah Bar Nahmani. One of the important Babylonian Amoraim
(c.270-330) who became principal of the academy of Pumbeditha (309).
Sharp and vitriolic, he was not popular but was admired for his
great scholarship.
/62/ Baba Ben Buta was one of the disciples of Shammai, and was
blinded by Herod when the latter persecuted the sages. Later, it is
said, Herod repented and asked his forgiveness.
/63/ Samuel Bar Abba (Mar Samuel), one of the most celebrated of
all Babylonian Amoraim. He was born about 180 CE and studied in
Palestine under Judah the Prince, whom he later cured of illness.
After the death of Abba Areka (Rab), his friend and intellectual
opponent, he was recognized as the leading authority in Babylonia.
He died in 257 CE.
/64/ Assi II. A number of Amoraim are known by this name, but
probably Assi II is here meant. A Palestinian Amora born in
Babylonia, he attended the academy of Samuel but later himself headed
the academy in Tiberias (270).
/65/ Samuel Ben (Bar) Nahman (Nahmani). A Palestinian Amora
(c.220-300) and famous haggadist, who was responsible for the dirge
dealing with the destruction of the Temple in Lamentations Rabbah.
/66/ Lagrange, *Marc*, p.300.
/67/ In addition to the texts cited on p.124, n.50, one should
also here compare P. Fiebig, *Rabbinische Wundergeschichten des
neutestamentlichen Zeitalters*, p.10, no.9 (KlT, 78); *Str-B*, I,
p.127 (d.) Mt.3.17 ad loc., p.759; IV.1 Excursus "Der Synagogenbann"
(II.A.6), pp.313-4 (α).
/68/ See *EJud*, 6, pp.619-23; Kolatch, *Who's Who*, pp.190-2.
/69/ It is said that Elijah, meeting one of the Rabbis, reported
that God himself, on hearing this declaration, had laughingly
exclaimed, "My sons have defeated me, my sons have defeated me."
/70/ For examples, see *Str-B*, II, p.234. See also Hunzinger,*ThDNT*,
7, p.758, fn.4; *supra*, pp.102-4.
/71/ *Str-B, ibid.*
/72/ See Hunzinger, *ThDNT,* 7, p.758, fn.5.
/73/ See *EJud*, 4, pp.228-39.
/74/ Cf. e.g. 2 Baruch 29.5 Irenaeus, Adv.Haer.V.33.3 (Papias Apoc.)
Enoch 10.19 Visio Pauli 22 B.Ket.111a-112b Sifre. Deut.317; etc.
See L. Ginzberg, *The Legends of the Jews*, I, p.112; V, pp.141-2,
fn.30.
/75/ Derrett, *HeythJ*, 14 (1973), p.253.
/76/ So, for example, Lohmeyer, *Matthäus* pp.271-4, 302-4. For
a critique, however, of Lohmeyer's position, see Grundmann, *Matthäus*

p.452, fn.5.

/77/ Cf. Harnack, *Sayings*, p.145; Loisy, *Évangiles Synoptiques*, II, pp.288-9

/78/ See Schrage, *Verhältnis*, pp.117-18.

/79/ J.R. Donahue, *Are You the Christ?*, pp.77-84, argues convincingly that in many places throughout Mark, the repetition of words, phrases and sentences indicate a compositional technique of the redactor. He frames inserted material by parallel repeated statements. Moreover, the framing repetitious words, phrases or verses draw attention to the inserted material and this inserted material usually contains motifs that are important to the major themes of Mark's gospel. He notes, too, that one or other of the evangelists usually alters the tautology in some way. The list of such insertions, given by Donahue in an appendix, is impressive.

/80/ *Cleansing*, p.250.

/81/ It is possible that Mark, in placing the mountain-moving saying here in chapter 11, and intending it to be understood as a reference to the destruction of the Temple, was not acting arbitrarily but had some substance in tradition for doing so. It is curious in the first place that John gives a similar replacement of the Temple logion *in the same context* as Mark here (Jn.2.19), while Mark has inserted a parallel form of this same logion elsewhere at an otherwise crucial place in his gospel, viz, the Trial scene (14.58, cf. Donahue, *op.cit.*, chap.III). In the second place, a number of other logia in Christian tradition do predicate of Jesus a negative attitude to the Temple; cf. e.g. Acts 6.14 Gospel of Thomas, logion 71; cf. also "I am come to do away with sacrifices, and if ye cease not from sacrificing, the wrath of God will not cease from you" (Gospel of the Ebionites; see E. Hennecke, *New Testament Apocrypha*, Vol.I, transl. R.McL. Wilson, ed. W. Schneemelcher, p.158).

Chapter V

THE OLD TESTAMENT BACKGROUND

Introduction

Thus far we have approached the problems of the fig-tree pericope from the point of view of its function within the Markan redactional scheme. We have sought to unravel the different redactional levels discernible within the pericope and to throw light on the hermeneutical development to which it has been subject. We shall be returning to the question of Mark's redactional purpose and procedure in chapters VII and VIII but having stated what we think the second evangelist intended his story to convey within its present context, we have now to consider the second half of the question that was raised at the end of chapter I. How was the Markan story likely to have been understood by the first-century reader for whom it was intended? Would he or she have necessarily interpreted the story in the eschatological and symbolic terms that we have suggested? How can we be sure?

To read Mark's gospel through the eyes of a first-century reader is of necessity to adopt an analytical stance that proves itself difficult for the twentieth-century reader who is accustomed to think in quite different conceptual categories and who often applies to what he reads (sometimes unknowingly) a set of cultural and philosophical presuppositions that would not be shared by the former. The task of exegesis, then, is a formidable one, if we are to 'think our way' into the life situation of those whose Weltan-schauung is so different from our own.

It is as aids for this task, however, that background studies have so important a place. By acquainting ourselves with apposite and correlative material from the Old Testament, late Jewish and early Christian world, we are able in some measure to construct the conceptual 'grid' through which that world was viewed, and hence to place ourselves tentatively and empathetically within the frame of reference that might have been adopted by these readers of long ago.

In our last chapter, we were examining the mountain-moving logion that Mark has attached to the fig-tree story, and the meaning and significance that was to be drawn from it. We suggested that an appropriate Sitz im Leben for the saying was an eschatological one, and that Mark has heightened this original eschatological import

by making the 'mountain' of the logion allude specifically to the
Temple Mount. It is in this light, we believe, that the first-
century reader would have understood it. But how would the first-
century reader have understood the fig-tree story itself? To
suggest an answer to this, we must make a systematic investigation
of the place of the fig/fig-tree in ancient religious and literary
usage. We must look at its employment in imagery and symbolism.
We shall attempt to chart both the variety and the limits of the
associations that it and other associated motifs connected with
the story held for the reader of the ancient world.

Our investigation will cover three main areas with results
compared in each. Mark and his readers were steeped in the *Old
Testament* tradition. We shall look at the story in the light of
this background, therefore. Early Christian exegesis was also both
conceived within and found itself in conflict with the scriptural
interpretation and religious orientation of *late Judaism*, and so
we shall look at the place of the tree in general, the place of the
fig-tree in particular, the efficacy of a curse, and other
associated motifs in that tradition too. The traditions of the
Markan gospel were in the last analysis understood and transmitted
within the more immediate world of early Christianity. Hence, no
investigation would be complete without the examination of the
fig-tree and related materials elsewhere in the *New Testament* for
the light that this will shed on this enigmatic story.

All three areas complement each other. The observations we
make on material exhibiting parallels with motifs and features
discernible in our story will help us to build a hermeneutical
framework in terms of which this story may be viewed. The
similarities and contrasts noted will provide, we believe, checks
and balances to the emerging pattern of associations, of related
ideas and concepts, out of which our interpretative frame of
reference is to be constructed.

The Influence of the Old Testament

"The Old Testament Scriptures formed part of the daily
environment of the writers of the New Testament, as the
writings of both testaments form part of our own daily
environment in the Christian Church."

This statement was made by the late Professor C.H. Dodd in his
According to the Scriptures, an important book appearing in the

post-war period /1/. Although it is by now a fundamental tenet,
almost a truism of New Testament scholarship, it is only
relatively recently that it has been taken up as an operative
principle in gospel research /2/.

In the earlier part of this century, Martin Dibelius, one of
the foremost advocates of the form-critical approach to the study
of the New Testament documents, had stressed the role of the Old
Testament in the formation of the gospel tradition. The Old
Testament, he claimed, had furnished proof-texts for the proclama-
tion and defence of the kerygma. But it had functioned not only
to serve the christological and apologetic purposes of a preaching
conducted in an eschatological situation. Numerous texts, he
further suggested, had also acted as catalysts for the composition
of whole pericopes created and designed to illustrate them. This
more radical view remained relatively undeveloped, although in more
recent times, particularly in the post-war period, the influence
of Dibelius' pioneering work has made itself felt /3/.

In *According to the Scriptures*, Dodd expressed his satisfaction
at the revival of interest in the Old Testament among New Testament
scholars /4/. His own contribution to this developing trend was
to isolate a common group of 'testimonia' passages that were most
used by the early church in the pre-literary period. These key
passages, which he further differentiated as primary sources of
testimonies and as subordinate and supplementary sources /5/,
functioned as 'quarries' for the 'regulative ideas' of primitive
theology /6/. The proof-texts drawn from them were hence not
arbitrarily selected from the Old Testament in toto /7/ but served
instead to evoke the wider context, the associated ideas and motifs
contained in the interrelated passages from which they were drawn.
In examining them, Dodd hoped "to get an opening into the
intellectual workshop of the early Church, and to watch its mind
at work"/8/.

Dodd's approach was more conservative than Dibelius' had been,
for the former took care to issue a warning against "speculation
and fancy, where associations of ideas arising in the critic's own
mind have been treated as evidence for original connections."
What was needed was "verifiable evidence that *this* New Testament
writer did in fact refer his readers to *that* passage of the Old
Testament in connection with this or that particular theme of the
Gospel or of Christian theology" /9/.

However, since 1952, when Dodd's book was published, scholars
working in this field have generally wished to apply less rigid

criteria to the search for the identification of certain Old
Testament passages with New Testament traditional material. Concern
has embraced *allusions* as well as *direct quotations* in the
determining of Old Testament influence. Willingness to believe
that the Old Testament may lie behind a New Testament tradition
without being specifically quoted or that the link with the Old
Testament may lie behind layers of tradition was strengthened in
particular by the publication and study of the Habakkuk Commentary
of the Dead Sea Scrolls in which the *pesher* and *midrash* methods of
interpretation and exegesis of scripture were clearly exhibited.
The pesher mode of biblical exegesis, which was current at the time
of the formation of our gospels, involved delicate alterations and
modifications of the biblical text and shifts of application that
accorded with the convictions and apologetic concerns of the
first-century commentators. The midrashic technique involved
amplification of the text or the rendering of the commentary on
the text in the form of a narrative. Such studies in turn have
thrown light on the formation of New Testament tradition and
scholars such as Barnabas Lindars have shown that whole narratives
are simply historicizations of the Old Testament /10/.

     In this respect, Matthew's gospel is particularly illustrative
of the Old Testament's link with the New. Matthew's "formula
quotations" constitute a specific appeal to the Old Testament as
'testimonia' /11/. But a measure of his special material, moreover,
consists, it has been argued, of a midrashic amplification of his
Markan Vorlage and of the Old Testament /12/. And if Matthew can
be seen at work amplifying and sometimes creating narrative material
from the sources at his disposal and in keeping with his apologetic
concerns and theological purposes, then is it not possible that Mark,
too, or his sources, has drawn on the Old Testament in this way?
Should we not look at the Old Testament indeed for the possible
source, origin or influence for the fig-tree story in particular?

     This possibility has been but little explored and the
suggestions that have been made have been, for the most part,
cautious and contradictory. This is not surprising, for the question
involves numerous difficulties. It calls for a methodology capable
of establishing links that may be already buried within layers of
tradition, or which merely percolated in the author's mind and as
allusions may be too recondite for scholarly suggestions regarding
them to be any more than speculation. To talk of the "influence"
of the Old Testament upon our story is in itself vague, for this
can mean a number of things. It can mean:

   a)   that the Old Testament furnished the *essential elements*
out of which (by midrash) the story was forged by Mark or the
pre-Markan tradition /13/.

   b)   that the tradition has been merely attached to certain
Old Testament passages, and has subsequently suffered *modification*
as a result of this association. This is the view of J.W. Doeve,
for example /14/.

   c)   that the story was recounted by Mark with certain Old
Testament passages in mind. It is the Old Testament *allusion*, in
other words, which gives the story its significance. This is the
view of C.H. Bird, for example /15/.

   d)   that certain Old Testament passages may actually have been
in Jesus' mind as he approached the tree and that Mark's story is
a misunderstood record of Jesus' intention on that occasion. This
is the view of A. de Q. Robin, J.N. Birdsall and J. Duncan M.
Derrett /16/.

   There are pitfalls, then, to be encountered in any exploration
of this question of "influence". The New Testament critic who
embarks on the course of establishing links between Mark's story
and the territory of the Old Testament less familiar to him may
well be voyaging between the Scylla of fancy and the Charybdis
of speculation. While recognizing this fact we shall try, however,
to describe, summarize and draw conclusions about the place of the
fig-tree in the Old Testament, touching on, at the same time, the
imagery of the tree in general and other related motifs from our
story paralleled there. In turn, we shall discuss certain specific
Old Testament passages which are, we believe, particularly
suggestive. And, in the last place, we shall attempt to say how
this background may have contributed to the way the story was
understood. Our concern, therefore, will be less with the search
for a pre-Markan origin for the story and more with the nature of
the influence wielded by the Old Testament, in keeping with our
redaction-critical orientation.

The Fig-tree in the Old Testament   /17/

   The fig-tree, with its large leaves, many branches and widely
spread boughs, was and still is one of the principal and
characteristic shade- /18/ and fruit-trees of the Mediterranean
region and of Palestine in particular. Along with the vine, with

which it is frequently linked /19/, it is one of the most
important trees of the Old Testament. Its cultivation, evinced
since Neolithic times /20/, and attributed originally, scholars
say, to the Semitic people of Syria /21/, was held by the
ancients to have been one of the principal harbingers and
blessings of the civilized life.

Existing in various species and producing numerous strains
of figs, this unusually productive tree normally yields two crops
in the course of a year, and over an extended bearing season. The
early figs or בכורים appear in May and June, and the main harvest
of late figs, summer figs or תאנים appear from the middle of
August until well on in October /22/.

Figs were a highly popular means of sustenance, and the
first-ripe fig or early fig was enjoyed with special relish /23/.
Particularly cherished, too, was the pressed fig-cake or דבלה /24/,
a delicacy to be placed before commoner (1 Sm.30.12), king
(1 Chr.12.40) or God /25/. Highly nutritious, figs were very
often the staple fare of the poor and of slaves /26/. Fig and
fig-cake alike were also used in medicine /27/, and the Old
Testament records that the latter was prescribed by Isaiah for
the curing of King Hezekiah's boil (2 Kgs.20.7 = Is.38.21) /28/.
All three properties, culinary, curative and cultic, reappear in
the wealth of halakic, haggadic and apocryphal material that we
shall touch upon in the next chapter.

The words תאנה (fig/fig-tree), בכורה (first-ripe fig or
early fig), פגה (immature early fig) or דבלה (fig-cake) appear in
some thirty-six passages of the Old Testament /29/. The use, in
fourteen cases, is in *narrative passages:* Gn.3.7 Nm.13.23; 20.5
Dt.8.8 1 Sm.25.18; 30.12 1 Kgs.4.25 2 Kgs.18.31 = Is.36.16
2 Kgs.20.7 = Is.38.21 1 Chr.12.40 Neh.13.15 1 Mc.14.12. The
fig/fig-tree appears in *poetic passages* (Ps.105.33 Ct.2.13), in
parable (Jgs.9.10,11) and in *proverb* (Prv.27.18), but its major
use is reserved for the imagery of the prophetic books where it
occurs some eighteen times: Is.28.4; 34.4 Jer.5.17; 8.13; 24
passim; 29.17 Hos.2.12; 9.10 Jl.1.7,12; 2.22 Am.4.9 Mi.4.4;
7.1 Na.3.12 Hab.3.17 Hag.2.19 Zech.3.10.

The fig-tree is rich in figurative and symbolic associations.
When one considers the above-mentioned passages, one cannot avoid
the impression that they produce, despite their diversity, certain
common factors of value to the understanding of Mark's fig-tree
story. The following three general observations are, we believe,

particularly pertinent.

In the first place, it is to be noted that the fig is *an emblem of peace, prosperity and security* and is prominent when descriptions of *the Golden Ages of Israel's history,* past, present and future, are given. It appears in *the garden of Eden,* where it furnishes leaves with which Adam and Eve cover their nakedness (Gn.3.7) /30/. Later tradition, indeed, was to fasten upon this association. In Moslem tradition, for example, figs were regarded as one of the fruits of Paradise /31/, and in the Apocryphal and Pseudepigraphical literature and in certain Rabbinic and Christian circles the tree from which Adam ate was commonly believed to have been the fig /32/. It is given as one of the trees of Egypt that God smote before *the Exodus* (Ps.105.33). It is for figs, among other things, that the Israelites pine when *in the wilderness* (Nm.20.5), a period that later tradition was to transform into a Golden Age /33/. In turn it is described as one of the principal fruits of *the Promised Land* (Nm.13.23), a distinguished member of the seven species (Dt.8.8), and hence regarded as one of God's blessings upon his chosen people /34/. It figures also in the idiomatic expression, "every man under his vine and under his fig tree", a popular image that in its varying forms designates a state of blissful peace, prosperity and happiness (2 Kgs.18.31 = Is.36.16). The picture is employed particularly with regard to the 'golden' reigns of *Solomon* (1 Kgs.4.25) and *Simon Maccabaeus* (1 Mc.14.12), under whom the nation experienced an unprecedented era of prestige, self-esteem and well-being. In Solomon's reign, the Temple in particular was built, and in that of Simon Maccabaeus it was replenished with sacred vessels and given a new splendour. It is not surprising then that the fig-tree image is one prominent element in the vision of felicity associated with *the New Age.* In Mi.4.4, on that day when "the mountain of the house of the Lord shall be established as the highest of the mountains", every man shall sit "under his vine and under his fig tree", or, as in Zech.3.10, shall invite his neighbour "under his vine and under his fig tree".

It has already been remarked that the fig-tree or its fruit appears as imagery *predominantly in the prophetic books* and it is further to be observed that it does so very often in passages with an *eschatological* import. Common to these passages are the following twin motifs. On the one hand, the blossoming of the fig-tree and its giving of its fruit is a descriptive element in passages which depict Yahweh's visiting his people with *blessing.* This has been already apparent in such passages as Dt.8.7-8, 1 Kgs. 4.24-25 and 1 Mc.14.12, but the blessing motif is even more

strongly accentuated in Hag.2.19 and the fig-tree is linked
specifically with the blessings of the Messianic Age in Mi.4.4 and
Zech.3.10.

On the other hand, the withering of the fig-tree, the
destruction or the withholding of its fruits is a descriptive
element in passages where Yahweh's *judgement* upon his people or
their enemies is stressed /35/. The judgement motif is, if
anything, more pronounced in the prophetic books. While the
failure of the fig or the vine is given merely as a sign of
distress in, for example, Jl.1.7,12 and Hab.3.17, the ravaged or
withered fig-tree is a vivid emblem of God's active *punishment* of
his people in Jer.5.17; 8.13 Hos.2.12; 9.10,16 and Am.4.9 (cf.
also Ps.105.33 Is.28.4; 34.4 Na.3.12). Within the context of a
number of passages, indeed, the reason given for God's wrathful
visitation particularly concerns cultic aberration on the part of
Israel, her running after false gods, or her condemnation for *a
corrupt Temple cultus and sacrificial system* (e.g. Jer.5.17-18;
8.12-23 Hos.2.11-13; 9.10-17 Am.4.4-13). In Mi.7.1 ff., God's
search for an uncorrupt and righteous people is pictured in the
express terms of a vain search for first-ripe figs!

The link between the fig-tree and the End-time of God's
blessing or judgement may even have extended to a pun upon both
words. In Am.8.1-3, the prophet is shown a basket of summer fruit
or קיץ (which were dried figs) /36/, whereupon the message is
proclaimed:

> "The end [or קץ] has come upon my people Israel;
> ... The songs of the temple shall become wailings
> in that day." /37/ (RSV)

Not all of these fig passages, of course, are eschatological
in import. It is worth noting at this point, however, that later
Jewish exegesis did often interpret certain of these originally
non-eschatological passages in this way. The blossoming fig-tree
of Ct.2.13, for example, the herald of springtime, becomes, in
Shir.R.II.13, the harbinger of the Messianic Age /38/. The
fig-tree and the vine that yield their fruit in Jl.2.22 become
proof, according to B.Ket.112b, that in the time to come all the
wild trees of the Land of Israel will bear fruit. In Pes.R.XXXIII.13,
a passage describing the joys of the Messianic Age, we even find a
whole collection of Old Testament fig verses strung together:

"They [sc. Adam] sinned at a fig tree: 'As the first-ripe
in the fig tree (Hos.9:10)'; and they were smitten -
snatched like figs from the trees: 'Nor figs on the fig
tree (Jer.8:13)'; yet they will be comforted by bearing
fruit like fig trees: 'The fig tree putteth forth her
green figs (Song 2:13)'"/39/.

Enough has now been said about the fig-tree's use in image
and symbol to justify the conclusion that Mark's readers, steeped
in the Old Testament tradition, would readily have understood
Jesus' cursing of the barren fig-tree as at the very least a
judgement upon Israel. But we can proceed further. The fig-tree,
as we have seen, is used in simile (Is.34.4 Na.3.12) and in
proverb (Prv.27.18), but its employment in figurative language
extends even further. Not only is it associated with the twin
motifs of blessing and judgement upon Israel, but in a number of
passages it is used expressly as a symbol *for the nation itself*
or for representative individuals within the nation. In Jotham's
parable of Jgs.9.7-15, it represents, along with the other trees,
those called to rule over Israel. In Jer.24 and 29.17, good and
bad figs together represent respectively the exiles of Judah at
the time of Zedekiah and the remnant who remained in Jerusalem
(who had provoked the prophet's displeasure). In Mi.7.1, the
first-ripe fig represents the godly within the nation for whom
God searches in vain. In Is.28.4 and in Hos.9.16 (cf. 9.10) the
imagery is specifically linked with the Northern Kingdom of
Ephraim and in Hos.9.10, in parallelism with the fruit of the
vine, the nation of Israel in the wilderness period is likened to
first-ripe figs on the fig-tree. This specifically symbolic usage
remains in evidence also in the literature of late Judaism and we
shall refer to it in our next chapter.

The fig-tree = Israel equation has been challenged, however.
J.W. Wenham, taking exception to C.H. Bird's espousal of this
view /40/, stated in a brief article in 1954 that a review of the
fig passages of the Old Testament revealed insufficient evidence
to justify the claim that in the Jewish mind 'fig-tree' meant
either 'Judaism' or 'the people of Israel'. Quoting Na.3.12, he
asked: "As far as the Old Testament is concerned, is there much
better ground for saying that Israel is very often compared to a
fig-tree, than there is for saying the same of the fortresses of
Nineveh?"/41/

Wenham's survey of the Old Testament fig passages, however,
is sketchy and superficial. His view is monochromatic. It has

not taken into account the colour or tenor of the contexts within
which the fig passages appear, or the related motifs associated
with the fig in these contexts. The fig-tree it is true, is not
used to symbolize Israel *exclusively*, but then the symbols for
Israel in the Old Testament are fluid. While the vine is a
prominent one, other trees are also mentioned without detracting
from this symbolism. Where the vine itself is concerned we have
already noted the close connection existing between it and the
fig-tree /42/. The symbolism of the one passes easily over to the
other /43/ (cf. esp. Hos.9.10), a fact that can be seen, moreover,
in Luke's parable (13.6-9) where a barren fig-tree (= Jerusalem?)
is situated in a vineyard (= Israel). Mark himself follows his
fig-tree story with the parable of the vineyard (12.1-12), a story
with an almost identical message. Fruit from the vineyard (= Israel)
is denied to the One with a rightful claim to it, and so judgement
follows.

The fact that the fig-tree is not used exclusively to symbolize
Israel need not blind us to the overwhelming symbolic force of its
employment in the Markan context. The precise symbolism of a
certain image depends ultimately on the specific use to which it
is put within its context. Mark here intends the fig-tree to
symbolize not Israel alone (he leaves this general use perhaps for
the parable of the vineyard), but, we believe, Israel's Temple
and its cultus. The symbolic dimension of his story, moreover, is
dependent not solely on the fact that it was a fig-tree that was
involved, although this particular tree is highly appropriate as
we have tried to show. It depends also on a number of associated
motifs whose symbolic import can be traced throughout the Old
Testament, and it is to these that we shall now turn.

Other Related Motifs

It is worth remarking, in the first place, that the *tree* in
general is employed regularly as an image for the spiritual
dimension of man and *for the religious life of Israel in particular*
/44/. The righteous individual in whom God delights is often
depicted as a fruitful tree (e.g. Ps.1.3 Jer.17.7-8 Ps.92.12-14;
cf. also Ps.Sol.14.1-3 where the trees in Paradise are the
righteous) /45/. The wicked individual by contrast is depicted as
a barren tree judged by God (e.g. Jb.18.16 Ps.37.35-36 Jer.17.5-6).
But more often it is the nation itself that is pictured as a tree,
its growth/blossoming or devastation/withering symbolizing the
nation's fate: Nm.24.5-7 (aloes, cedars) Ps.80.8-16 (vine)

Ct.8.12 (vineyard) Is.1.30 (oak); 5.1-7 (vineyard); 27.2 ff.
(vineyard/vine) Jer.2.21 (vine); 11.16-17 (olive); 12.10 (vineyard)
Ez.17 passim (cedar, willow, vine); 19.10-14 (vine) Hos.9.16 cf.
9.10 (vine/fig-tree); 10.1 (vine); 14.5-9 (poplar, olive, vine).
Although the vine is prominent /46/, these passages indicate that
different trees, according to the context, can represent Israel /47/.
The basic idea is of Israel as God's 'planting' established in the
Promised Land by his act of redemption, and watered and nourished
(as long as she is faithful) by his grace /48/.

A second dominant motif is that *the fertility of the land
bears a direct relationship to the spiritual fruitfulness of the
people*. Where the nation or a righteous remnant within the nation
are faithful, the land, and particularly the trees, will flourish.
Where the people are faithless, God will strike the land with a
curse. In Gn.3.17-19, Adam's disobedience is punished by a curse
that realizes itself in the unproductiveness of the soil. Isaac's
fidelity to Yahweh, on the other hand, provokes a blessing
expressed in terms of his reaping from the land a hundredfold
(Gn.26.12). In Dt.28, the people of Israel are assured that if
they obey the voice of the Lord their God

"... all these blessings shall come upon you (2) ...
Blessed shall be ... the fruit of your ground (4) ...
But if you will not obey the voice of the Lord your
God (15) ... Cursed shall be ... the fruit of your ground
(18) ... The Lord will smite you ... with blasting (22)
... You shall plant a vineyard, and you shall not use the
fruit of it (30) ... A nation which you have not known
shall eat up the fruit of your ground (33) ... All your
trees and the fruit of your ground the locust shall
possess (42) ... The Lord will bring a nation against
you from afar (49) ... and (they) shall eat ... the
fruit of your ground (51) ... and they shall besiege you
in all your towns throughout all your land (52) ... And
you shall eat the offspring of your own body ... in the
siege and in the distress with which your enemies shall
distress you (53)." (RSV)

This scenario is reproduced in countless OT passages, and it
is of further consequence for our enquiry that time and time again
*God's curse is actualized through the blasting, smiting or ravaging
of the trees* and especially of the vine and the fig-tree /49/. The
smiting of the trees, furthermore, is frequently described in terms
of their *withering* /50/, a descriptive image applied in numerous

other verses also for the fate of the wicked /51/, the mighty /52/
or mortals in general /53/.

The fact that God's curse is directed so often against the
tree may involve more than its status as a prominent and productive
genus of nature. It is worth reflecting that the tree in the
ancient world was an object of veneration and was regarded as
sacred by many. To the ancients, it was highly symbolical /54/.
The tree represented or symbolized the deity. It was, or
represented, the source of life by being a symbol of fertility, its
fruit and leaves possessing curative properties, and even bestowing
immortality. Hence the special significance of the fig /55/.

According to N. Perrot, the tree was in Mesopotamia and the
Near East a symbol of divinity rather than a thing worshipped
solely in and for itself. It was everywhere the abode of a god,
or as the sacred tree it guarded the Temple and the gate of the
rising sun /56/. As a symbol of divinity in its own right, therefore, it could be placed beside the altar of almost any god.

There is abundant evidence, too, that in all parts of the
Semitic area trees were adored as divine /57/. As the home of
gods or demons they were venerated or feared /58/. Gifts were
brought to them. They were associated with oracles and divination
/59/. Stylized trees as phallic symbols or אשרים (cf. maypole)
were features of Semitic sanctuaries, and a sacred tree, from which
the ăšērâ derives as a surrogate, was often the genesis for these
sanctuaries /60/.

Veneration for the tree or for the divinity it represented
was a persistent threat to Yahwism, although Yahweh himself is
described on one occasion as he "that dwelt in the bush" (Dt.33.16)
/61/. The Deuteronomic code forbade the planting of any tree as an
ăšērâ beside the altar of Yahweh (Dt.16.21) but, despite this,
elements of tree worship came to suffuse Israel's religion /62/.
The battle between Yahweh-transcendence and Baal-immanence waged
to and fro, with the prophets as the fiery spokesmen for the
former. Despite their fulminations, however, the Israelite laity
continued at times to worship "on every high hill and under every
green tree", the twin places of idolatry in the Old Testament /63/.

God's smiting of the trees, therefore, may not only embrace
the judgement dimension that we have explored so far. Involved also
may be the idea of *a superior exhibition of power*, a blow struck
simultaneously against the divinity residing in or associated with

the tree and against a false worship that had abandoned its true
God. The exhibition of power is certainly a feature of Mark's
story, and, viewed in this light, Jesus' cursing of the fig-tree
in the context of the Cleansing of the Temple would seem to take on
an added dimension /64/.

If Israel was warned against regarding the tree as sacred and
from worshipping on the hills or mountains, then we have also seen
that the tree, and especially the vine or fig, could be regarded as
the nation herself, which was sacred to Yahweh. Linked with this
idea of *'Israel'* as *God's 'tree'* or of *God's 'planting'*, and hence
sacred to himself, is the correlative notion of *the Temple* as the
mountain of mountains, *the high place par excellence,* Mount Zion,
the only legitimate sanctuary. These two motifs crop up time and
time again.

Israel, God's tree, will be planted on the mountain (cf. Ex.
15.17 Ps.78.54) /65/. There she shall be made to flourish (cf.
Is.27.6), her prosperity linked to that of the Temple, to which
the exiled of the nation will come as worshippers in the End-time
(Is.27.13). All other sanctuaries, high places or mountains shall
be brought low in that day /66/ but "the mountain of the house of
the Lord shall be established as the highest of the mountains and
shall be raised up above the hills; and peoples shall flow to it
(Mi.4.1 = Is.2.2, RSV)"/67/.

In Ezekiel 17, the imagery is even more colourful. Israel
is at first a cedar twig transported to a land of trade by an
eagle (Babylon) where it sprouts and becomes a spreading vine.
From the bed where it was planted, it is in turn transplanted
to other soil by a second eagle (Egypt) "that it might bring
forth branches, and bear fruit, and become a noble vine (8)." But
the prophet declares: "Thus says the Lord God: Will it thrive?
Will he not pull up its roots and cut off its branches, so that
all its fresh sprouting leaves *wither* (ξηραίνω)? It will not take
a strong arm or many people to pull it *from its roots* (ἐκ ῥιζῶν
αὐτῆς v.9; cf. Mk.11.20)." Hence God himself will take a sprig
from the cedar and "plant it upon *a high and lofty mountain;* on
the mountain height of Israel will I plant it, that it may bring
forth boughs and bear fruit, and become a noble cedar; and under it
will dwell all kinds of beasts; in the shade of its branches birds
of every sort will nest (cf. Mk.4.32 and parallels). And all the
trees of the field will know that I the Lord bring low the high
tree, and make high the low tree, dry up (ξηραίνω) the green tree,
and make the dry tree flourish. I the Lord have spoken, and I will

do it (17.22-24, RSV; cf. also 19.10-14; 36.8 ff., 36)."

The final point that we should consider is that *the fertility
of the land and of the trees, as also with the spiritual
fruitfulness of God's sacred plant Israel,* was *linked* habitually
in the Jewish mind with the maintenance and well-being of *the
Temple and its cultus* /68/. We have seen already that every man
had sat "under his vine and under his fig-tree" in the reigns of
men like Solomon and Simon Maccabaeus who had done so much for the
Temple. In Jl.1, devastation for the vine and the fig in turn
meant that "the cereal offering and the drink offering are cut
off from the house of the Lord (7,9,12,13)." "Since the day that
the foundation of the Lord's temple was laid", declares Haggai,
"consider: Is the seed yet in the barn? Do the vine, the fig
tree, the pomegranate, and the olive tree still yield nothing?
From this day on I will bless you (2.18-19)." Cultic aberration,
conversely, as we have previously remarked, is often described in
terms of God's judgement against the land and the trees.

In the End-time when the Temple is again elevated, every man
will once more "sit under his vine and under his fig tree (Mi.4.1,4)"
and in that day the fig-tree and vine will give their full yield
(Jl.2.22). In the Messianic Age, indeed, the Temple will be a
source of prodigious fruitfulness, water will flow from it /69/
and the earth will be exceedingly abundant /70/. These
interrelated motifs of the Temple, the prodigiously fruitful
tree, and the flow of life-giving water from the sanctuary in the
End-time all come together in Ezekiel 47 (cf. esp. v.12), a passage
that has had its influence on the New Testament (and perhaps even
on Mark's story) and which will be discussed presently.

Thus far, to sum up, then, we have examined the particular
imagery and symbolism of the fig-tree in the Old Testament. Our
aim has been to construct a nexus of associations within the
framework of which we believe Mark and his readers would have
understood the story. In asking after these associations we have
emphasized the need to take into consideration the more general
but related motifs of the sacred or symbolic tree, the representa-
tion of Israel as God's sacred 'planting', the twin ideas of
blessing and curse upon Israel being expressed or actualized in
terms of the land (and particularly the trees) offering or
withholding their fruit, the withering motif, the link between
the Temple and the notion of fruitfulness and so on. All these
impinge upon Mark's story and contribute to our understanding of
it, and all persist or are developed in later Judaism, as we shall

see in chapter VI.

Certain Primary Old Testament Passages Considered

In the course of this chapter, however, it remains for us to consider whether specific Old Testament passages may have been in Mark's mind as he recounted this story or which may have had a formative influence at some stage upon it. The possibility that this was so was raised earlier, and we should now return to the question. Of the passages to which we have already referred, five, we believe, are particularly suggestive. These are *Jer.8.13, Is.28.3-4, Hos.9.10,16, Mi.7.1* and *Jl.1.7,12*. Certain other supplementary passages such as Ez.47, Ct.2.13 and various echoes within the language of the Psalms will also be discussed, but the five we have listed are of primary significance and we shall take them one by one.

Jer.8.13

> "When I would gather them, says the Lord, there are no
> grapes on the vine, nor figs (σῦκα, LXX; תאנים MT) on
> the fig tree (pl. ἐν ταῖς συκαῖς; sing. בתאנה); even
> the leaves are withered (τὰ φύλλα κατερρύηκεν; והעלה נבל)."/71/

This lament for Judah and Jerusalem is given within the immediate context of Jeremiah's oracles uttered in the Temple (chaps.7-10). In the wider context of chapters one and following, a series of oracles are given which deal with both the Northern Kingdom and Judah, although they are deemed to have been delivered by the prophet in Jerusalem (2.2). The material is clearly composite /72/, yet certain keynotes are struck repeatedly and motifs already familiar to us run through these entire first ten chapters. Judgement is to be uttered against Judah and Jerusalem for their apostasy and that judgement is coming in the shape of foreign invasion (the Chaldeans) as it had come for the Northern Kingdom with the Assyrians (1.15-16). Israel, holy to the Lord, the first fruits of his harvest (2.3), his choice vine (2.21), nurtured by him in the wilderness (2.2,6) has made cakes for the queen of heaven (7.18) and has played the harlot "upon every high hill and under every green tree" (2.20; 3.6,13; 7.31). The Temple cultus is corrupt and no longer pleasing to God (6.20-21; 7.11,21 ff.) Yahweh's house has become a den of robbers (7.11). The leaders of the people - kings, princes, priests and prophets - are corrupt and shall be put to shame (2.8,26; 4.9; 5.31; 6.13; 8.8-10; 9.23-24).

Judgement is coming upon the nation. The invader who will be
God's agent will eat up Israel's vines and her fig-trees (5.17).
She will be gleaned as thoroughly as a vine (6.9). God's wrath
"will be poured out on this place, upon man and beast, upon the
trees of the field and the fruit of the ground" (7.20). The
mountains will move (4.24) and the fruitful land will become a
desert (4.26). Jerusalem itself will be laid waste (4.16; 7.34;
9.11), a mound will be raised against her (6.6) and her occupants
will be advised to flee (6.1). God will look for even one righteous
man to redeem his people but none shall be found (5.1-3). "There
are no grapes on the vine, nor figs on the fig tree" (8.13).

This section of Jeremiah is plainly one of the most prominent
'judgement' passages of the Old Testament. Its link with the
theme of 'catastrophe' is strong and persistent. The Jer.8.13
passage itself was read, according to B.Meg.31b, as the lection
from the Prophets (or haftarah) for the Ninth of Av fast-day. The
Ninth of Av was a day of mourning for the Jews, the day, according
to Talmudic tradition, when the First Temple had been burned, and
the day, therefore, upon which all subsequent major catastrophes
happening about that time were deemed to have taken place /73/.
It was the day upon which the Second Temple, too, was said to have
been destroyed, and the day in turn that would witness, according
to the Midrash, the birth of the Messiah /74/.

The New Testament also draws directly and possibly indirectly
upon these chapters /75/. Descriptive motifs concerning God's
wrath are echoed in some eschatological judgement passages in
Revelation (cf. e.g. 7.34 and Ap.18.23; 10.25 and Ap.16.1) and,
according to C.H. Dodd, there are echoes of Jeremiah language in
NT predictions of the destruction of Jerusalem /76/. J.W. Doeve,
for example, argues that Jer.6.6,14,15,21 lies behind Luke's
Lament for Jerusalem pericope (19.41-44) /77/ and Dodd himself
names Jer.7.1-15 specifically as a subordinate or supplementary
source for the early church's estimation of the Temple /78/.
Jer.7.11 indeed (combined with Is.56.7) is cited by Mark himself
as representing the substance of Jesus' attack on the Temple
cultus in chapter eleven.

The description of Israel as obdurate, "uncircumcised in
heart" (Jer.9.26; cf. 6.10) recurs in the New Testament (cf. Acts
7.51) and the motif of 'judicial blinding', applied likewise to
Israel in the Old Testament (cf. Is.6.9-10 Ez.12.2), occurs both
in Jer.5.21 and in Mark (e.g. 6.52; 8.17-18). It is possible
that in Mk.8.17-18 we have an echo of the Jeremiah passage (cf.

also Mk.4.12-13) although it may be noted in passing that the πώρωσις-motif is applied by Mark to the disciples here, as well as to Israel's religious leaders elsewhere (cf. Mk.3.5) /79/.

Does Jer.8.13 lie behind Mark's fig-tree story, however? Some scholars have suggested a link, although in the vaguest of terms. Nineham, for example, ventured the opinion that in the light of Old Testament passages such as Jer.8.13, Jl.1.7, Ez.17.24, Mi.7.1-6 and Hos.9.10,16 f., Jesus' action may well have been seen as a fulfilment of the scriptures /80/. Hiers, too, has cautiously stated that "the story of the fate of the fig tree may well have been influenced by Jer.8.13." /81/ Giesen has expressed the view that the 'hunger' datum of Mk.11.12 contains an allusion to Jer.8.13 and that Jesus' hungering for figs is to be seen as metaphorical in the same way as God's search for figs is understood here /82/.

On the positive side indeed we may say that the basic substance of the Markan story - the search for figs, the lack of fruit, the withered tree - is all here and the connection of this passage with the impending destruction of Jerusalem, the Temple and its corrupt cultus coincides with the redactional position in which the fig-tree story is found. The associated descriptional motifs found in the Jeremiah context (recounted above) likewise coalesce with those appearing in Mark, chapter eleven (the coming judgement upon Jerusalem and the Temple, wrath poured out on the trees of the field, the moving of the mountains and so on).

In the second place, we know that Mark was acquainted with Jer.7.11 (and, therefore, presumably with the surrounding context), for he cites it in 11.17. Jer.5.21 has already been compared with Mk.8.17-18 and one may also compare Jer.7.20 with our story, and Jer.7.25 with the parable of the vineyard (12.1-12), although the link in the case of these latter two references is not as strong, in our opinion, as J.W. Doeve has wished to make it /83/.

On the negative side, however, it is worth remarking that while the Massoretic text uses נבל for the withering of the leaves, the Septuagint has κατερρύηκεν rather than the more usual verb ξηραίνω. The LXX, too, does not refer to God's search for figs but renders the text with: "and (when) they shall gather their fruits ...". Reference is made also to fig-trees in the plural where the MT has בתאנה in the singular.

There is no evidence, therefore, of any direct verbal influence

upon our story, via the LXX, on the part of Jer.8.13, and for
this reason it would be hazardous to suggest that the fig-tree
story was an actual historicization of this one text. We have
yet to assess the possible contribution of the other fig-tree
passages, however, and hence we shall leave our final conclusions
until after these have been discussed.

Is.28.3-4

> "The proud crown of the drunkards of Ephraim will be
> trodden underfoot; [4]and the fading crown of its glorious
> beauty, which is on the head of the rich valley, will be
> like a first-ripe fig before the summer (MT כבכורה בטרם קיץ ;
> LXX ὡς πρόδρομος σύκου): when a man sees it, he eats it
> up as soon as it is in his hand." (RSV)

This passage is part of an oracle (28.1-6) which dates
probably from shortly before 721 BCE /84/. The revelling
leaders of Samaria, oblivious to their impending fate, are
depicted as wearing crowns of flowers which fade, droop and are
ultimately trodden underfoot. Samaria is at the same time at the
head of a fertile valley, which evokes, as an image of swift
judgement, the idea of their being eagerly devoured like a first-
ripe fig. The passage is placed here in order to serve as a
parallel between the imminent fate of the drunkards of Jerusalem
and the actual fate of Samaria which fell to the Assyrians in 721
BCE.

In the wider context of chapters 24 - 35 we are presented
with material that is again composite in nature. Chapters 24 - 27
are in essence an apocalypse on the theme of the coming judgement
and the New Age, and chapters 28 - 35 present a series of
prophecies of blessing and judgement that are mainly concerned
with Judah. Again, themes that were observed in Jer.1 - 10 make
their appearance. In the apocalyptic section, the devastation of
the world is foretold (24 passim), "a curse devours the earth"
(24.6), "the wine mourns, the vine languishes" (24.7) and the
nations shall be like gleaned trees (24.13). The inhabitants of the
height shall be made low, while the way of the righteous will be
made level (26.5,7). The foundations of the earth shall be shaken
(24.18-19) but God's hand will rest on Mount Zion (24.23; 25.10).
There, on "this mountain" (25.6,10) God's people will enjoy a
Messianic feast (cf. many gospel passages) and will rejoice in his
coming to save them (25.9). The veil between Jews and Gentiles will
be removed (cf. Mk.15.38), and death will be swallowed up (25.7-8;

26.19). Israel shall take root, blossom and fill the earth with
fruit (27.6) and the exiles from far and wide will flock to
Jerusalem to worship on the holy mountain (27.13).

In chapters 28 - 35, Judah's leaders - priests, rulers and
prophets - are indicted for their corruption (cf. 28.7-22 and
especially 29.9-14 where the notion of 'judicial blindness'
appears as it did in Jer.5.21). Judgement is coming, a decree
of destruction has been issued by the Lord God of hosts upon the
whole land (28.21-22), Judah will be visited, in an instant,
suddenly, by the Lord of hosts (29.6), "burning with his anger ...
his lips ... full of indignation ... his tongue ... like a
devouring fire" (30.27-28). Jerusalem will be besieged (29.3).
In Zion, a new building erected in righteousness is arising, "a
stone, a tested stone, a precious cornerstone", namely faith in
Yahweh (28.16). Other refuges will be swept away. Eschatological
hope and eschatological despair are described alternately in terms
of fruitfulness and barrenness (cf. 29.17; 30.23-26; 32.10-20;
33.9; 34.4). In the New Age, the land will be abundantly fertile
(29.17; 30.23-26; 32.15-20; 35) and the Temple exalted (27.13;
28.16; 29.8; 30.29; 31.4,5,9; 33.5,20,21; 35.10; cf. Ez.47.1-12
Zech.14.8-11).

There is evidence that the early church made considerable use
of these chapters, for echoes as well as direct quotations from
them abound in the New Testament /85/. Chapters 28 and 29, for
example, (esp. 28.11,12,16; 29.10,13,14) were frequently used in
connection with the rejection of the Jews /86/. The 'stone'
saying of 28.16 was particularly important in NT apologetic (cf.
e.g. Rom.9.33; 10.11 1 Pt.2.6) /87/ and Dodd names this passage
indeed as a primary source for the early church /88/. The
'judicial blindness' or πώρωσις passage of 29.9-14 is also named
by him as a supplementary source /89/ and was invoked frequently
along with Is.6.9-10 (cf. Mk.4.12) Jer.5.21 and Ez.12.2 to
'explain' the rejection of Jesus and the gospel by the Jewish
people (see e.g. Mt.15.8-9 Mk.7.6-7 1 Cor.1.19; cf. also 29.10
and Rom.11.8) /90/. The chapters were also drawn on to furnish
images and motifs for the church's eschatology /91/, such as the
'swallowing up of death' in the New Age /92/, judgement /93/,
the last trumpet /94/ and so on.

Mark himself knew these chapters, it would seem. In 7.6-7 he
too applies the 'blindness and hypocrisy' citation of Is.29.13 to
the Jewish leaders, and it would be interesting to speculate
whether the 'confounding of the wise' motif, found in Is.29.14 and

present also, interestingly, in the Jeremiah context (cf. esp.
Jer.8.9) has influenced his presentation of Jesus' encounter with
the representatives of the Jewish nation in chap.11.27 - 12.40.
The πώρωσις theme also, it was seen, figured in the Jeremiah
context (Jer.5.21) and was applied in Mk.8.17-18 to the disciples.
Mark quotes the 'stone' sayings, too, in 12.10-11, although here
the LXX version of Ps.118.22-23 is the text cited. Kee,
nevertheless, thinks that an allusion to Is.28.16 (LXX) is also
here in view /95/. He claims, moreover, that in the apocalyptic
imagery of Mk.13.24,25 and 27 Mark is quoting from both the 'fig'
verse of Is.34.4 (MT) and from Is.27.13 /96/.

These facts, then, would make it reasonable to suppose that
the essential ideas found in these chapters could well have had
some bearing on Mark's intention for and understanding of the
fig-tree story (as well as that of his readers), but is the
evidence strong enough to justify the view that Is.28.3-4 was
itself the starting-point for the story?

On the whole, it seems unlikely. The substance of the verse
provides less of a parallel than does Jer.8.13. The passage, it
is true, does present the devouring of the first-ripe fig as an
image of judgement, and it is certainly our contention that the
story was viewed in this light. But in Mark's story no figs were
found to be devoured, not even the first-ripe ones, and that is
the essential point.

The verbal links, moreover, are not strong. It is possible
that the 11.13d datum, "for it was not the season for figs", alludes to the image here of the first-ripe fig *before the summer* /97/
that is seen, plucked and eagerly devoured, and that the LXX
ὁ ἰδὼν αὐτό is echoed in καὶ ἰδὼν συκῆν (11.13), but this is
hardly conclusive. In any case, the story may not have been influenced by any *one* OT passage exclusively but by a number of
interrelated passages, a possibility bolstered by the early church's
(and Mark's) frequent practice of conflating scripture, and made
apparent in the material we are presently reviewing.

Hos.9.10,16

"Like grapes in the wilderness, I found Israel.
Like the first fruit on the fig tree,
in its first season
(כבכורה בתאנה בראשיתה MT; ὡς σκοπὸν /98/ ἐν συκῇ πρόϊμον LXX),
I saw your fathers.
****

16
    Ephraim is stricken (הכה; ἐπόνεσεν),
    their root is dried up
    (שרשם יבש; τὰς ῥίζας αὐτοῦ ἐξηράνθη),
    they shall bear no fruit
    (פרי בלי-יעשון; καρπὸν οὐκέτι μὴ ἐνέγκῃ).

This passage is set within the context of the prophet's
thunderous denunciation of Israel's cultic aberration and
particularly against those Baal-elements that had come to suffuse
Israel's religion. Although Hosea is fragmentary, badly preserved
and unskilfully redacted /99/, the keynotes struck within the
compass of the book as the early church would have had it are again
remarkably similar to those we have already encountered within the
context of the other fig passages.

The people have turned from Yahweh to play the harlot. "They
sacrifice on the tops of mountains, and make offerings upon the
hills, under oak, poplar and terebinth, because their shade is
good" (4.12-13; cf. also 2.13; 4.17-19; 6.9-10; 8.11-13; 9.10c;
10.2,8; 11.2; 12.11). Their leaders are rebels (9.15), their
prophets foolish (9.7), their traders dishonest (12.7), their
priests are thieves and robbers (6.9-10; cf. also 7.1 and 4.4-10;
5.1-2). The "people are destroyed for lack of knowledge" (4.6).
Their worship is corrupt and Yahweh has no delight in their
sacrifices and burnt offerings (6.6; 8.13; 9.4). The fruit of
righteousness is required instead (10.12).

In the wilderness period, a sacrificial cultus had been
unnecessary and there Israel had experienced Yahweh's grace
(9.10; 13.5). Such a time would come again (2.14-15; 3.4; 12.9)
if Israel were to repent ("After two days he will revive us; on
the third day he will raise us up ..." 6.2). In time to come,
Yahweh will make for them a covenant with the beasts (2.18; cf.
Is.11.6ff.) and "the earth shall answer the grain, the wine, and
the oil, and they shall answer Jezreel" (viz, 'God sows', 2.21-22).
Israel will again

    "blossom as the lily, he shall strike root as the
    poplar; his shoots shall spread out; his beauty
    shall be like the olive, and his fragrance like
    Lebanon. They shall return and shall dwell beneath
    my shadow, they shall flourish as a garden; they
    shall blossom as the vine, their fragrance shall
    be like the wine of Lebanon." (14.5-7)

Yahweh himself will answer and look after them.   "I am like an
evergreen cypress, from me comes your fruit" (14.8).

    But in the meantime judgement is coming for the nation (9.7).
God will strike against her vines and her fig-trees (2.12).
Ephraim and Judah shall be slain by the words of his mouth (6.5).
"They shall say to the mountains, Cover us, and to the hills, Fall
upon us" (10.8).   Israel, "a luxuriant vine that yields its fruit"
(10.1) will have her altars broken down, her pillars destroyed
(10.2).   Ephraim, "the first fruit on the fig tree" (9.10) will be
stricken, his roots withered, he will no longer bear fruit (9.16).
"Because of the wickedness of their deeds I will drive them out
of my house" (9.15). (!)

    According to Dodd, the whole of this short book of Hosea was
influential in early Christian thought, with chapters 1 and 2,
5.8 - 6.3 and perhaps chapter 13 having especial significance /100/.
From chapters 1 and 2 was drawn material for the theology of the
rejection of the old Israel and the adoption of the new /101/, a
quarry for which was also Is.28 and 29, as we have seen.   The book
furnishes frequent references to the "knowledge" of God as the mark
of the renewed Israel /102/, and the lack of "knowledge" as a mark
of the old.   This latter motif appears in 4.6 and was a feature
also of the previously cited 'judicial blindness' passages of Is.
and Jer. /103/.   The call for Israel to break up her fallow ground
and sow righteousness (10.12) is also repeated in Jer.4.3 and
Paul echoes this theme in respect of the Christian community in
2 Cor.9.6 ff. (cf. esp. v.10).   The citation of Hos.6.6 (mercy
rather than sacrifice) appears twice in Matthew as verba Christi /104/.

    The book's keynote themes of judgement and deliverance were
also of value to the early church in respect of its own understanding
of salvation history.   Luke employs both Hos.9.7 and 'the appeal to
the mountains' saying of 10.8 specifically within the context of
the destruction of Jerusalem and its Temple (Lk.21.22; 23.30 cf.
Ap.6.16), and it is noteworthy that the Jeremiah passages that we
reviewed were similarly employed /105/.   Hosea 13, Dodd suggests,
may also have had an influence upon the formation of the tradition
lying behind the "apocalyptic discourse" in the Synoptic gospels /106/.
Hos.13.14 was certainly used with regard to 'deliverance from
death' in the End-time, and here again there is a link with the
Isaiah context.   In 1 Cor.15.54-55, Hos.13.14 is conflated with the
'swallowing up of death' Is.25.8 passage /107/.   The national
deliverance or restoration metaphor ("after two days ... on the
third day") of Hos.6.2 is generally held to be the passage behind

the resurrection of Christ on the third day scheme alluded to by
Paul in 1 Cor.15.4 /108/, and there are also a number of other
scattered NT allusions to Hosea, and proof-texts, where the
surrounding context has been more obviously ignored /109/.

The specific use of Hosea by Mark himself is less pronounced
although echoes can perhaps be heard.   Kee thinks, for example,
that Mark is quoting from the LXX text of Hosea 6.6 in 12.33c as
well as alluding also to 1 Sm.15.22 and Prv.21.3 in that verse /110/.
In 14.1, he claims that there is an allusion to Hos.6.2, and Dodd,
too, has drawn attention to echoes of Hos.13 in the Markan
apocalypse, as we noted above.

The verbal parallels between Hos.9.10,15,16 and our story are
perhaps a little stronger than those we have examined in our
previous fig passages, although curiously little attention has been
drawn to them by those who have claimed to recognize a link between
this passage and the fig-tree story /111/.   One may compare τὰς
ῥίζας αὐτοῦ ἐξηράνθη, καρπὸν οὐκέτι μὴ ἐνέγκη (9.16), for example,
with μηκέτι ... ἐκ σοῦ μηδεὶς καρπὸν φάγοι (Mk.11.14) ... εἶδον τὴν
συκῆν ἐξηραμμένην ἐκ ῥιζῶν (Mk.11.20) ...ἴδε ἡ συκῆ ... ἐξήρανται
(Mk.11.21), or again the Cleansing scene, where Jesus begins to
cast out the money changers (ἤρξατο ἐκβάλλειν 11.15) from God's
house ('Ο οἶκος μου οἶκος προσευχῆς κληθήσεται 11.17) with διὰ τὰς
κακίας τῶν ἐπιτηδευμάτων αὐτῶν ἐκ τοῦ οἴκου μου ἐκβαλῶ αὐτούς (Hos.
9.15) /112/.   The reference to the seeing(εἶδον) /113/ and finding
(εὗρον) /114/ of Israel as the first-ripe fruit *in its first season*
(בראשיתה, as opposed to the regular season for figs later on in the
year) may possibly have some resonance too with Mark's "for it was
not the season for figs" (11.13d), although the LXX version of this
expression is confusing (ὡς σκοπὸν ἐν συκῆ πρόιμον) /115/.   The
substance of the passage, however, the first-ripe fig as a picture
of Israel, and her withering and consequent future barrenness as an
emblem of judgement, is particularly congenial to the Markan story.

Mi.7.1

"Woe is me! For I have become as when the summer fruit
has been gathered (כאספי-קיץ MT; ὡς συνάγων καλάμην ἐν
ἀμήτῳ LXX), as when the vintage has been gleaned: there
is no cluster to eat, no first-ripe fig which my soul
desires (בכורה אותה נפשי) /116/. [2] The godly man has
perished from the earth ..."

Here again, as in Jer.8.13, God is depicted as looking in vain
for the righteous of the nation as one would search for figs to no

purpose if the season were inopportune. Curiously, the prophet
has God, the speaker, seek for the בכורה, or first-ripe fig
(May-June) *after* the summer harvest (Aug.-Sept.) has been
gleaned (!) a fact that illustrates perhaps how verisimilitude
is often sacrificed when symbolism or allegory is intended. With
the moving image of God walking sorrowfully through the gleaned
vineyard, a lament is being raised against the moral corruption of
Israel and the absence of righteousness in the land. The parallel
with Jesus' search for figs is striking, and, at the very least,
would not have been overlooked, we believe, by Mark or the early
church.

As with the other fig passages, there appear likewise in the
context of this short book the same concomitant pattern of ideas
that we have seen emerge as we proceed. In chapters 1 - 3, which
are generally ascribed to Micah himself /117/, the coming judgement
upon the house of Israel (chap.1) is announced, the punishment and
restoration of Israel (chap.2) is forecast, and the princes,
prophets and priests (chap.3) are condemned (cf. esp. 3.11).
Yahweh "will come down and tread upon the high places of the earth.
And the mountains will melt under him and the valleys will be
cleft" (1.3-4). "Zion shall be ploughed as a field; Jerusalem
shall become a heap of ruins, and the mountain of the house a
wooded height" (3.12; cf. also 4.9-10; 5.1).

In chapters 4 and 5, we find prophecies of the New Age,
dating from the Exile or after. Jerusalem will be the world
capital, the mountain of the house of the Lord shall be elevated,
peace and prosperity will abound, and every man shall sit "under
his vine and under his fig tree" (4.1-4). The future Messianic
king will rise from Bethlehem (5.2-4) and the exiles of the
nation shall return to Zion (4.6-8; 5.3-4).

In the concluding prophecies of chapters 6 and 7, we are
presented with material again similar to that in chapters 1 - 3.
The note of judgement is strong. Yahweh pleads his case against
the defendant Israel before the mountains and hills, appealing to
salvation history to vindicate his long-suffering care for a
nation that has now become corrupt and which he must punish as a
result. An anticultic note is struck, and the 'mercy not
sacrifice' theme is sounded (6.6-8; cf. Hos.6.6 Jer.7.21-23;
etc.). As before, judgement is expressed in terms of the
withholding of fruit. "You shall sow, but not reap, you shall
tread olives, but not anoint yourselves with oil; you shall tread
grapes, but not drink wine" (6.15) ... "The earth will be desolate"
(7.13).

Micah figured less prominently in early Christian usage than
did our aforementioned Jeremiah, Isaiah and Hosea passages, but it
did, in 5.2-4, furnish a key proof-text for christology and the
birth narratives, as did Hos.11.1 /118/. Mark, however, did use
the book and possibly on more than one occasion /119/. In the
"apocalyptic discourse" of chapter 13, describing the tribulations
and woes to come and the destruction of Jerusalem and the Temple
in the End-time, he draws *from the very passage in which our fig-
text stands* a verse depicting the internecine warfare that will
exist in these days (cf. Mi.7.2,6 - brother against brother,
father against son - with Mk.13.12).   Mark's wording does not
follow the LXX, as Birdsall has pointed out /120/, but Kee claims
to have identified the source of Mk.13.12b as the Targum of Mi.7.2,6
/121/ (which is interesting, since the reference to the first-ripe
fig in 7.1 also exists only in the MT and not in the LXX).   There
is evidence, too, according to A. de Q. Robin /122/, that this
Micah chapter 7 passage was applied to times of national crisis in
contemporary Rabbinic circles. When one ponders that the destruction of the Temple prophecy in Mk.13.2 ("no stone upon another")
bears an uncanny resemblance to Mi.3.12 ("Jerusalem ...a heap of
ruins") /123/ and that the fig-tree (its withering an omen of
eschatological judgement in Mk.11) reappears in Mk.13 (its blossoming a sign of the imminence of the End-time), then the possibility
that this passage (Mi.7.1) lies behind our story becomes much
stronger.

But was Mi.7.1 the starting-point for the story? Robin,
Birdsall and Derrett, believing that the Markan report is basically
historical, all claim that the verse was actually in Jesus' mind
when he approached the tree, an inference that we have already
criticized as presupposing too optimistic a view of what the
exegete qua historian can recover from the story. At the same
time there are no close verbal links between Mk.11.12-14, 20 ff.
and Mi.7.1 and we are not at liberty to infer, therefore, that
Mark himself has composed the story specifically out of this
particular text. The substance of the passage, however, and
perhaps also the specific idea of the *untimely* search for figs
(cf. Mk.11.13d) is strikingly apposite and perhaps we can conclude,
therefore, that either the link with the passage lies further back
in the tradition and/or that Mark and his readers, as at least
seems certain, would have understood the story in the light of
this verse.

Jl.1.7,12

" (⁶For a nation has come up against my land ...)
⁷It has laid waste my vines,
   שם גפני לשמה MT; ἔθετο τὴν ἄμπελόν μου εἰς ἀφανισμόν LXX
and splintered my fig trees;
   ותאנתי לקצפה; καὶ τὰς συκᾶς μου εἰς συγκλασμόν
it has stripped off their bark and thrown it down;
their branches are made white.

¹²The vine withers
   הגפן הובישה; ἡ ἄμπελος ἐξηράνθη
the fig tree languishes.
   התאנה אמללה; καὶ αἱ συκαῖ ὠλιγώθησαν
....
all the trees of the field are withered;
   כל-עצי השדה יבשו
καὶ πάντα τὰ ξύλα τοῦ ἀγροῦ ἐξηράνθησαν."

In the eyes of the prophet, a calamitous plague of locusts
(the "nation" of 1.6) is taken as a portent of the coming Day of
the Lord, the devastation they cause being invested with
eschatological significance. In chapters 1 - 2.17 the prophet
issues a call to national repentance in the light of the
approaching day of divine wrath ("Lament like a virgin ...",
1,8,13,14). In 2.18-27, Yahweh responds to Israel's repentance
and promises of restoration are given, while in the remaining
section of the book (2.28 - 3.21) there is a magnificent
description of the coming Day of the Lord, the outpouring of the
spirit, the judgement of the nations and the renewal of Judah.

Yet again in the space of this very brief work, we encounter
motifs that have been previously discussed. Judgement is
actualized in the devastation of the land, but particularly in
that of the vine and the fig-tree (1.7,12). As a result, "the
cereal offering and the drink offering are cut off from the house
of the Lord" (1.9,13,16; 2.14). Blessing, however, will come in
the renewed fruitfulness of the land and of the trees: "... the
tree bears its fruit, the fig tree and vine give their full
yield" (2.22). Zion shall be pre-eminent in the New Age period,
and the Temple shall be a source of fruitfulness. "And in that
day the mountains shall drip sweet wine, and the hills shall flow
with milk, and all the stream beds of Judah shall flow with
water; and a fountain shall come forth from the house of the
Lord and water the valley of Shittim" (3.18).

This short book of Joel, and in particular chapters 2 and 3, was, according to Dodd, a primary source for the early church /124/. It was one of the chief 'quarries' from which the church's apocalyptic and eschatological imagery and conceptions were drawn /125/. The 'outpouring of the Spirit' passage of 2.28-32 was especially important, and was employed by early Christians to support their claim that they were living in the Last Days and that they had experienced this gift (cf. Acts 2.17-21). Jl.2.32 is also cited in Rom.10.13, and it is interesting to note that in the surrounding context of chapters 9 - 11, where Paul is found similarly referring to OT passages which appear to have been already current as testimonia, there appear once again passages from the Isaiah and Hosea contexts that we have already discussed /126/.

Mark, too, appears to have drawn on Joel for apocalyptic imagery. In 13.24-25 of his "apocalyptic discourse", for example, we have in all probability an allusion, inter alia, to the 'darkening of the sun and moon' motif occurring in Jl.2.10,31 and 3.15 /127/. In the 'putting in of the sickle for the harvest has come' of Mk.4.29 we have an even clearer reference to the harvesting/judgement image of Jl.3.13 /128/.

Has Mark or his source drawn on Jl.1.7,12, however, for the account of the fig-tree story? The verb ξηραύνω is used a great deal by the LXX in this passage /129/, although, as A. de Q. Robin points out, it is employed (strictly speaking) only in regard to the other trees /130/. Of the fig-trees it is said merely that they have been made to snap or splinter (שם..לקצפה; /131/ ἔθετο ... εἰς συγκλασμόν) or have become weak (MT אמללה) /132/ or few (LXX ὠλιγώθησαν). The constituent elements of the passage, it must also be said, do not form as close a parallel to the Markan story as do those, for example, of Jer.8.13, Hos.9.10,16 or Mi.7.1. The conception of the *blasted tree* as an emblem of *eschatological judgement*, however, *is* appropriate and would, we believe, have influenced Mark's, or the Markan reader's, *perception* of the story.

These, then, are the primary OT passages in the light of which we suggest Mark's fig-tree story should be viewed. Before we look at some supplementary passages for which an influence has also been claimed, it might at this point be valuable to give a short summary of the impressions we have gathered to date from this review. The following general observations were made:

1.   All five 'fig' passages occur in contexts that were 'mined'
      regularly by the early church for testimonia relevant for
      her theological self-understanding, mission and eschatology:
      the rejection of the Jews, the destruction of Jerusalem and
      the Temple, the new Israel, the outpouring of the Spirit, the
      arrival of the End-time, eschatological judgement and
      deliverance.

2.   The contexts of all five passages (as well as the individual
      testimonia) exhibit a number of *common* and *interrelated themes
      and motifs* which link them not only with each other but also
      with the features and surrounding context of the Markan
      story: the judgement against Israel, the corruption and
      consequent condemnation of the nation, her leaders, her
      Temple and its cultus, the appearance of Yahweh in wrath to
      curse the land and blast the trees, the moving of the
      mountains, the destruction of Jerusalem and its Temple; the
      blossoming of Israel, God's tree, in the New Age, the
      abundant fertility of this period, the elevation of the
      Temple Mount and its future exalted status.

3.   The five 'fig' passages themselves all without exception
      employ the language of figurative imagery and symbolism. The
      image of the fig or fig-tree, whether used in allegory,
      metaphor or simile, is intimately associated with the nation
      and the judgement upon it and in particular with the
      above-mentioned themes.

4.   Certain of these fig passages are also found employed in
      Rabbinic circles in connection with the theme of lament,
      mourning or catastrophe for the nation, and especially for its
      Temple (cf. Jer.8.13 Mi.7.1 ff.).

5.   Mark himself shows acquaintance with the contexts in which the
      'fig' passages are found, and in certain cases has drawn on
      these chapters in connection with the same themes as were
      enumerated in 1.

6.   While the essential elements of these 'fig' passages (esp.
      Jer.8.13 Hos.9.10,16 Mi.7.1) show a correspondence with
      Jesus' search for figs, the verbal links observed in each
      individual case have not in the main been particularly
      striking (though cf. Hos.9.10,15,16).

From this, it can be said that no one 'fig' verse seems to
have provided a starting-point for Mark's story. If the story did
develop out of the Old Testament then the link probably existed
with the pre-Markan tradition rather than solely with Mark, and
the contribution of a number of passages, rather than any single
one, is more in view. It is not inconceivable, in fact, that the
story was formed out of separate but interrelated OT passages,
for all its elements appear there, but it is unlikely that it was
a pure composition on the part of Mark. This is not to say,
however, that the OT did not directly influence Mark as well, both
in terms of his perception of the story and with regard also to
the verbal allusions and motifs he employed in transmitting it.
We shall see in a moment that further such echoes can be detected.
It is, however, to leave open the question of origin, and this
deliberately so, for, in enquiring after the form of the story
prior to Mark, we have yet to consider the place of the Lukan
parable in all this. The question of origin, therefore, will be
raised again when we come to examine the New Testament evidence
(chapter VII), although here again we must emphasize that
ultimately our concern is not with the story's origin but with
its function.

Some Supplementary Passages Considered

Our redaction-critical investigations upon the fig-tree
pericope have already indicated that Mark's hand is to be observed
at work on the story, but nowhere more clearly than in the first
half of the sequel (11.20-23) /133/. Here the especial influence
on him of the language of the Psalms can perhaps be detected.

Carrington /134/, for example, has drawn attention to the
parallel between 11.20-21 ([20]καὶ παραπορευόμενοι πρωῒ εἶδον τὴν
συκῆν ... [21] ... ἴδε ἡ συκή ...) and *Ps.37.35-36:*

"I have seen (εἶδον) a wicked man overbearing,
and towering like a cedar of Lebanon.
[36]*Again I passed by* (καὶ παρῆλθον), *and, lo* (καὶ ἰδού),
he was no more; though I sought him
he could not be found (οὐχ εὑρέθη ὁ τόπος αὐτοῦ)" /135/.

Carrington notes how in the Psalms "morning and evening,
evening and morning, are used for the passage of time, and the
withering of green vegetation for the shortness of human life or
the fate of the ungodly" /136/. He further suggests that this

same psalm (37.3-5) anticipates Jesus' words about trusting God
(11.22,23: ἔχετε πίστιν θεοῦ ... καὶ ἔσται αὐτῷ).

> "Trust in the Lord (ἔλπισον ἐπὶ κύριον) ... and he
> will give you the desires of your heart. ... trust
> in him (ἔλπισον ἐπ' αὐτόν) and he will act (καὶ αὐτὸς
> ποιήσει).

The Psalms were of course a primary source for the early church,
and particularly with respect to the passion narrative /137/.
Mark frequently quotes from them or alludes to them /138/. If
Carrington is right, then it is to be noted that *Ps.37.1-2* also
introduces the *withering* motif:

> "Fret not yourself because of the wicked ... for they
> will soon fade (ἀποξηρανθήσονται LXX; ימלו MT) like
> the grass, and wither (ἀποπεσοῦνται; יבולון)like the
> green herb."

Many other such 'withering' passages in the Psalms might also be
claimed as influences, however, and Carrington himself cites
Ps.90.6, where the morning/evening scheme also reappears:

> "(⁵Thou dost sweep men away ... like grass ...)
> ⁶In the morning, it flourishes and is renewed;
> τὸ πρωὶ ἀνθήσαι καὶ παρέλθοι
> in the evening it fades and withers.
> τὸ ἑσπέρας ἀποπέσοι, σκληρυνθείη καὶ ξηρανθείη

Jb.18.16, however, might also be cited:

> "His roots [the wicked's] dry up beneath,
> ὑποκάτωθεν αἱ ῥίζαι αὐτοῦ ξηρανθήσονται
> and his branches wither above.
> καὶ ἐπάνωθεν ἐπιπεσεῖται θερισμὸς αὐτοῦ" /139/

The Markan phrase (ἐξηραμμένην) ἐκ ῥιζῶν (11.20) is a New
Testament hapax legomenon /140/, although its meaning is clear
enough. It indicates how complete the fig-tree's destruction was
/141/. The phrase is in fact a classical expression, although it
occurs again in Job (28.9, 'the overturning of mountains ἐκ ῥιζῶν';
31.12) as well as in Ez.17.9. This latter reference is an
interesting one and has been commented on before /142/. Mk.4.32,
indeed, may contain an allusion to this allegory (cf. Ez.17.23;
31.6). Here in the Ezekiel passage we have Israel, the tree,
planted in foreign soil but in danger of being withered and plucked

up ἐκ ῥιζῶν. Its future lies in being planted upon *a high and
lofty mountain,* where it can only with difficulty be uprooted.
Mark's tree, however, *has withered,* and, indeed, the whole mountain
itself is capable, with faith, of being uprooted!

Eschatological imagery lies behind the 'uprooting of mountains'
motif, as we have seen, and in this respect some commentators have
also made reference to Zech.14.4 as lying behind this mountain-
moving logion (so, for example, R.M. Grant, Derrett). Mark's
gospel and especially the eleventh chapter has been shown to
contain numerous echoes of Zechariah, particularly chapters 9 - 14
/143/, and if Zech.14.4 is here reflected in Mk.11.23, then it is
of interest to note that in the immediate context of this passage,
certain familiar eschatological themes reappear. With the moving
of the mountains (14.4-5), "the whole land shall be turned into a
plain" although "Jerusalem shall remain aloft upon its site"
(14.10). "It shall be inhabited, for there shall be no more
curse" (14.11). The Temple shall be exalted "and there shall no
longer be a trader in the house of the Lord of hosts on that day"
(14.21). On that day, too, "living waters shall flow out from
Jerusalem, half of them to the eastern sea and half of them to the
western sea" (14.8).

This latter expectation, the flow of living waters from the
sanctuary, was one that we have met before in connection with
another Ezekiel passage (chap.47) that has been cited as having a
bearing on our story. In 47.12 we read:

"And on the banks, on both sides of the river, there
will grow all kinds of trees for food. Their leaves
will not wither (לא-יבול עלהו MT; οὐ μὴ παλαιωθῇ ἐπ' αὐτοῦ
LXX /144/) nor their fruit fail (ולא-יתם פריו; οὐδὲ μὴ ἐκλίπῃ
ὁ καρπός), but they will bear fresh fruit every month,
because the water for them flows from the sanctuary. Their
fruit will be for food, and their leaves for healing."

This passage is important for its witness to the Old Testament
expectation previously discussed, that the Messianic Age would be
an age of extraordinary fruitfulness, and that this fruitfulness
would stem from the Temple as its source. It stands within the
context (chaps.40-48) of Ezekiel's inspired depiction of the new
State and its Temple, "living under a prince of David's line and
devoted to the worship of Yahweh, who has now returned to his
House and his holy Land" /145/. Set down upon a very high
mountain (the Temple Mount), the prophet is given a vision of the
future Holy Land, City and Temple, which turns out to be, in

Lowther Clarke's words, "a masterpiece of Town and Country
Planning" /146/. As part of this vision, Ezekiel is shown a
river of water emanating from below the threshhold of the restored
Temple (cf. also Ps.46.4 Jl.3.18 Zech.14.8 Ap.22.1-5) and a
number of prodigiously fertile trees which are nourished by this
river and which bear fruit all the year round. Gustaf Dalman has
argued, indeed, that the fig-tree, in view of its successive and
excessive fruitage, is here without doubt the source of this
description and this view has been shared by B.W. Bacon /147/.

The early church made use of Ezekiel, and particularly
chapter 47 /148/, although it is not named by Dodd as a primary
or supplementary source. The 'Shepherd' passage of Ez.34, for
example, has influenced christology (cf. esp. Jn.10.1-6 /149/, but
also Mk.6.34 where Ez.34.8 and Zech.10.2 may be reflected), and
apocalyptic and eschatological imagery drawn from the book
reappears frequently in the New Testament, especially in the
Apocalypse. The parallel, for example, between Ap.22.1-5 and
Ez.47 has already been noted /150/.

Mark himself has apparently drawn on or alluded to Ezekiel on
a number of occasions. An echo of Ez.12.2 (blind eyes and deaf
ears; cf. also 11.19) may be detected in Mk.8.17-18 where the
incomprehension of the disciples is described, a motif ($\pi\acute{\omega}\rho\omega\sigma\iota\varsigma$)
that we have already discussed in relation to Jer.5.21 and Is.29.13-
14 /151/. Kee claims traces of the influence of Ezekiel in Mark's
"apocalyptic discourse" /152/. The 'darkening of the sun and
moon' image, for example, may owe something to Ez.32.7-8, as well
as to Jl.2.10,31 and 3.15 as described above /153/. Bird believes
that Ezekiel (40 - end) has influenced Mark's presentation of
Jesus' ministry in several ways /154/ and J. Schniewind states,
for example, that the significance of the Cleansing of the Temple
must have been Messianic and corresponds to Jewish eschatological
expectation such as is found in Ezekiel 40 - 48 /155/. Bird in
particular (who sees an allusion to Ez.47 also in Mk.1.16-17; 'the
fishermen of the New Age') maintains, as we have seen, that Mark,
with his allusive $\gamma\acute{\alpha}\rho$-clause of 11.13d, is interpreting the
fig-tree incident by Ez.47.12. The tree, if it had been a
'faithful' tree, bearing fruit unceasingly, should have presented
such fruit to its Messiah. The idea is certainly an attractive
one, although the verbal links with Ez.47.12 are not close /156/.
The link may reside in the Messianic 'perennial fruitfulness'
expectation, however, which Mark and the early church may have
shared. The theme was present in connection with a number of other
'fig' passages that we have mentioned. Only along with these and

in this one respect, therefore, may Ez.47.12 have a bearing on the
Markan story.

The same conclusion applies to the last of the 'fig' passages
that we shall mention, viz, *Ct.2.13:*

> "The fig tree puts forth its figs,
> MT התאנה חנטה פגיה LXX ἡ συκῆ ἐξήνεγκεν
> ὀλύνθους αὐτῆς and the vines are in
> blossom."

Ct.2.13 has been described as "one of the loveliest descriptions of
spring in all literature" /157/. The putting forth (חנטה) of the
פגים is a sign that the summer is on its way. The passage was
later interpreted eschatologically, the blossoming of the fig-tree
being the precursor of the Messianic Age (Shir.R.II.13; cf. Mk.13.
28-32). Both Samuel Cohon and John Bowman, as we have noted in
chapter I, have linked Ct.2.13 directly with the Markan fig-tree
story. Cohon's view /158/ that Jesus' action was seen by the
evangelists as a Messianic portent that had to be fulfilled, viz,
the 'embalming' or drying up of the fig-tree, is extremely dubious
and hangs upon a questionable rendering of the word חנטה. Immanuel
Löw has stated that the word has nothing whatsoever to do with
embalming /159/. Bowman's opinion /160/, on the other hand, that
Jesus was blasting the Messianic hopes of the Jews of the time,
rests ultimately on the supposition that his action was understood
over against the Rabbinical exegesis of this *particular* passage, an
exegesis, moreover, that occurs in a late Jewish source (about the
end of the tenth century) /161/. For that reason his view is
doubtful, although it is not unlikely that Mark and the early
church did in fact share the more general expectation that the
Messianic Age would be an age of prodigious fruitfulness in which
the fig-tree would figure, and this contention we shall strengthen
when we come to consider both the late Jewish and the New
Testament evidence. The theme is not confined to either Ez.47.12
or Ct.2.13, however, but adheres to numerous Old Testament passages,
as we have seen, as well as to the late Jewish exegesis of these
passages. Song of Solomon itself appears on the whole to have
been disregarded by Mark and the early church, although in a later
period it came to be seen as an allegory of Christ and the
church.

Summation

Our attempt to bring the background of the Old Testament to bear on the Markan fig-tree story is now complete, and we can only hope that we have been able to avoid "speculation and fancy", and to have guarded ourselves against the danger highlighted by the late Professor Dodd that "associations of ideas arising in the critic's own mind have been treated as evidence for original connections". We have throughout sought to show tangible links between the 'fig' verses of the Old Testament and the passages and contexts in which they appear *and* the early church's actual employment of such scriptural passages, particularly the acquaintance and use of them on the part of Mark himself. In our general review of the fig-tree in the Old Testament, we have detected a discernible pattern of interrelated motifs and associations that were also perceived and highlighted within the specific context of five primary 'fig' passages (Jer.8.13 Is.28.3-4 Hos.9.10,16 Mi.7.1 Jl.1.7,12) and several supplementary passages (the Psalms Ez.17; 47 Zech.14 Ct.2.13) that we believe are more clearly linked with our story. The contexts of these passages were almost all employed regularly by the early church and Mark, and 'mined' for a number of themes common to them. Their association in the mind of the early church, therefore, may suggest that the fig verses themselves were also connected. While our examination has uncovered no firm evidence that any *one* verse may have been the starting-point for the story, we suggest that *in toto* they may have exercised a formative influence, and this probably prior to Mark. Mark may perhaps have received the story either in the form of a parable, or of a story, but this is a view we shall discuss in Chapter VII. Our ultimate concern is not with the question of origin, however, but with the way Mark has shaped traditional material to his purposes and with the meaning that was conveyed to his readers thereby.

What then would have been the images, concepts and associations that the Markan reader steeped in the Old Testament would have brought to the story? To sum up, we have seen that the fig was an emblem of peace, security and prosperity and is prominent when descriptions of the Golden Ages of Israel's history, past, present and future, are given - the Garden of Eden, the Exodus, the Wilderness, the Promised Land, the reigns of Solomon and Simon Maccabaeus and the coming Messianic Age. It figures predominantly in the prophetic books and very often in passages with an *eschatological* import. Common to these passages are the twin motifs of *blessing* and *judgement*. The blossoming of the fig-tree and *its giving of its fruits* is a descriptive element in passages which depict Yahweh's visiting his people with *blessing,* while *the withering of the fig-tree,* the destruction or withholding of its fruit, figures in imagery describing *Yahweh's judgement* upon his people or their enemies. The theme of judgement is, if anything, more pronounced in the prophetic books. Very often the reason given for God's wrathful visitation is cultic aberration on the part of Israel, her condemnation for *a corrupt Temple cultus and sacrificial system.* In some cases, indeed, the fig or fig-tree is not only associated with the twin motifs of blessing and judgement upon Israel, but can be used expressly as a symbol *for the nation itself,* in this respect, therefore, resembling the vine with which it is otherwise frequently connected.

We have also examined a number of other related OT themes that likewise throw light on the Markan story. We have noted that *the tree* in general is employed regularly as an image for the spiritual dimension of man and for the religious life of Israel in particular. Religious literature on the whole knows very little, in fact, of non-symbolical trees. The tree in the Old Testament may stand for the righteous and the wicked, but more often it is an image for *the nation itself,* its growth/blossoming or devastation/withering symbolizing the nation's fate. *Israel is God's tree or 'planting',* established in the Promised Land by his act of redemption, and watered and nourished (as long as she is faithful) by his grace.

We have seen, too, that the fertility of the land bears a direct relationship to the spiritual fruitfulness of the people, that where the people are faithful, the land, and particularly the trees, will flourish and bear fruit and that, conversely, where the people are faithless Yahweh will visit the land with a *curse.* God's curse, moreover is frequently actualized *through the blasting, withering or ravaging of the trees,* and especially of the vine and the fig-tree. Such an image may serve, we have suggested, to exhibit Yahweh's superior power, the tree having been worshipped in the ancient world as the home of gods and demons. The cultic veneration of the tree was long an active threat to Yahwism, the people persistently sacrificing, to the exasperation of the prophets, "on every high hill and under every green tree". Israel alone was God's 'sacred tree', his especial 'planting'.

Linked with this idea was the correlative notion that *the Temple Mount,* the high place par excellence, was the only legitimate sanctuary, the mountain of mountains upon which God's 'planting', Israel, could take root and flourish securely. The fertility of the land and of the trees, as well as the

fruitfulness of the people, rested ultimately on the maintenance
and wellbeing of the Temple and its cultus. The land would
blossom, the trees bear fruit, if the Temple were functioning as
it should. Cultic aberration, on the other hand, would bring a
curse upon the land, and destruction to Jerusalem and its
sanctuary. In *the End-time,* however, all other sanctuaries, high
places or *mountains* would be shaken, *moved* or brought low, but
Zion would be elevated. That age would see *abundant fruitfulness,*
the trees would bear fruit prodigiously, and the Temple would be
its source, with waters flowing from beneath its threshhold to
nourish the land.

     Who could doubt, then, the extraordinary impact that Jesus'
cursing of the fig-tree would have produced upon the Markan reader,
schooled to recognize symbolism wherever it occurred? Who could
doubt that a *solemn judgement* upon the nation was here being
proclaimed; and in this context *a judgement directed against a
corrupt Temple cultus*? The nation could expect no peace,
prosperity or security. The Lord whom they sought *had* suddenly
come to his Temple (cf. Mal.3.1 and Mk.1.2) but had condemned
rather than restored it! Elijah the prophet *had* been sent before
the great and terrible day of the Lord (Mal.4.5; cf. Mk.9.12) but
they had done to him whatever they pleased (Mk.9.13)! Therefore the
Lord would come and smite the land with a curse (Mal.4.6) and the
blow *had* been struck against the barren fig-tree! For Mark and
his readers the scenario had already been written in the pages of
the Old Testament, and in their actual experience Jerusalem and
the Temple had, in 70 CE, been utterly destroyed! God's plant,
Israel, had been withered. Within the very lifetime of Jesus
himself, the promised curse had commenced (Mk.11.14) and only after
a short delay (Mk.11.20-21) was its efficacy perceived. "This
mountain", which was to be elevated in the Messianic Age, was in
fact to be uprooted and cast into the sea! For the Markan reader
the cursing of the fig-tree was an eschatological sign prefiguring
the destruction of Jerusalem and its Temple. For Mark, it was a
commentary upon his own time.

NOTES

/1/   *Op.cit.* (1952), p.132.
/2/   *Vide supra,* pp.19 ff., 24.
/3/   For an appreciation of Dibelius' work, and particularly his
treatment of the role of the Old Testament in the formation of the
Passion narrative, see J.R. Donahue's *Are You the Christ?* pp.12-19.
/4/   *Op.cit.,* p.28. For a bibliography on 'the Use of the Old
Testament in the Gospels', see, for example, B.M. Metzger,*Index
to Periodical Literature on Christ and the Gospels,* pp.523-37.
/5/   *Op.cit.,* pp.107-8.
/6/   Cf. Barnabas Lindars, *New Testament Apologetic,* p.14, who
gives there a brief appraisal of Dodd's work in this area.
/7/   In focusing attention on these related primary and
secondary source *passages* that served as special 'quarries' for
texts or testimonia, Dodd hereby discounted the hypothesis of Rendel
Harris that there was a primitive anthology or testimony-book of
isolated, arbitrarily selected *proof-texts* underlying the New
Testament tradition. "The composition of 'testimony-books' was the
result, not the presupposition, of the work of early Christian
biblical scholars," he declared. Selections were made
principally from Isaiah, Jeremiah, certain of the Minor Prophets,
and the Psalms, and the verses quoted were meant to conjure up the
total context of these passages. See Dodd, *op.cit.,* pp.126-7.
/8/   *Op.cit.,* p.28.
/9/   *Ibid.*
/10/   See Lindars, *Apologetic,* esp. chap.I, and Donahue, *Are You
the Christ?,* pp.15, 76 and fn.3.
/11/   Cf. K. Stendahl, *The School of St. Matthew,* and esp. pp.183-
202, where Stendahl compares Matthew's formula quotations with the
pesher method of quoting scripture illustrated in the Habakkuk
Commentary. *Vide supra,* p.85, n.15.
/12/   F.C. Grant, for example, (*IDB,* 'Matthew, Gospel of', pp.
306-7, 311) specifically termed part of Matthew's peculiar
material Christian "midrash" or "haggadah" - the imaginative
elaboration, in story form, of a striking text or series of
texts - and points, inter alia, to numerous examples in the birth,
passion and resurrection narratives of his gospel.
        M.D. Goulder in his *Midrash and Lection in Matthew,* goes
even further, and, combining a lectionary theory with a strong
emphasis on Matthew's midrashic creativity, holds that the first
gospel was the work of a 'scribe' who had only Mark before him and
who has expounded Mark in standard Jewish ways.
/13/   An example elsewhere in the gospel is furnished by J.R.
Donahue, who argues that the scene at the Trial, where Jesus faces

the testimony of false witnesses, has come straight from the pages
of the Old Testament (Ps.27.12, LXX; Ps.35.11, LXX).   See *Are You
the Christ?*, pp.71 ff.
/14/   *Vide supra*, pp.21-2.
/15/   *Vide supra*, pp.20-1.   More recently, Howard Clark Kee has made
a detailed examination of the scriptural allusions in the latter
half of Mark's gospel.   His article refers to the earlier work of
scholars such as A. Suhl (who limited himself to scriptural links
which corresponded to a known text and reproduced a text in a
known sequence) and S. Schulz (who aimed to demonstrate that Mark
had used scripture to undergird a particular kerygmatic affirmation
about Jesus).   Kee argues, however, that Mark's own oblique
allusions should also be considered, in view of the freedom
exhibited (in modification and arrangement of scriptural material)
by the Qumran scriptural method.   See "The Function of Scriptural
Quotations and Allusions in Mark 11 - 16" in *Jesus und Paulus*, Fs.
W.G. Kümmel, ed. E.E. Ellis, E. Grässer, pp.165-88.
/16/   *Vide supra*, pp.8,23-4.
/17/   For *works dealing with the fig or fig-tree in general*, see:
G.B. Winer, *Biblisches Realwoerterbuch* - henceforth *BRW*(Winer) -
3rd edn., Vol.I, 'Feigenbaum' ad loc.; *Handwörterbuch des biblischen
Altertums*, ed. E.C.A. Riehm - henceforth *HBA*(Riehm) - Vol.I,
'Feigenbaum' ad loc.; I.G.A. Benzinger, *Realencyklopädie für
protestantische Theologie und Kirche*, 3rd edn., ed. J.J. Herzog,
A. Hauck - henceforth *PRE*(Herzog-Hauck) - Vol.VI, 'Fruchtbäume in
Palästina' ad loc.; Hunzinger, *ThDNT*, 7, συκῆ ad loc.; *Real-
Encyclopädie des Judentums*, ed. J. Hamburger - henceforth *RE*(Ham-
burger) - Vol.I, 'Feige' ad loc.; F. Olck, *Real-Encyclopädie der
classischen Altertumswissenschaft*, ed. A. Pauly, G. Wissowa -
henceforth *RE*(Pauly-Wissowa) - Vol.VI, 'Feige' ad loc.; S. Klein,
"Weinstock, Feigenbaum und Sykomore in Palästina", in *Festschrift.
Adolf Schwarz*, ed. S. Krauss, pp.389-402; F. Goldmann, *La Figue en
Palestine à l'époque de la Mischna*; Löw, *Flora*, I, pp.224-54;
Dalman, *Arbeit*, passim; V. Reichmann, *Reallexikon für Antike und
Christentum*, ed. T. Klauser - henceforth *RAC* - Vol.7, 'Feige'
ad loc.; J. Feliks, *EJud*, 6, 'Fig' ad loc.; H. Graf zu Solms-Laubach,
*Die Herkunft, Domestication und Verbreitung des gewöhnlichen
Feigenbaums* - henceforth *Solms-Laubach*; Post, *DB*, 2, 'Figs' ad loc.;
Bacon, *DCG*, 1, 'Fig-Tree' ad loc.
/18/   See, for example, Dalman, *Arbeit*, I, pp.378-9, 506.
/19/   Cf. Nm.13.23; 20.5 Dt.8.8 Jgs.9.10-13 1 Kgs.4.25
2 Kgs.18.31 Ps.105.33 Ct.2.13 Is.34.4 Jer.5.17; 8.13 Hos.2.12;
9.10 Jl.1.7,12; 2.22 Am.4.9 Mi.4.4 Hab.3.17-18 Hag.2.19
Zech.3.10 1 Mc.14.12.
        This association extends further than the fact that they were

two of the principal fruit-bearing trees. Figs and vines were
often cultivated together, and Dalman records that there were
fig-trees in almost every vineyard, often with vines actually
climbing freely among their branches (cf. Lk.13.6-9). See Dalman,
Arbeit, I, pp.161, 378; IV, pp.315-16, 327-8; M. Noth,*The Old
Testament World,* p.36; Goldmann, *Figue,* p.3, fn.4; contr. Derrett,
HeythJ, 14 (1973) pp.262-3.

/20/   *EJud,* 6, p.1272.

/21/   Cf. *Solms-Laubach,* p.77. For the history and territorial
extent of the fig-tree's cultivation, see also: *RE*(Pauly-Wissowa),
VI, pp.2100-3, 2118-9; Löw, *Flora*, I, pp.224-36; Klein, *op. cit.,*
pp.396 ff.; *RAC*, 7, pp.640-3.

/22/   For our previous discussion on the relevance of the growth
cycle and bearing seasons of the fig-tree for our story, *vide supra*
pp.3 ff., and esp. n.16.

/23/   Cf. e.g. Is.28.4 Jer.24.2 Hos.9.10 Mi.7.1 Na.3.12.

/24/   Cf. 1 Sm.25.18; 30.12 2 Kgs.20.7 = Is.38.21 1 Chr.12.40,
and see Löw, *Flora*, I, p.244; Goldmann, *Figue*, pp.35-8 and *RE*
(Pauly-Wissowa), VI, p.2136.

/25/   Sweet cakes made from raisins and from figs were favourite
offerings to the gods in the Graeco-Roman religions (see, for
example, *RE*(Pauly-Wissowa), VI, p.2149; J. Murr, *Die Pflanzenwelt
in der griechischen Mythologie,* p.33) and there is some evidence
that their use was a feature of Israelite worship too, especially
at the popular level (cf. e.g. 2 Sm.6.17-19 1 Chr.16.1-3 Is.16.7
Jer.7.18; 44.19 Hos.3.1 Am.4.4-5). See W. Robertson Smith,
The Old Testament in the Jewish Church (1881), Lecture XI, Note 7,
p.434; H.W. Wolff, *Dodekapropheton.1. Hosea* (BK, XIV.1), Hos.3.1
ad loc., p.76.

/26/   See *RE*(Pauly-Wissowa), VI, pp.2135-7.

/27/   *BRW*(Winer), I, p.367; *RE*(Pauly-Wissowa), VI, pp.2138-42;
Löw, *Flora*, I, p.254.

/28/   This age-old remedy was known also to Pliny (cf. H.N. XXIII,
117-30). See also C.F.A. Schaeffer, *The Cuneiform Texts of Ras
Shamra-Ugarit,* p.41; J. Gray, *I & II Kings,* p.698; Goldmann, *Figue,*
p.40 and fn.3.

/29/   The Old Testament also makes reference to the word קַיִץ, which
the RSV usually translates as 'summer fruit(s)'. While originally
connoting the summer harvesting period, and hence the fruits
harvested then, qayiṣ primarily signifies the fig-harvest, and
hence 'figs' (or more particularly 'dried figs'). Cf. 2 Sm.16.1-2
Is.16.9 Jer.40.10,12; 48.32 Am.8.1-2 Mi.7.1 Jdt.10.5; and see
BRW(Winer), I, p.367, fn.3; Goldmann, *Figue,* p.14; Löw, *Flora,* I,
pp.239-40; *EJud*, 6, p.1273.

The "honey out of the rock" of Dt.32.13 and Ps.81.16 apparently refers also to the honey of figs, since the fig-tree was

noted for its ability to grow in rocky places (cf. e.g. P.Ber.IX.3,
Schwab, p.166). In later times the "honey" in the expression "a
land flowing with milk and honey" was likewise associated with
the honey of figs (cf. B.Ket.111b).
/30/   The sexual significance of the fig and its various parts
was especially strong in the Graeco-Roman world. See, for example,
V. Buchheit, "Feigensymbolik im antiken Epigramm", *RheinMus*, 103
(1960), pp.200-29; R. Eisler, *Orphisch-dionysische Mysteriengedanken
in der christlichen Antike*, p.108 and fn.5; A.B. Cook, ΣΥΚΟΦΑΝΤΗΣ,
CR, 21 (1907), pp.134-6. It is worth noting, however, that apart
from the possible link here between the fig leaf and the notion of
sexual shame, the Old Testament appears to know or recognize
little of the fig's erotic, and particularly phallic, symbolism.
Cf. *RAC*, 7, p.658; *RE*(Pauly-Wissowa), VI, p.2146.
/31/   Dalman, *Arbeit*, IV, p.161; J.G. Frazer, *The Golden Bough*,
II, p.316.
/32/   See, for example, A. Jeremias, *The Old Testament in the
light of the Ancient East*, Vol.I, chap.V, but esp. p.209; *vide
infra*, p.190.
/33/   *Infra*, pp.190-1. Already in the Old Testament the belief is
expressed that in the wilderness period God's grace had been
operative and that he had strengthened and succoured his people
(cf. e.g. Dt.32.7-14 Hos.2.14-15; 9.10; 12.9; 13.5). Nature had
been responsive to their needs and signs and wonders had been
performed on their behalf, especially through Moses and Aaron
(cf. e.g. Ex.15.22 ff., the tree cast into the water makes the
waters of Marah sweet; Ex.19.16 ff., the mountain that quakes;
Nm.17.8 ff., the rod of Aaron that sprouts; Nm.20.2 ff., the rock
that gushes water; etc.).
/34/   *Infra*, p.178. The association of the fig with the
"honey" in the expression "a land flowing with milk and honey" has
already been noted, *supra*, n.29.
/35/   Cf. Holtzmann ("Rasches Hinsterben und Welken der Blätter
oder Unfruchtbarkeit des Feigenbaumes symbolisiren Israels Unglück"),
HC, I, p.233; Bacon, *DCG*, 1, p.593 ("the girdled fig-tree an OT
emblem of the punishment of Israel"); Robin, *NTS*, 8 (1961-2),
p.279; Dowda, *Cleansing*, pp.223-4; *RAC*, 7, p.658 ("Wo Unglück
ausgemalt wird, wird daher auch Unfruchtbarkeit, Wegnahme oder
Zerstörung der F. erwähnt").
/36/   *Supra*, n.29.
/37/   See Löw, *Flora*, I, p.240; *RAC*, 7, p.659; cf. also Mk.13.28-
29 and *infra*, p.243, n.42.
/38/   *Supra*, p.23; cf. also p.19.
/39/   Pesikta Rabbati II, transl. W.G. Braude (New Haven/London,
1968), pp.656-7, *gratia* Derrett, *HeythJ*, 14 (1973), p.257.

/40/   *Supra*, p.37, n.138.
/41/   *JTS*(NS), 5 (1954), pp.206-7.
/42/   *Supra*, pp.132-3 and n.19.
/43/   See Holtzmann, *HC*, I, p.233; Carpenter, *Three Gospels*, p.157.
/44/   See, for example, T. Fawcett, *Hebrew Myth and Christian Gospel*, p.270.
/45/   According to Dalman, the ever-fruitful tree mentioned in both Ps.1.3 and Jer.17.8 as an image for the righteous man "ist am ehesten der Feigenbaum" (*Arbeit,* I, pp.100-1).
        For Ps.Sol.14.1-3, see the text and translation edited by H.E. Ryle and M.R. James (Cambridge: University Press, 1891), pp.111-13.
/46/   See Fawcett, *op.cit.*, p.276; Lohmeyer, "Von Baum und Frucht", *ZSTh,* 9 (1932), pp.377-97; Dowda, *Cleansing*, p.223, and the article by J.P. Brown, "The Mediterranean Vocabulary of the Vine", *VT,* 19 (1969), pp.146-70, cited there.
        The vine appearing in the chief butler's dream (Gn.40.9-11) was identified with 'Israel' by R. Jeremiah b. Abba (B.Ḥul.92a), although it is of note that a number of other identifications were also made by the Rabbis in that passage (the vine is the world, the Torah, Jerusalem, etc.).
/47/   See Münderlein, *NTS*, 10 (1963-4), p.100; Cousin, *Foi et Vie* (May, 1971), p.87.
        In Est.R.IX.2 a whole variety of trees, offering themselves as wood for Haman's cross, are said to be representative of Israel. The figure can also in some cases extend itself to other nations such as Egypt (cf. Ez.31, Pharoah = cedar) or Babylon (cf.Dn.4.4 ff., Nebuchadnezzar = a great tree).
/48/   Cf. Münderlein, *ibid,* and esp. fn.3; Cousin, *op.cit.*, p.90.
/49/   Cf. e.g. Ps.105.33 Is.24.6,7 Jer.6.6; 7.20 Hos.2.12 Am.4.9; cf. also Is.5.5-7; 11.4 Jl.1.6-7,11-12 Am.5.16-17 Mal.4.6. For further references to the eschatological curse that devours the land, see R.M. Grant, *JBL,* 67 (1948), p.300.
/50/   MT נבל or יבש, LXX ξηραίνω; cf. e.g. Jer.8.13 Hos.9.16 Jl.1.12.
/51/   Jb.8.12-13 Ps.37.1-2; 129.6; cf. also Sir.40.15 Mal.4.1.
/52/   Is.40.23-24; cf. also Lam.4.8 Sir.10.15 Ez.31.esp.5-6, 10 ff. Dn.4. esp.11-15. In these latter two passages (both of which have echoes in the NT: cf. e.g. Ez.31.5-6 and Dn.4.12,21 with Mk.4.30-32 and parallels) the fate of the tree is to be cut down rather than withered (cf. Lk.13.6-9).
/53/   Jb.14.2 Ps.90.5-6; 102.11 Is.40.6-8; 51.12, and see Münderlein, *op.cit.*, pp.100-1.
/54/   See, for example, Fawcett, *Myth,* p.269.
/55/   See E.R. Goodenough, *Jewish Symbols in the Greco-Roman period*, VII, pp.91 ff.; VIII, pp.140-1.

/56/   *Les Représentations de l'Arbre Sacré sur les Monuments de Mésopotamie et d'Élam* (Babyloniaca, ed. Ch. Virolleaud, Vol.17, 1937), p.19.

/57/   W. Robertson Smith, *Lectures on the Religion of the Semites* (1889), pp.169-80;,Fawcett, *Myth*, p.270.

/58/   Cf. B. Pes.111b and *RAC*, 7, p.664. A similar attitude has persisted even until recent times among Palestinians. Trees are regarded in some quarters still as inhabited by malignant spirits, and Dalman records, for example, that Arabs are wary of sleeping under the fig-tree for that very reason (*Arbeit*, I, p.57). Mrs. Grace Crowfoot and Miss Louise Baldensperger, with a wide experience of life in Palestine, report the fig-tree also as belonging to that group of trees considered uncanny, dangerous and very much to be feared (*From Cedar to Hyssop*, pp.106-7).

/59/   Cf. e.g. Gn.12.6 Dt.11.30 Jgs.9.37 Hos.4.12-13.

/60/   A.J. Wensinck, *Tree and Bird as cosmological symbols in Western Asia* (VAA, XXII, 1921), p.33; Robertson Smith, *Semites*, pp.169-80.

/61/   This fact led an idolater according to Bem.R.XII.4 (cf. also Shir.R.III.10.2) to pose the following question to R. Gamaliel: "'Why did the Holy One, blessed be He, reveal Himself to Moses out of a bush?' The other replied, 'If He had appeared on a carob-tree or on a fig-tree you would have asked me a similar question. I must not, however, let you go unanswered. It serves to teach you that there is no spot unoccupied by the Shekinah, and that He would communicate with Moses even from a bush.'" (Sonc., p.465).

/62/   Goodenough suggests that the especially mentioned presence of trees (palm-trees) in Solomon's Temple (cf. 1 Kgs.6.29,32,35; 7.36) was hardly for "pure decoration", and that they had probably a symbolic force (*Jewish Symbols*, VII, p.93, 125). They appear again in Ezekiel's Temple vision (Ez.40.16,22,26,31; 41.18-26; cf. 47.12). For later legends concerning the blossoming and withering of the trees in Solomon's Temple, *vide infra*, pp.191-2.

Trees and fruit also played an important role in the Jewish Feast of Tabernacles (cf. Lv.23.40 Neh.8.15), a festival in which Plutarch, for example, recognized many Bacchanalian elements and which he surmised therefore was connected with the cult of Dionysus (one of whose symbols was the fig/fig-tree). See A. Schalit, *EJud*, 6, 'Dionysus, Cult of' ad loc.

A certain hard-headed and realistic attitude, however, to the status of trees remains characteristic, in general, of the Old Testament, as also of late Judaism. Their economic value as food weighs against their needless destruction on the one hand (cf. Dt.20.19-20) and their excessive veneration on the other.

On the whole, as Fawcett has stated, the tree in Israel "came to
be de-divinized so completely that it could be identified with
Israel herself" (*Myth*, p.270).

/63/   See J. Schneider, *ThDNT*, 5, ξύλον ad loc., p.37; W. Foerster,
ThDNT, 5, ὄρος ad loc., and cf. e.g. 1 Kgs.14.23 2 Kgs.16.4;
17.10 2 Chr.28.4 Is.1.29; 57.5 Jer.2.20-21; 3.6,13; 17.2-3
Ez.6.13; 20.28-29 Hos.4.12-13. In these passages, the recurrent
refrain "on every high hill and under every green tree" or "on
the high places, and on the hills, and under every green tree"
is frequently heard. This link between the tree and the high
place or mountain (cf. esp. Is.2.12-14 Jer.17.2-3 Ez.6.13
Hos.4.13) is particularly suggestive when considered in the
light of our previous examination (chap.IV) of the tree- and
mountain-uprooting logia of Mk.11.23 and parallels. Might it be
that the uprooting of tree or mountain carried with it originally
a cultic overtone, a note that expressed the conviction that
faith in the God of Israel would remove the heathen places of
worship (cf. B.'A.Z.45a-47a B.Sanh.55a)? If so, this would
support our contention that Mark understood "this mountain" to
refer to the Temple Mount, a cultic centre to be considered no
greater than a heathen high place and to be swept into the sea
before the growing faith of the gospel movement.

/64/   In a recent book, Hyam Maccoby, for example, makes the
following unusual but interesting suggestion:

    "The reason for Jesus's angry reaction is probably this:
the Hebrew Prophets had foretold that the time of the Messiah
would be one of unprecedented fertility of plants and animals
(e.g. Joel ii.22: '...the fig-tree and the vine do yield their
strength'). Jesus, with his Galilean belief in evil spirits,
may have thought that the fig-tree contained an evil spirit that
was fighting against the kingdom of God." - *Revolution in Judaea.
Jesus and the Jewish Resistance*, p.176.

/65/   Later exegesis of Ps.78.54 clearly brings out that by
"the mountain" the Temple was understood. "The *Temple* is one
possession [one of God's four possessions in the world, the other
three being the Torah, heaven and earth and Israel], for it is
written, *'This mountain'* [sc. the Temple Mount], which His right
hand had acquired (Ps.78.54)'." - B.Pes.87b (Sonc., p.461,
italics mine; cf. also B.Git.56b and *infra*, p.204, n.84).

/66/   See Ps.46.2-5 Is.40.4; 45.2; 49.11; 54.10 Zech.4.7;
14.4,10; cf. also Ps.Sol.11.esp.vv.5,7 1Bar.5.7-8.

/67/   For the popular expectation that the Temple Mount would be
elevated in the Messianic Age and all other mountains or high
places abased, see Fawcett, *Myth*, p.173; Foerster, *ThDNT*, 5,
pp.481, 483, 486.

/68/   See Dowda, *Cleansing*, pp.155-7.

/69/   See Jl.3.18 Zech.14.8; cf. also Ps.46.4.
/70/   Cf. e.g. Is.35 Jer.31.12 Ez.34.27; 36.8-11,29-30,35 Am.
9.13 Zech.8.12, and see Grant, *JBL,* 67 (1948), pp.299-300; Hiers,
JBL, 87 (1968), pp.395-6; Derrett, *HeythJ,* 14 (1973), pp.253 ff.;
Dowda, *Cleansing,* pp.155-7.
/71/   The LXX Greek of the Prophets is as per *Septuaginta* (SLG,
Vols.13-16, ed. J. Ziegler, 1939-57); the Massoretic text is as
given by *Biblia Hebraica*³, ed. R. Kittel. The English translation
follows the RSV.
/72/   See, for example, W.K. Lowther Clarke, *Concise Bible
Commentary,* ad loc. (henceforth *CBC*).
/73/   Cf. B.Ta'an.29a-30b and *EJR,* 'Av, Ninth of', ad loc.
/74/   *EJR, ibid.*
/75/   Cf. e.g.*1.5* and Gal.1.15; *1.8* and Acts 18.9-10; *1.10* and
Ap.10.11; *5.21* and Mk.8.17-18 Mt.13.10-15; *6.16* and Mt.11.29; *7.11*
and Mk.11.17 Mt.21.13 Lk.19.46; *7.34* and Ap.18.23; *9.24* and
1 Cor.1.31 2 Cor.10.17; *9.26* and Acts 7.51; *10.25* and 1 Thes.4.5
Ap.16.1.
/76/   *Scriptures,* pp.86-7.
/77/   *NTS,* 1 (1954-5), pp.301-2.
/78/   *Scriptures,* p.107.
/79/   Cf. Dodd, *Scriptures,* p.38; Lindars, *Apologetic,* pp.162,166,
167 and fn.1.
/80/   *Mark,* p.299; cf. also Münderlein, *NTS,* 10 (1963-4), p.101.
/81/   Hiers, *JBL,* 87 (1968), p.394, fn.3.
/82/   *BZ,* 20 (1976), p.104. See also E. Schweizer, *Das Evangelium
nach Markus,* p.131 (cited by Giesen), who thinks that Jer.8.13
furnishes the nearest parallel in the OT to Mark's story.
/83/   *Supra,* pp.21-2. H.C. Kee, however, cites Jer.7.25 as having
had some influence on Mk.12.2 (*Jesus und Paulus,* p.168).
/84/   See Lowther Clarke, *CBC,* ad loc.
/85/   Cf. e.g. *24.8* and Ap.18.22; *25.8* and 1 Cor.15.54 Ap.7.17;
21.4; *26.11* and Heb.10.27; *26.20* and Heb.10.37 (Lindars,*Apologetic,*
p.231); *27.9* and Rom.11.27; *27.13* and Mt.24.31 1 Cor.15.52
1 Thes.4.16; *28.11-12* and 1 Cor.14.21; *28.16* and Rom.9.33; 10.11
1 Pt.2.6; *29.10* and Rom.11.8; *29.13-14* and Mt.15.8-9 Mk.7.6-7
1 Cor.1.19; *29.18-19* and Mt.11.5; *34.4* and Ap.6.13-14; *34.9-10* and
Ap.19.3; *35.3* and Heb.12.12; *35.5-6* and Mt.11.5 Lk.7.22.
/86/   See Lindars, *Apologetic,* pp.164, 175.
/87/   Dodd, *Scriptures,* pp.41-3; Lindars, *Apologetic,* pp.175-83.
/88/   *Scriptures,* p.107.
/89/   Dodd, *ibid.*
/90/   Dodd, *Scriptures,* pp.83-4; Lindars, *Apologetic,* pp.164-7.
/91/   Cf. e.g. *24.8* and Ap.18.22; *28.12* and Mt.11.29 (cf. Jer.6.16);
29.18-19 and *35.5-6* and Mk.7.37 Mt.11.5 Lk.7.22.

/92/   Cf. e.g.*25.8* and 1 Cor.15.54 Ap.7.17;21.4.
/93/   Cf. e.g.*26.11* and Heb.10.27 (Lindars, *Apologetic,* pp.230-1);
34.4 and Ap.6.13-14 (leaves from the fig-tree); *34.9-10* and Ap.19.3.
/94/   Cf. *27.13* and Mt.24.31 1 Cor.15.52 1 Thes.4.16.
/95/   *Jesus und Paulus,* p.168.
/96/   *Op.cit.,* p.169.
/97/   Is there a faint echo here once more of the קיץ/קץ pun (cf.
Am.8.2 Jer.8.20)? *Vide supra,* p.135. The LXX has πρόδρομος σύκου.
For the exact meaning of this term, see *ThDNT,* 7, p.751, fn.3; *RE*
(Pauly-Wissowa), VI, pp.2105 ff.; *RAC,* 7, p.641.
/98/   For comment on the usage of this uncommon word, see J. Ziegler
Septuaginta. Duodecim Prophetae, pp.48, 95 and *ThDNT,* 7, p.751, fn.4.
/99/   See Lowther Clarke,*CBC,* p.589.
/100/   *Scriptures,* pp.74-8, esp.78.
/101/   Cf. e.g. 1.6,9,10; 2.1,23 with Rom.9.25-26 1 Pt.2.10, and
see Dodd, *Scriptures,* p.75; Lindars, *Apologetic,* pp.242-3.
/102/   `Dodd, *Scriptures,* p.77.
/103/   *Supra,* pp.143-4,146.
/104/   Cf. Mt.9.13; 12.7 and Dodd, *Scriptures,* p.77; Lindars,
Apologetic, p.62, and Stendahl, *Matthew,* pp.128-9.
/105/   *Supra,* p.143.
/106/   *Scriptures,* p.76.
/107/   Dodd, *ibid.*
/108/   See Dodd, *Scriptures,* p.77; Lindars, *Apologetic,* pp.60-6.
A three-day schema is connected not only with Jesus' resurrection
but recurs curiously in a number of other puzzling passages; with
the Temple logion of Mk.14.58 and parallels, for example, in Lk.
13.32-33 (a lament for Jerusalem passage) and in Mark's
chronological scheme in chapter 11, as we have seen.
/109/   Cf. the celebrated *11.1* ("out of Egypt I called my son") and
Mt.2.15 (for comment, see Dodd, *Scriptures,* p.75; Lindars,
Apologetic, pp.216-17; Stendahl, *Matthew,* p.101); *12.8* and
Ap.3.17; *14.2* and Heb.13.15 and possibly also *6.9-10; 7.1* with Mk.
11.17, Jn.10.8, or the parable of the good Samaritan (Lindars,
Apologetic, p.62).
/110/   *Jesus und Paulus,* p.168.
/111/   Holtzmann, for example, *HC,* I, p.232, thinks that both
Hos.9.10 and Mi.7.1 were influences in the conversion of the Lukan
parable into the fig-tree story, but does not develop this further
(cf. also Klostermann, *Markusevangelium,* p.116; Bultmann, *History,*
pp.230-1; contr. *ThDNT,* 7, p.757, fn.52).
/112/   Cf. Münderlein, *NTS,* 10 (1963-4), p.101 and fn.1.
/113/   ... εἶδον πατέρας αὐτῶν ... (Hos.9.10); cf. ἰδὼν συκῆν
(Mk.11.13) ... εἶδον τὴν συκῆν (Mk.11.20) ... ἴδε ἡ συκῆ
(Mk.11.22).

/114/ ... εὖρον τὸν Ισραηλ ... (Hos.9.10); cf. ... εἰ ἄρα τι εὑρήσει ... οὐδὲν εὗρεν (Mk.11.13).

/115/ Bruno Bauer, it should be noted, believed that Mark had made this remark (11.13d) precisely on account of Hos.9.10. See Meyer-Dickson, I, p.178, and cf. also Kee,Jesus und Paulus, p.167.

/116/ The LXX lacks "no first-ripe fruit which my soul desires" and has οὐχ ὑπάρχοντος βότρυος τοῦ φαγεῖν τὰ πρωτόγονα. οἴμμοι, ψυχη,ὅτι κτλ.

/117/ See Lowther Clarke, CBC, ad loc.

/118/ See Mt.2.6 Jn.7.42 and Lindars, Apologetic, pp.192-4; Stendahl, Matthew, pp.99-101; cf. also Mi.7.20 and Lk.1.55.

/119/ See below, and cf. also Mi.5.1 (and Is.50.6) with Mk.14.65 (Kee, Jesus und Paulus, p.170).

/120/ ET, 73 (1961-2), p.191.

/121/ Jesus und Paulus, p.169.

/122/ NTS, 8 (1961-2), p.280; cf. M.Sot.9.9,15.

/123/ Kee thinks that Mi.3.12, along with Jer.26.6,18, is in fact being alluded to here (Jesus und Paulus, p.168).

/124/ Scriptures, pp.46-8, 62-4, 107; cf. also Lindars, Apologetic, pp.36-8.

/125/ Cf. e.g. 1.6 and Ap.9.8; 2.4-5 and Ap.9.7,9; 2.10 and Ap.9.2; 2.11 and Ap.6.17; 2.28-32 and Acts 2.17-21; 2.31 and Mk.13.24 Lk.21.25 Mt.24.29 Ap.6.12; 9.2; 2.32 and Acts 2.39 Rom.10.13; 3.13 and Mk.4.29 Ap.14.15,18,19; 3.18 and Ap.22.1.

/126/ Cf. e.g. Rom.9.20 and Is.29.16; 9.25 and Hos.2.23; 9.26 and Hos.1.10; 9.27 and Hos.1.10; 9.33 and Is.28.16; 11.8 and Is.29.10; 11.27 and Is.27.9; see Dodd, Scriptures, pp.47-8.

/127/ Cf. also Is.13.10; 34.4 (leaves from the fig-tree) Ez.32.7-8 and Kee, Jesus und Paulus, p.169. Mk.13.19 should also be compared with Jl.2.3.

/128/ Cf. also Ap.14.15,18,19 and Stendahl, Matthew, p.144.

/129/ Cf. 1.10 ... ἐξηράνθη οἶνος, ὠλιγώθη ἔλαιον; 1.11 ἐξηράνθησαν οἱ γεωργοί ...; 1.12 ἡ ἄμπελος ἐξηράνθη, καὶ αἱ συκαῖ ὠλιγώθησαν ... πάντα τὰ ξύλα ... ἐξηράνθησαν; 1.16 ... βρώματα ἐξῄρθη/ἐξηράνθη (v.l.); 1.17 ... ἐξηράνθη σῖτος.

/130/ NTS, 8 (1961-2), p.279.

/131/ According to Löw, the expression ḳĕṣāfā should properly be read as (brought) 'to mourning' or 'to grief', in line with the Palestinian-Aramaic ḳĕṣāfā that is here, he thinks, in view (Flora, I, p.228).

/132/ The Hebrew אמל (Pul) can mean 'to dry up, wither' as well as 'grow weak', but the usual withering verbs are יבש or נבל.

/133/ Supra, pp.56-7.

/134/ Mark, p.241.

/135/ Ps.36.35-36 in the LXX; cf. Septuaginta Gottingensis. Psalmi cum Odis, ed. A. Rahlfs (1931).

/136/ Mark, ibid.

/137/ See Dodd, Scriptures, esp. pp.31-6, 96-103, 108.

/138/ Cf. e.g. Mk.11.9-10 and Ps.118.25-26; 12.10-11 and Ps.118.
22-23; 12.36 and Ps.110.1; 14.18 and Ps.41.9; 15.24 and Ps.22.18;
15.29 and Pss.22.7; 109.25; 15.34 and Ps.22.1; 15.36 and Ps.69.21.

/139/ Septuaginta (1935), ed. A. Rahlfs, II, ad loc. Cf.
Holtzmann, HC, I, p.235; Münderlein, NTS, 10 (1963-4), p.101.

/140/ See Swete, Mark, p.259; Lohmeyer, Markus, p.238, fn.2.

/141/ See Cranfield Mark, p.360. As a result, some scholars
(e.g. Grundmann, Münderlein, Giesen) have suggested that this
datum points yet again to the symbolic dimension of the story, for
such withering "from the roots" could not have been visible to the
naked eye.

/142/ Supra, pp.140-1.

/143/ Cf. Mk.1.6 and Zech.13.4; 6.34 and Zech.10.2; 10.27 and
Zech.8.6 (LXX); 13.27 and Zech.2.6,10; 14.24 and Zech.9.11;
14.27,50 and Zech.13.7. For chapter 11, a list of parallels is
given in Grant's article, but see also that of C. Roth (supra,
pp.19-20).

/144/ The LXX here apparently mistranslates עלהו, "their leaves",
as "upon it", ἐπ' αὐτοῦ.

/145/ Lowther Clarke, CBC, p.567.

/146/ CBC, p.577.

/147/ Dalman, Arbeit, I, p.101; Bacon, DCG, 1, p.592.

/148/ See Bird, JTS, 4 (1953), p.176.

/149/ Cf. Dodd, Scriptures, p.84.

/150/ R.M. Grant (who thinks that Ez.47.12 lies behind Mark's
story) has even suggested that the Revelation passage (22.2-3),
in combining Ezek.47.12 with Zech.14.11 ('no more curse'),
represents the earliest Christian exegesis of the fig-tree story
(JBL, 67 (1948), p.299; cf. also Bird, op.cit., p.179). While
this is an intriguing possibility, on the whole it seems more
likely that the two Ezekiel and Zechariah passages were linked
via the 'living waters' motif (cf. Zech.14.8). There is little
else in Ap.22.1-5 to suggest that Mark's fig-tree story is being
alluded to.
        One may also compare Ez.47 with Jn.7.38 and chapter 21,
where echoes of the former may be in view (cf. Bird, op.cit., p.176,
citing the view of Hoskyns).

/151/ Supra, pp.143-4,146.

/152/ Cf. Mk.13.8 with Ez.5.12; 13.24 with Ez.32.7-8; 13.27 with
Ez.32.9-10 (inter alia);13.31 with Ez.13.1 ff.; cf. also Mk.12.35b
with Ez.34.23-24; 37.24 (inter alia);Mk.14.36 with Ez.23.31-34
and Kee, Jesus und Paulus, pp.168-70.

/153/ Supra, p.154.

/154/   *Op.cit.*, p.176.
/155/   *Markus*, p.150.
/156/   While the MT uses נבל, to wither, for example, the LXX does not employ ξηραύνω and other links are non-existent.
/157/   Lowther Clarke, *CBC*, p.516.
/158/   *Supra*, p.19.
/159/   *Flora*, I, p.229, fn.2.
/160/   *Supra*, p.23.
/161/   See Dowda, *Cleansing*, p.225.

176

Chapter VI

THE LATE JEWISH BACKGROUND

Introduction

In our last chapter we brought the Old Testament to bear on the fig-tree pericope, and we attempted to show how a first-century reader steeped in that background would most naturally have interpreted the story. The Old Testament and its interpretation is not, however, a static thing. Exegesis alters and develops over time, and it is important, therefore, to look at the late Jewish background in order to ascertain how far the associations mapped out in the Old Testament with regard to the fig-tree can be seen to have remained the same, at a later date, or to have developed. The study of this material will serve, we maintain, to strengthen the impressions and conclusions gained in chapter V, and will be of great interest in determining not only the variety but also the limits of the associations and symbolism that the fig/fig-tree and related themes carried in the Jewish mind.

In this chapter, then, we shall explore these themes. The thorny question of the dating of this material is often raised but we should remark that, for our purposes, the determining of precise chronology is not as pressing as it might be for studies of a different kind. Our aim is merely to construct a nexus of associated ideas and motifs within the interrelated literature of the Old Testament, New Testament and late Jewish 'worlds', such that the relevant elements of their common Weltanschauung are revealed. The examination of each area will provide checks on the other. The persistence in the late Jewish period of certain ideas and beliefs discernible in the Old Testament will make it reasonable to assume that they held sway in the New Testament period also, and our examination of the New Testament evidence (chapter VII) will bear this out. All three areas, we believe, can furnish insights to illuminate the Markan story.

The Estimation of the Fig-Tree in the Rabbinical Literature /1/

The fig-tree was one of the most characteristic, most fruitful and most important trees of Israel in Talmudic times /2/, as is evidenced by the fact that more than seventy expressions connected with the fig occur in the literature of the period /3/. Reference

has already been made to the growth cycle of the fig, and to the
different terms employed for each stage of maturation (paggîm,
bikkûrîm, t^{e}ēnîm, etc.) /4/. The paggîm could in fact be eaten,
although only after they had assumed a rosy appearance (lit. begun
'to glisten', B.Sheb.IV.7; cf. P.Sheb.IV.7, Schwab, pp.362-3).
The Talmud records the case of a woman who was beaten for having
eaten the (forbidden) unripe figs of the seventh year (B.Yom.86b).
That they would have been edible at Passover, however, is extremely
doubtful. Several kinds of figs were also mentioned in addition
to the common ones (Persian figs, for example, or white figs
בנות שוח, which ripened only every third year) /5/.

   The nutritional and medicinal value of the fig was noted in
our previous chapter, and in the Rabbinical literature, too, these
properties are foremost /6/. Stories and legends circulated of
the power of the fig to sustain life in extreme circumstances.
One legend credited this fruit with the sustenance of Noah and the
occupants of the ark /7/, while R. Zadok, fasting for forty years
to prevent the destruction of Jerusalem, is said to have survived
on figs alone /8/! Figs were given to the poor as alms /9/ and
were prescribed for the sick even if it meant plucking them on the
Sabbath (B.Men.64a-64b).

   Corresponding to the Jewish care for fruit-bearing trees, a
prohibition protected the fig-tree (regarded as the most fruitful
of all the trees, cf. B.Sheb.I.3) from being cut down, even though
it yielded only a small amount of fruit /10/. R. Ḥanina is said to
have credited the death of his son to the fact that the latter had
cut down a fig-tree "before its time" (B.B.Ḳ.91b, Sonc., p.530;
cf. also B.B.B.26a). If a tree was completely barren, however,
(אילן סרק cf. B.Kil.VI.3,5, Sonc., pp.121-2) it was justifiable
to destroy it for it was occupying valuable space and expending
the soil's resources (cf. Dt.20.20 M.B.B.2.11-13) /11/.

   While its cultivation was widespread, the fig is mentioned in
particular association with certain celebrated localities /12/. In
this connection, mention should be made of "the unripe figs of
Beth Hini" (בית היני) or "Bethania" (בית ינִיא) referred to, for
example, in B.Pes.53a and B.'Erub.28b. Some scholars have
identified this place-name with the Bethany of the gospels (cf.
Mk.11.1) /13/ but doubt has been expressed that this is so. S.
Klein, after a detailed examination of the evidence, has concluded
that the identity of the Talmudic 'Bethania' should be sought in
the 'Ānin that is east of Caesarea /14/. There is some doubt, too,
whether the Bethphage (בית פאגי, βηθφαγή) of both gospels (cf.

Mk.11.1) and the Talmud /15/ is to be derived from the description
'place' or 'house of unripe figs', a claim often made but as often
countered /16/. Apart from this dubious etymology, there is no
other evidence that Bethphage was celebrated for its cultivation
of figs.

The Fig-tree in the Halakah

References to the fig in the Mishnah, Tosefta and Talmud are
chiefly halakic in nature, a fact that is not surprising when we
consider the place of the fig-tree in the everyday life and economy
of the period. The fig was one of the seven species of fruit
(cf. Dt.8.8) that were seen as God's blessing on Israel. In
granting his people these fruits of the Promised Land, God had
granted Israel the means for a pleasant and peaceful life. As a
result, a series of blessings were required to be said over them,
whenever they were eaten /17/.

In common with much else in Jewish life, the utilization of
the fig-tree and its fruit was hedged about with a whole panoply of
legal prescriptions. There were sabbatical regulations to be
complied with and rules of ritual cleanness and uncleanness to be
observed /18/. Figs, as with all other fruits, were also subject
to tithe, the tithing procedure being particularly difficult,
however, because of the tree's prolonged bearing season /19/.
Wild figs and certain other strains were exempt from Demai /20/,
although pressed figs were not /21/. The fruit of the fig-tree,
since it did not appear all at once, was not subject to Pe'ah, the
law that a portion of the harvest should be left for the poor
(Lv.19.9-10 Dt.24.19 ff) /22/. For this reason it is difficult
to treat with any seriousness the views of certain scholars
(Lichtenstein, van Hasselt) /23/ who have argued that, in
sentencing the fig-tree to future infertility, Jesus was actually
punishing the owner of the tree for his greediness in picking the
tree clean before its fruit could be enjoyed by others!

It has also been suggested, however, that Jesus' action was
presumptuous since the tree must have had an owner /24/, but this
view has been countered in turn with the reflection that the tree
was probably a wild fig-tree, תאנה מדברות, growing by the wayside
(ἐπὶ τῆς ὁδοῦ, Mt.21.19) and hence designated by the Law a tree
whose fruits were of common right (מופקר) /25/.

While it is true that the Law did permit the casual plucking
of unwanted figs in certain circumstances, both in the case of

owned and ownerless trees /26/, the overall value of this halakic
material for our story is perhaps questionable. In the first place
we simply are not told whether the tree had an owner or not. In
the second place, we have seen reason to doubt that the fig-tree
anecdote was intended to be an empirically accurate record of an
actual historical event. Those elements of the story that appear
to contradict its verisimilitude are best explained in terms of
the pericope's underlying symbolic function rather than in terms
of the false problems and unnecessary considerations raised by an
historical rationalist approach. For this reason, the logical,
realistic and essentially mundane character of the Jewish Halakah
is a less appropriate guide to the interpretation of our story
than is the irrational, folklorish and richly symbolical ethos to
be encountered in the Haggadah, to which we shall shortly be
turning.

Before we now consider the fig's place in imagery and
symbolism, however, it is worth briefly remarking upon the
connection between the fig and the Temple cultus /27/, an
association that is interesting in view of the Markan link
between the Temple and fig-tree pericopes. The first-ripe fruits
of the land and of the trees were required to be brought to
Jerusalem and offered to the Temple (cf. Lv.19.23-25 Nm.18.13).
This took place at Pentecost. While these First-fruits or
Bikkûrîm were brought only from the fruit of the seven species
(cf. Dt.8.8 and B.Bik.I.3), figs are generally acknowledged to
have played the major role /28/. A vivid description of the
Bikkûrîm procession at Pentecost is given in B.Bik.III, and
figs are frequently mentioned /29/. These First-fruits of the
fig-tree, moreover, that were brought to the Temple as Bikkûrîm /30/,
were the exclusive right and property of the priests, and were
regarded as sacrosanct (cf. B.Bik.III.12 B.Me'il.13a B.'Erub.29b).
This link, therefore, between the fig-tree and the Temple, may
possibly add a cultic dimension to the associations surrounding the
fig-tree and its fruit. Such a dimension may not perhaps have been
lost on the Markan reader who is shown his Lord both hungry for
and in turn claiming the first-ripe fig for himself, and at the
same time preventing this fig-tree in the vicinity of the Temple
from ever supplying such fruit again /31/.

The Fig/Fig-tree in Rabbinic Imagery and Symbolism

In our examination of the Old Testament, we saw that the
fig-tree played a prominent role in figurative language and
symbolism. The righteous and the wicked, for example, were

depicted as good and bad figs (Jer.24; 29.17 Mi.7.1). More
specifically, the fig was also seen in these passages to be an
emblem for *Israel*, for the nation itself (Is.28.4 Jer.8.13 Hos.
9.10), for the wicked and righteous remnant of the nation (Jer.24;
29.17 Mi.7.1) or for representative individuals within the
nation, for Israel's rulers (Jgs.9.10-11) and so on. This
symbolic usage is also widely attested in the Rabbinical literature.

We find, in the first place, the image of the fig similarly
employed for *the righteous and the wicked*. B.'Erub.21a-21b (Sonc.,
p.148) records the following exegesis of the Jer.24 passage:

"R. Ḥisda [a Babylonian Amora of the third century]
further stated, Mari b. Mar made this exposition:
What [is the significance] of the Scriptural text,
'And behold two baskets of figs set before the temple
of the Lord; one basket had very good figs, like the
figs that are first-ripe, and the other basket had
very bad figs, which could not be eaten, they were so
bad'? 'Good figs' are an allusion to those who are
righteous in every respect; 'bad figs' are an allusion
to those who are wicked in every respect."

The identification of the first-ripe fig (or bikkûrâ) with
the righteous of the nation made in Mi.7.1, for example, is
rendered even more explicit by the Targum of this passage. Words
from Mi.7.2 which explain the symbolism, appear already in verse 1,
and the 'grape-cluster' and the 'first-ripe fig' appear simply,
without metaphor, as 'good men' /32/.

The same verse, Mi.7.1, is quoted, moreover, in the Mishnah
(M.Soṭ.9.9, Danby, p.305), a passage mourning the passing of the
prophets, the destruction of the Temple, the dissolution of the
Sanhedrin and the death of distinguished Rabbis. Here, however,
it is the 'grape-cluster' image of Mi.7.1 that is applied
specifically to two *Rabbis* of exceptional learning, and the
passing away of these righteous men is mourned as a profound loss
for the nation:

"When Jose b. Joezer of Zeredah and Jose b. Johanan of
Jerusalem died /33/, the 'grape-clusters' ceased, as it is
written, 'There is no cluster to eat, my soul desireth
the first-ripe fig.'"

Conversely, the unripe figs or paggîm of Ct.2.13 are
identified by the Midrash as certain wicked individuals of the

nation, "the sinners of Israel who died in the three days of
darkness" (Shir.R.II.13.1, Sonc., p.123, cf. Ex.10.21 ff. and
Shem.R.XIV.3).

Unripe figs can also be used to signify the righteous, in
particular those who die prematurely. The following story is told
in connection with R. Johanan b. Nappaha (190–279 CE) who is said
to have wept over the words of Jb.15.15 ('Behold, He putteth no
trust in His holy ones'):

> "One day he was going on a journey and saw a man gathering
> figs: he was leaving those that were ripe and was taking
> those that were unripe. So he said to him: Are not those
> [the ripe ones] better? He replied: I need those for a
> journey: these will keep, but the others will not keep.
> Said [R. Johanan] this is the meaning of the verse: 'Behold
> He putteth no trust in His holy ones'" (B.Hag.5a, Sonc., p.18).

God, then, like a man gathering figs, is afraid that the
righteous, his ripe figs, will later be drawn into sin, and hence
he plucks them before their proper season. The search for and the
plucking of figs is hence, as in the Old Testament, a ready and
common image for God's dealings with his people.

A similar analogy is drawn in Ber.R.LXII.2 (Sonc., pp.550–1)
/34/. Here the death of young men, as opposed to the old, is
compared (unfavourably) with the premature plucking of figs.

> "R. Abbahu [an Amora of the third century] said: when
> a fig is gathered at the proper time, it is good for
> itself and good for the tree; but if it is gathered
> prematurely, it is bad for itself and bad for the tree."

God's coming to pluck the righteous, moreover, is illustrated in
this selfsame passage by the story of R. Hiyya /35/ and his
disciples who are said to have moved from under a certain fig-
tree (where they were studying the Torah) because they believed
the owner suspected them of stealing his figs, and for this
reason was rising early in the morning to pluck its fruit. The
man persuaded them to return, however, assuring them that his
practice of early plucking was motivated simply by the desire to
prevent the figs becoming wormy later in the day when the sun shone.

> "Said they: 'The owner of the fig-tree knows when the
> fruit is ripe for plucking, and he plucks it.' In the

same way, the Holy One, blessed by He, knows when the
time of the righteous has come, whereupon He removes them."

The fig is employed, in the second place, specifically as a
symbol for *the nation itself* or for its *representatives*. Reference
has already been made to the 'Haman's cross' legends /36/. There
the fig-tree is said to have exclaimed, when offering its wood for
the Jewish persecutor's gallows: "I am ready to serve, for I am
symbolic of Israel, and, also, my fruits were brought to the
Temple as first-fruits" /37/.

The Targum to the Song of Songs, treating the book as an
allegory of Israel's salvation history from the Exodus to the
Messianic Age, identifies the unripe figs of Ct.2.13 explicitly as
the Assembly of Israel at the Red Sea:

"The fig tree putteth forth her green figs, and the
vines in blossom give forth their fragrance. Arise, my
love, my fair one, and come away.
"The Assembly of Israel, likened unto the first-fruits
of the fig tree, opened her mouth and sang praises at
the Red Sea; even children and sucklings praised with
their tongues the Lord of the Universe; /38/ whereupon the
Lord addressed them, saying: 'Arise, O Assembly of
Israel, My beautiful love, depart hence unto the land
which I have promised unto thy fathers.'" /39/.

The picture of Israel as God's 'grape-cluster' or 'first-ripe
fig' that was vividly presented in Hos.9.10, recurs likewise in
late Jewish literature. In Bem.R.II.6 (Sonc., p.27), for example,
we find Dt.32.10 ("He found him" [Israel] "in a desert land")
linked with the Hosea passage, with Israel being described as
God's great find in the wilderness:

"It was a great find that the Holy One, blessed be He,
came across in Israel, as it is said, 'I found Israel
like grapes in the wilderness.'"

Sometimes the first-ripe fig of Hos.9.10 is identified more
closely with the fathers of Israel, *the patriarchs*. Six things are
said to have preceded the creation of the world, and the patriarchs
are named as one of these:

"The creation of the Patriarchs was contemplated,
for it is written, I saw your fathers as the first-ripe

in the fig-tree at her first season."
(Ber.R.I.4, Sonc., p.6; cf. also Bem.R.XVI.24).

This identification of the fig with the leaders and fathers of
Israel can become in turn even more specific. In Ber.R.LIII.3
(Sonc., p.462), for example /40/, we find Abraham himself singled
out in connection with the exegesis of Hab.3.17 and Hos.9.10.

"'For though the fig-tree doth not blossom', etc.
(Hab.III,17). This alludes to Abraham, as in the
verse, 'I saw your fathers as the first-ripe in the
fig-tree at her first season (Hos.IX,10).' 'Neither
is there fruit in the vines (Hab.loc.cit.)' alludes
to Sarah, as you read, 'Thy wife shall be as a fruitful vine (Ps.CXXVIII,3).'"

Jotham's parable (Jgs.9.7-15) was also a fertile breeding-ground
for Rabbinic speculative exegesis and we find R. Me'asha (a third-
century Palestinian Amora), for example, identifying the fig-tree
(9.10-11) with Deborah /41/.

In all these examples, then, where direct symbolism is
involved, the fig appears consistently to signify either the wicked
or the righteous, the nation itself, its representative leaders and
pious men, its Rabbis, patriarchs or rulers. The good fig is the
godly man, or collectively God's righteous people, and the image
of the individual seeking and gathering figs passes easily over to
that of Israel's God, the owner of the fig-tree, seeking out his
own, as in the Old Testament. For this reason we can scarcely
doubt that in Jesus' search for figs the same allegorical
significance would have been perceived.

The direct symbolism of the fig for Israel or for the
righteous of the nation does not, however, exhaust the figurative
associations that this tree held for the Jewish mind. Different
aspects of the fig-tree's growth and maturation led to a number
of other metaphorical comparisons. Chief among these was the
phenomenon of the tree's gradual fruitage, the harvest of figs
being collected progressively, over an extended bearing season.
The physical development of a woman, for example, was expressed
in terms of the different stages of the fig's maturation. The
child was referred to as 'an unripe fig' (paggâ), the maiden as
'a fig in its early ripening stage' (bohal), and 'a ripe fig'
(şemel) was an epithet for the mature woman (cf. B.Nid.47a-47b,
Sonc., pp.327-9) /42/.

The successive fruitage phenomenon was also employed as a symbol for good memory retention, knowledge being secure if it was acquired in steady progressive stages. This is expressed, for example, in the 'interpretation of dreams' passage of B.Ber.57a (Sonc., p.352):

> "If one sees a fig tree in a dream, his learning will be preserved within him, as it says: 'Whoso keepeth the fig tree shall eat the fruit thereof.' (Prv.27.18)" /43/.

In B.'Erub.54a-54b (Sonc., p.379) the metaphor is applied specifically to knowledge of the Law, the tree's fruitage being likened in this respect to the words of *the Torah*:

> "R. Ḥiyya b.Abba [the Palestinian Amora of the third century] in the name of R. Joḥanan expounded: With reference to the Scriptural text, 'Whoso keepeth the fig tree shall eat the fruit thereof', why were the words of the Torah compared to the 'fig tree'? As with the fig tree the more one searches it the more figs one finds in it so it is with the words of the Torah; the more one studies them the more relish he finds in them." /44/.

In Ber.R.XLVI.1 (Sonc., p.389), the people of Israel are again likened to the fig-tree, *the growth of the nation* constituting the point for comparison:

> "R. Judan [a Palestinian Amora of the fourth century] said: At first the fruit of a fig-tree is gathered one by one, then two by two, then three by three, until eventually they are gathered in baskets and with shovels. Even so, at the beginning, 'Abraham was one' (Ezek.XXXIII, 24); then there were Abraham and Isaac; then Abraham, Isaac and Jacob. Until eventually, 'And the children of Israel were fruitful, and increased abundantly, and multiplied, etc. (Ex.I,7)."

The image was applied also to the creation of the world, the argument being that the heaven and the earth and the hosts ('generations') created with them, while created together, were nevertheless completed on separate days. In this respect they were said to resemble a crop of figs which all take shape at the same time, but do not all ripen at the same time:

"Said R. Nehemiah: They [the 'generations'] were like
those who gather figs, when each appears in its own time."
        (Ber.R.XII.4, Sonc., pp.89-90)

The application of fig-tree imagery to the resolution of a
debate on *cosmogony* /45/ such as we have in this last passage
recalls the similar use of the fig-tree motif in the *eschatological*
imagery of Is.34.4. There the host of heaven shall fall "like
leaves falling from the fig tree" (cf. Ap.6.13-14). This latter OT
passage is cited in P.R.E.LI (Friedlander, pp.410-9), a passage
important for the study of late Jewish eschatology, and one vividly
describing the nature of the new creation, the new heavens and the
new earth:

"Just as the leaves fade from off the vine and the fig
tree, and the latter remain standing as a dry tree,
and again they blossom afresh and bear buds and produce
new leaves and fresh leaves. Likewise in the future
will all the host of heaven fade away like a vine and
a fig tree, and they will again be renewed before Him
to make known that there is passing away [which] does
not [really] pass away."
        (Friedlander, p.411; cf. Mk.13.28-31)

This connection of the fig with eschatology is one that we
have noted before and one that we shall presently discuss further
in relation to the Haggadah. One final comparison should, however,
be noted. In describing the new heavens and the new earth, Jewish
eschatology, as we have seen, gave a prominent role to the Holy
City, and according to Pes.R.172b and Shir.R.VII.5.3, *the new
Jerusalem* itself is to develop like a fig-tree:

"As the fig tree, rooted deep in the earth and sending
up a straight trunk with branches spreading out on all
sides, is called beautiful, so, too, Jerusalem is called
"beautiful because of its spreading branches" - that is,
[the influence of] Jerusalem is destined to keep
enlarging and ascending, as is said 'And there was an
enlarging, and a winding about still upward (Ezek.41:7).'"
        -Pes.R.172b (Braude, II, p.725)

"What does R. Johanan make of the verse, 'And the city
shall be builded upon her own mound (Jer.XXX,18)?' (He
replies): It will be like a fig-tree which is narrow
below and broad above. So Jerusalem will expand on all
sides and the exiles will come and rest beneath it, to

> fulfil what is said, 'For thou shalt spread abroad on
> the right hand and on the left (Isa.LIV,3).'"
>   -Shir.R.VII.5.3 (Sonc., p.287) /46/

Our examination of the Rabbinical use of the fig/fig-tree in
direct and indirect imagery and symbolism has hence revealed a
persistent correspondence between this usage and that of the Old
Testament where the fig, too, can stand for the righteous, the
wicked, Israel or its representatives, as well as being
associated more loosely with the eschatological themes of
judgement and blessing in the New Age. If anything, precise
symbolic identification is more common in this later period.
Münderlein has argued that in the Old Testament, while the tree
or its fruit is indeed employed as a symbol for the godly or wicked
man, or for the people of Israel collectively, it never stands for
an object, such as the Temple /47/. Late Jewish exegesis does,
however, show a fondness for a more *specific* one-to-one correlation,
and the above passage, while it does not evince the use of the
fig-tree in direct symbolism, indicates at least that the tree
could be compared with the city of Jerusalem. Notwithstanding, the
fig-tree's withering within the context of the Temple 'Cleansing'
would most readily have suggested, we believe, an eschatological
judgement upon this institution.

In our examination of the Old Testament, however, we have
focused not only on the fig's use in direct symbolism but also on
related motifs connected with it and present also in our Markan
story. In pursuit of similar links we shall now turn specifically
to the Jewish Haggadah.

The Fig-tree Story and the Haggadah

The value of the Haggadah cannot be overestimated. Haggadic
stories in particular show close similarities, in form, content,
and 'atmosphere', to our own fig-tree pericope, a discovery first
brought to light by R.H. Hiers, and developed by J.D.M. Derrett /48/.
They evince motifs and themes similar to those that were noted in
the Old Testament, but viewed often at a later stage of development,
they allow us in some measure to gauge what might have been
believed in New Testament times. They show, hence, the kind of
ideas and associations that were possible in the first-century
world, and so illuminate the fig-tree story for us. The stuff of
folklore and legend, they reveal symbolic intent as well as
displaying elements of the fantastic and the miraculous.

The modern reader finds Mark's story puzzling for many reasons, not the least of which is that Jesus should speak to the tree as if it were a person and curse it for not serving his needs /49/. The notion that it should likewise wither at his command, is also foreign to a twentieth-century mentality. But examination of haggadic stories in which trees figure reveals a world of ideation in which such things were accepted as 'natural', and indeed expected. The haggadic view of nature is of a world *endowed with human characteristics*. The trees, for example, are sensitive to the moral dimension. They encourage a man to be righteous or put obstacles in his way. They are like barometers accurately recording fluctuations in the moral climate. A tree belonging to R. Ḥiyya b. Abba (the Palestinian Amora of the third century) is said to have yielded him progressively less fruit every day that he failed to return to his sacred duty of teaching his pupils the Torah (B.Ket. 111b). The trees in the Garden of Eden are said to have actively responded to the Fall of Adam, as we shall presently see. God's curse had fallen not only on the first Man and Woman, but also on the earth, for the latter, too, had disobeyed God. The trees were moral agents and, in producing only succulent fruit had revealed a resistance to the Divine Will that had dictated that *every* part of a tree should be edible (Ber.R.V.9) /50/! Conversely, they exhibit their fervour for justice by offering themselves as wood for Haman's cross, a public-spiritedness that God rewards by granting each of them a blessing /51/.

In the world of the Haggadah talking to trees is nothing unusual /52/. Communication exists between man and nature. The tree may be invoked in a halakic dispute, as is shown by the aforementioned story of R. Eliezer and the carob /53/, a Rabbinic miracle story that Bultmann considers in fact a distant parallel to the Markan story /54/. This particular story illustrates more-over the importance ascribed in ancient times to the words of a Rabbi, which were regarded, like the serpent's bite /55/, as possessing an uncanny and, very often, a death-dealing potency /56/. After the Rabbi's excommunication a series of calamities are said to have smitten the world and everything at which Eliezer cast his eye was burned up. The curse of a sage, indeed, even when unmeri-ted, was not deemed to go unfilfilled (B.Sanh.90b).

An even more interesting tradition is that concerning R. Jose of Yoḳereth /57/. The story is given in B.Ta'an.24a (Sonc., p.122):

"Once R. Jose had day-labourers [working] in the field; night set in and no food was brought to them and they

said to his son, 'We are hungry'. Now they were resting
under a fig tree and he exclaimed: Fig tree, fig tree,
bring forth thy fruit that my father's labourers may eat.
It brought forth fruit and they ate. Meanwhile the
father came and said to them, Do not bear a grievance
against me; the reason for my delay is because I have
been occupied up till now on an errand of charity. The
labourers replied, May God satisfy you even as your son
has satisfied us. Whereupon he asked: Whence? And they
told him what had happened. Thereupon he said to his
son: My son, you have troubled your Creator to cause
the fig tree to bring forth its fruit *before its time*
(שלא בזמנה) /58/, may you too be taken hence before your
time!"

In thus describing a fig-tree's response to the request of a
Rabbi's son, this haggadic tale furnishes perhaps a closer
parallel to our Markan story than does any other. The address to
the tree, the request made of it and the assumption that it will
respond to the speaker are typical features of such stories. In
relation to Mark's account, this episode constitutes a converse
miracle /59/, for here the fig-tree *does* meet the needs of the
persons involved and does so notably by bearing fruit *out of
season*. This story demonstrates, then, the kind of ideas that
were possible in a Jewish environment. Mark's fig-tree *could,*
after all, have supplied Jesus with fruit although "it was not
the season for figs". Such a scenario was not impossible for a
first-century tradition, no more than it was for the series of much
later traditions in which we read of a fig-tree that bent over and
offered its fruit to the infant Jesus, of a fig-tree that opened
up and protected the holy family from robbers, of the trees that
bore homage to Jesus, and so on /60/. If the fig-tree had, in
fact, produced fruit for Jesus, it would have suited the lessons
of the sequel far better. The fact that *it did not* emphasizes that
in Markan intention the *cursing* of the tree and the judgement upon
it was the central point of the story, and not any object lessons
on the efficacy of faith and prayer that might be drawn from it.

In the Talmudic story, the reaction of the father is a curious
and, indeed, a shocking one. The son is condemned for what might
seem a considerate action. While the father's cursing of his son
might issue simply from a profound abhorrence of his son's
presumption in disturbing the natural order /61/, one wonders if
this is the whole story. Could it be that an eschatological
dimension is also here in view?

We have already seen much evidence to link the fig-tree with
the Messianic Age. The host of heaven in that Age will fade and
be renewed like the vine and the fig-tree (Is.34.4 Ap.6.13-14
Mk.13.28-32 P.R.E.LI). The New Jerusalem will develop like the
fig-tree (Pes.R.172b Shir.R.VII.5.3). Israel is to be comforted
in the New Age "by bearing fruit like fig trees: 'The fig tree
putteth forth her green figs'" (Pes.R.XXXIII.13, Braude,II, p.657).
These very words of Ct.2.13 are likewise the starting-point for a
midrash on the Second Deliverance to usher in the Messianic Age
(Shir.R.II.13) /62/. All the wild trees that blossom in that Age,
moreover, will bear fruit, and will do so perennially (B.Ket.112b)
/63/.

The father's curse may possibly reflect, therefore, an
additional facet, namely his offence at his son's presumption in
advancing the conditions that were associated with the Messianic
Age, an act that was considered to be the prerogative of God
himself or his Messiah. If this were so, the parallel with our
story is even closer, except that here *the fig-tree itself* is
cursed for refusing Jesus fruit, so emphasizing its failure to
recognize and respond to the signs of the New Age that had, in
Jesus, begun.

These haggadic tales, then, are imbued with an atmosphere so
similar to that of the Markan fig-tree story that it seems reasonable
to suppose that the latter was conceived within the same general
climate of ideas and associations. The trees are involved in the
world of men. They are sensitive to human affairs. They can be
addressed. They can be held morally responsible. They are
responsive to man, and his needs. Nowhere is this more apparent
than in the haggadah relating to *Israel's Golden Ages,* the selfsame
periods with which the fig and fig-tree were found to be
associated in the Old Testament. Here, in these traditions, all
restraint is lost, the miraculous and the fanciful are given free
reign, and nature is especially responsive to the righteous. Here
again the fig and the fig-tree crop up as do other related motifs
discussed in regard to the OT evidence and linked with our story.

We note first of all the legends surrounding *Eden* and the
Fall of Man. In these days, according to R. Phinehas (a Palestinian
Amora of the fourth century), even non-fruitbearing trees yielded
fruit (Ber.R.V.9). Before the Fall, the fruit of the tree was
one of the six precious gifts enjoyed by Adam, but it was taken
from him (and hence from Israel and mankind), and was only to be
fully restored by the Messiah in the age to come (cf. e.g. Ber.R.XII.
6 Bem.R.XIII.12) /64/. At the Fall, when Adam tried to cover his

nakedness, the trees are said to have refused him their leaves,
declaring with righteous indignation, "There is the thief that
deceived his Creator. Nay, the foot of pride shall not come
against me, nor the hand of the wicked touch me. Hence, and take
no leaves from me!" /65/ A similar tradition is given in the
Apocalypse of Moses /66/. There, the leaves of all the trees
are said to have withered as soon as Eve had eaten of the forbidden
fruit (Apoc.Mos.20) /67/ - all the trees, that is, except the
fig-tree. The latter retained its leaves, supplying them as a
covering for the disgraced pair /68/. Only when God himself
entered the garden are the bare trees said to have blossomed
again (Apoc.Mos.22) /69/.

The prominent part played by the fig-tree in these Fall
legends is exemplified by the widespread tradition (found not
only in Rabbinic sources but also in Tertullian, the Apocalypse
of Moses and in numerous Christian apocryphal Books of Adam from
the fifth century onwards) that the fig-tree was the Tree of
Knowledge of Good and Evil, and was responsible, therefore, for
bringing sorrow, mourning and death into the world /70/. No
definite determination of the Tree of Life, on the other hand,
can be found in the early Rabbinical literature, although the
apocryphal tradition, conversely, is replete with such speculation
/71/.

The trees of Eden, then, in their withering and diminished
fruitfulness, exhibit and reflect a moral attitude to the human
plight. They were involved in the disobedience of mankind's first
parents. Even after the Fall, when Cain murdered Abel, his crime
is said to have had baneful consequences for all of nature. The
trees refused to yield their fruit, and although they recovered
somewhat at the birth of Seth, they would only again regain their
pristine powers in the Age to come /72/.

The wilderness period was another era that the haggadic imagination transformed into a Golden Age /73/. Here nature showed
itself extraordinarily responsive to Moses and the Israelites, and
the signs and wonders performed on their behalf quite outdo those
recorded in the Old Testament /74/. A branch of the bitter laurel
(according to some traditions, of the Tree of Life) was cast into
the waters of Marah to make them sweet /75/. So much manna fell
as to satisfy the needs of sixty myriads of people, through two
thousand years /76/. In the future world, such manna would be set
before the righteous ////. In company with the rock struck by
Moses, a fantastic well followed the Israelites wherever they

journeyed, its waters continually gushing forth, when bidden, to
slake their thirst /78/. Trees of every conceivable kind,
nourished by these waters, bore them fresh fruits every day,
a gift that would again be enjoyed in Messianic times /79/.
Aaron's rod, blossoming overnight and yielding almonds,
validated his priesthood, and was used henceforth by the Judaean
kings until the time of the Temple's destruction, after which it
miraculously disappeared. In the Age to come, it would be
fetched by Elijah and handed over to the Messiah /80/. Though
highly fanciful, somewhat similar beliefs appear to have been
entertained in the first century /81/, with the wilderness being
seen as the place of Messianic deliverance, the location where
God would once again liberate and succour his people /82/.

A further avenue that was explored in our examination of the
Old Testament background was the conceptual links that appeared to
exist between the tree and Israel, the mountain and the tree, the
tree and the Temple. We saw there that the tree was highly
symbolical, that its blossoming or withering reflected both
blessing or judgement upon the nation. We saw, too, that the
fruitfulness of the tree was a function of the health and
well-being of the Temple cultus, and that in the time to come
waters would flow from it and make the land abundantly fertile.
These and similar themes are likewise to be encountered in the
haggadah relating to *the Temple* both *in the reign of Solomon* and *in
the Messianic Age.*

The connection of trees with Solomon's Temple has already been
noted /83/. A Rabbinic legend, recorded in B.Yom.21b (Sonc., p.93),
tells how Solomon planted trees of gold in the Temple which
periodically yielded fruit. They are said to have withered,
however, when the heathen entered but would again blossom and
bear fruit in the Messianic Age.

"Did not R. Oshaia *[a Palestinian Amora of the third
century]* say: When King Solomon built the Sanctuary,
he planted therein all kinds of *[trees of]* golden
delights, which were bringing forth their fruits in
their season and as the winds blew at them, they would
fall off, as it is written: 'May his fruits rustle
like Lebanon' /84/ (Ps.72.16), and when the foreigners
entered the Temple they withered as it is written:
'And the flower of Lebanon languisheth' (Na.1.4); and
the Holy One, blessed be He, will in the future restore
them, as it is said: 'It shall blossom abundantly and

rejoice, even with joy and singing; the glory of Lebanon
shall be given unto it'? (Is.35.2)."

Other versions of the legend ascribe the withering of the Temple
trees to the idolatry introduced by Manasseh /85/. Everything
connected indeed with the Temple was said to have blossomed or
grown prodigiously, the rod of Aaron, the cedars of Hiram, the
staves of the Ark /86/. The withering of the trees, on the other
hand, as here, was a sign of misfortune brought on by cultic
aberration /87/.

Fruitfulness was dependent upon the Temple service /88/.
According to A.R.N.4 (Goldin, pp.33-4):

"So long as the Temple service is maintained, the world
is a blessing to its inhabitants and the rains come
down in season .... But when the Temple service is not
maintained, the world is not a blessing to its inhabitants
and the rains do not come down in season .... But if you
will busy yourselves with the service of the Temple, I
shall bless you as in the beginning; as it is said,
'Consider, I pray you .... from the four and twentieth
day of the ninth month, even from the day that the
foundation of the Lord's temple was laid .... Is the
seed yet in the barn? Yea, the vine, and the fig tree,
and the pomegranate, and the olive tree hath not brought
forth - from this day will I bless you (Hag.2:18-19).'"

The destruction of the Temple, conversely, produced a blight
on the land that affected the fruits.

"Rabban Simeon b. Gamaliel says in the name of R. Joshua
[Tannaim of the first century]: Since the day that the
Temple was destroyed there has been no day without its
curse; and the dew has not fallen in blessing and the
fruits have lost their savour. R. Jose [a Tanna of the
second century] says: The fruits have also lost their
fatness" (M.Soṭ.9.12, Danby, p.305).

All this would be reversed in the Messianic Age. With the
sanctuary as their source, the waters of creation would once again
spring forth to make the land fertile. The Water Gate of the
Temple was so named, according to R. Eliezer b. Jacob (a Tanna
of the first century), because. "Through it 'the waters trickle
forth' (Ez.47.2), and hereafter they will 'issue out from under

the threshhold of the House' (Ez.47.1)" /89/. The belief (based
on Ez.47) becomes even more elaborate in later Jewish legend.
According to P.R.E.LI (Friedlander, pp.416-19), every field and
vineyard that would not normally yield fruit would do so when
watered from these streams. Trees would bear fruit every month,
some for food and others for growing: "and the fruit thereof shall
be for meat, and the leaf thereof for healing."

The Messianic Age will witness such marvellous productivity
as was not seen since the days of Eden. From Ps.72.16 ('There will
be a rich cornfield in the Land upon the top of the mountains') the
Rabbis inferred that "there will be a time when wheat will rise
as high as a palm-tree and will grow on the top of the mountains"
(B.Ket.111b, Sonc., p.721). From Deut.32.14 they inferred that
"in the world to come a man will bring one grape on a wagon or a
ship, put it in a corner of his house and use its contents as [if
it had been] a large wine cask, while its timber [the stalk] would
be used to make fires for cooking. There will be no grape that
will not contain thirty kegs of wine, for it is said in Scripture,
'And of the blood of the grape thou drankest foaming wine' (Dt.32.14),
read not 'foaming' [חָמֶר] but ḥomer [חֹמֶר]." (!) /90/ According to
R. Gamaliel (one of the earliest of the Tannaim; cf. Acts 5.34)
the trees were destined to bear fruit every day (B.Shab.30b) /91/.

That similar beliefs respecting the Age to come were
entertained in the New Testament is a view that has come to be
increasingly shared by scholars /92/, and we shall be considering
the evidence for this in our next chapter. It was within such a
climate that, we believe, Mark's story was conceived, and it is
against such a background that it must be interpreted. To Mark and
to his readers a fig-tree in the vicinity of the Temple in the
Messianic Age should have produced fruit for its Messiah. The fact
that it did not, and was sentenced to infertility as a result, was
an omen of the greatest significance for the well-being of that
institution.

Summation

Our examination, then, of late Jewish material can be said to
have strengthened the impressions that were gained in respect of
both the variety and the limits of the associations connected with
the tree and the fig-tree in the Old Testament. We have seen how
important the fig-tree was in the everyday life of Palestine, and
the high esteem with which this, the most fruitful of all the

trees, was regarded. The nutritional, life-sustaining and
curative powers of the fig are lauded in both Halakah and
Haggadah. References to the fig abound in the Halakah, although
in general we have found this material of less significance for the
understanding of the Markan story than the Haggadah in which
trees, and especially the fig-tree, appear. Note was taken,
nevertheless, of the fig-tree's special connection with the Temple
cultus, its fruits being among the principal First-fruits to be
brought to the sanctuary.

It is the fig-tree's prominent place in Rabbinic imagery and
symbolism, however, that is the significant factor of value for
our story. As in the Old Testament, the image of the fig is
employed for the righteous and the wicked. First-ripe figs, the
bikkûrîm, figure as the nation's 'good men'. Unripe figs, the
paggîm, figure as the righteous, particularly those who meet their
deaths prematurely or, conversely, represent the wicked of the
nation. Overall, the search for and the plucking of figs is a
ready and common image for God's dealings with his people.

The fig is employed specifically as a symbol for the nation
itself or its representatives. The unripe figs of Ct.2.13 are the
Assembly of Israel at the Red Sea, the first-ripe fig of Hos.9.10,
God's great find in the wilderness, or the patriarchs, or even
Abraham. Deborah is identified with the fig-tree of Jotham's
parable.

In all the examples that we have considered, therefore, the
use of the fig in direct symbolism is broadly consistent. The
good fig is the godly man, or collectively God's righteous people,
and the search for figs a picture of Israel's God, seeking out
those who are his own. Viewed in this light, we find it difficult
to believe that Mark and his readers would not have attached a
similar allegorical significance to Jesus' visit to Jerusalem and
his search, in that context, for figs from the fig-tree.

The fig's employment in indirect image and symbol was also
explored and we found, for example, that the phenomenon of the
tree's gradual fruitage could be figuratively linked with female
sexual development, the acquisition of knowledge and the words of
the Torah. It was also, however, a picture for the growth of
Israel, and it figured, too, in imagery of a cosmological and
eschatological nature. The generations of the heaven and the
earth are said to have developed like the fig crop, and the new
heavens and the new earth are to come into being in like fashion.

The image may even be applied specifically to the New Jerusalem,
which will, like the fig-tree, expand and grow in the New Age.
It is in these latter respects that Rabbinic fig-tree imagery has
links with the New Testament, for in Mk.13.28-32 the blossoming
of the fig-tree is likewise seen as a suitable model for
eschatological events.

From the Rabbinic use of the fig/fig-tree in figurative
language and symbolism we turned to the place of both the tree
and the fig-tree in the Jewish Haggadah. Herein we found a world
of ideation within the context of which the Markan story has its
rightful place. Features of the story that are problematic for
the modern reader were found to be consonant with the haggadic
view of nature and the affairs of men. In these stories, the
world is endowed with human characteristics. The trees are
sensitive to the moral dimension. They can be addressed. They
can give or withhold their fruit in response to human need
(whatever the season). Their blossoming or withering has moral
and symbolic significance. In the world of the Haggadah, the
Rabbi's curse has an incontrovertible efficacy. Nature is
responsive to the righteous.

Nowhere was this more true than in the haggadah relating to
Israel's Golden Ages, the selfsame periods with which the fig and
fig-tree were found to be associated in the Old Testament. We
looked at the legends of Eden recounting the response of the
trees to the Fall of Adam, and noted the part played by the fig-tree
in these traditions. We examined likewise the legends surrounding
the wilderness period, during which the trees, for example, were
said to have borne fresh fruit daily for Israel. Reference was
made to the trees associated with the Temple, their withering being
an omen of misfortune brought on by cultic aberration. We took
note, too, of the connection existing in the Jewish mind between
the fruitfulness of the trees and the maintenance of the Temple
service. According to Rabbis of the first and second centuries,
the fruits had lost their savour when the Temple had been destroyed,
a state of affairs that was, however, to be reversed in the
Messianic Age, according to a number of the sources that were
referred to. Such an Age would see a return to conditions
prevalent before the Fall, and would witness signs and wonders as
had been performed on Israel's behalf in the wilderness. Waters
would issue from under the threshhold of an exalted and elevated
Temple, and all the trees in its vicinity would bear fruit
prodigiously, month after month and day after day.

What is problematic in Mark's story for us would not then
have been problematic for the Markan reader, and what was striking
for him we might easily ourselves pass over. For him the coming
of the Lord in the Last Days to the Holy City, the search for figs,
the lack of fruit, the curse, the withering, the judgement - all
have rich symbolic content. Although it was not the season for
figs, the fig-tree in the Messianic Age should have rendered to
its rightful owner its fruit, and the nation to the Son of God
those who would follow him. By placing the story, moreover, in
the context of Jesus' visit to the Temple, Mark has dramatically
indicated that the expected fruitfulness associated with that
institution is not to be. Its destiny is rather to be withered,
and that - ἐκ ῥιζῶν!

NOTES

/1/   For works dealing with the fig or fig-tree in general, *vide
supra*, p.165,n.17.
/2/   Goldmann, *Figue*, p.3 and fns.3,4; *RAC*, 7, pp.662-3.
/3/   *EJud*, 6,p.1273; Löw, *Aramaeische Pflanzennamen*, pp.390-3.
/4/   For our previous discussion of the growth cycle, bearing
seasons and edibility of the fig, and their relevance for our
story, *vide supra*, pp.3 ff., 133.   Cf. also *PRE* (Herzog-Hauck),
VI, pp.303-4; Goldmann, *Figue*, pp.10-17,22-9 and (esp.) pp.38-40;
contr. Löw, *Flora*, I, p.245; *RAC* 7, p.663.
/5/   Cf. e.g. P.Sheb.V.1 (Schwab, pp.366-8) and see *Str-B*, I,
p.857; Edersheim, *Life and Times*, II, p.246; Löw, *Flora*, I, pp.241-
2; Bacon, *DCG*, 1, p.592. In the view of J. Lightfoot, it was
this latter species of fig-tree that Jesus had approached when
seeking figs (*vide supra*, p.27, n.8).
/6/   See Löw, *Flora*, I, pp.244-5,254; Goldmann, *Figue*, pp.38-40.
/7/   Cf. e.g. Ber.R.XXXI.14. For other references to this
legend see Ginzberg, *Legends*, V, p.181, fn.37.
/8/   B.Giṭ.56a Ekah R.I.5.31.
/9/   Klein, *Fs. A. Schwarz*, p.398.
/10/   Cf. Dt.20.19 and Edersheim, *Life and Times*, II, p.246;
Goldmann, *Figue*, p.6 and fn.6.
/11/   Edersheim, *op.cit.*, p.247; Derrett, *HeythJ*, 14 (1973),
p.260 and fn.3.
/12/   See Klein, *Fs. A. Schwarz*, pp.396-9; Löw, *Flora*, I,
pp.225-7; Dalman, *Arbeit*, I, p.337-8 for a description of these.
For Josephus' (doubtless exaggerated) claim, regarding the figs
of Gennesaret, *vide supra*, p.27, n.8.

/13/   So, for example, A. Neubauer, *La Géographie du Talmud,*
pp.149-50; Bowman, *Mark,* pp.224-5.
/14/   Klein, *Fs. A. Schwarz,* p.398 and fns.; cf. also Löw, *Flora,*
I, pp.225-6; Goldmann, *Figue,* p.18 and fn.3; A. Schlatter, *Der
Evangelist Matthäus,* pp.616-7; *Str-B,* I, pp.855-6.
/15/   For the numerous references to Bethphage in the Rabbinical
literature, see e.g. Dalman, *Sacred Sites and Ways,* pp.252 ff.
/16/   So, for example, Klein, *Fs. A. Schwarz,* p.396, fn.2; Olck,
RE(Pauly-Wissowa), VI, p.2105. See also Bowman, *Mark,* pp.224-5,
and, by way of contrast, Goldmann, *Figue,* pp.19-22, esp. p.19,
fn.2; Löw, *Flora,* I, p.225; E.G. Kraeling, R.A.S. Macalister, *DB*[2]
(ed. F.C. Grant, H.H. Rowley), 'Bethphage' ad loc.; L. Gautier,
DCG, 1, 'Bethphage' ad loc.; *ThDNT,* 7, p.752, fn.9, and *supra,* p.11.
/17/   Cf. e.g. B.Ber.44a and see *ETal,* 1, 'Tree' ad loc., p.652.
/18/   See Löw, *Flora,* I, p.247, and *ETal,* 1, pp.646-54.
/19/   See Lightfoot, *Horae,* II, pp. 279-81.
/20/   Lit. 'dubious', 'suspicious' i.e. produce over which doubt
exists whether the rules relating to the priestly and levitical
dues and ritual cleanness and uncleanness have been strictly
observed; cf. e.g. B.Dem.I.1 B.Ber.40b B.'Erub.18a.
/21/   Cf. B.Dem.II.1.
/22/   Cf. e.g. B.Pe'ah.I.4 B.Nid.50a B.Shab.68a, and
Edersheim, *Life and Times,* II, p.247; Löw, *Flora,* I, p.247.
/23/   F.J.F. van Hasselt, "De vijgeboom, waaraan Jezus „niets dan
bladeren" vond", *NThS,* 8 (1925), pp.225-7; for the earlier view
of Lichtenstein, see Wohlenberg, *Markus,* p.299, fn.49.
/24/   Cf. e.g. Bradley, *LCQ,* 9 (1936), p.187.
/25/   Cf. J. Lightfoot, *Horae,* II, p.277, and Loisy, *Évangiles
Synoptiques,* II, p.284 ("Comme la Loi permettait de prendre
quelques fruits en passant, la démarche de Jesus n'a rien d'insolite
ni de choquant"). It should be pointed out in passing, however,
that the fruit of the wild fig-tree is in general quite unpalatable
(see *Solms-Laubach,*p.5; *RE*(Pauly-Wissowa), VI, p.2101; Murr,
Pflanzenwelt, p.34). If a wild fig-tree were here in view, morever
the proper term ἐρινός or ἐρινεός rather than συκῆ (the cultivated
fig-tree) would probably otherwise have been used. See *RE*(Pauly-
Wissowa), VI, pp.2103,2105; *RAC,* 7, p.641.
/26/   Cf. e.g. B.'Erub.32a B.Pes.6b. A caretaker was often
assigned by an owner to guard his figs, and his presence indicated
that the figs were liable to tithe and forbidden to be sampled.
The risk that one took in plucking such figs is illustrated by the
story of the third-century Palestinian Amora, Resh Laḳish (B.M.Ḳ.17a,
Sonc., pp.107-8), who ordered an unfortunate fellow, who had eaten
figs from an orchard the Rabbi had been guarding, to be "under a

shammetha" (a judicial curse)! On another occasion, a Rabbi
(R. Jose b. Judah, a second-century Tanna) was himself challenged
by a caretaker when he attempted to pluck some figs (P.Dem.I.1,
Schwab, p.123). An owner could renounce his figs, so permitting
all and sundry to take them (P.Dem.I.1, Schwab, pp.122-3), or,
conversely, he could declare them Korban (i.e. dedicated to God),
in which case no one, with the possible exception of his father
and brothers (cf. B.Ned.25b-26a), was henceforth allowed to pluck
them. Workmen were, however, allowed to eat fruit from the trees
they worked with (P.Dem.I.1, Schwab, p.122; cf. also B.Ta'an.24a).
/27/   This link was already noted in our examination of the OT
background, cf. e.g. Jl.1.7,9,12,13,16; 2.14,22.
/28/   See Klein, Fs. A. Schwarz, p.397, fn.6 ("Bei בכורים ist in
erster Reihe an Feigen zu denken"); Löw, Flora, I, p.247 ("Dafür
spielen sie [Feigen] unter den Erstlingen die erste Rolle"), and
Dalman, Arbeit, I, pp.420,464 ff.,585.
        The special role of both fig and vine in supplying first-
fruits for the Temple is stated expressly in the later legends
surrounding Haman's cross (Est.7.10). Each of the trees is said
to have vied for the privilege of providing the wood to hang
Haman on. The fig-tree and the vine are named first. "The
fig-tree said: 'I am ready to serve, for I am symbolic of Israel,
and, also, my fruits were brought to the Temple as first-fruits.'
The vine said: 'I am ready to serve, for I am symbolic of Israel
and, also, my wine is brought to the altar.'" See Ginzberg,
Legends, IV, pp.443-4; VI, p.479 and fn.184.
        Later Jewish exegesis of Ct.2.13, in addition, supplies
evidence for this association: "The fig-tree putteth forth her
green figs: this refers to the baskets of firstfruits. And the
vines in blossom give forth their fragrance: this refers to the
drink-offerings" (Shir.R.II.13, Sonc., pp.124-5).
/29/   Although the vine precedes the fig in Dt.8.8, in B.Bik.III.
1,3 the fig is mentioned first. See Goldmann, Figue, p.3 and fns.
3,4; Löw, ibid.
/30/   The same word used for the First-fruits in general, as for
the first-ripe fruits of the fig-tree in particular, shows the
pre-eminent role that the latter played in Jewish life; cf. also
qayis = summer fruit(s) or figs, supra, p.166, n.29.
/31/   It is curious that in the only other passage in the gospel
where Mark employs ἐπείνασεν (2.25), a cultic note is introduced.
In this parallel passage of 2.23 ff., it is Jesus' disciples this
time who are shown to be hungry. To satisfy their hunger they
pluck whatever is available from the fields through which they are
passing. When they are challenged for breaking the Sabbath, Jesus
defends their action by appealing to the precedent of David's having

eaten the shewbread of the Temple which was specially reserved for
the priests. By introducing this reference to the Temple, Mark
may not only be suggesting that Jesus was Lord of the Sabbath but
(in an indirect way) Lord of the Temple, too.

/32/   לית גבר דליה עובדין טבין לטביא חמידת נפשי Targum Jonathan,
Mi.7.1 ad loc. (cf. A. Sperber, *The Bible in Aramaic*, Vol.3,
ad loc.) and J.N. Birdsall, "The Withering of the Fig-Tree", *ET*,
73 (1961-2), p.191; Derrett, *HeythJ*, 14 (1973), p.257, fn.1.

/33/   These two Rabbis lived in the first half of the second
century BCE and were the first of the 'Zugoth' or 'Pairs' of
teachers who preserved and transmitted the Torah-lore accumulated
by the men of the Great Assembly (cf. A. Cohen, B.Soṭ.47a, Sonc.,
p.249, fn.4.).

/34/   Cf. also Qoh.R.V.11.2 Shir.R.VI.2.1.

/35/   Ḥiyya bar Abba, a Palestinian Amora of the third century.
The story is also associated with R. Hoshaya (third - fourth century)
and R. Akiba (c.50-135 CE).

/36/   *Supra,* n.28.

/37/   The legend appears in a number of sources, and in different
forms; see Ginzberg, *Legends,* IV, pp.443-4; VI, p.479 and fn.184
and cf. e.g. Est.R.IX.2. It is interesting to note, however, that
the vine is not given precedence as *the* symbol for Israel par
excellence. Here each of the trees claims this symbolic status
(cf. *supra,* pp.136-7).

/38/   The same motif occurs, interestingly, in Matthew's account
of the Cleansing of the Temple; cf. Mt.21.14-16, and Edersheim,
Life and Times , II, p.379 and fn.2.

/39/   Transl. H. Gollancz (1908), ad loc.

/40/   Cf. also Ber.R.XLVI.1 (Sonc., p.389); Pes.R.177b (Braude,
II, pp.746-7); and Löw, *Flora,* I, pp.250-1; *RAC,* 7, p.661; Derrett,
HeythJ, 14 (1973), p.257, fns.1 and 3.

/41/   The olive is said to be Othniel, the vine Gideon, and the
thorn-bush Abimelech; see Ginzberg, *Legends,* IV, p.41; VI, p.201
and fn.103; Löw, *Flora,* I, p.249; *RAC,* 7, p.661.

        Pseudo-Philo also gives a version of this parable in which
the fig-tree (named first), the vine, the apple-tree and the
bramble appear. The trees are told by the bramble that if they
were electing him in good faith, they would lie down in his shade.
If not, fire would proceed from the bramble and devour the trees of
the field, 'for then the apple-tree would be a judge, and *the
fig-tree the people,* and the vine the hangman' (P. Riessler,
Altjüdisches Schrifttum ausserhalb der Bibel, pp.814-5 - italics
mine; see also *RAC,* 7, p.660).

        The Church Fathers, too, drew from the parable a wide range
of allegorical nuances; see *RAC,* 7, pp.674-5.

/42/   Cf. also B.Sanh.107a (Sonc., p.731) where it is stated that
although Bathsheba was predestined for David, "he enjoyed her
before she was ripe" (lit. "as an unripe fig" or "paggâ"); see
Löw, *Flora*, I, p.241; *RAC*, 7, p.661.

/43/   See *RE*(Hamburger), I, p.360; *DCG*, 1, p.592; Löw, *Flora*, I,
p.252.

/44/   Cf. also Bem.R.XII.9; XXI.15, and *Str-B*, I, pp.857-8; II,
pp.26-7; Löw, *Flora*, I, p.251.

/45/   The generative potency of the fig-tree makes it a fitting
image for cosmogonic speculation and its use in this respect is
attested in a number of quite diverse traditions. Dr. R.D.H.Brown has
drawn my attention to its presence in the Hindu tradition, where
the cosmos is likened to an "eternal fig tree", whose root is
Brahman (Katha Upanishad, VI,1; cited by H.D. Lewis, R.L. Slater,
World Religions, p.44). Cf. also *RAC*, 7, p.640.

      Hippolytus records that the Docetists held a similar view,
claiming that God (or the first God) was the seed of a fig and
out of him, as from a fig-tree, the cosmos sprang into being.
From God emerged three Aeons corresponding to the branches, leaves
and fruit of the fig-tree (cf. *Philosophumena*, VIII.8-11, transl.
F. Legge, Vol.II, pp.99-105). This passage is interesting for it
gives a cosmological interpretation of both Mk.11.12-14, 20 ff.,
and Mk.13.28-32, treating God, among other things, as the fruit
that was sought. Ginzberg (*Legends*, V, p.98, fn.70) thinks that the
Docetic view may bear a close relation to the tradition, attested
in both Jewish and Christian circles, that the fig-tree was the
Tree of Knowledge, but a possible influence may also have come
from the Hindu tradition (cf. e.g. *Phil*.VIII.7, Legge, p.99).

/46/   Cf. also Pes.K.143a and *RAC*, 7, p.663 (which cites P. Volz,
Eschatologie der jüdischen Gemeinde (1934), p.372); Löw, *Flora*, I,
p.250.

/47/   *NTS*, 10 (1963-4), p.101.

/48/   *Supra*, p.23.

/49/   This problem has continued to plague scholarly exegetes even
up to the present day; cf. Haenchen, *Weg*, p.380: "Wie soll er da
einen Baum verflucht haben, an dem er keine Frucht fand? Jesus ist
doch kein Kind, das den Schemel schlägt, der „ihm weh getan hat";
er weiss, dass der Baum keine Person ist, die schuldig werden kann."

/50/   See J.G. Kahn's article, *supra*, p.23 and n.149.

/51/   *Supra*, n.28.

/52/   Derrett, *HeythJ*, 14 (1973), p.252.

/53/   *Supra*, pp.113-14.

/54/   *History*, p.235.

      According to a mediaeval source, R. Abraham b. Solomon's
Supplement (flor. late fifteenth century) to R. Abraham b. David's

Chronicle, 'The Book of Tradition' (comp.1161 CE), a certain Rabbi
Netanel is also said to have cursed a fig-tree, after losing a
precious ring in connection with it. Three years later, when the
tree was being cut down for bearing no fruit, the ring was
discovered amid great rejoicing. Thereafter the tree blossomed
as it had done before and was referred to henceforth as the
fig-tree that R. Netanel had cursed ויקראו שמן כן רבי נתנאל מקלל
התאינה (A. Neubauer, *Mediaeval Jewish Chronicles*, p.105; *gratia*
Löw, *Flora*, I, p.253).
/55/   The Rabbi's curse was described as "the serpent of the
Rabbis" (cf. e.g. B.Shab.110a, Sonc., pp.534-5), whose bite was
believed incurable.
/56/   For a whole series of examples, see *Str-B*, I, pp.858-9;
Schlatter, *Matthäus*, p.618.
       Even in more recent times, such powers have been credited
to the religious leaders of certain communities. J.E. Carpenter
(citing Turner, *Samoa*, p.23) recounts, for example, how in Samoa
"the eye of a certain high priest and prophet bearing the title
Tupai had the same deadly power: 'If he looked at a cocoa-nut
tree, it died; if he glanced at a bread-fruit tree, it withered
away' (*Three Gospels*, p.158, fn.2).
/57/   A contemporary of R. Ashi and R. Jose b. Abin who lived
in the fourth century.
/58/   See Goldschmidt, *Der babylonische Talmud*, III, p.496;
italics mine.
/59/   J.E. Carpenter cites another such converse miracle, this
time occurring in the Buddhist tradition. "As the great minister
Basita stood at the gates of the Lumbini garden when the infant
Buddha was born, he saw the trees and flowers bursting into life.
'See,' he observed to his colleagues, 'how all the trees are
blossoming *as if the season had come*.' The wondrous verdure had
its own meaning. 'It referred,' said the narrator, 'to the
faith which those were able to arrive at who heard the first
teachings of the sage.'" (Beal, *Romantic History of Buddha*,
pp.45,46; cited Carpenter, *Three Gospels*, p.158, fn.1.).
/60/   For an account of these legends, see O. Dähnhardt,
Natursagen, Vol.II, pp.25, 31 ff., 34-5, 46-7; Löw, *Flora*, I,
p.253; *RAC*, 7, p.686.
/61/   As J.G. Kahn suggests (*NovTest*, 13 (1971), p.39 and fn.2).
/62/   See Bowman, *Mark*, pp.221-2.
/63/   See also Derrett, *HeythJ*, 14 (1973), pp.253-4, and *supra*
pp.134-6.
/64/   The other gifts were his lustre, his immortality, his
(extraordinary) height, the fruit of the earth, and the light of
the sun and the moon, which were all reduced. For further

references to this tradition, see Ginzberg, *Legends*, I, p.86; V,
pp.113-4 and fn.105.
/65/   See Ber.R.XV.7 and Ginzberg, *Legends*, I, p.75; V, pp.97-8
and fn.70.
/66/   A pseudepigraphical work, also known (more aptly) as the
Book of Adam and Eve or the Life of Adam and Eve. The conjectured
date of composition is the late Second Temple Period. Its author-
ship has been ascribed to Jewish mystic circles, possibly the
Essenes. See *EJR*, p.12.
/67/   See R.H. Charles, *The Apocrypha and Pseudepigrapha of the
Old Testament*, Vol.II, p.146; E. Kautzsch, *Die Apokryphen und
Pseudepigraphen des Alten Testaments*, Vol.II, p.522; Ginzberg,
Legends, I, pp.96-7.
/68/   Cf. also P.R.E.XX (Friedlander, p.144); The (Ethiopic) Book
of Adam and Eve, chaps.XXXVI-XLI (transl. S.C. Malan, pp.39-44).
/69/   Charles, *op.cit.*, p.147; Kautzsch, *op.cit.*, p.522; Ginzberg,
ibid.
/70/   Cf. e.g. B.Ber.40a B.Sanh.70a-70b Ber.R.XV.7 Qoh.R.V.10.1
Pes.R.XLII.1 (Braude, II, p.736) Apoc.Mos.20 (Charles, II, p.146;
Kautzsch, II, p.522); The Book of the Bee, chaps.XV-XVI (Budge,
pp.20-3); The Testament of Adam, 3.13-14 (Riessler, p.1087); cf.
also Est.R.V.1 - the vine was also put forward as a candidate,
along with the wheat plant and the ethrog (citron).
        The Church Fathers in particular exploited this speculative
identification. Starting from verses such as Ps.96.10 (v.1), "The
Lord reigns from the tree", highly fanciful links were made between
the Tree of Knowledge of Good and Evil, the Tree of Life and the
Cross. Christ had been nailed, for example, to the wood of the
fig-tree whose fruit Adam had eaten (*RAC*, 7, p.669). The link was
even extended to the cursing pericope. According to one tradition,
Christ had cursed the fig-tree so that it would no longer give
occasion for the human race to sin as in Eden (*RAC*, 7, p.672). Cf.
also Trench, *Miracles*, p.481 and fn.2.
        *For further references and for discussion on this Tree of
Knowledge tradition,* see Ginzberg, *Legends*, I, pp.75, 96-7; V, pp.
97-8 and fn.70; Dalman, *Arbeit*, I, p.57; *Str-B*, I, p.858; Löw,
Flora, I, p.249; *Pflanzennamen*, p.390, fn.1; R.M. Grant, *JBL*, 67
(1948), p.299; *RAC*, 7, pp.659-60, 666 ff.; *ThDNT*, 7, p.752, fn.19;
J. Jeremias, "Die Berufung des Nathanael", *Angelos*, 3 (1930), p.3.
For background material on the apocryphal Books of Adam, see, for
example, *EJud*, 2, pp.234-47. For the Cave of Treasures group, too,
see, for example, J. Bowker, *Targums*, pp.91-2.
/71/   See Ginzberg, *Legends*, V, p.119 and fn.113. In the Wisdom
literature the Tree of Life was identified with Wisdom and,
according to Fawcett, this idea was in fact taken up in Rabbinic

literature where the Tree of Life was regularly understood as a
symbol of the Torah (*Myth*, p.271; cf. also B.Ta'an. 7a). E.R.
Goodenough (*Jewish Symbols*, VII, pp.127-30) states that the tree's
place in eschatology was known to the Rabbis but usually avoided,
presumably on account of its popular and pagan veneration as a
cult object (cf. e.g. B.'A.Z.45a-47a M.P.A.3.8, and see also
Fawcett, *ibid.*). One may compare, however, Shem.R.XXV.8 (Sonc.,
pp.309-10), where God, it is said, will prepare a great banquet
for the righteous in the New Age, and "will bring them fruit from
the Garden of Eden and will feed them from the Tree of Life" (cf.
also B.Pes.119b).

The notion that the righteous will eat of the Tree of Life in
Paradise is one that is frequently met with in the apocryphal
tradition; cf. e.g. Apoc.Mos.28.2-4 (Charles, II, p.148); T. Levi
18.11 (Charles, II, p.315); 4 Ezra 8.52 cf. 7.123 (Charles, II,
pp.597, 591); 2 Enoch 8.2-5 (Charles, II, p.434); Enoch 24.4 -
25.5 cf. 32.3-6 (Charles, *The Book of Enoch*, pp.52-3, 60-1). It
is encountered, too, in the New Testament (Ap.2.7; 22.1-5 cf. also
Ez.47.12). See Goodenough, *Jewish Symbols*, VII, pp.126-7; Schneider,
ThDNT, 5, p.40; Fawcett, *Myth*, p.274.

Christian tradition and exegesis drew a great deal on such
notions, the Tree of Life being linked from Patristic times onwards,
for example, with the Cross of Jesus. For a survey of the
Patristic material, see *RAC*, 7, pp.668 ff., and Goodenough, *Jewish
Symbols*, VII, pp.119 ff.; for the mediaeval legends, see, for
example, Crowfoot, Baldensperger, *From Cedar to Hyssop*, pp.130-3.

/72/   See Ginzberg, *Legends*, I, p.112; V, pp.141-2 and fns.29,30.
/73/   *Vide supra*, p.134 and n.33.
/74/   See Ginzberg, *op.cit.*, III, pp.36 ff.
/75/   Ginzberg, III, p.39; VI, p.14 and fns.81 and 82.
/76/   Ginzberg, III, p.45; VI, p.18 and fn.105.
/77/   Ginzberg, III, p.44; VI, p.17 and fn.97.
/78/   Ginzberg, III, pp.52-3; VI, p.21, esp. fn.129.
/79/   Ginzberg, III, p.53; VI, p.21 and fns. 130 and 131.
/80/   Ginzberg, III, pp.306-7; VI, pp.106-7 and fn.600.
/81/   Cf. e.g. the wilderness feeding miracles and esp. Jn.6 where
Jesus is identified as the manna that came down from heaven; cf. also
Jn.4.13-14 & 1 Cor.10.1-5.
/82/   Josephus, for example, furnishes many examples of Messianic
pretenders or prophets who urged the people to follow them into
the wilderness where again Yahweh would reveal his power through
signs and wonders and lead and strengthen his people as he had in
days of old. See W.R. Farmer, *Maccabees, Zealots and Josephus*,
pp.116-22.
/83/   *Supra*, p.169, n.62.

/84/   Lebanon was identified with the Sanctuary; cf. 1 Kgs.10.21
and B.Giṭ.56b, Sonc., p.258: "Lebanon refers to the Sanctuary, as
it says, 'This goodly mountain and Lebanon' (Dt.3.25)." Cf. also
Fawcett, *Myth,* p.175, and *supra,* p.170, n.65.
/85/   The legend reappears in B.Yom.39b, a passage describing the
portents in the forty years before the Fall of Jerusalem which had
presaged the Temple's destruction; cf. also P.Yom.IV.4 (Schwab,
p.208) Bem.R.XI.3;XII.4 Shem.R.XXXV.1 Shir.R.III.10.3, and
Ginzberg, *Legends,* IV, p.154; VI, p.294 and fn.58; III, p.163; V.,
p.122 and fn.125. Josephus, Ginzberg notes, gives a rationalistic
rendering of this same legend (see Ant.VIII.136 and *Legends,* VI,
p.294 and fn.58).
/86/   Ginzberg, *Legends,* III, pp.162-3; VI, p.66 and fn.342.
/87/   The withering of the trees is also seen as an omen of
misfortune in the Job story; cf. Targum on Job 2.11, cited
Ginzberg, *Legends,* V, p.387 and fn.30.
/88/   See Dowda, *Cleansing,* pp.155-6.
/89/   M.Mid.2.6 (Danby, p.593); cf. also B.Sheḳ.VI.3 and Dowda,
Cleansing, pp.155-7.
/90/   *Ibid.*
/91/   For further references to the belief in the wonderful fertilit
of the earth in Messianic times, see Ginzberg, *Legends,* V, p.141 and
fn.30.
/92/   *Vide supra,* p.23.

Chapter VII

THE NEW TESTAMENT BACKGROUND

Introduction

Our investigations to date into the Old Testament and late Jewish background have enabled us to construct a nexus of interrelated themes and associations with respect to the tree and the fig-tree in the ancient world. Though disparate in time and origin, this material has nonetheless introduced us into a common 'world' in which nature was seen as responsive to the human situation, in which trees in particular would *literally* offer or refuse their fruit to the righteous or wicked, in which a marvellous display of productivity was deemed to attend the Golden Ages of Israel's experience.

We have seen, too, that the tree was also highly *symbolical* for the ancient world. The blossoming of the trees was a sign of good fortune, the withering of the trees an omen of impending disaster. The tree was a common symbol for the religious life of the ancients and the fig-tree itself was compared in Jewish tradition with the nation of Israel, its representatives and even its Holy City. This highly symbolic tree was observed, too, to have a special connection with the Temple and the Messianic Age, its blossoming and fruitfulness an emblem for the blessings of that Age, its withering a sign of eschatological judgement.

The overwhelming force of this evidence suggests, then, that the fig-tree story in Mark's gospel was intended at the Markan level to be understood both literally and symbolically and, indeed, would have been so understood. At the pre-Markan level, the climate of eschatological belief regarding the expected fruitfulness of the Messianic Age has suggested a plausible creative milieu for the story before Mark took it and gave it an added symbolic dimension. It will be the purpose of this chapter, therefore, to determine whether the more immediate 'world' of the New Testament lends support to these conclusions. Was the abundant fertility of the New Age a belief entertained in New Testament times? Is the New Testament use of tree imagery in general symbolic? Can an eschatological and/or symbolic dimension be perceived with respect to the New Testament's other references to the fig-tree? We shall begin by examining briefly the character of the New Age as it is revealed in the gospels.

End-time Expectation in the Early Church

No one who reads these documents can avoid the impression
that for the early church the New Age of Jewish expectations had
dawned with the coming of Jesus. The question of how he himself
envisaged this Age, whether he expected it to come in his lifetime
or with his death, has been much debated /1/. Nevertheless, to
his followers in the years immediately after his crucifixion, the
conditions of that Age had begun with his appearance and would
shortly be consummated with his Parousia. The 'world' described
by the evangelists and their sources is a world in which the
extraordinary and the miraculous are deemed to have been witnessed.
Nature was responsive to Jesus. Winds and waves had obeyed him
(Mk.4.35-41 and parallels). He had walked across the water (Mk.6.
45-52 and parallels). Demons had been exorcized by the finger of
God (Mt.12.28 = Lk.11.20), the blind were made to see, the deaf to
hear, the lame to walk (Mt.11.5 = Lk.7.22). Jesus himself had
seen Satan fall from heaven (Lk.10.18).

The signs of the Kingdom's coming, then, were all around to
see (Mt.16.2-3; cf. Lk.12.54-56) and the present generation would
not pass away before that Kingdom had been finally manifested
(Mk.9.1; 13.30 and parallels). The immediate followers of Jesus,
the Twelve who had represented perhaps the new Israel /2/, had
themselves experienced the powers that the faithful would possess
in the New Age. They had healed the sick and exorcized demons
(Mk.6.13 and parallels). They had witnessed the miraculous in the
wilderness, participating in a banquet for thousands which had
been manufactured from a few loaves and fishes (Mk.6.30-44; 8.1-10
and parallels). For the author of the longer ending of Mark, they
were promised immunity from snake bites and deadly poison (Mk.16.
18; cf. Lk.10.19 Acts 28.3-6). For the sacrifices they had made
they would be repaid "a hundredfold in this present age" and in
the world to come, eternal life (Mk.10.29-30 and parallels).

The 'hundredfold' repayment, which also calls to mind the
harvest expected from the sowing of the word (Mk.4.8) leads one
naturally to wonder if the more specific belief that the Messianic
Age would be a time of abundant fruitfulness was entertained in New
Testament times. In the stimulating article that we have referred
to frequently hitherto /3/, R.H. Hiers has presented compelling
evidence that this is so. Hiers draws examples from the wide
range of pre- and post-Christian sources, viz, the Old Testament,
the Apocrypha and Pseudepigrapha and the Rabbinic literature,
material that we ourselves have surveyed, and from the New Testament

and the Church Fathers in addition. As a result he concludes:
"there is abundant evidence that many Jews, both before and
after Jesus' time, believed that in the messianic age the fertility
of nature would be so transformed that the ground would yield a
continuous harvest, and tree and vine would be everbearing /4/.

There are good grounds for assuming, therefore, that this
belief was a familiar part of the tradition in the first century.
Hiers, however, goes somewhat further and maintains that such
ideas can be attributed directly to Jesus himself. The evidence
for this bolder claim is to be found, he asserts, in two early
Christian sources /5/. It is found in Ap.2.7b and 22.2 where the
Tree of Life, as in Enoch 24 - 25 (cf. Ez.47.12) will be transplanted to the heavenly Jerusalem and fruit from that tree (Jesus
says) will be presented by him to the righteous /6/. In the
so-called 'Papias Apocalypse', moreover, Jesus himself is said to
have claimed (according to a tradition going back to the disciple
John) that in the New Age vines would grow with ten thousand
branches, grains of wheat with ten thousand ears and all other
fruit-bearing trees, and seeds, and grass, would produce in similar
proportions (cf. 2 Baruch 29.5) /7/.

It is by no means certain, however, that these two Christian
sources necessarily reflect Jesus' own End-time conceptions, far
less, indeed, his actual words, and Hiers is even ready to admit
this. What these sayings indubitably do indicate, on the other
hand, is that such ideas were not alien to the followers of Jesus
in the century following his ministry (as Hiers rightly states),
and the New Testament evidence, though scanty, suggests likewise.
Again the passages highlighted by Hiers are suggestive. The
parable of the Mustard Seed (Mk.4.30-32) with its extraordinary
growth may represent, he supposes, an example of the kind of
fertility that was expected to obtain in the Kingdom of God.
Behind the miracle of the transformation of water into wine at
Cana (Jn.2.1-11) may lie the popular notion that the miraculous
production of wine was to be a normal phenomenon of the Messianic
Age /8/. In the wilderness feeding miracle(s), there may be
reflected the idea of the Messianic banquet (Mk.6.30-44; 8.1-10 and
parallels), a conception attested elsewhere /9/, and one that is
perhaps also to be discerned in the account of the Last Supper
where Jesus looks forward to drinking new wine with his disciples
in the Kingdom of God (Mk.14.25 and parallels) /10/.

In thus drawing attention to the haggadic and eschatological
conceptions that prevailed in New Testament times, Hiers has

presented us with a fitting background against which the fig-tree
story may be understood as its *primary* level. On the negative side,
nonetheless, his treatment of Mk.11.12-14, 20 ff. has overlooked
the different redactional levels that are to be discerned in the
pericope. Hiers accepts that the story reflects in the main /11/
a genuine historical tradition that when Jesus himself had
entered Jerusalem he believed that the Messianic Age was about to
begin and, therefore, that a fig-tree such as the one he encountered
should have borne him fruit no matter what the season. In
disappointment, he "hopes, vows, or commands, that no one eat of
its fruit again, at any rate, until the arrival of the coming age."
/12/ In taking a broadly historical approach to the story, Hiers
fails to recognize that this pericope is an insertion by the second
evangelist and that its connection with the Jerusalem traditions
is secondary. As a result, he is not constrained to account for
the pericope's curious position in the gospel. He accords to the
story no symbolic intent and yet the search for figs from the
fig-tree is a figurative and symbolic motif that also has, as we
have seen, midrashic and haggadic attestation. In short, his
treatment is completely without regard for a literary- and redaction-
critical perspective and this is its shortcoming. While this
enigmatic story may originally have had a haggadic background and
an eschatological Sitz im Leben of the kind that Hiers points to,
it is the recognition of its added symbolic function in Mark that
is the clue whereby it may be completely unravelled. The New
Testament, indeed, furnishes good grounds for our belief that both
an eschatological *and* a symbolic dimension would have been
perceived, and it is, therefore, to its use of tree imagery in
general that we shall now turn.

Trees and Fig-trees in the New Testament

The use for symbolic purposes of tree imagery and its
related themes of fruit and fruitfulness is as common in the New
Testament as it is in the Old. In the latter we saw that the
tree could stand for the wicked or the righteous, but more often
it stood for the nation itself, its growth, blossoming and bearing
of fruit, or, conversely, its barrenness, withering and devastation
symbolizing the nation's fortunes. We noted that Israel, though
often identified with the vine, was yet also compared to the fig-
tree. Judgement was expressed upon the nation by God's blasting
of the trees, but particularly by his smiting of vine and fig-tree.
A link in the Jewish mind between 'tree' and 'Temple' was also
recognized, the proper observance of the cultus being allied with

both the literal fruitfulness of the earth, and the spiritual
'fruitfulness' of the people.

In the New Testament, too, such motifs appear. We see them
in Paul, for example. In 1 Cor.3.5-17, not Israel but the
Christian community is God's 'planting' and, at the same time,
significantly, his building (οἰκοδομή), his living Temple (ναός).
Here, too, a note of eschatological judgement is sounded, for when
the Day comes, fire will test how adequately the community's
Christian foundation has been laid (3.13-15) /13/.

We find such symbolism in John. In Jn.15.1-8, for example,
Jesus, not Israel, is the true vine and Christians are the
branches whose function it is to bear fruit. Again a cautionary
note is struck. Branches not bearing fruit are cast forth and
wither (ἐξηράνθη). They shall be gathered, thrown into the fire
and burned (15.6)! /14/

In the Apocalypse, as we have seen, apocalyptic Tree of Life
imagery makes its appearance, with Jesus himself offering fruit
from this Tree "to the one who conquers" (2.7). In the New
Jerusalem, after the old city has passed away, waters will flow,
not from the Temple, as in Old Testament and late Jewish
expectation, but from the throne of God and of the Lamb, and
Trees of Life (again symbolic) will bear perennial fruit
(22.1-2,14,19).

In Hebrews, nature imagery is likewise employed for figurative
purposes (cf.6.7-8) with members of the Christian community who
have committed apostasy being compared to once fruitful ground now
barren.

"For land which has drunk the rain that often falls
upon it, and brings forth vegetation useful to those
for whose sake it is cultivated, receives a blessing
from God. But if it bears thorns and thistles, it is
worthless and near to being cursed; its end is to
be burned." (RSV)

The theme of an eschatological judgement that is actualized in
the smiting of the tree finds its expression, too, in the Synoptic
gospels. In Lk.3.9 (= Mt.3.10), John the Baptist warns the Jewish
crowds (in Matthew, the representatives of the nation, the
Pharisees and the Sadducees) that "even now the axe lies at the root
of the trees (ἤδη δὲ καὶ ἡ ἀξίνη πρὸς τὴν ῥίζαν τῶν δένδρων κεῖται);

every tree, therefore, not bearing good fruit is cut down and
thrown into the fire." Ernst Lohmeyer has devoted an article to
the Matthean logion /15/ in which he argues forcibly that the
"trees" of the first part of the logion refer to *vines*, and that
the nation of Israel collectively is here to be understood. The
second part of the logion is an individualizing supplement, and
the force of the saying is that the true and future Israel will
not be represented by those claiming heredity or blood affiliation
("We have Abraham for our father", Mt.3.9 = Lk.3.8) but by those
individuals who do God's will (cf. Rom.9.6-8).

In view of the almost exact concurrence between Mt.3.10 and
Lk.3.9, however, Harald Sahlin /16/ maintains that the Lukan text
has been subject to a later harmonization with Matthew. In Luke's
text, he asserts, and originally also in Q, the logion simply ran:
ἤδη δὲ καὶ ἡ ἀξίνη πρὸς τὴν ῥίζαν κεῖται. Matthew has added the
generalizing and individualizing verse 10b (under the influence of
Mt.7.19 which is also Matthean) and in view of the plurality of
trees has added τῶν δένδρων after τὴν ῥίζαν. The upshot is that
a Q saying which originally referred to a single tree has been
reshaped theologically in an individualizing direction. The single
tree originally referred to was the vine, and the reference was
clearly to Israel.

Not all scholars would recognize here a specific reference to
the vine. Indeed, it might even be argued that the fig-tree was
here in view since in Luke's parable (13.6-9) the figure employed
by John the Baptist is developed in fuller form /17/. No
particular tree, on the other hand, may be intended but what is
significant for our purposes is that the image of the 'tree', be
it vine, fig-tree or any other, is clearly being used figuratively
for Israel, as in the Old Testament, and that the nation is being
threatened with eschatological judgement by means of this figure /18/

This notion of Israel as God's tree or 'planting' may also be
reflected in Mt.15.13 where Jesus, on hearing of the offence taken
by the Pharisees at his words, replies: "Every plant (πᾶσα φυτεία)
/19/ which my heavenly Father has not planted will be rooted up
(ἐκριζωθήσεται)." By insinuating that the religious leaders of
Israel were not necessarily of God's planting, Jesus, too, like
John the Baptist, may possibly be seen as tilting against this
popular conviction that mere physical descent from Abraham
conferred on the Jewish people the right to be considered God's
Chosen Ones. Those Pharisees who so believed would soon discover
that they were alien plants, and were doomed to be uprooted!/20/.

Another judgement saying in which the tree figures as an
analogy for the nation is to be found on the lips of Jesus on his
way to be crucified. Having prophesied to the women of Jerusalem
the terrible destruction that would one day befall the city, he
finishes by asking: "if they do this, then, when the wood is green,
what will happen when it is dry?" (Lk.23.32; cf. Ez.17.24). The
point is clear. If Jesus himself, 'a green tree', filled with the
sap of innocence, has not been spared, then what hope is there for
a guilty nation, 'a withered tree', dry and bare, fit only for the
fire /21/?

The use of fruitfulness and harvest imagery to convey spiritual
and symbolic meaning is above all to be seen in Mark himself. The
fact indeed that Mark uses καρπός in 11.14 instead of figs indicates,
thinks Münderlein, that we are standing "im Bereich der verschiedenen
Sprüche über Baum und Frucht" /22/. The theme of 'fruitfulness' as
a symbol for the response by faith to the Son of God is seen in
Mark, chapter 4, for example. In the parable of the Sower, an
obedient and *faith*-ful response to the word of Jesus, results in
abundant *fruit* (καὶ ἐδίδου καρπὸν ἀναβαίνοντα καὶ αὐξανόμενα 4.8).
Seed falling on rocky ground, on the other hand, represents a
shallow and ephemeral response to the word, which, *having no roots*,
withers (καὶ διὰ τὸ μὴ ἔχειν ῥίζαν ἐξηράνθη 4.6). Three key words
used in the fig-tree story, then, καρπός, ῥίζα and ξηραίνω are here
found employed in Mark in an obviously symbolic way /23/. The word
καρπός is also used figuratively in 4.29 in the parable of the
Growing Seed, where again the nature-image, growth culminating in
a final harvest (θερισμός), is a picture for the Kingdom of God and
the coming Age /24/. The marvellous growth associated with the
Kingdom is depicted in the parable of the Mustard Seed (4.30-32)
and has been commented on already.

The supreme example, however, of the symbolic use of fruit and
fruitfulness imagery in Mark's gospel is perhaps his parable of the
Vineyard (12.1-12). This parable, we believe, has a symbolic
content which is similar to that conveyed in the fig-tree story.
When the season has come (τῷ καιρῷ 12.2; cf. Mt.21.34 ὅτε δὲ ἤγγισεν
ὁ καιρὸς τῶν καρπῶν) the owner claims from those he has put in
charge of his vineyard the fruit that is rightfully his (ἵνα παρὰ
τῶν γεωργῶν λάβῃ ἀπὸ τῶν καρπῶν τοῦ ἀμπελῶνος 12.2). When this
fruit is withheld, a solemn judgement is announced. The lord
(ὁ κύριος) of the vineyard will come and kill these tenants and
hand over his vineyard to others (12.9) /25/.

The term καιρός (time, or season) here used (12.2) appears
also in 11.13d and on three other occasions in Mark's gospel (1.15;

10.30; 13.33). In these three latter cases the word is not to be understood purely in a chronological sense. It has, as Giesen points out /26/, an "Entscheidungscharakter", that is, it conveys the notion of a fateful and decisive point in human affairs, the divinely appointed opportunity granted for men to repent or perish /27/. In 12.2, therefore, the term may signify not only that it was the season for fruit but also that it was, in Münderlein's words, an "eschatologisch qualifizierte Zeit" /28/. The failure of Israel and her leaders 'at the decisive time' to render the fruit of faith and obedience to the Son of God, and the consequent destruction of the nation are here in view.

The evidence that we have considered, then, suggests that tree, fruit and harvest imagery was employed in the New Testament, as in the Old, almost exclusively in a spiritual and symbolic sense, that it was frequently applied in respect of both the old Israel and the new, and very often with the express notion of an eschatological judgement upon the former. Mark himself has confirmed this view. Giesen, indeed, declares that all references to fruit and/or fruits in Mark are to be symbolically understood /29/. Little further doubt should remain, therefore, that his fig-tree story is meant likewise to be understood in this way. Nevertheless it is further to be observed that not only the tree but *even the fig-tree itself* is found employed elsewhere in Mark and in the New Testament in general in *symbolic* and/or *eschatological contexts.*

We earlier noted, for example, that the fig-tree's casting of its leaves was a descriptive motif for the End-Time of God's judgement (Is.34.4). This Isaianic picture reappears in a more developed form in Ap.6.13-14 /30/. The fig also appears in figurative imagery in Mt.7.16 = Lk.6.44 (cf. Mt.12.33) and Jas.3.12. Here, a saying about the impossibility of obtaining figs from thistles (Mt.7.16), figs from thorns (Lk.6.44) or figs from vines (Jas.3.12) is used analogously to support a spiritual lesson /31/. The three remaining fig-tree passages are the Markan parable of chapter 13.28-32 (= Mt.24.32-36 = Lk.21.29-33), the enigmatic reference to Nathanael "under the fig-tree" (Jn.1.48,50) and Luke's own barren fig-tree parable (13.6-9). Since all three of these fig-tree passages have light to shed on the meaning of our own story, we shall discuss each of them in turn.

The Markan Parable of the Fig-Tree
(Mk. 13.28-32)

The little parable of the fig-tree in Mk.13.28-32 is fraught
with difficulties. Before we comment on its significance for
Mk.11.12-14, 20 ff., it is worth questioning whether the common
designation 'parable' is really appropriate here. It is only Luke
after all who specifically terms it such ("And he *told* them *a
parable*", 21.29). Mark's opening words are different, with no
mention of Jesus narrating a parable in the normal sense of that
word: /32/ "From the fig-tree *learn the lesson* (τὴν παραβολήν)" or
perhaps "the veiled meaning" or to accurately paraphrase, "Learn
the lesson that the fig-tree has to teach" (13.28; so also Matthew).
With its branches green in springtime and its proud show of leaves,
the fig-tree is a sign that the summer or harvest (or harvest-
judgement?) is soon to come. The lesson or veiled message that
the disciples (οὕτως καὶ ὑμεῖς) and hence Mark's readers, are
invited to draw from the fig-tree is that when they see "these
things" (ταῦτα) happen they are to know that 'he' or 'it' is
"near to the gates (ὅτι ἐγγύς ἐστιν ἐπὶ θύραις)."

The words and syntax of verses 28 and 29 are extremely
puzzling and their precise meaning obscure. Is the reference to
the fig-tree here to be understood generically or does Mark or
his source have a particular fig-tree in mind, viz, that in 11.12-14,
20 ff.? Is it the natural blossoming of fig-trees in springtime
that is here being employed as an analogy for an eschatological
claim, or does Mark or his source have a definite eschatological
event in mind which will happen or has happened to this specific
tree? Does the word θέρος here mean simply 'summer' or 'harvest-
time' or does it too have eschatological overtones /33/? The
moods of the two verbs γινώσκετε are unclear. Are they indicative
or imperative, or indicative in the one case and imperative in the
other? Why are both in the second person plural, when the οὕτως
καὶ ὑμεῖς of verse 29 suggests a change of person /34/. How indeed
is this awkward οὕτως καὶ ὑμεῖς to be taken? Does καὶ qualify and
hence emphasize ὑμεῖς ("likewise when *you also* see these things ...")
or does it actually qualify the entire preceding verse, although
attracted to the personal pronoun ("So, too - as in the case of
the fig-tree - when you see these things ...")? /35/ What precisely
is meant by "these things"? Does the ταῦτα refer to its immediate
antecedent, the Parousia of the Son of Man (13.26-27) or to the
eschatological events preceding the Parousia which are described
throughout the chapter (cf. e.g. 13.6-8,14,21-22,24-25)? What,
moreover, is the subject of ἐγγύς ἐστιν? Is it the 'harvest-
judgement' of verse 28 (so Schwartz, Bacon), the Son of Man or the

Messiah (so Wendling, Jeremias), the Messianic Age (so Derrett) or
the Kingdom of God (so Luke)? What, finally, is the source-redactional relationship between the individual components of this
pericope (13.28-32) as also that between the pericope and the
entire Apocalyptic Discourse (13.3-37)? Is the 'parable' a Markan
composition or has he taken it over from another source? Does this
source go back to Jesus? Can a distinction be drawn between the
original meaning of the 'parable' and its meaning in the Markan
context?

Given these manifest difficulties, it is not surprising
that the passage has been subject to a variety of interpretative
emendations, the earliest of which were made by Luke himself. While
Matthew for the most part reproduces Mark, Luke has considerably
altered his Vorlage /36/. He has remodelled Mark's introduction,
describing Jesus' words as a definite parable told by him to his
disciples. In so doing, he has subtly shifted the Markan sense
of the word παραβολή here, has disguised the abrupt and unannounced
mention of the fig-tree that is a curious feature of the Markan
text, and hence has removed any sign that a tradition- or redaction-
connection might exist between 13.28-29 and 11.12-14. He shortens
the description of the fig-tree's putting forth its leaves and adds
the generalizing "and all the trees (καὶ πάντα τὰ δένδρα)", hence
indicating his failure to appreciate the especial fitness of the
fig-tree as a symbolic harbinger of both θέρος and ἔσχατον. He has
also created, as we have noted, a closer linkage between verses 28
and 29 by adding βλέποντες ἀφ' ἑαυτῶν after γινώσκετε (21.30; cf.
Lk.12.57) and has given "the Kingdom of God" as the subject of
ἐγγύς ἐστιν.

Despite these changes, it is widely admitted that Luke has
done little to bring out the proper sense of the passage, and,
indeed, in the view of many exegetes, he has actually disguised
its original or Markan significance /37/. Luke's attempt to smooth
over the difficulties of the passage serves rather to highlight the
disturbed nature of the text. In view of such undoubted awkwardness,
therefore, a considerable number of scholars would now hold that
Mark has attempted to press into service material in which a fig-tree
was mentioned and which originally had a different meaning and
context.

The view that Mark's 'parable' is a 'Fremdkörper' has received
its most celebrated expression in Schwartz's article of 1904 which
we summarized in chapter I /38/. In pre-Markan tradition, the
fig-tree of Mk.13.28 was a specific fig-tree in the vicinity of

Jerusalem which Jesus was believed to have condemned to barrenness
until his coming Parousia, and which prior to that time would again
blossom forth.

Such a tradition-connection had been earlier suspected by
Wellhausen, for why, he asked, had Mark not spoken of the trees in
general /39/? Having read Schwartz's treatment of the pericope, he
espoused this view with greater vehemence. After all, he declared,
the rising of the sap in trees is not really a sign that the θέρος
was close at hand, if θέρος is taken to mean the summertime or
harvest. And why only in the fig-tree? A definite eschatological
event must therefore be meant /40/.

This opinion has not commanded widespread support. The
definite article before συκῇ in the singular, it has been objected,
does not necessarily point to a single, specific tree but simply
means fig-trees in general /41/. Moreover, the reason that the
fig-tree is here given special mention is simply because it was
the most characteristic springtime tree /42/.

For these reasons, many scholars think that the 'parable' has
a *general* application only in Mark (so Bacon, Münderlein, Jeremias,
Dupont), the (present) summer or harvest expectation engendered by
the early verdure of this characteristic springtime tree providing
an analogy for the (future) imminent approach of the End-time.
Nonetheless, it is still doubtful whether this was the 'parable's'
original application. J. Jeremias points out that chapter 13 is,
after all, a secondary composition, and that the fig-tree symbol
points, in fact, in a different direction from what we would
expect. The blossoming of the fig-tree is normally a sign of the
coming *blessing* (cf. Jl.2.22), whereas here it is employed
(inappropriately, Jeremias thinks) for the *dreadful portents* that
herald the end. In Jesus' mouth, he asserts, the simile had
originally directed the disciples "not towards the horrors of the
end of the age, but towards the signs of the time of salvation" /43/.

J. Dupont has also claimed that the 'parable' goes back to
Jesus and that within the framework of his life and teaching the
analogy was applied not to the future Parousia of judgement but to
the present signs of the imminent Kingdom of God. Mk.13.28b is
pre-Markan, therefore, and corresponds to such logia, he suggests,
as Mt.12.28 = Lk.11.20 Mt.11.5 = Lk.7.22 Lk.12.54-56 (cf. Mt.16.
2-3) /44/. He also questions if it was Mark's practice to
illustrate a religious message by drawing a parallel from nature
(a point that is surely debatable!) /45/. Mk.13.29, on the other

hand, is (he states) clearly Markan /46/, and this can readily be
conceded.

The source-redactional position adopted by Jeremias, Dupont
and others has, in general, much to be said for it. It certainly
appears to account for the disturbed nature of this pericope. While,
too, one may also concur in regarding as purely speculative (and
ultimately undemonstrable) the aetiological saga hypothesis
advanced by Schwartz and Wellhausen, it may not be altogether fair
to dismiss outright the supposition that a connection does in fact
exist between 13.28-29 and 11.12-14. This connection need not
after all lie at the pre-Markan level as Schwartz and Wellhausen
have suggested. It may exist *at the redactional level*. Even were
it accepted that 13.28 is not a pure Markan composition /47/ and
that pre-Markan material (unrelated to 11.12-14) with a different
original meaning and context has been pressed into Mark's service,
one cannot avoid the suspicion that the evangelist may intend his
readers to think back to his previous mention of the fig-tree while
pondering what Jesus has to say here.

Certain considerations make this supposition a reasonable one.
In the first place, the reference to the fig-tree in chapter 13 is
sudden, abrupt, completely unannounced, a fact highlighted, as we
have noted, by Luke's remodelling of the Markan introduction.
This would be less inexplicable if Mark had intended his readers
to think back to the fig-tree in chapter 11.

In the second place, we should note that the fig-tree's
withering in chapter 11 was intended in our view to be seen as an
eschatological sign prefiguring an imminent *judgement* upon the
Jewish people, but in particular upon their Temple. In Chapter 13,
the disciples, and hence the readers, are invited to look upon the
fig-tree's *blossoming* as a sign likewise prefiguring an
eschatological event, viz, the coming Age of both *blessing* and
judgement. Here, then, Mark may perhaps be seen reflecting the
two different sides of the fig-tree's eschatological symbolism, that
is, its withering as a sign of judgement, its blossoming as a sign
of blessing (at least for Christians).

The parallel that exists (however awkwardly) between these two
sole references to the fig-tree in Mark is heightened considerably
when we take into account the symmetry that can be discerned
throughout chapter 11 to 13. This symmetry was commented on before
/48/ and marks the evangelist as a careful redactor who knew what
he was about /49/. The material in all three chapters, though

composite, is held together by the unifying theme of Jesus' first
and last visit to Jerusalem and its Temple. In 11.1, Jesus appears
on the Mount of Olives prior to that visit /50/; in 13.3, he is
found there again at its conclusion. In 11.1-10, we are presented
with Jesus' *triumphant entry* into Jerusalem, an anticlimactic event
which for Mark had betokened rejection for the *Son of God* /51/.
In 13.24-27, 32-37 we are told of Jesus' *triumphant return,* a
climactic event signalling vindication for the *Son of Man,*
judgement for the Jews and *blessing* for the Christian community.
In 11.11, he visits the Temple for the first time: in 13.1, he
leaves it for the last time. In 11.17, he utters his rebuke
against it; in 13.2, he pronounces its destruction. In 11.27-33,
Jesus' authority is called into question; in 13.24-27, it will be
made manifest. In 11.12-14, the fig-tree withers as a sign of an
eschatological judgement; in 13.28-29, it blossoms as a sign of an
impending Parousia!

     This entire scheme, then, is highly suggestive. However, were
this suggested link between both fig-tree passages merely accidental,
the latter passage would still serve a valuable function in casting
light upon our story. In its source-redactional relation to the
rest of chapter 13, the 'parable' pericope reveals the very concerns
and redactional procedure that were seen to operate in chapter 11.
For let us see what Mark has done.

     The "these things" that the disciples are to see happening
and which are to herald the imminent advent of either the harvest-
judgement, the Son of Man, the Messiah or the Messianic Age (each
interpretation may, in the end, add up to the same thing) cannot
be the events described in verses 26-27, for the Parousia of the
Son of Man described there *is* the end (τέλος) itself. Mark's
"*all* these things" (ταῦτα πάντα) of verse 30 (which are to occur
within the experience of Mark's readers) may, of course, embrace
both the dreadful portents *and* the final Parousia, but the ταῦτα
of verse 29 can only refer to the catalogue of premonitory signs
listed throughout the chapter (verses 7,8,11,14 etc.). But these,
it is to be observed, are all answers given to the twofold
question posed in verse 4 ("Tell us when these things - ταῦτα -
shall be, and what is the sign - τὸ σημεῖον - when all these things
- ταῦτα πάντα - are about to be fulfilled") and the ταῦτα here, one
notes, refers specifically in turn to *the destruction of the Temple*
(13.1-2).

     The discourse then following proceeds to answer the first half
of this question - *when* shall these things be (πότε ταῦτα ἔσται) -

by listing the catastrophes leading up to the Temple's destruction
(13.7 *when* you hear of wars and rumours of war ... 13.11 *when* they
arrest you and hand you over ... 13.14 *when* you see 'the abomination
of desolation' standing where it does not belong ...). This
catalogue of catastrophes reaches its climax in the words of 13.26
where the reader is told "*then* (τότε) they will see the Son of Man
coming in (the) clouds with great power and glory." In other words,
the catastrophes leading up to the destruction of the Temple are to
be understood by the disciples, and hence by Mark's readers /52/,
as eschatological events intimating the proximity of the Parousia.

Having reached this climax, Mark then invites his readers to
see *in the fig-tree* the sign (could this be the sign - τὸ σημεῖον,
sing.- asked for in the second half of the question posed in verse
4?) that these events are to happen and happen soon. If Mark has
indeed used source material for his 'parable', then it is equally
important to recognize what he has done with it. He has used a
fig-tree logion in the service of an *eschatological lesson* regarding
the destruction of the Temple and the imminence of the Parousia.
And this, it must be emphasized, is precisely what we have argued
he has done in chapter 11! The two pericopes may not be
intentionally related. The latter passage may not be Mark's
explanation (albeit clumsy) for the former. The redactional
concerns in each, however, are undeniably similar. This is
sufficient for our case, but a lingering question does remain.
Can it be *merely fortuitous* that Mark should invite his readers,
and the disciples even more strongly /53/, to see in *each* of his
two sole references to the fig-tree a sign portending the End-time
in which the Temple will be destroyed?

Nathanael 'under the Fig-Tree' (Jn. 1.48, 50)

The eschatological associations that the fig-tree and its
fruit have been found to possess in the Old Testament, late Judaism
and also in the New Testament suggest that such a background may
serve to illumine what for many has been seen as *the* other
enigmatic fig-tree passage of the New Testament, viz, Nathanael
'under the fig-tree' (Jn.1.43-51).

John recounts that a certain Nathanael was invited to meet
Jesus, whom his friend Philip deems to be the One spoken of by
Moses and the prophets. Nathanael is sceptical.   However, when
Jesus addresses him as "a true Israelite in whom there is no
guile ("Ἴδε ἀληθῶς Ἰσραηλείτης, ἐν ᾧ δόλος οὐκ ἔστιν 1.47)" and

declares that before Philip had called him, he "saw him (being)
under the fig-tree (ὄντα ὑπὸ τὴν συκῆν εἶδόν σε 1.48)", Nathanael
is completely disarmed and confesses him to be the Messiah without
reservation /54/. The puzzled reader, however, is hereby at a
loss to understand why Nathanael should have been so completely
won over by what appears to be a very trivial exhibition of either
keen observation, acute insight or supernatural knowledge!

That the story carries a symbolic intent is both obvious and
widely recognized. Attempts, on the other hand, to identify
Nathanael with known historical persons such as the Bartholomew
of the Synoptic gospels (cf. Mk.3.18) have been, on the whole,
unconvincing /55/. It is more likely that Nathanael is "that
exquisite creation of a devout imagination "(Cheyne) /56/ and is
intended to represent an ideal type. The Nathanael of John's
gospel is the pious, well-trained, God-fearing (but sceptical) Jew,
a member of God's Chosen People by spiritual birth rather than by
heredity (cf. Rom.9.6-8), the ideal Israelite (Ἰσραηλείτης) as
opposed to the unbelieving Jew (Ἰουδαῖος) who with his nation has
rejected the Messiah /57/.

This much, then, is apparent. Disagreement, however, has
centred around the question whether the reference to Jesus' seeing
Nathanael "under the fig-tree" should likewise be seen in a
symbolic light, or has some deeper meaning or hidden association
which would throw light on the incident. Some scholars have
denied this emphatically. The datum is purely incidental, and
quite insignificant (so Dalman, Hunzinger) /58/.

One wonders, however, if this abrupt and unexplained mention
of the fig-tree can be so easily dismissed as a contingent
topographical detail which tradition or "local colouring" has by
chance supplied. John's gospel is replete, after all, with hidden
meanings and veiled allusions and is given to the free rendering
of Synoptic-type material at the hand of an allegorizing fancy
(cf. e.g. Jn.10.1-18). When all is said and done, we are still at
a loss to explain why Nathanael should have been so ready to accord
Messianic status to Jesus simply because the latter had seen him
"under the fig-tree". If Nathanael's being "under the fig-tree"
is a datum as immaterial to the story as the possibility, perchance,
that he had been spotted in the market-place, then Nathanael's leap
from scepticism to faith is inexplicable. Pious Jews in John's day
were not so easily won over /59/!

This objection, nevertheless, has invited the reply that it was, in essence, the exhibition on the part of Jesus of a very accurate /60/ or even supernatural knowledge of Nathanael's character and whereabouts that evoked this response /61/. Although the idea of supernatural 'seeing' is not automatically suggested by the word εἶδόν, on the whole it is probable that Jesus' 'seeing' of Nathanael "under the fig-tree" does carry a 'visionary' or 'clairvoyant' overtone. The motif occurs elsewhere in the gospel (cf. 2.24-25; 4.17-19,29; 6.61,64,71; 13.1,11,27-28; 16.19,30; 18.4; 21.17).

Given the truth of this, however, we are still entitled to ask if the implied possession by Jesus of clairvoyant powers is enough to place the incident within a Messianic dimension. Nathanael after all is said to recognize and affirm Jesus as *the Messiah* merely in view of his having apparently shown knowledge of both his character and his "being under the fig-tree". Would a visionary or clairvoyant gift per se have necessarily supplied the link? There is reason to doubt it.

The possession of supernatural knowledge, clairvoyance or visionary powers was attributed in the ancient world to numerous individuals and groups. Josephus states that such gifts were possessed by members of the Essene community /62/. Judas the Essene, for example, is said to have been able to foresee the future, and to have passed this gift on to his disciples /63/. The Essene Manaēmus or Menahem was likewise credited with the remarkable gift of inspired insight into the human character. Menahem, it was said, had been able to read Herod's character when the latter was still a boy and had predicted both his advancement to kingship and good fortune and his consequent impious cruelty. It was for such supernatural knowledge, Josephus tells us, that Herod held the Essenes in honour and respect /64/.

A number of individuals were said to have had dreams or visions that revealed knowledge of the future and others still were credited with the power to interpret them. Herod himself is described as "springing in horror from his bed", having dreamt of the death of his brother moments before messengers arrived with the news /65/. Prior to his summons by Caesar, Archelaus is reported to have had a premonitory dream similar to that of Pharaoh in Genesis (and to have had it interpreted for him by a certain Simon the Essene). Five days later he was summoned to his trial and subsequently deposed (6 CE) /66/.

The gift of clairvoyance was also attributed to the Pharisees

/67/. Even Josephus himself, who was a Pharisee, claimed such a
gift for himself /68/. In consequence of a self-serving
prediction that Vespasian and his son Titus would accede to the
imperial throne, he recounts how he was subsequently liberated
from captivity and his fortunes reversed when his prophetic insight
had later been vindicated /69/.

The accrediting by the ancients of supernatural knowledge to
these various individuals and groups hence reveals that the gift
of such knowledge *per se* would not necessarily indicate that its
possessor was to be identified specifically with *the Messiah*.
Something more is needed to make sense of Nathanael's response and
the clue must surely lie in the mention of the fig-tree and the
associations it carried to the Johannine reader.

Scholars who have acknowledged the significance of this datum
have nevertheless been divided with regard to what that significance
precisely is. Proceeding very often from an historical rationalist
point of view, they have sought to determine what Nathanael might
actually have been *doing* under the tree. J. Lightfoot, for
example, felt sure that Nathanael had retired there from the view
of men "either for prayer, meditation, reading, or some other
religious performance", an act of piety which Jesus with his
supernatural knowledge had seen and applauded /70/. With a
similar assumption, T.K. Cheyne even suggested that the expression
"when thou wast under the fig-tree (ואתה תחת התאנה)" was a
mistranslation of a Hebrew original which read "when thou wast
making supplication (ואתה מתחנן)" /71/. B.W. Bacon, who criticised
this view, theorized, on the other hand, that the evangelist, in
compiling his gospel from disparate sources, had suppressed
intentionally or unintentionally an element of the narrative that
would in fact have explained this allusion /72/.

Few scholars have been willing to leave the story with an
exegetical or logical lacuna. By far the most common view has been
the suggestion that "under the fig-tree" was a traditional site
for *the study of the Torah* /73/, and that Nathanael was therefore
the type of the Jewish expert in the Law, searching the scriptures
but coming to believe in the One of whom they spoke (cf. Jn.5.39-40)
/74/. Jeremias even suggests that a contemporary reader would
have understood Nathanael to have been sitting under the tree that
represented the Knowledge of God and his Word /75/.

The passages that are adduced to support this contention,
however, Ber.R.LXII.2 = Qoh.R.V.11.2 = P.Ber.II.8 (Schwab, p.48) =

Shir.R.VI.2.2, relate only a *single* incident (*supra,* pp.181-2),
albeit ascribed to different Rabbis, in which the Rabbi in
question, and his disciples, move away from under a *certain fig-tree*
(where they had been studying the Torah - an incidental detail) to
prevent their being accused of stealing its fruit. This is hardly
conclusive evidence for a widespread practice, or, as J.D.M.
Derrett has so well expressed it, "one can hardly say that to be
under a fig-tree is to be a Torah-student, for at that rate
sleepy Arab camel-drivers would be Torah-students" /76/.

It should also be noted that the other examples given by
Strack-Billerbeck refer to trees other than the fig-tree. The
Rabbinical evidence, moreover, as we reviewed it in chapter VI,
does not support the view that the link between the fig-tree and
the notion of Torah-study was exceptionally strong or deep-rooted,
or that the fig-tree itself (unlike the Tree of Life) was ever a
direct symbol for the Torah /77/.

Where, then, does that leave us? The clue to a correct
understanding consists, we feel, not in asking what Nathanael was
doing under the fig-tree, but in asking what Jesus might have
meant, according to John, when he claimed that he had 'seen'
Nathanael "(being) under the fig-tree".

In an article in *The Expository Times* /78/, J.R. Michaels
made the pregnant suggestion that the key to Jesus' enigmatic
utterance lay in Hos.9.10. Having already linked Nathanael with
the Jacob (Israel) of the past (1.47), Jesus could be saying, he
suggests, that he had discovered the new Israel in the same way
that his Father had discovered the old ("Like grapes in the
wilderness, I found *Israel*. Like the first fruit on the *fig tree,*
in its first season, I *saw* your fathers"). Michaels' attempt to
link the Johannine passage with the Old Testament and the fig-
tree's symbolic associations there, is very attractive. It must
be said, however, that the connection he wishes to make between
Hos.9.10 itself, where Israel is the first-ripe fruit *on* the
fig-tree, and Jn.1.48,50, where Nathanael was seen to be *under*
the fig-tree, is not entirely convincing.

J.D.M. Derrett, more recently, has linked the saying with
Zech.3.10 and this is even more suggestive /79/. Though perplexing,
Zech.3, he notes, is a chapter that is obviously Messianic. In the
New Age, God's servant, the Branch, is to come forward, and the
iniquity of the land will be removed in one day (3.8-9). Joshua
the high priest (LXX 'Jesus') and his companions are to participate

in the events of this period and are described as men fit for a
sign (3.8) /80/. On the day when this Joshua's obedience, and his
companions' fitness, are fulfilled then each "will give and
receive invitations under his vine or his fig-tree as the case
would be" (3.10) /81/. In Zech.4 and 6.11-13, Zerubbabel (or
Joshua) is introduced as the Branch (the Messiah) who will rebuild
the Temple. The companions of Joshua can be seen, then, as "a
company assembling to see the Messiah's work begin" /82/.   Jesus,
consequently, claims Derrett, had seen Nathanael being invited
under a fig-tree (symbolic of the dawning of the New Age), had
connected this with Zech.3.10 (reading it with 3.8, which certified
the 'companions'' fitness for a sign and their connection with
the Messiah) and so had recognized Nathanael as a potential recruit
to whom participation in the story of Redemption could be promised.

The weakness in Derrett's position, in our opinion, is that
he has approached the story with too historical a perspective, by
placing the burden of its interpretation too narrowly upon a
particular Old Testament passage (whose amalgam of Messianic
allusions he himself admits is perplexing and obscure) and on
Jesus' own (conjectured) exegesis of it /83/.

His highlighting of the fig-tree's *eschatological* significance,
however, is undoubtedly on the right lines, and is borne out by
all the evidence that we have until now considered. The statement
made in Zech.3.10 (as in Mi.4.4) may be seen as reflecting the
general belief that sitting under the fig-tree (a sign of peace and
prosperity) would be one of the blessings experienced by those
privileged to witness that Age. It is this belief that supplies a
fitting key to the incident, and not necessarily the specific
ramifications of the Branch-Joshua-Zerubbabel story.

The ancient world, as we have remarked, was fascinated by
dreams and attached great significance to them /84/. This was
especially true of the Jews /85/. Interest was also keen among
pious Jews over the question of who would and who would not share
in the blessings of the Messianic Age, and it was a matter of great
import when someone had a dream or vision with Messianic
significance. "If one sees a choice vine", it was said, for
example, "he may look forward to seeing the Messiah, since it says,
'Binding his foal unto the vine and his ass's colt unto the choice
vine' (Gn.49.11)" /86/.

In declaring that he had 'seen' Nathanael "under the fig-tree",
we therefore suggest, Jesus was saying in effect that Nathanael was

one of those who would participate in the world to come, in the
Messianic Age. In a vision, in a dream perhaps, by clairvoyant
powers at any rate, Jesus had seen Nathanael as a true Israelite,
as one being without guile, as one "being", in the Messianic Age,
"under the fig-tree". The response of the pious Nathanael then
becomes immediately intelligible. If he is to share in the
beatitude of this New Age, then Jesus' ability to predict, to
foresee, even perhaps to bestow, this privilege leads Nathanael
to accord Messianic status to him. The Messiah alone knows who will
be his own. Surprised that Nathanael is now willing to believe in
him because he had intimated the latter's worthiness for the coming
Age, Jesus then proceeds to predict the even greater wonders that
are in store: "You will see heaven opened, and the angels of God
ascending and descending upon the Son of Man" (1.51).

The Lukan Parable of the Fig-Tree
(Lk. 13.6-9)

     The eschatological associations attached to the fig-tree have
thrown light, we believe, on the otherwise puzzling Nathanael
passage of Jn.1.43-51. In this passage, however, it is the
associations of the fig-tree rather than its direct employment
in symbolism that has provided a clue to its understanding, and in
this respect the Nathanael passage does not contribute greatly to
our Markan pericope, apart from supplying a further pointer to the
kind of background and Sitz im Leben in which it might have been
conceived. The situation is quite different with our next passage,
the Lukan parable, which not only evinces once again the fig-tree's
employment within a judgement context, but also its use in direct
symbolism.

     The parable stands in the same eschatological context as
Jesus' warning to the Jews to read the signs of the times in view
of the coming judgement (12.54-56) and of his exhortation to the
disciples to be watchful in view of the coming Parousia (12.35-48 =
Mt.24.42-51 = Mk.13.33-37). The parable and the 'slain Galileans'
passage with which it is connected (Lk.13.1-5) stand at the climax
of this section /87/. Both passages (it is generally agreed)
derive from Luke's 'special source' /88/ and are linked by the
redactional 'repent or perish' motif (13.3,5,9), a theme already
introduced in 12.54 ff /89/. The formal method of construction, as
Grundmann points out (viz, an exchange between Jesus and the crowd,
followed by a parable) corresponds to that of earlier pericopes
(cf. 12.13-21, 12.54-59) /90/.

A number of views have been expressed with regard to the
parable's origin and original meaning and application. J.
Wellhausen, for example, suggested that it was based on the
aforementioned Q logion Mt.3.10 (= Lk.3.9) /91/. W.L. Knox, on
the other hand, thought it was drawn from a popular magic recipe
for barren trees /92/. Others still have seen a parallel in the
story of Ahikar where an unfruitful tree pleads (unsuccessfully)
to be given another chance /93/.

On the whole, the case that the parable reflects a piece of
popular folklore is plausible, whether one holds that it goes back
to Jesus /94/, or, conversely, that it is a Gemeindebildung that
has been placed in his mouth /95/. If the former, then the
parable, as adapted by Jesus, would doubtless have provided a
simple but forceful illustration for his 'repent or perish' call
to the Jewish people, its essential point being that even an
unfruitful tree cannot expect an undue amount of care and concern.
Eventually it must be cut down /96/. If the parable, on the other
hand, is a 'community-formation', then it may reflect the missionary
situation of the Palestinian church discouraged over the relative
failure of its mission to the Jews /97/.

The details of the parable have been subject to an elaborate
allegorization in the course of Christian exegesis /98/. Theodor
Zahn, for example, argued that the *owner* of the vineyard was *God*,
that the *vineyard* itself was *Israel*, the *fig-tree* within it
Jerusalem, the *vinedresser* (ἀμπελουργός) *Jesus*, and the period of
three years during which the owner had come searching for fruit,
the period of *Jesus' ministry* from the time that John had first
issued his call for national repentance /99/.

Few scholars since Zahn have been willing to allegorize the
parable to this extent, although many would still see Israel (or
God's world) in the reference to the vineyard /100/, Israel again
(the Jewish people or the Jewish state /101/), the individual /102/,
or even Jerusalem /103/ in the reference to the fig-tree, and
Jesus /104/ (either as the Messiah /105/, or the second Adam /106/),
in the reference to the vinedresser.

With the publication of Jülicher's *Die Gleichnisreden Jesu*
(Vol.I, 1888; Vol.II, 1899) a powerful broadside was issued against
the tendency thus to allegorize the gospel parables. Such
allegorization was completely unjustified, Jülicher claimed, for
parables uttered by Jesus in the cut-and-thrust of debate would
have had only one simple message. They would not, indeed, have

been comprehensible to his original audience if they had carried
either the subtle nuances or the full-blown Christian
Heilsgeschichte that later exegetes have found in them. In the
Lukan parable, no references to God's intention to punish Israel
or Christ's pleading on their behalf are to be read in, for none,
he claimed, exist /107/.

Jülicher's argument, however, is overstated, for it is just as
important to ask what *Luke* intended the parable to convey and how
the *Lukan reader* would have interpreted it as it is to speculate
on the parable's Sitz im Leben in Jesus' ministry and its effect
upon his original hearers. If the Church Fathers can allegorize
traditional material, then why not Luke himself? If the later
church found allegorical meanings in the parables, then why not
the early church? Indeed, if this parable were a Gemeindebildung,
as some have suggested, then it is not unreasonable to expect that
it would have been conceived and transmitted with Christian themes
of theology and christology in mind.

The allegorization of a detail such as the mention of "three
years" is, of course, extreme. This datum which Zahn considered
"strangely chosen" is in fact quite a natural one. It appeared,
for example, in the R. Netanel story to which we earlier referred,
and quite without allegorical significance /108/. Some fig-trees
only bear fruit in their third year, although most do so every year
/109/. In the normal course of events, then, if a tree had not
borne fruit after three years, it would be unlikely to do so /110/.
It would hence be a drain on the earth's resources and could legally
be cut down /111/. Within the context of the parable, the period
of three years probably signifies no more than a short interval or
a period of grace sufficiently long to allow the tree to show proof
of its fertility /112/.

Arguments that the *principal elements* of the parable (vineyard,
fig-tree and the owner's search for fruit) have no symbolic function,
however, are less cogent. The practice of planting fig-trees in
vineyards was commonplace, it is claimed /113/, and this is certainly
true /114/. One cannot ignore, nevertheless, the symbolic
associations that the image of the vineyard and the fig-tree would
have conjured up in the Jewish mind. Both were common and widespread symbols for the Jewish nation, a fact borne out by our
investigations of both Old Testament and late Jewish material.
Lagrange states that in the Old Testament Israel was compared to
'figs' and not the 'fig-tree' /115/, but such a distinction is
surely casuistic. The tree and its fruit are to be considered

together. The owner of the fig-tree was after all seeking *figs* from
his *fig-tree*, and this, as we have seen, is a common image for God
and his dealings with Israel. One can scarcely avoid the conclusion,
therefore, that it was in this light that the parable would have
been understood.

That the image of the nation should here be conjured up by the
twofold symbols of fig-tree *and* vineyard is perhaps a little
strange, and it does seem natural, therefore, to look for a more
specific identification for the *fig-tree* that is said to be *in*
the vineyard. Edersheim draws attention to the fact that the
vineyard is elsewhere in the New Testament the symbol of the
Kingdom of God, as distinct from the nation of Israel /116/. It
is conceivable, then, that the increasing use by Christians of
the vineyard symbol for the Kingdom might have manufactured a
necessity for a symbol that on its part more specifically suggested
the old Israel. In this case, the fig-tree would have been
appropriate. Indeed, this might be borne out by Mark's choice of
the *fig-tree* story in 11.12-14 *and* the *vineyard* parable in 12.1-12,
for what amounts to an identical message. In the former, the
nation (in respect of its Holy City and Temple) is clearly in
view, while in the latter the vineyard, one notes, is to be given
to others (12.9) and hence represents the (spiritual) Kingdom
rather than the (physical) nation.

However, there is also much still to be said for the view of
Zahn, Bornhäuser, Grundmann and others that, in the Lukan parable,
the fig-tree in the vineyard may represent *for Luke and his*
readers the Holy City of *Jerusalem*, even if at a pre-Lukan stage
this allegorical link was not intended. Luke after all connects
the parable with the double-saying on the 'slain Galileans' and
the 'tower of Siloam', incidents that both appear to have
happened *in the capital* and which are taken as warnings for the
people to repent. The combining of both pericopes would indicate
that Luke recognized a thought relationship between the two /117/.
Later in the chapter, moreover, Luke again reveals that the Jewish
metropolis is on his mind for he refers to Jesus' prospective
journey there (13.31-33) and at the same time represents Jesus as
having made repeated efforts (like the ἀμπελουργός of the parable)
to prevent its destruction (13.34-35). Although Jesus has not
yet reached the city - he does not reach it until 19.41 - it
appears that Luke at any rate has already travelled ahead of him!

The possibility here of a symbolic link between Jerusalem and
the fig-tree has an obvious bearing on the Markan fig-tree story,

and would tend to support the view that we have been taking of
Mark's intention for that pericope. But even were it admitted
that such a precise identification is the product of an overactive
allegorizing fancy on the part of the exegete, it surely remains
abundantly clear that Luke had, at the very least, the Jewish
nation in mind, and even, indeed, its fate in 70 CE. By placing
the parable after 13.1-5 he reveals that this is so /118/. Jesus
is presented as offering to the nation a last opportunity for
repentance. Time is running out. Behind the call to repentance
there is the threat of judgement, an impending destruction that
Jesus' audience is invited to see prefigured for them in the
massacre of the Galileans at their sacrifices or in the collapse of
Siloam's tower.

Attempts to identify these two incidents historically have
been largely unsuccessful, although Pilate's action against the
Galileans accords well with what we otherwise know of his
character and ruthlessness /119/. For Luke at any rate, the
incident reflects the lesson that "the Roman power may yet prove
the instrument of divine justice upon the whole people" (W. Manson)
/120/. It has been also remarked, however, that the incidents
here described call to mind the similar atrocities and calamities
that Josephus reports in connection with the Fall of Jerusalem
and the events leading up to it. The fact, for example, that
Galilee was a hot-bed of revolution and that Galileans played
a major role in the Revolt of 66-70 /121/ has led K.H. Rengstorf
to argue that the significance of this passage lies precisely in
the point that Jesus is being asked to reveal where he stands
vis-à-vis Zealotism, by expressing his opinion on an incident with
Zealotic implications /122/. By presenting Jesus as offering no
express sympathy for the revolutionaries, but as reminding his
hearers that they were no more guilty than the rest of the nation
(which, unless it turned from its present course, would suffer a
similar fate) Luke, then, may well be thinking of the events of the
Romano-Jewish War /123/.

The message of the parable is 'repent or perish' but Luke
knew, after all, that the Jewish nation *had* for the most part
rejected Jesus' message (cf. 13.34-35; 19.41-44; 23.28-31). He
knew, too, that judgement *had* come upon the Jews in the Revolt.
The effect of 13.1-9 is to show that a period of grace had been
offered to the nation before this, that Jesus himself had
repeatedly called upon his people to produce the fruits of
repentance, and that the fate of the nation, as of the barren
fig-tree, rested ultimately on its response to that call. If this

is so, and we believe it is, then Luke's parable provides the
nearest parallel we have to the Markan fig-tree story, and a
comparison between them, therefore, is of especial significance.

It has been a matter of frequent comment that the fig-tree
story is lacking in Luke, who here has a fig-tree *parable*, and that,
conversely, the fig-tree parable is lacking in Matthew and Mark,
who yet both have the *story*. In consequence of this, a number of
scholars have wished to argue that there is hence a source-relation
between the two, that the story developed out of the parable (or
even vice-versa). This need not be so. The question of origin
is a separate one, and must be settled on a number of other
grounds. We shall presently, indeed, be considering it. At this
point it is pertinent, however, to ask why the Markan story is
lacking in Luke and what significance, if any, is to be attached
to this fact.

Scholars have ventured various opinions. Some have declared
that it is lacking simply because Luke did not find it in his
version of Mark (so, for example, Hirsch, Helmbold, Bartsch /124/).
Most have claimed, however, that Luke had the Markan story before
him but, recognizing that it conveyed the same message as the
parable, omitted it for this reason (so Loisy, Rawlinson). A
number have suggested in fact that Luke viewed the parable as a
substitute for the Markan story (so Creed, Schmid), perhaps because
its symbolic message (which he recognized) was still not sufficiently clear or, conversely, was all too clear, even offensive (so
Chapman, Münderlein /125/). Jülicher, on the other hand, has
denied that the omission was prompted by any regard for the
story's resemblance to his parable. It was prompted rather by Luke's
disregard for a miracle story with no obvious religious significance,
and one, moreover, whose teaching-content had been covered by
material already given in chaps.11 - 18 (esp. 17.6) /126/.

What then can be said with regard to Luke's redactional
situation and procedure? In the first place, we should affirm that
in all likelihood Luke did have Mark's version of the fig-tree
story before him. The position adopted by scholars such as Hirsch
and Helmbold was discussed in chapter II and found to be
unsatisfactory. Modern scholarship on the whole has proceeded
upon the tried and tested assumption that Mark's gospel was Luke's
primary source /127/, and if convincing reasons can be given for
Luke's omission of this particular pericope, then it is unnecessary
to abandon this widely-held position. Our examination of the
interrelationship between the mountain-moving sayings in Mark and

Matthew and the sycamine-saying of Lk.17.5-6 (chap.IV) led us to
conclude that Luke does in fact reveal his knowledge of the Markan
pericope.

One should also note in turn that the Lukan parable is to be
found in that section of Luke's gospel, the "travel narrative",
where large blocks of disparate, didactic material (the "great
interpolation", 9.51 - 18.14) have clearly been inserted into the
framework of Jesus' journey to Jerusalem /128/. In Lk.9.51 (=
Mk.10.1), Jesus is on his way to the Holy City. From 18.15
onwards (= Mk.10.13 ff.), he is found blessing the children
(Lk.18.15-17 = Mk.10.13-16), meeting the rich young ruler and
discoursing on riches (Lk.18.18-30 = Mk.10.17-31), prophesying
his imminent Passion (Lk.18.31-34 = Mk.10.32-34) and finally
reaching the metropolis via Jericho (Lk.18.35 - 19.29 = Mk.10.46-
52; 11.1). When the intervening didactic material is removed,
therefore, it can clearly be seen that the basic narrative thread
coincides with the Markan order of events. This "central section",
indeed, has been seen as a composition by the evangelist himself
"who has widened the situation advanced in Mk.10:1; 11:1 for the
insertion of his disparate material" /129/.

The fact, moreover, that Luke, shortly after he has given
his parable in chap.13, presents Jesus as declaring that "today
and tomorrow" he would cast out demons and "on the third day"
attain his end (13.32) and that "today and tomorrow and the
next day" he must go on in order to meet his death in Jerusalem
(13.33), clearly indicates that the evangelist is already
anticipating the events surrounding Jesus' arrival in the Holy
City, events that are reported in his Markan Vorlage shortly after
the point at which he departs from it. Jesus is heard to lament
over the city (13.34-35), a passage that looks forward to Lk.19.
41-44 (which occupies the same position as the absent fig-tree
pericope). He will not arrive until the time when the people of
Jerusalem cry, "Blessed is he who comes in the name of the Lord!",
a cry heard in the Triumphant Entry (19.38) /130/. It is
difficult, therefore, to avoid the conclusion that the events of
Mark chapter eleven were in Luke's mind when he presented this
material in chapter thirteen. The enigmatic words of 13.31-33
may best be understood, indeed, as his attempt to *prolong* Jesus'
journey for the moment in order to smooth over the insertion of
so much material into his Vorlage.

Luke, then, has deliberately removed the Markan fig-tree
story from its position sandwiching the Cleansing of the Temple

pericope, and instead has presented a parable of a barren fig-tree within the context of Jesus' projected journey to the Jewish metropolis. Why has he done so? The clue is to be found in those very differences between parable and story that have led scholars to disclaim any connection, even at a redactional level, between them. It lies, we hold, in the respective attitudes of both evangelists to the destruction of Jerusalem and its Temple.

In the Lukan parable, as commentators have frequently pointed out, a period of grace is granted to the barren tree. The owner has been patient but his patience is running out. By virtue of the vinedresser's pleading, however, a further but limited time is given for the tree to produce some fruit. The outcome is ostensibly unknown, although for Luke the fate of the 'fig-tree' is scarcely in doubt (13.34-35; 19.41-44; 23.28-31).

In the Markan story, conversely, no such grace is offered. There is no hint of God's redeeming patience or ἀνοχή. Time has run out. The fig-tree is judged for its barrenness. It withers as a result of Jesus' *curse*.

For Mark, it is *Jerusalem and its Temple* that have fallen under this curse. Their raison d'être has been removed. The Markan attitude, therefore, is a harsh one, though understandable for one caught up in the eschatological fervour of the Romano-Jewish War and the expectation of an imminent Parousia. An eschatological judgement has been pronounced upon the city and its exalted shrine. For Mark and his community, Jesus himself was the agent of that judgement. Had he not after all *cursed* the barren fig-tree?

For Luke, however, writing some ten to fifteen years after passions have cooled, and at a time when salvation history is replacing eschatology /131/, this attitude may have been too harsh, even offensive. Looking back and reflecting on the tragic events of his generation and their relation to the ministry of Jesus, Luke sees the Lord of the church less as an instrument of judgement upon his people (cf. 9.52-56), but more as the one who had pleaded for them, but to no avail. Grace and an opportunity for repentance had been offered to Israel (13.1-9) and the destruction of Jerusalem and its Temple was a result of the nation's rejection of that message (13.34-35; 19.41-44; 23.28-31). For Luke, then, the overwhelming emotion is one of regret or pity rather than the vehement anger or fear of those caught up more immediately in the events of 66-70 CE.

This sense of regret for the nation's catastrophe and a
corresponding respect for its national shrine are characteristic
of Luke. It can be seen in general in the attitude he takes
elsewhere to the Temple, an attitude, as R.E. Dowda points out /132/,
that is a *positive* one. Some twelve references to the Temple in
Luke's gospel are peculiar to the evangelist (1.9,21,22; 2.27,
37,46; 18.10; 19.47; 21.37,38; 22.52; 24.53). The total impact
of these passages, claims Dowda, is to accord to the Temple a
positive role in the story of salvation /133/. The revelation
concerning John's birth is received in the Temple (1.8 ff.). Mary
and Joseph are shown observing the cultic requirements of the Jewish
Law in regard to Jesus' birth (2.39). People connected with the
Temple such as Anna and Simeon are portrayed sympathetically.
Jesus himself is found there at an early age listening to the
teachers and asking them questions (2.41-51). At the temptation,
the Temple episode is made by Luke the climactic one, the effect
of which, Dowda suggests, is to make the Temple become the point
from which Jesus begins his ministry (4.9-13, 14ff.) /134/. Luke,
moreover, softens the opposition to the cultus that is to be
discerned in Mark. The 'Cleansing' account is abbreviated.
Mk.11.16 is omitted and attention focuses elsewhere on Jesus'
teaching activity (cf. Lk.19.45-48 and parallels) /135/. The
charge levelled at Jesus that he had threatened to destroy the
Temple (Mk.14.58) is removed, as also is Mk.15.29-30.

The net effect of these alterations, in Dowda's opinion, is
to modify the theme of the Temple's destruction and to allow it
to serve a positive function. It is the place of prayer and
teaching, though not of sacrifice, the place where God reveals
his will, the place where Jesus and the early church prayed, taught
and preached the message of salvation (cf. Lk.19.47; 21.37-38
Acts 2.46; 3.1 ff.; 5.42; 21.23 ff.; 22.17; 24.6,17-19; 25.8), the
place where redemptive history is fulfilled and from which the
saving message of the gospel proceeds. Only when that gospel is
moving outwards from the Jew to the world, from Jerusalem eventually
to Rome, does the Temple lose its significance and may hence be
denounced (Acts 7.42 ff.) /136/. In Dowda's words: "Luke-Acts is
the story of the church set free from its roots in Jerusalem and
carried to the ends of the earth. It is the story of how the
temple surrendered its redemptive significance to Jesus and his
church. In a sense, "Mount Zion" is no longer the temple in
Jerusalem but wherever the new Christian community exists" /137/.

This, then, is the attitude of Luke to the Temple and it is
this attitude, we think, that more than any other has led him to

omit Mark's harsh fig-tree story and to replace it with his
parable. If any other proof were needed, then it would reside in
the fact, previously noted, that at the precise point at which his
Markan Vorlage presented this offensive story, Luke has substituted
a *lament* on the part of Jesus for the destruction that he sees
coming (19.41-44). Jesus' concern for the city is so important
for Luke, indeed, that he repeats this theme (cf. 23.28-31, where
again the withered tree motif appears!). Jerusalem has not
recognized "the time of her visitation" (19.44 καιρός cf. Mk.11.13;
12.2), a time when grace and salvation had been offered to her.
As a result, her enemies would not leave "one stone upon the
other" within her (19.44 λίθον ἐπὶ λίθον cf. Mk.13.2). For Luke,
Jesus was one who had pleaded and wept for the barren fig-tree.
For Mark, he had *cursed* it. By replacing Mark's story with a
lament for Jerusalem, Luke shows that he recognized the full import
of that story (as Matthew may also have done) and confirms for
that reason the view of its significance that we ourselves have
argued for.

The Question of Origin

At various points throughout this study the question of the
origin of the Markan fig-tree story has been raised but so far
has not been discussed with a view to final conclusions. This has
not been accidental, for our investigation in the first place has been
concerned primarily with the story as it stands within Mark's
gospel, with its function within his redactional scheme. In the
second place, we doubt whether, in the final analysis, any one
precise literary source can be pinpointed that would constitute
a source, origin or starting-point for the story. Our discussion
of the Lukan parable, however, has raised this question afresh,
and while the search for an origin is no easier than the search
for the proverbial needle, it would be unsatisfactory not to
attempt to say something at least about the haystack!

To date we have examined three areas in which a possible
formative influence upon the story at a pre-Markan level can
perhaps be detected. We refer to the Old Testament 'fig' verses
(chap.V), the Jewish Haggadah pertaining to the Messianic Age
(chap.VI) and finally the Lukan parable. We have seen that the
various elements of the fig-tree story (the search for figs, the
barren or unfruitful tree, the curse, the smiting of the fig-tree,
the withering motif, etc.) are all present in the Old Testament
and in passages that were frequently mined by the early church.

We have noted the similarities existing between features of Mark's
story and Jewish haggadic tales pertaining to trees, particularly
in respect of Israel's Golden Ages, and especially with regard to
the Messianic Age (communication between men and trees, the
response of trees to the needs of the righteous, the expected
abundant fruitfulness of trees in the Messianic Age, etc.). We
have observed the close parallel between Luke's parable and Mark's
fig-tree story. How may these different areas of possible
influence be reconciled, if at all? While each may not necessarily
exclude the other, all can hardly be claimed as sources in the
determination of the story's origin.

Let us first consider the Lukan parable, for this is
undoubtedly the closest parallel that we possess. Has Mark
historicized Luke's parable? An historical survey of the
course of this debate was presented in chapter I (pp.12 ff.) and
need not therefore be repeated. We should note again, however,
the arguments that have been advanced on either side.

Defenders of this theory have in general advanced four main
considerations:

1.   In substance, both accounts are similar. The essential idea
      of the parable has become materialized in the story, viz, if
      the fig-tree = Israel cannot show itself fit for the Kingdom,
      it must perish (so, for example, Carpenter).

      The similarity between both, it has been claimed, extends
      even to the matter of wording (so Wendling /138/);

      Cf. Mk.11.13 ἦλθεν εἰ ἄρα τι εὑρήσει ἐν αὐτῇ,
                    καὶ ἐλθὼν ἐπ' αὐτὴν οὐδὲν εὗρεν εἰ μὴ φύλλα

      Lk.13.6 ἦλθεν ζητῶν καρπὸν ἐν αὐτῇ καὶ οὐχ εὗρεν

2.   ·The 'disappointed search for figs' theme of the parable would
      have made it a ready subject for allegorization. When once
      connected with the events of Jesus' ministry and particularly
      with his visit to Jerusalem, it would have been a short step
      to develop the parable further and to represent the tree as
      having been definitely condemned. The nature of events in
      66-70 CE could in turn have given a spur to a tendency which
      culminated in the historicization (perhaps by Mark himself)
      of the parable (so Loisy, J. Weiss).

3.   Parabolic teaching can in certain circumstances be converted
      into historical fact. Examples that have been cited have
      been the story of the Widow's Mite (Mk.12.41-44, so Smith
      /139/) and the Stater in the Fish's Mouth (Mt.17.24-27, so
      Bacon /140/). Reference has also been made to the fact
      that such parables as the Good Samaritan have long been
      regarded as historical, even up to the present /141/.

4.   While Matthew and Mark have the story, they lack the parable.
      Luke, on the other hand, has the parable, but lacks the
      story. This state of affairs is best explained, therefore,
      by the supposition that Luke has omitted Mark's story because
      he regarded it as a double of his parable (so, for example,
      Bacon).

      In reply, however, the following counter-arguments have been
advanced.

1.   The point of similarity between the parable and the story
      limits itself purely to the fact that in both accounts figs
      are sought from a barren tree. In all other respects they
      are different (so Jülicher).

      a) They are different in spirit (so Meyer-Weiss, Goguel,
      Jülicher, Hatch, Münderlein, Giesen). In the parable a
      period of grace is granted to the tree. There is a desire
      to save it. In the story the tree is condemned at once.
      It is cursed.

      b) They are different in content. In the parable, a well-
      cultivated tree in a vineyard is merely threatened with
      being cut down. In the story, a fig-tree by the wayside is
      cursed and (actually) withers (so Hirsch, Branscomb,
      Münderlein).

      c) They are different in respect of the moral drawn from each
      (so Hatch, Carrington). The parable is a warning against
      spiritual unproductiveness, while the fig-tree of the story
      is destroyed, not for unproductiveness per se, but for its
      deceptive show of productiveness (so Plummer). The lessons
      of the sequel, moreover, are concerned with faith, prayer and
      forgiveness and do not indicate that the fig-tree has an
      allegorical dimension (so Lagrange).

d) They are different in style. Mark's narrative supplies
details which indicate that it is based on eye-witness
testimony (so Burkitt, Lagrange, Cranfield, Robin).

2. While a miracle story can be seen developing out of a saying
/142/, it is unusual for a complete parable to supply the
starting-point. The process has not been convincingly
demonstrated, and the examples given are for the most part
inappropriate or speculative. The fig-tree story remains
largely by itself, for, as Bultmann has stated, a parabolic
origin is hardly possible with any other miracle story /143/.

3. According to scholarly consensus, Luke uses Mark as his source,
and not vice versa. Yet the original parable must have been
transformed by Mark before Luke found it and wrote it down in
its original form (so C.W.F. Smith). It is something of an
oddity then that the earliest gospel should present the later
form of the fig-tree story, while the later gospel should
present the earlier form of the pericope. If the parable has
been converted into a story, why is it so chaotic (so Bradley)?
It would have been more natural for Luke to have removed an
obvious difficulty than for Mark to invent one (so R.M. Grant).
And how would the parable to which Mark had access have run
(so Münderlein)?

These, then, are the arguments and counter-arguments. In
regard to the latter, however, the following qualifying remarks
should perhaps be made. In the first place, the difference in
spirit between both accounts does not necessarily imply that
parable and story have no relation to one another. The delay
accorded to the tree, which represents Israel or Jerusalem, is,
as we have argued, consistent with the Lukan perspective on
salvation history, and the curse on the tree with Mark's
historical situation and eschatological concern. As regards
the apparent differences in their respective teaching-content,
it should be noted again that the Markan sequel is after all a
secondary one and that Mark's redaction of the pericope and his
attachment to it of the mountain-moving saying (11.22-23) do show
a symbolic intent. The argument, moreover, that Mark's story
cannot be based on Luke's parable because it came directly from an
eye-witness such as Peter is one that would not commend itself to
many scholars today.

The remaining counter-arguments, however, are still cogent.
While a relation between story and parable does exist, we believe,

at a redactional level, the respective presence-absence of both
story and parable in either gospel is not a sufficient reason to
conclude that the one was a *source* for the other, especially when
such a derivation is considered unusual. The parable and the
story *are* very similar *(pace* Jülicher) and hence serve to
illuminate each other. The question of the story's *origin* from
the parable, however, must still in our opinion, remain an open
one.

        If the derivation from the Lukan parable cannot be considered
certain, can anything more be said for our other two possibilities,
the Old Testament and the Jewish Haggadah? Here it should be
remarked that both these areas do not necessarily exclude each
other. The various elements of the fig-tree story were found to
exist in the Old Testament, with echoes of Old Testament language
possibly also being detected in Mark's retelling of the story.
There we observed the fig-tree's association with Israel's Golden
Ages and with the Messianic Age in particular. There, too, we have
the seeking of figs as an image for God's dealings with Israel and
the smiting of the fig-tree as a picture of his judgement. In the
Jewish Haggadah these motifs were also present, but in a more
developed state, with eschatology playing a more significant role,
and with the belief being more extravagantly expressed that trees
in the Messianic Age would bear fruit at any time for the
righteous and for their Messiah.

        This background, then, might best account for the genesis of
such an odd story. It may have been in such a climate of belief
that the fig-tree story was conceived. The trace of such ideas
has been found in the New Testament, and such conceptions were
not foreign to the followers of Jesus after his death. The
pre-Markan story may not, therefore, have been a parable, but
a haggadic tale based on the Old Testament whose creative milieu
was Judaeo-Christian and whose import was eschatological and
perhaps also symbolic. Like the God of the Old Testament, Jesus
the Messiah had approached the fig-tree which should have presented
him with fruit in recognition that the Age had dawned with his
appearance. Like the God of the Old Testament, too, Jesus the
Messiah, at a deeper symbolic level, had sought Israel as figs,
but had been denied her fruit.

        Whatever the origin, however, it is important to recognize
what Mark has done. He has heightened any previous eschatological
and/or symbolic import attending the story by bringing it
specifically into connection with Jesus' visit to Jerusalem and

his so-called 'Cleansing' of the Temple. In so 'doing, the tree's
lack of response and its subsequent withering could be seen as a
solemn, proleptic sign that judgement had been pronounced on the
Temple, and that this judgement had finally been consummated in
the eschatological events of 70 CE. This, we have consistently
maintained, is how Mark's story would have been interpreted, and in
this respect the evidence of *all* three areas, the Old Testament
'fig' verses, the late Jewish Haggadah on the trees, and the Lukan
parable, can be claimed in support of our contention. Doubt may
still exist with regard to how the story was *conceived*. Little
doubt can exist with regard to how it was *perceived*.

Final Summation

Before we conclude, in chapter VIII, by relating this view
of Mark's treatment of the fig-tree story to some redactional
themes of his gospel as a whole, we should now briefly summarize
what appears to us to have been the source-redactional history
of this enigmatic pericope.

1.   The *origin* of the story remains obscure, with arguments
     regarding its derivation from the Lukan parable being in
     the main inconclusive. A connection does exist, we think,
     between the story and Old Testament 'fig' passages, as also
     with features discernible in the Jewish Haggadah pertaining
     to the trees and the Messianic Age. The story may have been
     a free-floating tradition, with a Judaeo-Christian background,
     a haggadic tale perhaps based on the Old Testament in which
     Jesus was said to have been refused fruit from a fig-tree
     (also perhaps symbolic of Israel) which did not recognize
     that the Messianic Age had dawned. Conclusive claims as
     to origin, however, cannot in view of the evidence be made.
     An original *eschatological* import for the story, nevertheless,
     is strongly suggested, and if such material does not provide
     an origin, then at the very least it would have influenced
     the story's perception.

2.   Whatever the origin, however, the story has been deliberately
     brought into connection with the tradition of Jesus' visit to
     Jerusalem and the so-called 'Cleansing' of the Temple. By
     sandwiching his story on either side of the Cleansing
     account, Mark indicates that he wishes the fate of the
     unfruitful tree to be seen as a proleptic sign prefiguring
     the destruction of the Temple cultus. The Markan import of

the story, therefore, is both *eschatological* and *symbolic*.

3.   The harsh import of Mark's story was recognized by Luke who
     decided to omit it. The third evangelist replaced the
     pericope with a characteristic lament for Jerusalem and
     earlier has Jesus recount a parable of a barren fig-tree to
     which a period of grace was granted. The Lukan parable
     intimates that in Jesus' ministry a time for repentance was
     offered to Israel and its Holy City. An *allegorical* tendency
     is hence discerned in Luke, in keeping with his view of
     salvation history.

4.   The significance of Mark's story was perhaps also perceived
     by Matthew who chose to alter it, however, rather than omit
     it. The miraculous element in the story is heightened and
     the story is rearranged and reinterpreted to serve as a
     point of departure for a lesson on the efficacy of faith
     and prayer. For Matthew, therefore, the Markan story has a
     thaumaturgic and *didactic* import.

5.   The didactic trend begun by Matthew is continued by later
     glossators of the Markan gospel who, influenced by the
     first evangelist, have added to the Markan text the sayings
     about forgiveness (11.25,26) and possibly prayer (11.24).
     These sayings betray Matthean language and style. For
     these later glossators, the Markan story has a *moral* and
     pietistic import.

It can thus be clearly seen that a number of redactional and
hermeneutical strata exist in the development of this hitherto
puzzling pericope. This work has sought to demonstrate that it
is only in the unravelling of these different layers that light
can be shed on its problems.

NOTES

/1/   Cf. e.g. R.M. Grant, *JBL*, 67 (1948), pp.297-303; H. Schürmann, *BiLeb*, 11 (1970), pp.29-41, 73-8.
/2/   See Schürmann, *op.cit.*, p.37.
/3/   "Not the Season for Figs", *JBL*, 87 (1968), pp.394-400. *Vide supra*, p.23.
/4/   *Op.cit.*, p.395.
/5/   *Op.cit.*, p.396.
/6/   *Vide supra*, pp.158-60,203 (n.71).
/7/   For the Latin text of this passage, see W.W. Harvey, *Sancti Irenaei*, II, pp.416-18. See also the more recent critical edn. by A. Rousseau, *Irénée de Lyon. Contre les Hérésies* (SC, 152-3), II, pp.414-17, which is based on the Armenian and Latin Versions. For an English translation, see *Irenaeus. Adversus Haereses* (ANL, IX), ed. A. Roberts, J. Donaldson, pp.145-6.
/8/   Bultmann, it should be noted, has claimed that this miracle was taken over from the Dionysus tradition (*History*, p.238). Were this so, its use by the early church and/or the fourth evangelist may still reflect the belief that such a miracle should have been done by the One who ushered in the New Age. Cf. also Derrett, *HeythJ*, 14 (1973), p.261, fn.2.
/9/   Cf. Mt.8.11 = Lk.13.29 Lk.22.29-30 Ap.19.9. *Vide supra*, pp.190-1 and esp. ns. 71,81 and 82.
/10/   Hiers suggests (*op.cit.*, pp.397-8) that the saying of Mk. 14.25 may in fact be a close parallel to Jesus' words to the fig-tree (Mk.11.14). The meaning conveyed in both sayings is that, in Jesus' expectation, neither fruit from the fig-tree nor fruit from the vine was yet to be enjoyed because the Kingdom for the present had not come. Despite the disappointment expressed in these words, Hiers claims, Jesus did nevertheless expect that the Kingdom would very shortly be coming. While attractive, this interpretation requires that one translate "May no one eat of your fruit εἰς τὸν αἰῶνα" as "until the coming age" rather than as an emphatic negative ("May no one *ever* ...") and this rendering is questionable. It also accounts insufficiently for Jesus' *cursing* of the tree, and for the redactional connection of this pericope with the Cleansing account.
/11/   He does concede that the sequel is probably legendary, with the fate of the tree perhaps influenced by Jer.8.13 (*op.cit.*, p.394 and fn.3).
/12/   *Op.cit.*, p.398.
/13/   Fawcett, however, makes the interesting comment that in Rom.11.16-24 the tree of Judaism is not destroyed but pruned, and the wild branches of the Gentiles grafted in (*Myth*, p.278, fn.24).

For Mark, on the other hand, its destruction is complete.

/14/   It is worth recalling here the view of J.E. Roberts (*supra*, p.16) that by virtue of the similarity in symbolic content between Jn.15.1-8 and Mk.11.12-14,20 ff. there was even a tradition-connection between both passages. Cf. also Cousin, *Foi et Vie* (May, 1971), p.93.

/15/   "Von Baum und Frucht", *ZSTh*, 9 (1932), pp.377-97.

/16/   *Studien zum dritten Kapitel des Lukasevangeliums*, pp.34-7.

/17/   See Bacon, *DCG*, 1, p.593, and Gaston, *No Stone*, p.312 ("The axe is already against the root of the tree" was not originally a prediction of the coming of the Gentiles, claims Gaston, but a warning to Israel. "The threat is of judgement against, even the complete destruction of Israel, the fig-tree.")

/18/   G. Dalman notes that the symbolic use of this everyday image has in fact completely overshadowed the otherwise *useful* and practical purpose served by the burning of unfruitful trees. "Unfruchtbar gewordene Reben (Joh.15,6) und Fruchtbäume wie Oliven und Feigen (Matth.3,10; 7,19, Lk.3,9; 13,7.9) haben als Brennholz gedient, obwohl bei der bildlichen Verwendung dieser Tatsache der darin liegende Nutzen unbeachtet bleibt, so dass es aussieht, als handele es sich nur um Vernichtung" (*Arbeit*, IV, p.6).

/19/   The Gospel of Thomas version of this saying (logion 40) refers specifically to a vine (see Guillaumont, p.25).

/20/   Lohmeyer, *op.cit.*, pp.389-90.

/21/   Cf. J. Schneider, *ThDNT*, 5, p.38; Trench, *Miracles*, p.483 and fn.1, and *supra*, pp.140-1.

/22/   Münderlein, *NTS*, 10 (1963-4), p.95; cf. also Giesen, *BZ*, 20 (1976), pp.105-6.

/23/   See Münderlein, *op.cit.*, p.95-6; Giesen, *op.cit.*, p.106.

/24/   Giesen, *ibid*.

/25/   Matthew adds: διὰ τοῦτο λέγω ὑμῖν ὅτι ἀρθήσεται ἀφ' ὑμῶν ἡ βασιλεία τοῦ θεοῦ καὶ δοθήσεται ἔθνει ποιοῦντι τοὺς καρποὺς αὐτῆς (Mt.21.43).

/26/   *Op.cit.*, p.105.

/27/   See G. Delling, *ThDNT*, 3, καιρός ad loc.

/28/   *Op.cit.*, p.99.

/29/   *Op.cit.*, p.106. A metaphorical or symbolic meaning is also, Giesen claims, to be discerned in the hunger datum of the fig-tree pericope (11.12b), the use of καιρός (11.13d), the withering of the tree, and of its doing so "from the roots" (11.20).

/30/   See, for example, Bacon, *DCG*, 1, p.592; Dalman, *Arbeit*, I, p.100; *RAC*, 7, pp.665-6; C.-H. Hunzinger, *ThDNT*, 7, p.757, and *supra*, pp.146 and n.93, 189.

/31/   The saying appears to have been in common use in the ancient world since similar versions of the metaphor occur also in

Graeco-Roman sources (esp. in Stoic literature) as well as in the
gospel of Thomas (logion 45). Hunzinger notes that the Synoptic
versions have an OT or Palestinian colouring in that they combine
grapes with figs (*vide supra*, p.133) and thorns with thistles (cf.
e.g. Gn.3.18 Is.5.6; 7.23-25; 32.13; 34.13 Hos.10.8 Mi.7.4;
cf. also Heb.6.8). The interrelationship between the different
New Testament versions is complex, with each writer employing the
analogy in different contexts and with differing didactic
purposes.

     For a more detailed discussion, see Hunzinger, *ThDNT*, 7, pp.
753-5. Cf. also *RE* (Pauly-Wissowa), VI, pp.2126,2143; Dalman,
Arbeit, I, p.407; IV, p.341.

/32/ The term παραβολή has a considerable range (see F. Hauck,
ThDNT, 5, παραβολή ad loc.). Though usually associated with the
teaching of Jesus, and especially denoting the specific oral or
literary *form* of the teaching method employed by him, the term can
also signify a piece of teaching that either vividly illustrates,
illuminates or establishes a difficult point or, on the other hand,
that carries a veiled meaning, a concealed message, or a profound
lesson. In the latter sense, the emphasis comes to rest on the
specific character of this teaching, not on its form, and hence in
turn on the teaching-*content* of what is signified. The translation
'lesson' for παραβολή is here, therefore, appropriate.

/33/ In classical usage, θέρος may mean either the 'summer' or
the 'summer fruits', 'harvest' or 'crop' (H.G. Liddell, R. Scott,
Greek-English Lexicon, 1968, p.794). In Semitic usage, the word
קיץ which the LXX translates as θέρος, can also mean the 'summer',
'summer fruit(s)' or even the 'fig-harvest' or 'dried figs' in
particular (*supra*, p.166, n.29). The term קיץ was used, as we
have seen, in a pun with the word קץ denoting the *end* that was to
come upon Israel (cf. Am.8.1-3 and *supra*, p.135). Like its
derivative θερίζω (to reap) and θερισμός (harvest), therefore,
θέρος may have eschatological overtones. The harvest, like the
wedding and the wine, is a well-established symbol of the New Age
and especially of the Last Judgement with which that Age is to
begin. See Jeremias, *Parables*, pp.118-19, who furnishes numerous
examples, and for a contrary view J. Dupont, "La parabole du
figuier qui bourgeonne", *RB*, 75 (1968), pp.541-2. Dupont's
article gives an ample Bibliography and a survey and critique of
exegesis on the passage.

/34/ This difficulty has led some scholars to prefer the more
poorly attested variant γινώσκεται in verse 28; cf. Wellhausen,
Marci (1903), p.113; contr. Schwartz, *ZNW*, 5 (1904), p.81; Dupont,
op. cit., p.527 and fn.2. This reading, however, as Dupont points
out, has few defenders today, and even Wellhausen in the second

edition of his commentary (1909) found himself thinking again after
he had read Schwartz's article.

/35/   Cf. Schwartz, *op.cit.*, p.82. By adding βλέποντες ἀφ'
ἑαυτῶν before the first γινώσκετε, Luke appears to have taken it
in this latter sense (21.30).

/36/   See Dupont, *op.cit.*, pp.533-6.

/37/   See, for example, Bacon, *DCG*, 1, p.593; Schwartz, *ibid.*;
Dupont, *ibid*. The effect of Luke's redaction of Mark 13.28 ff.,
as of the Apocalyptic Discourse in toto, has been to make the
anticipation of an imminent Parousia far less pronounced. In
keeping with the fact that Luke was writing considerably after
the Romano-Jewish War and the destruction of Jerusalem, he has
prolonged the eschatological scheme, a procedure otherwise
characteristic of apocalyptic and one that Wellhausen claims is
already to be seen in Mark (*Marci*^{2}, pp.106-7). The catastrophes
that surround the destruction of the Temple are not for Luke a
sign of the imminent end of the world and the advent of the
Parousia but a stage in salvation history, the start of a new
world period (cf. Lk.21.7,8,9,11,12,19,20,24,28 with the Markan
parallels, and see Dupont, *ibid.*).

/38/   *Supra*, p.11.

/39/   *Marci*^{1}, p.113.

/40/   *Marci*^{2}, pp.106-7. The mood of γινώσκετε in verse 28 is,
therefore, imperative, thinks Wellhausen. Verses 28 and 30
belong together as pre-Markan traditional material. Both verses
stem from the period before the destruction of Jerusalem in which
the Parousia was regarded as imminent. Verses 29 and 31-37,
however, reflect the belief of a later Christian generation.
Written after the Fall of Jerusalem, they no longer connect the
Parousia with that event, and introduce, with regard to its
actual timing, a qualifying and indeterminate note.

/41/   So Münderlein, *NTS*, 10 (1963-4), pp.92-3, who cites
Jn.4.35 as a parallel.

/42/   So E. Meyer, *Ursprung*, I, p.127, fn.1; Jeremias, *Parables*,
p.120; *ThDNT*, 7, p.757, fn.56. It must be added, however, that
the fig-tree's association with eschatology furnishes an additional
qualification for its fitness for the image here described. It
is even possible that the קץ/קיץ pun may underlie the logion. Cf.
Derrett, *HeythJ*, 14 (1973), p.259, although contr. Dupont, *RB*, 75
(1968), p.542.

/43/   *Parables*, pp.119-20. This latter point may possibly be
overdrawn, for the blossoming fig-tree is the harbinger for a
New Age in which both blessing and judgement are expected
concomitants. For Christians at any rate the advent of the Son
of Man would be a time of blessing.

/44/   In such logia, Jesus draws the attention of his hearers to
those signs of the coming Kingdom that are already *present* in their
experience, if only they will recognize them. In Lk.12.54-56,he
disparages his hearers for being able to make accurate observations
on nature and yet unable to read 'the signs of the times'. In Mt.
16.1-4, he explicitly refuses the request for a definite
supernatural sign. See Dupont, *op.cit.*, pp.543-6.
/45/   *Op.cit.*, p.540.
/46/   *Op.cit.*, pp.538-9.
/47/   Some scholars, indeed, have questioned the 'parable's'
authenticity; so for example, P. Lambrecht (see Dupont, *op.cit.*,
p.540).
/48/   *Supra,* p.39.
/49/   Trocmé, *Formation*, p.66.
/50/   The Mount of Olives was associated in the minds of the Jews
with Messianic expectations (cf. e.g. Zech.14.4 B.J.II.261-3
Ant.XX.169-72). See Dowda, *Cleansing*, pp.190-1.
/51/   *Infra*, chap.VIII.
/52/   Cf. Mark's note to the reader in 13.14.
/53/   The οὕτως καὶ ὑμεῖς of verse 29, therefore, may refer to
the disciples in particular, while Mark may intend the γινώσκετε
(imperative) of verse 28 for his readers as a whole. (In verse 37,
it should be noted, there is a return from the *you* - the disciples -
to *all*.) If so, the tenor of the following chapter, as also
elsewhere, would indicate that for Mark the disciples failed to
recognize the significance of Jesus' teaching, person and work
(*infra,* pp.258-9).
/54/   Ραββει, σὺ εἶ ὁ Υἱὸς τοῦ θεοῦ, σὺ Βασιλεὺς εἶ τοῦ Ισραηλ
1.49. In the Johannine context, both titles, according to R.
Bultmann, mean essentially the same as Μεσσίας. See *The Gospel of
John*, p.104, fn.7.
/55/   For a survey and critique of such attempts, see, for
example, T.K. Cheyne, *EncBib*, III, 'Nathanael' ad loc.; Bultmann,
John, p.103, fn.4; C.K. Barrett, *The Gospel according to St John*,
p.153, 1.45 ad loc.
/56/   *Op.cit.*, p.3339 (following Spaeth).
/57/   See E. Hirsch, *Das Vierte Evangelium*, pp.116-17. Nathanael
is a 'true Israelite' in the sense in which Paul speaks in Rom.9.
6-8, states Hirsch. The term 'Israelite' for John is 'ein
religiöser Ehrenname' while the term 'Jew' is a pejorative
designation for the members of that nation in their capacity as
'unbelievers', as sons of Cain (8.44). "Damit wird, im Gegensatz
zum Judentum, Gotteskindschaft von der Bedingung der Zugehörigkeit
zum jüdischen Volke gelöst und dem jüdischen Volke der Charakter
als Gottesgemeinde abgesprochen" (*op.cit.*, p.116).
        Bultmann remarks that Ἰσραηλείτης as distinct from Ἰουδαῖος

is the name used in the saving history; cf. Rom.9.4; 11.1 2 Cor.
11.22 (*John*, p.104, fn.4).

It is also worth remarking that the description of Nathanael
as "a true Israelite in whom there is no guile" may be meant to
conjure up the story of Jacob/Israel in Gn.27. Jeremias ("Die
Berufung des Nathanael" in *Angelos,* 3 (1930), p.3) thinks the
allusion is to Ps.32.2, but this is less likely. The Jacob-Bethel
story is further echoed in 1.51 (cf. Gn.28.12). See Barrett,
John, p.154.

/58/   G. Dalman ("Under the Fig-tree", *ET*, 32 (1920-1), pp.252-3)
is disinclined "to search for some special doing of Nathanael
under the fig-tree". The fig-tree, he declares, was in Jesus' day
the favourite 'shadow-tree' (*supra*, p.132) and no other
explanation is necessary for Nathanael's having been seen there.
Local colouring may have mentioned this place as the previous
meeting of Jesus with Nathanael, but any other setting would have
been equally appropriate and equally insignificant. C.-H.
Hunzinger, too, (*ThDNT,* 7, p.753) thinks that the fig-tree datum
has no particular significance in the account of the meeting of
Jesus and Nathanael and that "the text offers no indication that
the judgement of Jesus in v.47 rests on what Nathanael was doing
under the fig-tree." Both Bultmann (*John*, p.104, fn.6) and Barrett
(*John,* p.154) are guardedly of the same opinion.

/59/   This objection was recognized as early as the seventeenth
century by John Lightfoot when he asked: "What doing there? Doubtless not sleeping, or idling away his time, much less doing any
ill thing. *This would not have deserved so remarkable an
encomium as Christ gave him*" (*Horae*, III, pp.246-7, italics
mine).

/60/   So C.F.D. Moule, "A Note on 'Under the Fig Tree' in John
I.48,50", *JTS*(NS), 5, (1954), pp.210-11.

/61/   So e.g. Bultmann, Dalman, Barrett, Hunzinger.

/62/   B.J.II.159.

/63/   He had, in particular, foreseen the death of Antigonus,
Josephus records; cf. Ant.XIII.311-13 B.J.I.78-80.

/64/   Ant.XV.373-9.

/65/   B.J.I.328 (Loeb, Vol.II, pp.154-5) Ant.XIV.451.

/66/   Ant.XVII.345-8 B.J.II.112-13.

/67/   Ant.XVII.41-3.

/68/   B.J.III.351-4.

/69/   B.J.III.399-408; IV.622-9.

/70/   *Horae*, III, p.247.

/71/   *EncBib*, III, pp.3338-9.

/72/   *DCG*, 1, p.594.

/73/   See, for example, Dalman, *Arbeit*, I, pp.379,506; *BRW*(Winer),
I, p.366, fn.3; *HBA*(Riehm), I, p.441.

/74/   So, for example, Hirsch, *op.cit.*, p.116; *Str-B*, II, p.371;
RAC, 7, p.662, and, with reservations, Bultmann, *John*, p.104, fn.6,
and Barrett, *John*, p.154.
/75/   *Angelos*, 3 (1930), p.3. *Vide supra* , p.190.
/76/   *HeythJ*, 14 (1973), p.262; cf. also Hunzinger, *ThDNT*, 7,
p.753, fn.25.
/77/   Cf. *supra*, pp.184,190 and n.71.
/78/   "Nathanael Under the Fig Tree", *ET*, 78 (1966-7), pp.182-3.
/79/   *Op.cit.*, pp.261-4.
/80/   The reconstitution of the priesthood and the completion and
governance of the future Temple - the stone (cf. note in Jerus.Bib.
Standard edn., 3.9 ad loc.) - are a feature, too, of this Age, and
are tasks entrusted to Joshua.
/81/   Derrett, *op.cit.*, p.263.
/82/   Derrett, *ibid*.
/83/   C.F.D. Moule had earlier pronounced a link with Zech.3 "far
fetched", although C.H. Dodd had tentatively suggested such a link
to him (*op.cit.*, pp.210-11). Cf. Derrett's rejoinder to this,
op.cit., p.264, fn.2.
/84/   Cf. e.g. Ant.XVII.166,349-53 B.J.II.114-16.
/85/   Cf. Dt.13.1 ff., for example, and the famous 'dreams' passage
in the Talmud, B.Ber.IX.
/86/   B.Ber.57a.
/87/   Bacon, *DCG*, 1, p.593.
/88/   See, for example, W. Manson, *The Gospel of Luke*, *p.*163;
K.H. Rengstorf, *Das Evangelium nach Lukas*, p.171; Grundmann, *Lukas*,
p.274.
/89/   Lagrange, *Luc*, p.378.
/90/   Grundmann, *ibid*. According to Grundmann, the "Doppellogion"
of 13.1-5 is the first of a series of passages from Luke's 'special
source' which are concerned with the connection between the
rejection of Jesus and the fate of Jerusalem.
/91/   Wellhausen, *Das Evangelium Lucae*, p.72; contr. Loisy,
Évangiles Synoptiques, II, p.115, fn.1. Comparisons between both
passages have been invited by several scholars; so, for example,
A. Plummer, *The Gospel according to S. Luke*, p.341; E. Klostermann,
Das Lukasevangelium, p.143; Rengstorf, *Lukas*, p.172.
/92/   Knox, *Some Hellenistic Elements in Primitive Christianity*,
p.19 and fn.4.
/93/   See Charles, *Pseudepigrapha*, II, p.775, and Grundmann, *Lukas*,
p.275. Cf. also Derrett, *HeythJ*, 14 (1973), p.259, fn.5; *ThDNT*, 7,
p.756, fn.44; Jeremias, *Parables*, p.170.
/94/   So, for example, Jeremias, *ibid*.
/95/   So (but cautiously) Bultmann, *History*, p.204.
/96/   So, for example, A. Jülicher, *Die Gleichnisreden Jesu*[2], II,

p.442. For Derrett, the original message of the parable was more
closely linked with the Coming of the End, which explains the
particular mention of the fig-tree: "Just as a barren tree is
spared until proper treatment has been shown to fail, so the Age
to Come, in which all trees and plants will bear prodigiously, is
postponed until the immediately suitable 'treatment' has been
applied to the existing Age, which is the precursor of the next"
(*op.cit.*, pp.260-1).
/97/ So, for example, Gaston, *No Stone*, pp.342-3.
/98/ For an exegetical survey, see Jülicher, *Gleichnisreden*[2], II,
pp.440-1.
/99/ Zahn, *Introduction*, III, p.169 and fn.2.
/100/ So Derrett.
/101/ So Holtzmann, J. Weiss, Bacon, Menzies, Loisy, Plummer (but
also the individual), Schmid, Geldenhuys (but also the individual).
/102/ So Wellhausen, Plummer, Geldenhuys.
/103/ So Grundmann, Bornhäuser.
/104/ So Jeremias.
/105/ So Edersheim.
/106/ So Derrett.
/107/ See *Gleichnisreden*[2] (1910), II, pp.441 ff. Jülicher admits,
however, that in recounting the parable to a concrete Jewish
audience (the τινες of 13.1 and the πάντες - Galileans and
Jerusalemites - of 13.3,5), Jesus would also have had the Jewish
people as a whole in mind (although not because the fig-tree
carried this symbolism). Cf. also Lagrange, *Luc*, p.380; Manson,
Luke, p.163, and *ThDNT*, 7, p.756, fn.45.
/108/ *Supra*, p.200, n.54.
/109/ *Vide supra*, pp.27 (n.8), 133, 176-7. Maimonides, notes
Edersheim, curiously mentions three years as the utmost limit
within which a tree should bear fruit in the land of Israel (*Life
and Times,* II, p.247).
/110/ *ThDNT*, 7, p.755, fn.43. Some scholars have drawn attention
to the fact that a fruit-tree is said in the Old Testament to reach
maturity *within three years* (cf. Lv.19.23-25). A newly planted
fig-tree, therefore, should have produced fruit within this period
(so Plummer, Jeremias). However, as both Jülicher and Hunzinger
point out, there is actually no suggestion here that the fig-tree
in question had *never* borne fruit. Had it been a young tree, then
we would not have been told that the owner had been coming *every
year* for the past three years to look for fruit (13.7), and had
been disappointed. Even had it produced for the first time, its
fruit could not have been (legally) eaten anyway, for such fruit,
according to Lv.19.23-25, had to remain untouched until the
fourth year, at which time it was consecrated to Yahweh. In the

case of a newly planted tree, then, an owner could not have expected to enjoy its produce until the fifth year.

/111/ *Vide supra*, p.177.

/112/ So Holtzmann, Loisy. Jülicher (*Gleichnisreden*[2], II, p.441)
and Klostermann *(Lukasevangelium,* p.143) take issue with the word
'short', however, and maintain that under the circumstances the
period of grace granted to the tree was in fact a relatively long
one!

/113/ Jülicher, *op.cit.*, p.434; Lagrange, *Luc*, p.380.

/114/ *Vide supra*, p.166, n.19.

/115/ Lagrange, *ibid*.

/116/ *Life and Times*, II, p.247.

/117/ Zahn, *Introduction*, III, p.172.

/118/ See J.M. Creed, *The Gospel according to St. Luke,* p.181.

/119/ Josephus reports, for example, that Pilate on one occasion
commandeered money from the Temple treasury to build an aqueduct
into the city. When the Jews protested, he sent in his soldiers,
who clubbed many to death (Ant.XVIII.60-2 B.J.II.175-7). Zahn
thought that the Siloam accident was connected with the project
that led to the incident. Wellhausen (following Theodor Beza)
linked the Galilean massacre, on the other hand, with Pilate's
brutal suppression of a Samaritan disturbance at Mount Gerizim in
35 CE (Ant.XVIII.85-7). H.J. Holtzmann thought, however, that the
insurrection in which Barabbas had figured (Mk.15.7 Lk.23.18-19)
might be here in view, while Eisler claimed that Lk.13.1-2 referred
to a counter-attack that Pilate had actually made on the Galileans
who had entered the Temple with Jesus (*The Messiah Jesus and John
the Baptist,* pp.502-6).

/120/ *Luke*, p.163.

/121/ Cf. e.g. Acts 5.37 Vita 87 Ant.XVII.213-8,254-64 B.J.II.
60-5,66-71,441-8 and Holtzmann, *HC*, I, p.233; Rengstorf, *Lukas*, p.
171; Grundmann, *Lukas*, p.276.

/122/ Rengstorf, *Lukas*, pp.171-2.

/123/ Cf. also Holtzmann, *ibid*.; Klostermann, *Lukasevangelium*,
p.143; Loisy, *Évangiles Synoptiques*, II, p.113; contr. J. Schmid,
Das Evangelium nach Lukas, p.229.

/124/ The hypothesis of H.-W. Bartsch that Mk.11.12-14 contains
a primitive apocalyptic saying predicting Jesus' Parousia = Resurrection before the fig season, was described in chapter I (p.8 and
n.61). Bartsch thinks that Luke either did not know the Markan
pericope or that, if he did, he knew it only in its more primitive
form (viz, in the form of a Chria and without the sequel interpreting
it as a curse). This he omitted because it had not been fulfilled
(*ZNW*, 53 (1962), p.259).

/125/ "Lk. either thinks more explanation is needed for Gentiles,
or that it is an unsuitable parable of the rejection of the Jews"

(Chapman, *Matthew, Mark and Luke*, p.138). See also Münderlein, *NTS* 10 (1963-4), p.103, fn.3.

/126/ *Gleichnisreden*², II, p.446.

/127/ See Trocmé, *Formation*, pp.172-3.

/128/ Cf. Kümmel, *Introduction*, pp.93,99.

/129/ Kümmel, *op.cit.*, p.93.

/130/ Differing interpretations have been advanced for Lk.13.35. T.W. Manson has claimed that Jesus' words were a promise that Jerusalem would not see him until the Feast of Tabernacles, since these words from Ps.119 were sung with special significance as part of the Hallel at this great pilgrim festival (*BJRL*, 33 (1951), p.279, fn.1). Others have claimed to see here a reference to the Parousia. Rejecting this view, J. van Goudoever also rightly argues that the Entry into Jerusalem is in Luke's mind. He suggests, too, that Luke therefore has prolonged Jesus' journey, although he accords an historical significance to this Lukan notice. By prolonging Jesus' journey, Luke intends to say that Jesus entered Jerusalem not at the Feast of Tabernacles (in the autumn) but six months later, at Passover (in the spring). Chapter 13 of Luke's gospel, he claims, falls in the autumn season. The parable hence is a correction of the Markan story which is presented as taking place in the spring, but which only makes sense, Goudeover claims, if it was originally seen as happening in the autumn during the season for figs (see *Calendars*, pp.264,266).

/131/ Luke's gospel is not eschatological, J. van Goudoever has stated, and the fact that he has written his Acts is one of the best proofs of this (*Calendars*, p.266 and fn.24).

/132/ See Dowda, *Cleansing*, chap.VII; cf. also Gaston, *No Stone*, pp.96-7, 365-9.

/133/ *Op.cit.*, p.325.

/134/ *Op.cit.*, pp.327-8.

/135/ It is worth here also recalling how Luke has made the "these things" for which Jesus was challenged in Mk.11.28 refer to his teaching activity (*supra*, p.48).

/136/ In Dowda's opinion, Luke may have omitted Mk.14.58 and removed it in modified form to the story of Stephen (Acts 6.14) in order that Jesus should not be seen to have been charged with denouncing the Temple before the ministry of the disciples had been completed there. "That work having been done, Stephen may now be allowed to denounce the temple (7:42 ff.)." Dowda, *op.cit.*, pp.328,356.

/137/ *Op.cit.*, p.359.

/138/ *Entstehung*, p.150. *Vide supra*, p.12.

/139/ Smith, *Parables of the Synoptic Gospels*, p.67; cited Knox, *Hellenistic Elements*, p.19. fn.4.

/140/ *DCG*, 1, p.594.
/141/ Bacon, *op.cit.*, p.593; cf. also Hatch, *JPOS*, 3 (1923), p.9.
/142/ Bultmann, *History*, pp.230-1.
/143/ *Ibid*.

Chapter VIII

CHRISTOLOGY AND THE MESSIANIC SECRET IN MARK CHAPTER ELEVEN: A POSTSCRIPT

Few books have had such a profound influence upon studies of Mark's gospel than that of W. Wrede. Published in 1901, his *Das Messiasgeheimnis in den Evangelien* /1/ drew scholarly attention to the contrast within the gospel between the public nature of Jesus' miracles on the one hand, and his curious and persistent injunctions that they be kept secret on the other. Wrede argued that, viewed historically, there were intrinsic contradictions in such a presentation of Jesus' life /2/. "Nothing is more obvious," he declared, "than that Mark understood the miracles as manifestations of the Messiah " /3/. That the earliest recoverable traditions regarding Jesus' life viewed them in this light was, however, unlikely. The secrecy with which Jesus' healing and teaching activity is surrounded, the implausible commands to silence /4/, the veiled nature of his parabolic teaching /5/ and his frequent sessions with his disciples in private /6/ all led Wrede to view this Messianic Secret motif as a secondary and therefore unhistorical theological idea developed out of traditions which originally did not represent Jesus' life as having been Messianic in character. The earliest tradition, he maintained, held a belief in Jesus' *future* Messiahship. It was by virtue of the *resurrection*, in other words, that Jesus had been designated Messiah and he would appear shortly, as such, in glory and power. The idea of Jesus' secret Messiahship, therefore, could only have arisen at a time when nothing was known of an open Messianic claim on the part of Jesus in his lifetime, and when there was a tendency at the same time to carry the notion of Jesus' future Messiahship back into the period of his life /7/.

To Wrede, then, the key event in the development of christology was the resurrection. With the resurrection there was effected a transformation in the disciples' understanding of Jesus' significance. By virtue of the resurrection, and not before, they proclaimed that Jesus was Messiah /8/. Traditions regarding his life, teaching and activity were originally non-Messianic in character /9/. The Messianic Secret motif operates in Mark, therefore, such as to 'update' these traditions and present them 'sub specie resurrectionis', as it were.

It is not the purpose of this concluding chapter to make a detailed evaluation and critique of Wrede's work /10/, but rather

to look for the redactional thread that unites the various
pericopes of chapter eleven with each other and with the gospel
as a whole, and to do this in the light of Wrede's important
thesis. Does an examination of our chapter support, modify or
weigh against his views? Can we discern, in the first place, the
Secrecy motif in these passages? If the motif is present, are we
justified in accepting Wrede's view that a christological tendency
has been at work so as to invest essentially non-Messianic
material with a Messianic ⁻iew of Jesus? Is Wrede right in
thinking that the purpose of the Secrecy motif (deriving either
from Mark or from a tradition influencing him) was to present
Jesus even in his earthly life as the bearer of the concealed
dignity of the Messiah? Is it true to say, as he does, that
nothing in the traditional material used by Mark implied that he
had been acknowledged to be the Messiah during his lifetime?

Our first possible allusion to the Secrecy motif occurs in
the story of blind Bartimaeus, a pericope whose strategic
position in Mark's redactional scheme has been frequently
commented upon /11/. Jesus and his followers have come to
Jericho but, according to 10.46, are to be found (just as soon)
on their way out. Bartimaeus, who is named, but given no further
introduction beyond the (possibly etymological) one that he is
"the son of Timaeus", appears by the wayside, begging. Hearing
that it is Jesus ὁ Ναζαρηνός, he begins to cry out, Υἱὲ Δαυειδ
Ἰησοῦ, have mercy upon me." We are then told that many (πολλοί)
rebuked him (ἐπετίμων αὐτῷ), telling him to be silent (ἵνα σιωπήσῃ).
Undeterred, he cries out all the more, "Υἱὲ Δαυειδ, have mercy
upon me."

This story is puzzling. Whence came the blind man's confession
of Jesus as the Son of David /12/? We are told no more than that
he had heard that it was Jesus, the Nazarene. Are we to understand
that he had heard Jesus confessed as such, or had drawn this
conclusion for himself on hearing of Jesus' miraculous deeds? We
are not told. The Son of David title occurs here abruptly,
unannounced and for the first time in the gospel. However, we may
take it, the Secret is definitely out, and what is surprising is
that no command to silence issues from Jesus himself. Instead,
there is a rebuke from the undefined πολλοί, a group who presumably
embrace both the Jewish crowd and the disciples (cf. 10.46).

Wrede himself believes that this passage has nothing to do
with the Messianic Secret /13/. Though the verb ἐπιτιμάω is often
used in this connection, he regards the 'rebuking' in this case as
concern on the part of the "many" that Jesus should not be detained

and burdened by the man's request and cries. He cites 10.13 as
a parallel.

In this respect, Wrede, we think, is right. It would be
strange and contradictory indeed if Mark intended that the πολλοί
here should be thought of as silencing the man's Messianic
confession of Jesus, when in 11.8-10 members of the same group
(πολλοί ... ἄλλοι ... καὶ οἱ προάγοντες καὶ οἱ ἀκολουθοῦντες ...)
welcome Jesus in such terms.

However, we have still to reckon with the abrupt and
reiterated use of this Messianic title. The story intimates that
Jesus was addressed publicly as Son of David, and no apparent
attempt is made by him to silence this confession. What purpose
can Mark have had, then, in relating such a story when it appears
to run contrary (if Wrede is right) to his emphasis on the secret
nature of Jesus' Messiahship? Is the abrupt and reiterated
mention of the title meant to attract the reader's attention, and
perhaps also to point forward to 11.8-10 where, in the Triumphal
Entry scene, Jesus is once more greeted in Messianic terms by a
group, again undefined, but doubtless consisting, as before, of
the disciples and the crowd of 10.46 ff.? Is any significance to
be attached, moreover, to the fact that it was a *blind* man who
addressed Jesus as Υἱὸς Δαυειδ /14/, and that cured *thereafter* of
his blindness he followed Jesus "on the way" (ἐν τῇ ὁδῷ) /15/.

The Triumphal Entry story itself poses further awkward
questions. Its Messianic overtones have in general been recognized
/16/, although the restraint discerned in the Markan account (when
compared with that of Matthew or Luke) has led some scholars to
vouch for its historical worth /17/. Leaving aside, however, the
question of its historical value, it remains clear at least that
it represents a tradition which apparently knows nothing of a
secret Messiahship on Jesus' part. Not only does he fail to
silence those who salute him as Messiah but he apparently encourages
such a view by taking the initiative in sending for the ass, thus
precipitating the ensuing action.

This point has been commented upon by a number of scholars /18/,
although Wrede himself recognized this apparently curious
contradiction in the Markan presentation. "But why," he asks,
"did Jesus alter his behaviour at the entry into Jerusalem and why
did he let himself quietly become the object of a Messianic ovation,
and indeed not without some initiative on his own part?" /19/. He
admits further that this tradition runs counter to Mark's Secrecy

motif and that for that reason there must have existed in Mark's day, and previously, certain traditions that were already opposed to the idea of the secret Christ /20/.

If this is so, then we may question why Mark recounts such a tradition. What function does it perform within his christological scheme? If it runs counter to the Messianic Secret, then what purpose is served by its inclusion? Does Mark actually intend that his readers should conclude that Jesus understood himself to be the Υἱὸς Δαυειδ, the Messianic deliverer whom God would send to liberate the Jews? The salutation of verses 8-10 certainly implies that Jesus' disciples and followers so understood him, according to Mark. The words of verse 10a, which run in parallel with the Ps.118.25-26 citation of verse 9b, do not belong to that psalm. They are undoubtedly, therefore, the comment of either the Markan redactor (so Kelber) or the Christian community (so Ambrozic) on the words of that psalm. Either way, the addition serves here to indicate that "he who comes (ὁ ἐρχόμενος) in the name of the Lord" was interpreted by those who fêted Jesus, as the one who would usher in "the coming Kingdom of our father David", viz, the Son of David /21/.

This difficulty in exegesis is further compounded by 12.35-37. In this passage Jesus, while teaching in the Temple, is made to expressly *repudiate* the Son of David title. By means of a characteristically Rabbinic form of argumentation, Jesus questions how the Christ can be the Son of David. If David in Ps.110.1 can call the Christ his 'Lord', how can the Christ then be David's 'Son'? The implication is clear. For Jesus, and hence for Mark, the designation Χριστός is to be understood as and equated with the title Κύριος and not the title Υἱὸς Δαυειδ. For Mark and the community he represents, Jesus as Χριστός means Jesus is Κύριος.

The title Κύριος occurs elsewhere in Mark. In a number of cases it is a reference to God, but, where it does refer to God, the Κύριος is anarthrous /22/. In all but one of these cases (13.20), the reference to God is, moreover, an Old Testament quotation. In 2.28, the Son of Man (another favourite christological title of Mark) is κύριος ... καὶ τοῦ σαββάτου. In 7.28, Jesus is addressed as Κύριε by a Gentile woman. In 5.19, Jesus instructs the cured Gerasene demoniac, a Gentile, to announce to his own people what ὁ Κύριος has done for him. The reference here, in our opinion, is to Jesus, as the parallel verse 20 shows. "He began to announce what ὁ Ἰησοῦς had done for him." If God were meant, then one would have expected Κύριος to be anarthrous as elsewhere in the gospel.

This latter verse is also interesting in that, along with the Triumphant Entry, it too appears to break the Messianic Secret by having Jesus instruct the man to announce the miracle rather than attempt to conceal it. Wrede denies this, arguing that in sending the man to his house and to his friends, Jesus is to be understood as seeking to contain the secret /23/. Verse 20, by contrast, records that this effort, as in the case of the leper and of the deaf-mute (1.45; 7.36; cf. 7.24) was frustrated. Although the 'house' in Mark is often a place of secrecy /24/, it does not always have this implication, as Wrede himself admits /25/. Wrede's interpretation, moreover, does not sufficiently reckon with the force of Jesus' command to *announce* the miracle (ἀπάγγειλον), which occurs in no other Messianic Secret passage. Verse 20, in addition, appears to develop the thought of verse 19. It is in parallel with it and not in obvious contrast with it /26/. In 5.19, then, as in 2.28 and 12.35-37, Mark betrays, by his use of Κύριος, the christological perspective of the Christian community to which and for which he speaks.

Having said this, we must now reiterate our earlier question. Why does Mark recount two stories in 10.46 - 11.10 which intimate that Jesus was acknowledged to be the Son of David, if according to 12.35-37 that title was repudiated by Jesus? In the light of the above, is it possible that 11.3 gives the faint glimpse of an answer? In this verse we are told that Jesus instructs his disciples to inform anyone who might challenge their taking of the ass that ὁ κύριος has need of it. This verse is curious. The awkwardness of its grammar and syntax have been commented on and it has occasioned a number of variants /27/. The first aorist form of λέγειν (εἴπατε) occurs frequently elsewhere in the gospel, though, interestingly, only from chapter 8 onwards /28/. The verb ἀποστέλλω is a common item of Mark's vocabulary, as are the words εὐθύς and πάλιν /29/. Is it possible, then, that Mark's own hand is here to be discerned especially fashioning or influencing the content of this obviously legendary story /30/.

What is also of note is that the story of the finding of the ass, as presented here, hints at, though it does not explicitly state, the question of Jesus' authority (ἐξουσία). Apparently it is enough for the disciples to say that ὁ κύριος has need of it for it to be immediately despatched. For this reason, there is some resemblance between 11.3 and 11.27 ff., where the question of Jesus' ἐξουσία is likewise raised by the chief priests, scribes and elders. The double question: Ἐν ποίᾳ ἐξουσίᾳ ταῦτα ποιεῖς; ἡ τίς σοι ἔδωκεν τὴν ἐξουσίαν ταύτην ἵνα ταῦτα ποιῇς; of verse 28

is similar to the Τί ποιεῖτε᾽τοῦτο; of verse 3. The authority
for both actions (ταῦτα, τοῦτο) is in each case being questioned.
For the Temple authorities the nature and source of Jesus'
ἐξουσία is concealed. For Mark's readers, however, it is Jesus.
ὁ Κύριος who sequesters the ass and rides into Jerusalem!

If we now consider 11.27-33, the question about Jesus'
authority, or Vollmachtsfrage, the function of this pericope
becomes clear. The christological question, explicit in Matthew
(21.10), is here being raised by Mark. Τίς ἐστιν οὗτος who enters
Jerusalem and "cleanses" the Temple? Moreover, the Secrecy motif,
to which Wrede has drawn so much attention, is also present here.
"Neither then do I tell you by what authority I do these things"
(v.33). Jesus refused to disclose his identity openly. The
Secret is withheld.

On the other hand, while explicitly refusing to disclose the
source of his ἐξουσία in 11.33, Jesus, nevertheless, proceeds to
reveal in implicit terms what that identity is! Mark allows the
Secret to be divulged through the medium of a parable.

For Mark, the parable is the characteristically dominical
form of teaching by means of which the secret or μυστήριον can be
both revealed and yet paradoxically concealed at one and the same
time (cf. 4.10-12,33-34). The parable thus invites its listeners
to comprehend the concealed message for which it is the vehicle.
Whoever has ears to hear, let him hear!

Jesus tells, therefore, of the vineyard which has been hired
out to tenants who refuse to offer the owner its fruits. Their
wickedness even extends to the killing of the owner's *beloved and
only son* (12.1-12) /31/.

Although the Jewish authorities are said to have perceived
that he was speaking against them (v.12), so understanding that
they were to be identified with the wicked tenants, it is not
entirely clear whether they equally perceived that Jesus was
identifying himself with the beloved son. That Mark's readers
were supposed to 'get the point', however, is almost certain, for
the expression υἱὸς ἀγαπητός is a clear echo of two earlier
crucial passages. The gospel had begun with the baptism of Jesus.
The voice from heaven had declared (1.11): "You are my beloved Son
(ὁ Υἱός μου ὁ ἀγαπητός), in you my favour rests." There seems
little doubt, therefore, that this opening statement reveals a

major Markan christological emphasis /32/. What better means can
there be for stating and reinforcing one's own christology than by
letting it be known that it had had the divine seal of approval!
If this were not enough, the formula is expressly repeated at the
commencement of the second half of the gospel in the Transfiguration
scene (9.7): "This is my beloved Son (Οὗτός ἐστιν ὁ Υἱός μου ὁ
ἀγαπητός), give heed to him (ἀκούετε αὐτοῦ)." It occurs again at
the climactic crucifixion scene, where the Roman centurion, a
Gentile, declares (15.39): "Truly this man was (the) Son of God
('Αληθῶς ὅυτος ὁ ἄνθρωπος Υἱὸς θεοῦ ἦν)."

If we may sum up at this point, then, the general course of
our observations thus far, we may say the following. It would
appear that there is conveyed, on the one hand, by the Entry and
Cleansing traditions, a conception of Jesus as being publicly
acclaimed as Messiah in a narrowly Jewish and particularistic
sense, as the Υἱὸς Δαυειδ, in other words. There is conveyed,
on the other hand, by means of the Secrecy motif and the Vineyard
parable (and perhaps, too, by the κύριος reference in 11.3) a
conception of Jesus as the concealed Υἱὸς θεοῦ. That the former
of these conceptions is being resisted by Mark is shown by 12.35-37.
May the contradictions of the Markan presentation be explained,
therefore, by the suggestion that Mark is seeking by means of the
Secrecy motif to oppose an 'open Messiahship' tradition that
interpreted the term Χριστός in its narrowly Jewish, particularistic
and perhaps political sense - in Υἱὸς Δαυειδ terms, in other words?
He has opposed this tradition, however, not by ignoring it but by
reinterpreting it. For Mark and the community he represents, the
term Χριστός is to be understood in terms of ὁ Υἱὸς θεοῦ, ὁ Υἱὸς
τοῦ ἀνθρώπου, ὁ Κύριος. For Mark, the one who enters Jerusalem,
who comes ἐν ὀνόματι Κυρίου, who "cleanses" the Temple and
pronounces its destruction, is the Lord, the Son of God, and not
the Son of David. This same one, who is shortly to return in
power and glory and is to preside over the world torn by civil war,
famine and plague, will not be the Jewish Messiah, moreover, but
the victorious Son of Man (chapter 13).

It follows from this that we are not entirely justified in
speaking, as Wrede and others have done, of a 'Messianic' Secret.
The Secret, according to Mark, was not that the one who lived, died
and rose again was the Messiah incognito, as the Jews understood
that term. He was rather the concealed Son of God, a semi-divine
figure with attributes compatible with Gentile conceptions (cf.
e.g. 5.25-34; 6.45-52; 9.2-8). In Mark we have not, strictly
speaking, a 'Messiasgeheimnis', but a 'Gottessohngeheimnis' /33/.

If the above exegesis is correct, then we may perhaps proceed further. According to both the Bartimaeus and the Triumphant Entry pericopes, the blind man and the followers of Jesus together apparently have this in common, that they understand Jesus to be the Son of David (cf. 10.47-48; 11.8-10). Curiously, too, both Bartimaeus and Peter, the representative of the disciples, employ the Jewish appellation Ραββουνει or Ραββει when addressing Jesus (10.51; 11.21) /34/. This title appears in only two further places in Mark. It is used, again by Peter, in the Transfiguration story (9.5), where the context suggests that Peter and those with him, overcome with fear, do not comprehend who Jesus really is. The voice from heaven, however, informs them: "This is my *beloved Son,* give heed to him." It is used also by Judas (whom Mark twice informs his readers is one of the Twelve) when this disciple is betraying Jesus in the garden (cf. 14.10,43,45). There, dramatically, no other words save "Rabbi" are spoken by the betrayer when he approaches with a crowd from the chief priests, scribes and Pharisees.

Other passages, too, suggest that, although the disciples, in company with Jesus, had been repeatedly made a party to the Secret /35/, they were nevertheless, according to Mark, endowed with a quite remarkable obtuseness /36/. Mark's harsh treatment of the disciples is noted by most commentators and was touched on by us in chapter III /37/. They are represented as barring others from coming to Jesus or being reckoned as one of their group /38/. They are fearful, afraid, cowardly even /39/. They are exhorted to have faith and admonished for not possessing it /40/. For lack of such faith they are even unable to perform miracles /41/. They are ashamed of him, betray him, are unable to keep watch for him, forsake him, deny him, fail to take up their cross and follow him /42/. They are also status-conscious /43/. Although previously intimated to them /44/, even the event of the resurrection, and Jesus' promise to go before them to Galilee, is in the final analysis withheld from them. In the closing words of the gospel, they are left behind in the dark, the Secret undivulged (16.8).

In view of this portrayal, it is all the more remarkable that a great many commentators can conclude with Wrede that "if anyone for one moment entertained the idea that Mark was ill-disposed towards the disciples he would soon dismiss it again" /45/. The gospel not only emphasizes that the disciples failed to understand the significance of Jesus, but particularly after 8.27 the notion that they positively *misunderstood* Jesus becomes more prominent /46/. This *blindness* of the disciples, indeed, has led scholars such as

Tyson, Schreiber and Schulz to argue that Mark is in fact involved
in polemics and apologetics. His gospel is a polemic against the
Urgemeinde and an apologia for the christology of the Hellenistic
Gentile church /47/.

There is much to be said for this position, for if Mark had
intended his readers to identify themselves, as fellow-Christians
under the gospel, with the disciples in their weakness, then we
would have expected, as with Matthew, Luke or John, some notice
concerning their *restoration* under that same gospel. None is
given.

It is not the object of this postscript, however, to engage
the wider question of the overall background, purpose and intention
of Mark's gospel. We may ask, nevertheless, if there is any
indication that Mark may be developing the Secrecy motif in this
chapter with particular reference to the disciples. Tyson argues
that the preoccupation of the disciples with the question of rank,
particularly in 10.35-45, indicates that his immediate followers,
according to Mark, understood their Master in terms of a royal
Messiahship /48/. This would also explain why the notion of
personal suffering and·death, on their own part and on that of
Jesus, was so foreign to them. Mark, Tyson believes,was aware
of a significant difference between his own view of Messiahship
and that of the early disciples. Throughout the gospel, as Wrede
has noted, Jesus is shown to instruct his disciples in scenes
where they are taken aside or are alone /49/. In these private
sessions they are invited to understand the significance of his
actions and of his words (cf. e.g. 7.17 ff., 8.14 ff.). Frequently,
also, they are said not to comprehend despite this personal
invitation on Jesus' part (cf. 8.17-21; 9.32). We may also accept
that in these private sessions it is Mark's purpose to inform his
readers of his own view of the significance of Jesus' person,
actions and words. If Mark had intended to comment on the
significance of the tradition regarding Jesus' Entry into Jerusalem
and his "Cleansing" of the Temple, then we might have expected
some such private session with his disciples.

When we look again at the stories presented in 10.46 - 11.33,
we note there are five scenes of any substance: the story of the
blind Bartimaeus, the Triumphal Entry, the cursing of the fig-tree,
the Cleansing of the Temple, the sequel to the cursing and the
Vollmachtsfrage. Of these scenes, the first two intimate that
Jesus is accompanied by a crowd that also includes his disciples
(10.46; 11.8-10). The scenes are public /50/. So, too, are the

Cleansing of the Temple /51/ and the questioning of Jesus by the
Jewish authorities. However, 11.11 intimates that Jesus retired
to Bethany with only the Twelve. In the fig-tree story and its
sequel, moreover, all trace of the crowd surrounding Jesus has
gone. The crowd is present in 10.46; 11.8,9,18,32; 12.12,37, but
does not appear in 11.12-14 or 11.20 ff. The cursing of the fig-
tree scene, then, is a private one, and appears to be enacted for
the benefit of the disciples alone. Indeed, Mark's specific
reference to the Twelve in 11.11 may indicate this.

This observation prompts us to suggest, therefore, that in
the fig-tree story itself there can be discerned, yet again, the
operation of the Secrecy motif. In this enigmatic scene, the
disciples are being invited to understand the significance of what
Jesus has done. This is surely what is implied in the curious
notice of 11.14c: "And his disciples heard (him)" /52/. 'Seeing'
(ἰδεῖν) and 'hearing' (ἀκούειν) are favourite Markan words, and
the verb ἀκούω frequently carries with it the notion of
discernment, of comprehension. To 'hear' for Mark, is to be
invited to understand, and, having done so, to respond /53/. The
'remembering' motif, which frequently functions in the gospels to
interpret or draw attention to the significance of a dominical
action or saying (cf. e.g. Jn.2.17), occurs here in v.21 and links
the sequel with vv.12-14, and especially with 14c: "And his
disciples *heard* (him) ... and Peter *remembered* and said ..." In
8.18 the disciples were asked if they did not *remember* the feeding
miracle and were berated by Jesus for the obtuseness they were
showing. In 14.72, Peter is again said to *remember* what Jesus had
said regarding his denial, words which he had failed to heed, as
Mark emphasizes (14.27-31).

We have considered already the possibility that Mark has
recounted the Entry story because it intimated to his readers that
Jesus' followers had fêted him as the Son of David, despite all
that he had said and done to disabuse them of this idea. They
shared this understanding, moreover, with Bartimaeus, a man who
nevertheless, in consequence of his faith, had subsequently been
cured of his blindness. If this is so, then how might the
disciples, in turn, have understood the significance of Jesus'
Cleansing of the Temple?

In his Doctoral Dissertation for Duke University, Dowda points
out that Temple-cleansing was a traditional activity associated
with the restoration of the Israelite or Jewish kingdom /54/. In
later times, he notes, Judas Maccabaeus and his brothers cleansed
the sanctuary, signalling the newly-won independence of the Jewish

state (1 Mc.4.36-61 2 Mc.10.1-8). The Zealots, too, had carried
out a cleansing of the Temple. Zeal indeed for the Temple came to
be the most important expression of national feeling (cf. Jn.2.17).

Though the precedent of Temple-cleansing might indicate a
purely political intent, he further notes that Temple-restoration
also figured prominently in prophetic-apocalyptic thought about
the Messianic Age, and a more thorough cleansing of a corrupt
Temple became part of the eschatological expectation of many at
this time /55/. "In a general way, then," he concludes, "the temple
reform and renewal were associated with the inauguration of a new
era, at least in some of the literature, as preparatory to the
beginning of the messianic age" /56/.

Such conceptions, then, may well have coloured the thinking
of Jesus' disciples. According to Mark, they appeared to have
seen Jesus' Messiahship, not in terms of suffering and death, but
in terms of victory and glory, the restoration of the Kingdom to
Israel. In that mighty event, they expected to play a prominent
part and to enjoy the ensuing benefits of peace, prosperity and
status. It is equally possible that they may have seen the Temple
as the focal point for the renewal and restoration of national,
political and religious life in the eagerly awaited New Age. Luke,
as we have seen, tells us of the connection of the Urgemeinde with
the Temple /57/. These two traditions of Triumphant Entry and
Cleansing, therefore, may originally have reflected such a view.
Jesus was the promised Υἱὸς Δαυειδ who had come to purify the
Temple cultus and inaugurate the Messianic age.

What, then, in the final analysis, does the cursing of the
fig-tree signify? Does it not invite the disciples (and thereby
Mark's readers) to understand the Entry into Jerusalem and the
Cleansing story, not as a Messianic purification of the cultus,
but rather as a visit in judgement by one who for Mark and his
community is both ὁ Κύριος and ὁ Υἱὸς Θεοῦ? Jesus comes not to
restore and renew the Jerusalem Temple but to announce its
destruction, that "henceforth no one will ever eat fruit from
you again!" Its spiritual authority is a sham and its pretense
to uniting man and God fruitless. For Mark and his readers it
had, indeed, with the Zealots, become a σπήλαιον λῃστῶν, "a
brigands' cave" /58/. Hence, in Jesus' words, "there will not
be left one stone upon another, that will not be cast down" (13.2).
In this way, Mark has given an entirely different slant to an
earlier Messianic tradition which regarded Jesus' action as a
purification of the Temple cultus, and he has done so, we believe,

to prepare his readers theologically for the brute fact of its
demise under the Romans in 70 CE /59/.

The overall picture that has emerged, then, can be summarized
as follows. Mark presents three stories, the healing of a blind
man, the Triumphant Entry into Jerusalem and the Cleansing of
the Temple, which imply that Jesus was openly and publicly
acknowledged as the Son of David or the Messiah and had apparently
acted as such. According to the gospel, this belief appears to
have been shared by his disciples. Mark wishes, however, to show
that Jesus repudiated this title (12.35-37). By means of the
Secrecy motif (11.27-33) and the parable of 12.1 ff., Mark conveys
to his readers that, in fact, Jesus is to be understood as the
Υἱὸς Θεοῦ. 11.3 also introduces the Κύριος title. Further, by
inserting the story of the fig-tree on either side of the Cleansing
of the Temple account, a scene that appears to be enacted for the
benefit of the disciples, he invites them (and his readers) to
understand the Entry and Cleansing traditions as a visit of
judgement upon the Jewish people and their Temple, rather than
the *restoration* expected with the coming of the Son of David.

That the disciples manage to break out of a more narrowly
nationalistic and particularistic concept of Jesus' person,
actions and words is not apparent in the gospel. For them, Jesus
is always Ραββει, Διδάσκαλος, or at most Χριστός in the Υἱὸς Δαυειδ
sense. He never, for them appears in any other than a Jewish
garb, despite the Transfiguration. Never is there in Mark a
recognition and confession by the disciples that Jesus is the
Son of God. It remains for a Roman soldier, a Gentile, to
recognize this. For Mark and his community, the term Χριστός
has become synonymous with Jesus himself. As with the term among
Christians today, it is part of his proper name (cf. 1.1; 9.41).
It is a term, moreover, that for Mark has to be qualified by both
the Son of God and Son of Man titles (cf.14.62) to avoid the
danger of its being narrowly interpreted in a Jewish Messianic
Son of David sense.

For Wrede's thesis, then, this section of the gospel is in
many respects damaging. The Secrecy motif is indeed present, but
the christological tendency that is here at work appears,
conversely, to be investing essentially Messianic material with
a non-Messianic or rather a transformed Messianic view of Jesus.
The Secrecy motif, rather than presenting Jesus as the *concealed*
Jewish *Messiah* (a strange ambiguity), serves to present him as
the concealed *Son of God*, in terms that harmonize well with a

Gentile or Hellenistic Jewish perspective. The distinction
between these two terms is not, of course, always clear, but
unless it is to some extent made, the contradictions in the
Markan presentation in these chapters are difficult to reconcile.
In short, Mark appears to be here incorporating and reinterpreting
Messianic material concerning the life of Jesus, which Bultmann,
as we have seen, acknowledges to be Palestinian in origin. By
being connected with Mark's treatment of the disciples, is it
possible that it goes back to the Urgemeinde?

NOTES

/1/   An English translation by J.C.G. Greig entitled *The Messianic
Secret* (LTT) was published in 1971. References throughout are to
the 1901 German edition.
/2/   *Messiasgeheimnis*, pp.46-51, 124-9. The senselessness of this
prohibition, if historical, appears most readily in the story of
the Raising of Jairus' daughter (cf. 5.43 and Wrede, pp.48-9).
/3/   *Op.cit.*, p.16.
/4/   Cf. 1.34,44; 3.11-12; 5.43; 7.36; 8.26,30; 9.9.
/5/   Cf. 4.10-12,33-34; 7.17 ff.
/6/   Cf. 4.10 ff.,34; 7.17 ff.; 8.14 ff.; 9.2 ff.,28-29,30 ff.;
10.10-12.
/7/   *Op.cit.*, pp.224-9.
/8/   "Ist die Messianität ursprünglich von der Auferstehung
datiert worden, so liegt der Gedanke sehr nahe, dass nun auch erst
der Glaube entstand, Jesus sei der Messias, und dass eben diese
Erkenntnis der Messiaswürde als der Inhalt der Erleuchtung
empfunden wurde" (*op.cit.*, p.235).
/9/   Mark had no knowledge, Wrede claims, of a time when Jesus
was acknowledged to be the Messiah, nor indeed had he in the
historical sense any interest in this question (*op.cit.*, p.115).
/10/   For a list of articles published on Wrede's thesis (up until
1961) see B.M. Metzger's *Index to Periodical Literature*, pp.139-40.
In particular, see F.C. Burkitt, *AJT*, 15 (1911), pp.175 ff. for the
reaction of a staunch defender of the gospel's historicity, and
A. Schweitzer's *Geschichte der Leben-Jesu-Forschung* (1913),
pp.368 ff. for that of a thoroughgoing eschatologist. For a
discussion and critique of Wrede and his subsequent influence, see
D.A. Aune, "The Problem of the Messianic Secret", *NovTest*, 11 (1969),
pp.1-31. Cf. also Weeden, *Mark*, pp.24-5, and Donahue, *Are You the
Christ?*, p.46, who in footnotes give further Bibliography. One
should also compare the more recent article by Professor C.F.D.

Moule, "On Defining the Messianic Secret in Mark", in *Jesus und Paulus,* Fs. W.G. Kümmel, pp.239-52. With especial relevance to the material in Mk.11.1 - 13.37 is T.A. Burkill's "Strain on the Secret: An Examination of Mark 11[1]-13[37]", *ZNW,* 51 (1960), pp.31-46.
/11/ The passage is seen by some as the conclusion of the fourth major section of the gospel (8.27 - 10.52), by others as the introduction to the fifth (10.46 - 13.37). Noting the parallel existing between 8.22-26 and 10.46-52 (two healing miracles in respect of blind men), N. Perrin regards each of these pericopes as "transitional giving-of-sight stories". "These stories," he declares, "enclose the fourth section of the gospel (8:27 - 10:45), in which Jesus attempts to lead his disciples to "sight" (i.e. understanding) and fails to do so. They are certainly used in ironic symbolism, and their function here is therefore quite different from the previous functions of miracle stories in the gospel" (*Introduction,* p.155; *vide supra,* p.84).
/12/ Υἱὸς Δαυειδ is here almost certainly a Messianic designation, king David of old being for the Jews a type of the Messiah. In popular expectation, the ben dāvīdh, or King Messiah (malkā meš̄īhā), would appear as a warrior-hero to wipe out Israel's enemies and once again to establish the nation's freedom and sovereignty. This Messiah, according to some Rabbis, would even be *named* David (cf. P.Ber.II.4, Schwab, p.42 = Ekah R.I.16.51, Sonc., p.138). See Jeremias, *Angelos,* 3 (1930), p.2; Burkill, *ZNW,* 51 (1960), p.33; *Meyer-Dickson,* I, p.177.
/13/ *Messiasgeheimnis,* pp.278-9.
/14/ W. Kelber, for example, thinks that it is not accidental that Bartimaeus addresses Jesus as Son of David *before* his eyes are opened. "The Son of David confession is made by a man *oculis captus*!" Approaching Jesus still *in statu erroris,* he goes on to greet Jesus as "Rabbi", a title clearly rejected by Mark, who takes care to introduce Jesus in this pericope as "the Nazarene" (10.47 cf. also 1.9,24; 14.67; 16.6 and *The Kingdom in Mark,* pp.94-5). See also Bowman, *Mark,* p.220.
/15/ The ὁδός motif recurs frequently in Mark but especially in the fourth section of the gospel (1.2,3; 8.3,27; 9.33,34; 10.17,32, 46,52; 11.8; 12.14). According to J. Schreiber (following Bultmann) the motif has theological overtones. The "road" that takes Jesus to Jerusalem is also his "Leidensweg", the "way" that leads the Son of Man (and all who follow him) to ultimate exaltation through suffering and death. Cf. Schreiber, "Die Christologie des Markusevangeliums", *ZThK,* 58 (1961), p.160.
/16/ Cf. Dowda, *Cleansing,* pp.188 ff.
/17/ For a detailed source-redactional analysis of this pericope, see Ambrozic, *Hidden Kingdom,* pp.32-45, and *vide supra,* p.47 and

especially n.39. The restraint here apparent is clearly visible
when we compare the more strongly christological nature of
Matthew's account. Matthew has the threefold Κύριε address to
Jesus in 20.29-34 while Mark merely has Ραββουνει (10.51). The
Messianic significance of the Entry and Cleansing is more sharply
accentuated both by the use of Messianic proof-texts in 21.5
(= Zech.9.9 Is.62.11) and 21.16 (= Ps.8.3 LXX - a psalm
interpreted Messianically in NT times; see Schniewind, *Matthäus*,
p.215) and by an even greater emphasis on the Son of David title
(cf. 21.9b,15-16), a designation that is elsewhere prominent in
Matthew (cf. e.g. 1.1; 9.27; 12.23; 15.22 and see McNeile,
Matthew, Introd., pp.xvii f.; Dowda, *Cleansing*, pp.288 ff.).
There is in Matthew, too, the heightened impression of a popular
enthusiasm for and participation in the event (cf.21.8,9,10,11,
14-16 and parallels), with Jesus' expulsion of the tradesmen and
miracles of healing implying a Messianic reconsecration of the
Temple (*supra,*p.83 and especially n.101).There is, too, in 21.10-11,
the specific raising by Matthew of the christological question
Τίς ἐστιν οὗτος;). By heightening the Messianic overtones of the
Markan account, however, Matthew may nevertheless be showing himself
more loyal to the original nature of these traditions, a point
observed in our earlier discussion of his redactional procedure
(*supra*, pp.71,91, n.85).
/18/ Cf. e.g. Gould, *Mark*, pp.205-6; J. Weiss, *Schriften*, I, p.176;
Montefiore, *Synoptic Gospels*, I, pp.263 ff.; Burkill, *ZNW*, 51 (1960),
pp.31-2.
/19/ *Messiasgeheimnis*, p.40.
/20/ *Op.cit.*, p.237.
/21/ The Matthean parallel is more explicit. In place of Mk.11.10a,
Matthew has the crowds exclaim, "Hosanna to the *Son of David*" (21.9b),
a fact that led Hilgenfeld to conclude that the second evangelist
was in 11.10a actively seeking to *avoid* the use of this title (see
Meyer-Dickson, I, p.177; B. Weiss, *Marcusevangelium*, p.368).
/22/ Cf. 1.3; 11.9; 12.11,29,30,36; 13.20.
/23/ *Messiasgeheimnis*, pp.139-41.
/24/ Cf. 7.17 ff.,24; 8.26; 9.28-29,33 ff.; 10.10-12.
/25/ Cf. e.g. 1.29; 2.1,11,15, etc. (*vide supra*, p.106 and n.37).
/26/ If a contrast had been intended between Jesus' command and
the man's subsequent action, then we might have expected v.20 to
run: ὁ δὲ ἀπελθὼν ἤρξατο κηρύσσειν ... (cf.1.45) rather than
καὶ ἀπῆλθεν καὶ ἤρξατο κηρύσσειν ...
/27/ The verse is ambiguous. Most commentators take ὁ κύριος
to refer to Jesus, either as exalted Lord (so Plummer) or
simply as Master (so Gould, Menzies, Bartlet).   Some, however,

take it to mean the owner of the ass (so Taylor, Cranfield) or even God (Allen). The words "and will send (sends) him here again immediately" have also occasioned difficulty. Most commentators take them as a reassuring promise by Jesus and, therefore, as part of what the disciples are to say (so B. Weiss, Holtzmann, Bruce, Swete, Menzies, Plummer, Bartlet). Some, however, view them as a statement by Jesus about what the disciples are to expect, viz, the instant despatch of the ass on the part of either the owner (so Taylor, Cranfield) or the person challenging them (so Meyer, Merx; cf. Mt.21.3). Some of the Versions, it should be noted, appear to have taken αὐτοῦ with κύριος, to give the translation "*Its* Lord/ (owner) has need (of it)" (so, e.g. sy[s.c] eth arm and Ephraem; see Merx, *Markus und Lukas,* pp.130-1; Burkitt, *Evangelion da-Mepharreshe,* II, pp.121-3). The reference, in our opinion, is to Jesus throughout, since otherwise the implication would be that the ass was to be obtained under false pretences. It is sheer conjecture to assume, as Cranfield does, that this alleged owner was with Jesus at the time (*Mark,* p.350).
/28/ Cf. 8.5,28; 9.18; 10.4,37,39; 11.3,6; 12.7,16; 14.14; 16.7,8.
/29/ See Ambrozic, *Hidden Kingdom,* pp.32-3, and *supra,* pp.46, 87, n.33.
/30/ According to Vincent Taylor, this narrative (11.1-7,11) and that of 14.12-18a were each composed by Mark on the basis of tradition (*Mark,* pp.535-6). Ambrozic draws attention, however, to the unusual amount of familiar Markan vocabulary that is to be found in the first three verses of the pericope in particular (*ibid*).
      According to Loisy, the subsequent and elaborate detailing of the finding of the ass (11.4-6; contr. Mt.21.6) may serve to emphasize the point that what the Lord says comes true (*Marc,* p.317). This emphasis certainly adheres to the fig-tree story (11.14,20) and may also underlie the reference to the removal of the Temple Mount (11.22-23; 13.2). There may be a certain warrant, therefore, for Bird's suggestion that the exhortation to the Christian disciple in 11.23 "to believe that what *he* is saying (ὃ λαλεῖ), happens" is in fact an exhortation "to believe that what *the Lord* says, comes to pass" (*JTS*(NS), 4 (1953), p.178, italics mine).
/31/ In an article discussing the interrelationship of the Synoptic and Thomas versions of this parable, J.A.T. Robinson draws attention to the fact that while Matthew's version reveals the highest degree of allegorization, Mark shows the greatest christological development in his description of the person of the son in 12.6. The owner of the vineyard, having sent his servants is said "still" to have had "one" (ὅτι ἕνα εἶχεν), "an only-beloved son" (υἱὸν ἀγαπητόν) whom he sent "at the last"

(ἔσχατον - a word with possible theological overtones). In this
one particular verse, Robinson exclaims, Mark's version appears
to be the *most* allegorical and Matthew's the least (*NTS*, 21 (1974-5),
pp.443-61, esp. pp.447,451,454). The addition of the word ἀγαπητόν
to his Vorlage, therefore, is a clear reflection of Mark's
christological emphasis.

/32/ It is this, perhaps, that explains the otherwise abrupt and
apparently adventitious reference to John's baptism in the
Vollmachtsfrage pericope (*vide supra*, p.43 and n.20). At the
redactional level, this reference may invite Mark's readers to
think back to John's baptism of Jesus in 1.9-11 at which a voice
"from heaven" (ἐκ τῶν οὐρανῶν) had declared Jesus to be *the Son of
God*. If John's act of baptism had a heavenly authority, if it was
indeed "from heaven" (ἐξ οὐρανοῦ 11.30), then why had the Jewish
authorities not believed 'him' (Διὰ τί ... οὐκ ἐπιστεύσατε αὐτῷ
11.31, viz, John's witness to Jesus, 1.7-8) or perhaps 'it' (viz,
John's act of baptism in which a Bath Qôl had revealed Jesus' true
identity)?

/33/ Cf. S. Schulz, "Markus und das Alte Testament", *ZThK*, 58
(1961), p.186.

/34/ *Vide supra*, p.56.

/35/ Cf. 1.24,34; 3.11; 4.11,34; 5.7; 8.31 ff.; 9.7,9 ff., 30-32;
10.32-34.

/36/ Cf. 4.13,40-41; 6.52; 7.18; 8.14-21,33; 9.10,32.

/37/ *Supra*, pp.81-2.

/38/ Cf. 9.38; 10.13-14.

/39/ Cf. 4.40-41; 6.50-51; 9.6,32; 10.32; 14.50.

/40/ Cf. 4.40; 9.19; 11.22.

/41/ Cf. 9.18,19,23.

/42/ Cf. 14.10-11,20-21,27-31,37-42,43-50,54,66-72. Mark's
presentation of the disciples' conduct in chapter 14 should be
compared with what Jesus says to the crowd in 8.34 - 9.1.

/43/ Cf. 9.33-37; 10.28-31,35-45.

/44/ Cf. 8.31; 9.9,31; 10.34; 14.28.

/45/ *Messiasgeheimnis*, pp.106-7.

/46/ Cf.8.31-33; 9.33-37; 10.35-45.

/47/ See J.B. Tyson, "The Blindness of the Disciples in Mark",
JBL 80 (1961), pp.261-8; Schreiber, *ZThK*, 58 (1961), pp.154-83;
Schulz, *ZThK*, 58 (1961), pp.184-97. While also supporting the
contention of these scholars that Mark is engaged in a polemic
against the disciples, T.J. Weeden presents the case that Mark's
presentation is a dramatization of what was for him a fundamental
conflict of christology in the early church. For the second
evangelist, the disciples are the representatives of a theios-aner
christology which has no place for a Messiahship that is authenti-

cated by suffering and death (see *Mark - Traditions in Conflict*, esp. pp.23-69).

/48/ *Op.cit.*, pp.264-5.

/49/ Cf. 4.10 ff.,34; 7.17 ff.; 8.14 ff.; 9.2 ff.,28-29,30 ff.; 10.10-12.

/50/ The abrupt appearance of this crowd, moreover, is commented upon by J. Weiss. Within the context of Mark's narrative, it seems, he remarks, to have suddenly "sprouted out of the ground" (*Ält.Evang.*, p.267).

/51/ Mark's intention in the Cleansing scene, however, is apparently to concentrate attention solely upon the action of Jesus, a point made by Taylor (*Mark*, p.457; cf. also J. Weiss, *ibid.*). No specific indication is given that the disciples participated in this dramatic act of his.

/52/ Cf. Lohmeyer, "Ebenso ist der Schlusssatz seltsam: es hörten's die Jünger. Denn es kommt nicht darauf an, dass die Jünger die Worte Jesu akustisch verstanden, sondern dass sie über das Gehörte nachsannen" (*Markus,* p.234).

/53/ Cf. 4.3,9,12,15 ff.,23,24,33; 6.11; 7.14; 8.18; 9.7; 12.29, 37.

/54/ Cf. 2 Kgs.18.4 ff.; 22.3 - 23.25   2 Chr.29.12 ff.; 34.3 ff. Neh.13.4-9.

/55/ Cf. Ez.22.8,26; 23.37-39; 37.26-28; 40 - 48   Tb.14.5-6 Jub.1.28-29 Enoch 90.28-29 Sib.Or.5.414-33 Ps.Sol.17.33.

/56/ See Dowda, *Cleansing*, pp.237-9, and *supra*, p.92, n.101.

/57/ *Supra*, p.232.

/58/ See G.W. Buchanan, "Mark 11.15-19: Brigands in the Temple", *HUCA*, 30 (1959), pp.169-77.

/59/ A similar procedure, it should be remarked, is in evidence in Mark's Trial narrative, where Jesus is charged with seeking to destroy the Temple (14.56-59). Luke, as we have seen (*supra*, pp.232-3), chose, in his gospel, to omit any reference to such a charge. In this passage, according to J.R. Donahue, Mark has taken over an apologetic tradition which had used select Old Testament texts to affirm the innocence of Jesus before false and lying witnesses. He has modified this tradition of "falseness" to "not in agreement" and has inserted into this context a saying of Jesus. This Temple saying (14.58) is a twofold one, the combination by Mark of two traditions, one attributing to Jesus "a threat or prophetic saying against the temple (13:2)", the other "an early Christian theologoumenon of those groups who viewed themselves as the nucleus of the new *naos.*" "The combined saying," he declares, "pictures Jesus in opposition to the Jerusalem temple and as founder of the new community" (*Are You the Christ?*, pp.135-6). Donahue's thesis is valuable, for it

traces in the remaining chapters of the gospel the anti-Temple
theme which we have claimed to discern in chapter eleven (*op.cit.*,
pp.113 ff.). For further discussion on 14.58 see, for example,
Dowda, *Cleansing*, pp.266 ff.; S.G.F. Brandon, *The Fall of Jerusalem
and the Christian Church*, pp.38 ff.; Trocmé, *Formation*, pp.85 (and
esp. fn.55),178-9; Gaston, *No Stone*, pp.65 ff.

270

BIBLIOGRAPHY

A. PRIMARY SOURCES, TEXTS AND TRANSLATIONS

Aland, K. *Synopsis Quattuor Evangeliorum*. 8th edn. Stuttgart: Württembergische Bibelanstalt, 1973.
Aland, K./Black, M./Metzger, B.M./Wikgren, A. (eds.). *The Greek New Testament*. London: United Bible Societies, 1966.
Bover, J.M. *Novi Testamenti Biblia Graeca et Latina*. 4th edn. Madrid: Talleres Gráficos Montaña, 1959.
Braude, W.G.(transl.). *Pesikta Rabbati* (YJS, XVIII). New Haven/London: Yale University Press, 1968.
Budge, E.A.W.(ed.). *The Book of the Bee* (AO, Sem.Ser.1.II). Oxford: Clarendon Press, 1886.
Burkitt, F.C. *Evangelion da-Mepharreshe*. Cambridge: University Press, 1904. 2 Vols.
Charles, R.H. *The Apocrypha and Pseudepigrapha of the Old Testament*. Oxford: Clarendon Press, 1913. 2 Vols.
The Book of Enoch. Oxford: Clarendon Press, 1912.
Danby, H.(transl.). *The Mishnah*. Oxford: Clarendon Press, 1933.
Epstein, I.(ed.). *The Babylonian Talmud*. Hebrew-English edn., in selected tractates. London: The Soncino Press, 1960-74.
The Babylonian Talmud. English transl. edn. 34 Vols. and Index Vol.(J. Slotki, 1952). London: The Soncino Press, 1935-48.
Fiebig, P.(ed.). *Rabbinische Wundergeschichten des neutestamentlichen Zeitalters* (KlT, 78). Bonn: A. Marcus and E. Weber, 1911.
Freedman, H./Simon, M.(eds.). *Midrash Rabbah*. London: Soncino Press, 1939. 9 Vols. and Index Vol.(J. Slotki).
Friedlander, G.(transl.). *Pirḳê de Rabbi Eliezer*. London: Kegan Paul, Trench, Trubner & Co., Ltd., 1916.
Ginzberg, L. *The Legends of the Jews*. Transl. H. Szold, P. Radin, 6 Vols. and Index Vol.(B. Cohen). Philadelphia: The Jewish Publication Society of America, 1911-38.
Goldin, J.(transl.). *The Fathers according to Rabbi Nathan* (YJS, X). New Haven: Yale University Press, 1955.
Goldschmidt, L. *Der babylonische Talmud*. Hebrew-German edn. Berlin: S. Calvary & Co., 1897-1935. 9 Vols.
Gollancz, H.(transl.). *The Targum to 'The Song of Songs'* (et al.). London: Luzac & Co., 1908.
Guillaumont, A., et al.(eds.). *The Gospel according to Thomas*. Leiden: E.J. Brill; London: Collins, 1959.
Harvey, W.W.(ed.). *Sancti Irenaei*. Cambridge: University Press, 1857. 2 Vols.

Hennecke, E.   *New Testament Apocrypha*.   Ed. W. Schneemelcher.
    Transl. R. McL. Wilson.   London: Lutterworth Press, 1963/1965.
    2 Vols.
Hippolytus.   *Philosophumena*.   Transl. F. Legge (TCL, Ser. 1).
    London: SPCK, 1921.   2 Vols.
Josephus.   *Vita*.   *Contra Apionem*.   *Antiquitates Judaicae*.   *Bellum
    Judaicum* (Loeb Classical Library; Greek-English transl. H. St.J.
    Thackeray et al.).   London: W. Heinemann, Ltd., 1926-65.
    9 Vols.
Kautzsch, E.   *Die Apokryphen und Pseudepigraphen des Alten
    Testaments*.   Tübingen: J.C.B. Mohr, 1900.   2 Vols.
Kittel, R.(ed.).   *Biblia Hebraica*.   3rd edn., ed. P. Kahle, A. Alt,
    O. Eissfeldt et al.   Stuttgart: Priv.Württ. Bibelanstalt,
    1929-37.
Legg, S.C.E.   *Novum Testamentum Graece*.   Oxford: Clarendon Press,
    1935 *(Marcum)*, 1940 *(Matthaeum)*.
Malan, S.C.(transl. ed.).   *The Book of Adam and Eve*.   London:
    Williams and Norgate, 1882.
Merk, A.   *Novum Testamentum Graece et Latine*.   7th edn. Rome:
    Pontifical Biblical Institute, 1951.
Nestle, Eberhard.   *Novum Testamentum Graece*.   25th edn., ed. E.
    Nestle, K. Aland.   London: United Bible Societies, 1967.
Nestle, Erwin/Kilpatrick, G.D.   *H KAINH ΔIAΘHKH*.   2nd edn., ed.
    E. Nestle, G.D. Kilpatrick.   London: The British and Foreign
    Bible Society, 1958.
Neubauer, A.(ed.).   *Medieval Jewish Chronicles* (AO, Sem.Ser.1.IV).
    Oxford: Clarendon Press, 1887.
Pliny.   *Historia Naturalis*.   Latin-English transl. H. Rackham,
    W.H.S. Jones (Loeb Classical Library, 10 Vols.).   London:
    W. Heinemann, Ltd., 1961-8.
Rahlfs, A.(ed.).   *Septuaginta*.   Stuttgart: Priv. Württ. Bibelanstalt,
    1935.   2 Vols.
    Septuaginta. Psalmi cum Odis (SSG, Vol.10).   Göttingen:
    Vandenhoeck & Ruprecht, 1931.
Riessler, P.   *Altjüdisches Schrifttum ausserhalb der Bibel*.   2nd
    edn. Heidelberg: F.H. Kerle Verlag, 1966.
Roberts, A./Rambaut, W.H.(transl.).   *Irenaeus. Adversus Haereses*
    (ANL, V, IX; ed. A. Roberts, J. Donaldson).   Edinburgh:
    T. & T. Clark, 1868-9.
Rousseau, A.(ed.).   *Irénée de Lyon. Contre les Hérésies. Livre V*
    (SC, 152-3).   Édition critique. Paris: Les Éditions du Cerf,
    1969.   2 Vols.
Ryle, E./James, M.R.(transl.).   *The Psalms of Solomon*.   Cambridge:
    University Press, 1891.

Schwab, M.   *Le Talmud de Jérusalem*.   French transl. edn. 11 Vols.
    and Index Vol.   Paris: J. Maisonneuve, 1871-90.
Soden, H. Freiherr von.   *Die Schriften des Neuen Testaments*. Pt.I,
    Untersuchungen.   Berlin: A. Duncker; A. Glaue, 1902-1910.
    Pt.II, *Text mit Apparat*.   Göttingen: Vandenhoeck & Ruprecht,
    1913.
Souter, A.   *Novum Testamentum Graece*.   2nd edn. Oxford: Clarendon
    Press, 1947.
Sperber, A.   *The Bible in Aramaic*.   Leiden: E.J. Brill, 1959-62.
    4 Vols.
Tischendorf, C. von.   *Novum Testamentum Graece*.   8th edn. 3 Vols.
    (Vol. III, Prolegomena, ed. C.R. Gregory).   Leipzig: Giesecke
    & Devrient/J.C. Hinrichs, 1869-94.
Vogels, H.J.   *Novum Testamentum Graece*.   2nd edn. Düsseldorf:
    L. Schwann, 1922.
Weiss, B.   *Die vier Evangelien im berichtigten Text*.   Leipzig:
    J.C. Hinrichs, 1900.
Westcott, B.F./Hort, F.J.A.   *The New Testament in the original
    Greek*.   Cambridge: Macmillan and Co., 1881.   2 Vols.
Whiston, W.(transl.).   *The Work of Flavius Josephus*.   London:
    Simms and McIntyre, 1852.
Ziegler, J.(ed.).   *Septuaginta. Duodecim Prophetae. Isaias.
    Ieremias. Ezechiel* (SLG, Vols.13-16).   Göttingen: Vandenhoeck
    & Ruprecht, 1939-57.

B.   INTRODUCTIONS, COMMENTARIES AND SPECIAL STUDIES

Allen, W.C.   *The Gospel according to Saint Mark* (OCBC).   London:
    Rivingtons, 1915.
    *A Critical and Exegetical Commentary on the Gospel according to
    S. Matthew* (ICC).   Edinburgh: T. & T. Clark, 1907.
Ambrozic, A.M.   *The Hidden Kingdom. A Redaction-Critical Study of
    the References to the Kingdom of God in Mark's Gospel* (CBQMS,
    2).   Washington: Heffernan Press, Inc., 1972.
Arndt, W.F./Gingrich, F.W.   *A Greek-English Lexicon of the New
    Testament*.   Chicago: Univ. of Chicago Press, 1957.
Aune, D.E.   "The Problem of the Messianic Secret", *NovTest*, 11
    (1969), pp.1-31.
Bacon, B.W.   *Dictionary of Christ and the Gospels* (ed. J. Hastings).
    Vol.1, 'Fig-Tree' ad loc. Edinburgh: T. & T. Clark, 1906.
Barclay, W.   *The First Three Gospels*.   London: SCM Press, Ltd.,
    1966.
Barrett, C.K.   *The Gospel according to St. John*.   London: SPCK,
    1970.

"The House of Prayer and the Den of Thieves" in *Jesus und Paulus*, Fs. W.G. Kümmel, ed. E.E. Ellis, E. Grässer, pp.13-20. Göttingen: Vandenhoeck & Ruprecht, 1975.

Bartlet, J.V.   *St. Mark* (The Century Bible). Edinburgh: T.C. & E.C. Jack, Ltd., 1922.

Bartsch, H.-W.   "Die „Verfluchung" des Feigenbaums", *ZNW*, 53 (1962), pp.256-60.

"Early Christian Eschatology in the Synoptic Gospels", *NTS*, 11 (1964-5), pp.387-97.

Beck, N.A.   *Efficacious Symbolic Acts of Jesus Christ during his Public Ministry* (Dissertation for Princeton University, 1967. Supervisor: B.M. Metzger).

Benzinger, I.G.A.   *Realencyclopädie für protestantische Theologie und Kirche*, 3rd edn., ed. J.J. Herzog, A. Hauck, Vol. VI, 'Fruchtbäume in Palästina' ad loc. Leipzig: J.C. Hinrichs, 1899.

Berlin, M.(ed.).   *Encyclopedia Talmudica* (transl. ed. I.Epstein, H. Freedman). Jerusalem: Talmudic Encyclopedia Publ., Ltd., 1969.

Best, E.   "Mark's Preservation of the Tradition" in *L'Évangile selon Marc. Tradition et rédaction* (BETL, 34), ed. M. Sabbe, pp.21-34. Leuven: University Press, 1974.

Beyer, K.   *Semitische Syntax im Neuen Testament* (SUNT, 1). Göttingen: Vandenhoeck & Ruprecht, 1962.

Bird, C.H.   "Some γαρ Clauses in St. Mark's Gospel",*JTS*(NS), 4 (1953), pp.171-87.

Birdsall, J.N.   "The Withering of the Fig-Tree", *ET*, 73 (1961-2), p.191.

Black, M.   *An Aramaic Approach to the Gospels and Acts*. 3rd edn. Oxford: Clarendon Press, 1967.

Blass, F./Debrunner, A.   *A Greek Grammar of the New Testament and Other Early Christian Literature*. Transl. ed. R.W. Funk (from 9/10th German edn.). Cambridge: University Press, 1961.

Blunt, A.W.F.   *The Gospel according to Saint Mark* (Clarendon Bible). Oxford: Clarendon Press, 1929.

Boehmer, J.   "The Cursing of the Fig-Tree", *ET*, 21 (1909-10), pp.328-9.

Boismard, M.-É.   "Influences matthéennes sur l'ultime rédaction de l'évangile de Marc" in *L'Évangile selon Marc. Tradition et rédaction* (BETL, 34), ed. M. Sabbe, pp.93-101. Leuven: University Press, 1974.

Bornkamm, G./Barth, G./Held, H.J.   *Tradition and Interpretation in Matthew*. Transl. P. Scott. London: SCM Press, Ltd., 1963.

Bornkamm, G.   "Matthäus als Interpret der Herrenworte", *THLZ*, 79 (1954), pp.341-6.

Bowker, J.   *The Targums and Rabbinic Literature*.   Cambridge:
    University Press, 1969.
Bowman, J.   *The Gospel of Mark. The New Christian Jewish
    Passover Haggadah* (SPB, 8). Leiden: E.J. Brill, 1965.
Box, G.H.   *St. Matthew* (The Century Bible).   Edinburgh: T.C. &
    E.C. Jack, Ltd., 1922.
Bradley, W.P.   "The 'Cursing' of the Fig Tree", *LCQ,* 9 (1936),
    pp.184-96.
Brandon, S.G.F.   *The Fall of Jerusalem and the Christian Church*.
    2nd edn. London: SPCK, 1957.
Branscomb, B.H.   *The Gospel of Mark* (Moffatt). London: Hodder
    and Stoughton, 1937.
Bruce, A.B.   *The Synoptic Gospels (ExpGT, I)*. London: Hodder
    and Stoughton, 1897.
Brun, L.   *Segen und Fluch im Urchristentum* (SNVAO, l). Oslo:
    l 'Kommisjon Hos Jacob Dybwad, 1933.
Buchanan, G.W.   "Mark 11.15-19: Brigands in the Temple", *HUCA,*
    30 (1959), pp.169-77.
Buchheit, V.   "Feigensymbolik im antiken Epigramm", *RheinMus,*
    103 (1960), pp.200-29.
Bultmann, R.   *Die Geschichte der synoptischen Tradition*.   5th
    edn. Göttingen: Vandenhoeck & Ruprecht, 1961.
    The History of the Synoptic Tradition.   2nd edn., transl.
    J. Marsh (from 2nd German edn., 1931, with corrections and
    additions from the 1962 Supplement). Oxford: Basil Blackwell,
    1972.
    The Gospel of John.. Transl. G.R. Beasley-Murray (from
    German edn., 1964, with 1966 supp.). Oxford: Basil Blackwell,
    1971.
Burkill, T.A.   "Strain on the Secret: An Examination of Mark 11[1]-
    13[37]", *ZNW,* 51 (1960), pp.31-46.
Burkitt, F.C.   "The historical character of the Gospel of Mark",
    AJT, 15 (1911), pp.169-93.
Butler, B.C.   *The Originality of St. Matthew*. Cambridge:
    University Press, 1951.
Carpenter, J.E.   *The First Three Gospels. Their Origin and
    Relations*. 3rd edn. London: Philip Green, 1904.
Carrington, P.   *The Primitive Christian Calendar*. Cambridge:
    University Press, 1952.
    According to Mark. Cambridge: University Press, 1960.
Chapman, J.   *Matthew, Mark and Luke*. Ed. J.M.T. Barton. London:
    Longmans, Green and Co., 1937.
Charles, P.   "Non enim erat tempus ficorum (Marc, 11, 13.)",
    NRTh, 61 (1934), pp.514-6.

Cheyne, T.K.(ed.). *Encyclopaedia Biblica*. London: Adam and
    Charles Black, 1899-1903. 4 Vols.
    Encyclopaedia Biblica, Vol.I, 'Bethphage' ad loc. London:
    Adam and Charles Black, 1899.
    Encyclopaedia Biblica, Vol.II, 'Fig Tree' ad loc. London:
    Adam and Charles Black, 1901.
    Encyclopaedia Biblica, Vol.III, 'Nathanael' ad loc. London:
    Adam and Charles Black, 1902.
Clarke, W.K. Lowther. *Concise Bible Commentary*. London: SPCK,
    1952.
Cohon, S.S. "The place of Jesus in the religious life of his
    day", *JBL,* 48 (1929), pp.82-108.
Cook, A.B. "ΣΥΚΟΦΑΝΤΗΣ", *CR,* 21 (1907), pp.133-6.
Cousin, H. "Le figuier désséché. Un exemple de l'actualisation
    de la geste évangélique" in *Foi et Vie* (Cahiers Bibliques -
    special edn., May, 1971), Fs. S. de Dietrich, ed. J. Ellul,
    pp.82-93. Paris: Foi et Vie, 1971.
Cranfield, C.E.B. *The Gospel according to Saint Mark* (CGTC).
    Cambridge: University Press, 1959.
Creed, J.M. *The Gospel according to St. Luke*. London:
    Macmillan and Co., Ltd., 1930.
Crowfoot, G.M./Baldensperger, L. *From Cedar to Hyssop*. London:
    The Sheldon Press, 1932.
Dähnhardt, O.(ed.). *Natursagen*. Leipzig/Berlin: B.G. Teubner,
    1907-10. 3 Vols.
Dalman, G. *Arbeit und Sitte in Palästina* (BFChTh). Gütersloh:
    C. Bertelsmann, 1928-42. 7 Vols.
    Sacred Sites and Ways. Transl. P.P. Levertoff (from 3rd
    German edn.). London: SPCK, 1935.
    "Under the Fig-tree", *ET*, 32 (1920-1), pp.252-3.
Daube, D. *The Sudden in the Scriptures*. Leiden: E.J. Brill,
    1964.
Delling, G. *Theological Dictionary of the New Testament*
    (ed. G. Kittel; transl. ed. G.W. Bromiley), Vol.3, καιρός
    ad loc. Grand Rapids, Mich.: W.B. Eerdmans, 1965.
Derrett, J.D.M. "Figtrees in the New Testament", *HeythJ*, 14
    (1973), pp.249-65.
Dibelius, M. *Die Formgeschichte des Evangeliums*. 5th edn.,
    ed. G. Bornkamm. Tübingen: J.C.B. Mohr, 1966.
    The Message of Jesus (ILCK). Transl. F.C. Grant. London:
    Nicholson and Watson, 1939.
Dobschütz, E. von. "Zur Erzählerkunst des Markus", *ZNW*, 27 (1928),
    pp.193-8.
Dodd, C.H. *According to the Scriptures*. London: Nisbet & Co.,
    Ltd., 1952.

276

The Parables of the Kingdom. London: Nisbet & Co., Ltd., 1935.

Doeve, J.W. "Purification du Temple et dessèchement du figuier", *NTS*, 1 (1954-5), pp.297-308.

Donahue, J.R. *Are You the Christ? The Trial Narrative in the Gospel of Mark* (Dissertation for the University of Chicago, 1972. Supervisor: N. Perrin. Publ. SBL Diss.Ser. 10, 1973).

Dowda, R.E. *The Cleansing of the Temple in the Synoptic Gospels* (Dissertation for Duke University, 1972. Supervisor: W.D. Davies).

Dupont, J. "La parabole du figuier qui bourgeonne", *RB*, 75 (1968), pp.526-48.

Edersheim, A. *The Life and Times of Jesus the Messiah*. 3rd edn. London: Longmans, Green and Co., 1886.

Eisler, R. *Orphisch-dionysische Mysteriengedanken in christlichen Antike* (VBW, II.2). Berlin: B.G. Teubner, 1925.
The Messiah Jesus and John the Baptist. Transl. ed. A.H. Krappe. London: Methuen & Co., Ltd., 1931.

Enslin, M.S. *Christian Beginnings*. New York: Harper & Row, 1956. Pts. I, II, III in 2 Vols.

Farmer, W.R. *Maccabees, Zealots and Josephus*. New York: Columbia University Press, 1956.
The Synoptic Problem. New York: The Macmillan Company, 1964.

Fawcett, T. *Hebrew Myth and Christian Gospel*. London: SCM Press Ltd., 1973.

Feliks, J. *Encyclopaedia Judaica* (ed. C. Roth, G. Wigoder), Vol.6, 'Fig' ad loc. Jerusalem: Keter Publishing House, 1971.

Filson, F.V. *The Gospel according to St. Matthew* (Black). 2nd edn. London: Adam & Charles Black, 1971.

Foerster, W. *Theological Dictionary of the New Testament* (ed. G. Friedrich; transl. ed. G.W. Bromiley), Vol.5, ὄρος ad loc. Grand Rapids, Mich.: W.B. Eerdmans, 1967.

Frazer, J.G. *The Golden Bough*. London: Macmillan and Co., Ltd., 1911-15. 12 Vols.

Fuller, R.H. *A Critical Introduction to the New Testament*. London: G. Duckworth & Co., Ltd., 1966.

Gaston, L. *No Stone on Another. Studies in the Significance of the Fall of Jerusalem in the Synoptic Gospels* (NovTSup, XXIII). Leiden: E.J. Brill, 1970.

Gautier, L. *Dictionary of Christ and the Gospels* (ed. J. Hastings), Vol.1, 'Bethphage' ad loc. Edinburgh: T. & T. Clark, 1906.

Geldenhuys, N. *Commentary on the Gospel of Luke* (NLC). London: Marshall, Morgan & Scott, 1971.

Giesen, H. "Der verdorrte Feigenbaum - Eine symbolische Aussage?", *BZ*, 20 (1976), pp.95-111.

Goguel, M. *L'Évangile de Marc* (BEHE, 22). Paris: Ernest Leroux, 1909.

The Life of Jesus. Transl. O. Wyon (from 1st edn., 1932).
London: George Allen & Unwin Ltd., 1933.
Goldmann, F.   *La Figue en Palestine à l'époque de la Mischna*.
Paris: La Librairie Durlacher, 1911.
Goodenough, E.R.   *Jewish Symbols in the Greco-Roman Period* (BS,
XXXVII). New York: Bollingen Foundation, 1958.   13 vols.
Goudoever, J. van. *Biblical Calendars*. Leiden: E.J. Brill, 1961.
Gould, E.P.   *The Gospel according to St. Mark* (ICC). Edinburgh:
T. & T. Clark, 1896.
Goulder, M.D.   *Midrash and Lection in Matthew*. London: SPCK, 1974.
"The Composition of the Lord's Prayer", *JTS*(NS), 14 (1963),
pp.32-45.
Grant, F.C.   *The Interpreter's Dictionary of the Bible* (ed.
G.A. Buttrick), 'Matthew, Gospel of' ad loc. New York:
Abingdon Press, 1962.
Grant, R.M.   "The Coming of the Kingdom", *JBL*, 67 (1948), pp.
297-303.
Gray, J.   *I & II Kings* (OTL). 2nd edn. London: SCM Press Ltd.,
1970.
Green, F.W.   *The Gospel according to Saint Matthew* (Clarendon
Bible). Oxford: Clarendon Press, 1936.
Grundmann, W.   *Das Evangelium nach Markus* (ThHK, 2). 2nd edn.
(1st edn., F. Hauck). Berlin: Evangelische Verlagsanstalt,
1959,
Das Evangelium nach Matthäus (ThHK, 1). Berlin: Evangelische
Verlagsanstalt, 1968.
Das Evangelium nach Lukas (ThHK, 3). 2nd edn. (1st edn.,
F. Hauck). Berlin: Evangelische Verlagsanstalt, 1964.
Gundry, R.H.   *The Use of the Old Testament in St. Matthew's
Gospel* (NovTSup, XVIII). Leiden: E.J. Brill, 1967.
Guy, H.A.   *The Gospel of Matthew*. London: Macmillan and Co., Ltd.,
1971.
Haenchen, E.   *Der Weg Jesu*. Berlin: Alfred Töpelmann, 1966.
Hamburger, J.(ed.).   *Real-Encyclopädie des Judentums*, Vol.I,
'Feige' ad loc. Leipzig: K.F. Koehler, 1896. 3 Vols.
Harnack, A.   *The Sayings of Jesus* (CThL, XXIII). Transl.
J.R. Wilkinson. London: Williams & Norgate, 1908.
Hasselt, F.J.F.   "De vijgeboom, waaraan Jezus „niets dan bladeren"
vond", *NThS*, 8 (1925), pp.225-7.
Hastings, J.(ed.).   *Dictionary of the Bible*. Edinburgh: T. & T.
Clark, 1898-1904. 5 Vols.
Dictionary of Christ and the Gospels. Edinburgh: T. & T.
Clark, 1906-8. 2 Vols.
Hatch, W.H.P.   "The Cursing of the Fig Tree", *JPOS*, 3 (1923),
pp.6-12.

278

Hauck, F. *Das Evangelium des Markus* (ThHK). Leipzig: A. Deichert, 1931.
Theological Dictionary of the New Testament (ed. G. Friedrich; transl. ed. G.W. Bromiley), Vol.5, παραβολή ad loc. Grand Rapids, Mich.: W.B. Eerdmans, 1967.

Helmbold, H. *Vorsynoptische Evangelien*. Stuttgart: Ehrenfried Klotz Verlag, 1953.

Hiers, R.H. "Not the Season for Figs", *JBL*, 87 (1968), pp.394-400.

Hirsch, E. *Frühgeschichte des Evangeliums. I. Das Werden des Markusevangeliums* (1940), 1951². *II. Die Vorlagen des Lukas und das Sondergut des Matthäus*, 1941. Tübingen: J.C.B. Mohr, 1940-1, 1951.
Das vierte Evangelium. Tübingen: J.C.B. Mohr, 1936.

Hirsch, S. "Die Verfluchung des Feigenbaumes", *NThT*, 27 (1938), pp.140-51.

Holtzmann, H.J. *Die Synoptiker* (HC, Vol.I). Freiburg i.B.: J.C.B. Mohr, 1889.

Hunter, A.M. *The Gospel according to Saint Mark* (Torch). London: SCM Press, Ltd., 1948.

Hunzinger, C.-H. *Theological Dictionary of the New Testament* (ed. G. Friedrich; transl. ed. G.W. Bromiley), Vol.7, συκῆ ad loc. Grand Rapids, Mich.: W.B. Eerdmans, 1971.

Jeremias, A. *The Old Testament in the light of the Ancient East* (ThTL, XXVIII). Transl. C.L. Beaumont (from German 2nd edn.). Ed. C.H.W. Johns. London: Williams & Norgate, 1911.

Jeremias, J. *Jesus als Weltvollender* (BFChTh, 33). Gütersloh: C. Bertelsmann, 1930.
The Parables of Jesus. 3rd edn. Transl. from German 8th edn., 1970, but based on that of S.H. Hooke from 6th edn., 1962, with revisions. London: SCM Press Ltd., 1972.
The Eucharistic Words of Jesus (NTL). Transl. N. Perrin (from 3rd edn., 1960, with author's revisions to July, 1964). London: SCM Press Ltd., 1966.
"Die Berufung des Nathanael (Jo 1, 45-51)", *Angelos*, 3 (1930), pp.2-5.

Johnson, S.E. *The Gospel according to St. Mark* (Black). 2nd edn. London: Adam & Charles Black, 1972.

Jülicher, A. *Die Gleichnisreden Jesu*. 2nd edn. Tübingen: J.C.B. Mohr, 1910.

Kahn, J.G. "La parabole du figuier stérile et les arbres récalcitrants de la Genèse", *NovTest*, 13 (1971), pp.38-45.

Kee, H.C. "The Function of Scriptural Quotations and Allusions in Mark 11 - 16" in *Jesus und Paulus*, Fs. W.G. Kümmel, ed. E.E. Ellis, E. Grässer, pp.165-88. Göttingen: Vandenhoeck & Ruprecht, 1975.

Kelber, W.H.   *The Kingdom in Mark. A New Place and a New Time.*
    Philadelphia: Fortress Press, 1974.
Kilpatrick, G.D.   *The Origins of the Gospel according to St.
    Matthew.* Oxford: Clarendon Press, 1946.
Kittel, G.(ed.).   *Theological Dictionary of the New Testament* (ed.
    G. Kittel, G. Friedrich; transl. ed. G.W. Bromiley).
    Grand Rapids, Mich.: W.B. Eerdmans, 1964-74.   9 Vols.
Klein, S.   "Weinstock, Feigenbaum und Sykomore in Palästina" in
    Festschrift. Adolf Schwarz (ed. S. Krauss), pp.389-402.
    Berlin and Vienna: R. Löwit, 1917.
Klostermann, E.   *Das Markusevangelium* (HNT, 3).   4th edn. Tübingen:
    J.C.B. Mohr, 1950.
    Das Matthäusevangelium (HNT, 4).   2nd edn. Tübingen:
    J.C.B. Mohr, 1927.
    Das Lukasevangelium (HNT, 5).   2nd edn. Tübingen:
    J.C.B. Mohr, 1929.
Knox, W.L.   *Some Hellenistic Elements in Primitive Christianity.*
    London: British Academy, 1944.
    The Sources of the Synoptic Gospels. Cambridge: University
    Press, 1953, 1957.   2 Vols.
Kolatch, A.J.   *Who's Who in the Talmud.* New York: Jonathan David,
    1964.
Kraeling, E.G./Macalister, R.A.S.   *Dictionary of the Bible* (2nd
    edn., ed. F.C. Grant, H.H. Rowley), 'Bethphage' ad loc.
    Edinburgh: T. & T. Clark, 1963.
Kuhn, H.-W.   *Ältere Sammlungen im Markusevangelium* (SUNT, 8;
    ed. K.G. Kuhn).   Göttingen: Vandenhoeck & Ruprecht, 1971.
Kümmel, W.G. *Introduction to the New Testament* (NTL). Transl.
    A.J. Mattill, Jr. (from 14th edn.).   London: SCM Press Ltd.,
    1966.
    *The New Testament. The History of the Investigation of Its
    Problems.*   Transl. S. McLean Gilmour, H.C. Kee.   London:
    SCM Press, Ltd., 1973.
    Jesus und Paulus. Fs. W.G. Kümmel.   Ed. E.E. Ellis, E. Grässer.
    Göttingen: Vandenhoeck & Ruprecht, 1975.
Lagrange, M.-J.   *Évangile selon Saint Marc* (EBib).   5th edn.
    Paris: J. Gabalda et Fils, 1929.
    Évangile selon Saint Matthieu (EBib). 2nd edn. Paris:
    J. Gabalda, 1923.
    Évangile selon Saint Luc (EBib).   2nd edn. Paris: J. Gabalda,
    1921.
Lewis, H.D./Slater, R.L.   *World Religions.* London: C.A. Watts &
    Co. Ltd., 1966.
Liddell, H.G./Scott, R.   *Greek-English Lexicon.*   Revised edn.
    (ed. H.S. Jones). Oxford: Clarendon Press, 1968.

Lightfoot, J. *Horae Hebraicae et Talmudicae*. Ed. R. Gandell. Oxford: University Press, 1859 (first published 1658-78). 4 Vols.

Lightfoot, R.H. *History and Interpretation in the Gospels*. London: Hodder and Stoughton, 1934.
The Gospel Message of St. Mark. Oxford: Clarendon, 1950.

Lindars, B. *New Testament Apologetic*. London: SCM Press Ltd., 1961.

Lohmeyer, E. *Das Evangelium des Markus* (MeyerK). Repr. 10th edn., 1937. Göttingen: Vandenhoeck & Ruprecht, 1957.
Das Evangelium des Matthäus (MeyerK). 3rd edn. Ed. W. Schmauch. Göttingen: Vandenhoeck & Ruprecht, 1962.
Lord of the Temple. Transl. S. Todd. Edinburgh: Oliver and Boyd, 1961.
"Von Baum und Frucht", *ZSTh*, 9 (1932), pp.377-97.

Loisy, A. *Les Évangiles Synoptiques*. Ceffonds,près Montier-en-der (Haute-Marne): chez l'auteur, 1907-8. 2 Vols.
L'Évangile selon Marc. Paris: Émile Nourry, 1912.

Löw, I. *Die Flora der Juden* (VAKMF, Vols.2,3,4,6). Leipzig/Wien: R. Löwit Verlag, 1924-34.
Aramaeische Pflanzennamen. Leipzig: Wilhelm Engelmann, 1881.

Maccoby, H. *Revolution in Judaea: Jesus and the Jewish Resistance*. London: Ocean Books Ltd., 1973.

McConnell, R.S. *Law and Prophecy in Matthew's Gospel* (Dissertation submitted to the Theological Faculty of the University of Basel, 1964. Publ. ThD, II, ed. Bo Reicke). Basel: Friedrich Reinhardt, 1969.

McNeile, A.H. *The Gospel according to St. Matthew*. London: Macmillan and Co., Ltd., 1915.

Manson, T.W. *The Sayings of Jesus*. London: SCM Press, Ltd., 1949.
"The Cleansing of the Temple", *BJRL*, 33 (1950-1), pp.271-82.

Manson, W. *The Gospel of Luke* (Moffatt). London: Hodder and Stoughton, 1930.

Marxsen, W. *Introduction to the New Testament*. Transl. G. Buswell. Oxford: Blackwell, 1968.
Mark the Evangelist. Transl. J. Boyce et al. Nashville: Abingdon Press, 1969.

Maurer, C. *Theological Dictionary of the New Testament* (ed. G. Friedrich; transl. ed. G.W. Bromiley), Vol.7, σκεῦος ad loc. Grand Rapids, Mich.: W.B. Eerdmans, 1971.

Menzies, A. *The Earliest Gospel*. London: Macmillan and Co., Ltd., 1901.

Merx, A. *Die vier kanonischen Evangelien*. Berlin: G. Reimer, 1897.
Die Evangelien des Markus und Lukas. Berlin: G. Reimer, 1905.

Das Evangelium Matthaeus. Berlin: G. Reimer, 1902.

Metzger, B.M. *Index to Periodical Literature on Christ and the Gospels* (NTTS, VI). Leiden: E.J. Brill, 1966.

Meyer, E. *Ursprung und Anfänge des Christentums*. Stuttgart and Berlin: J.G. Cotta, 1921-3. 3 Vols.

Meyer, H.A.W. *Die Evangelien des Markus und Lukas* (MeyerK, 8th edn.; ed. B. Weiss, J. Weiss). 1st Div., Pt.2. Göttingen: Vandenhoeck & Ruprecht, 1892.
The Gospels of Mark and Luke (MeyerK, transl. R.E. Wallis, ed. W.P. Dickson, fr. 5th edn.). Edinburgh: T. & T. Clark, 1880. Vols. I & II.

Michaels, J.R. "Nathanael Under the Fig Tree", *ET,* 78 (1966-7), pp.182-3.

Micklem, P.A. *St. Matthew* (Westminster). London: Methuen & Co., Ltd., 1917.

Montefiore, C.G. *The Synoptic Gospels*. 2nd edn. London: Macmillan and Co., Ltd., 1927. 2 Vols.

Moule, C.F.D. *An Idiom Book of New Testament Greek*. 2nd edn. Cambridge: University Press, 1959.
"A Note on 'Under the Fig Tree' in John I.48,50", *JTS* (NS), 5 (1954), pp.210-1.
"On Defining the Messianic Secret in Mark", in *Jesus und Paulus,* Fs. W.G. Kümmel, ed. E.E. Ellis, E. Grässer, pp.239-52. Göttingen: Vandenhoeck & Ruprecht, 1975.

Moulton, J.H. *A Grammar of New Testament Greek*. 3 Vols. (Vol. II, ed. W.F. Howard; Vol. III, ed. N. Turner). Edinburgh: T. & T. Clark, 1906-63.

Münderlein, G. "Die Verfluchung des Feigenbaumes (Mk.XI.12-14)", *NTS,* 10 (1963-4), pp.89-104.

Murr, J. *Die Pflanzenwelt in der griechischen Mythologie*. Innsbruck: Wagnersche Univ.-Buchhandlung, 1890.

Nestle, E. *Philologica Sacra*. Berlin: Reuther & Reichard, 1896.
"Zwei Varianten in der Gadarener-Geschichte", *ThStKr,* 3 (1896), pp.323-4.
"Etymologische Legenden?", *ZWTh* , 5 (1897), pp.148-9.

Neubauer, A. *La Géographie du Talmud*. Paris: Michel Levy Frères, 1868.

Nineham, D.E. *The Gospel of St. Mark* (PGC). 2nd edn. London: Adam & Charles Black, 1968.

Noth, M. *The Old Testament World*. Transl. V.I. Gruhn (from 4th German edn., 1964). London: Adam & Charles Black, 1966.

Olck, F. *Real-Encyclopädie der classischen Altertumswissenschaft,* ed. A. Pauly, G. Wissowa, Vol. VI, 'Feige' ad loc. Stuttgart: J. B. Metzler, 1909.

O'Neill, J.C. "The Synoptic Problem", *NTS,* 21 (1974-5), pp. 273-85.

282

Pallis, A.   *Notes on St. Mark and St. Matthew*. 2nd edn. London:
    Humphrey Milford, 1932.
Pearson, E.O.   "Matthew xvii.20", *ET*, 25 (1913-14), p.378.
Peloni, A.   "Faith as a grain of mustard seed", *Exp* (2nd Ser.), 8
    (1884), pp.207-15.
Perrin, N.   *The New Testament. An Introduction*. New York:
    Harcourt Brace Jovanovich, Inc., 1974.
Perrot, N.   *Les Représentations de l'Arbre Sacré sur les Monuments
    de Mésopotamie et d'Élam* (Babyloniaca, 17; ed. Ch. Virolleaud).
    Paris: Paul Geuthner, 1937.
Plummer, A.   *The Gospel according to St. Mark* (CBSC). Cambridge:
    University Press, 1915.
    *An Exegetical Commentary on the Gospel according to St.
    Matthew*. 2nd edn. London: James Clarke & Co. Ltd., 1961.
    The Gospel according to S. Luke (ICC). Edinburgh: T. & T.
    Clark, 1896.
Post, G.E.   *Dictionary of the Bible* (ed. J. Hastings), Vol.2, 'Figs'
    ad loc. Edinburgh: T. & T. Clark, 1899.
Rawlinson, A.E.J.   *St. Mark* (Westminster). London: Methuen & Co.,
    Ltd., 1925.
Reichmann, V.   *Reallexikon für Antike und Christentum,* ed. T.
    Klauser, Vol.7, 'Feige' ad loc. Stuttgart: Anton Hiersemann,
    1969.
Rengstorf, K.H.   *Das Evangelium nach Lukas* (NTD, 3). 6th edn.
    Göttingen: Vandenhoeck & Ruprecht, 1952.
Riehm, E.C.A.   *Handwörterbuch des biblischen Altertums,* Vol.I,
    'Feigenbaum' ad loc. Leipzig: Velhagen & Klasing, 1893.
Roberts, J.E.   "The Parable of the Vine. Its place in the Fourth
    Gospel", *ET*, 32 (1920-1), pp.73-5.
Robertson, A.T.   *A Grammar of the Greek New Testament in the light
    of historical Research*. 3rd edn. New York: Hodder & Stoughton,
    1919.
Robin, A. de Q.   "The Cursing of the Fig Tree in Mark XI. A
    Hypothesis", *NTS*, 8 (1961-2), pp.276-81.
Robinson, J.A.T.   "The Parable of the Wicked Husbandmen: A Test
    of Synoptic Relationships", *NTS*, 21 (1974-5), pp.443-61.
Robinson, T.H.   *The Gospel of Matthew* (Moffatt). London:
    Hodder & Stoughton, 1928.
Roth, C.   "The Cleansing of the Temple and Zechariah xiv 21",
    NovTest, 4 (1960), pp.174-81.
Roth, C./Wigoder, G.(eds.).   *Encyclopaedia Judaica*. Jerusalem:
    Keter Publishing House, 1971. 16 Vols.
Sabbe, M.(ed.).   *L'Évangile selon Marc. Tradition et rédaction*
    (BETL, 34). Leuven: University Press, 1974.
Sahlin, H.   *Studien zum dritten Kapitel des Lukasevangeliums*
    (UUÅ 1949:2). Uppsala: A.-B. Lundequistska Bokhandeln, 1949.

Sande Bakhuyzen, W.H. van de. "De vervloeking van den vijgenboom",
   NThT, 7 (1918), pp.330-8.
Schaeffer, C.F.A. *The Cuneiform Texts of Ras Shamra-Ugarit*.
   London: The British Academy, 1939.
Schalit, A. *Encyclopaedia Judaica* (ed. C. Roth, G. Wigoder),
   Vol.6, 'Dionysus, Cult of' ad loc. Jerusalem: Keter
   Publishing House, 1971.
Schlatter, A. *Der Evangelist Matthäus*. Stuttgart: Calwer
   Vereinsbuchhandlung, 1929.
Schmid, J. *Das Evangelium nach Markus* (RNT, 2). Regensburg:
   Friedrich Pustet, 1963.
   Matthäus und Lukas (BSt, 23). Freiburg i.B.: Herder & Co.
   G.M.B.H., 1930.
   Das Evangelium nach Lukas (RNT, 3). 4th edn. Regensburg:
   Friedrich Pustet, 1960.
Schmidt, K.L. *Der Rahmen der Geschichte Jesu*. Berlin: Trowitzsch
   & Sohn, 1919.
Schneider, J. *Theological Dictionary of the New Testament* (ed.
   G. Friedrich; transl. ed. G.W. Bromiley), Vol.5, ξύλον
   ad loc. Grand Rapids, Mich.: W.B. Eerdmans, 1967.
Schniewind, J. *Das Evangelium nach Markus* (NTD, 1). 7th edn.
   Göttingen: Vandenhoeck & Ruprecht, 1956.
   Das Evangelium nach Matthäus (NTD, 2). 8th edn. Göttingen:
   Vandenhoeck & Ruprecht, 1956.
Schrage, W. *Das Verhältnis des Thomas-Evangeliums zur
   synoptischen Tradition und zu den koptischen Evangelienüberset-
   zungen* (BZNW, 29). Berlin: Alfred Töpelmann, 1964.
Schreiber, J. "Die Christologie des Markusevangeliums", *ZThK*, 58
   (1961), pp.154-83.
Schulz, S. "Markus und das Alte Testament", *ZThK*, 58 (1961),
   pp.184-97.
Schürmann, H. "Die Symbolhandlungen Jesu als eschatologische
   Erfüllungszeichen. Eine Rückfrage nach dem historischen
   Jesu", *BiLeb*, 11 (1970), pp.29-41, 73-8.
Schwartz, E. "Der verfluchte Feigenbaum", *ZNW*, 5 (1904), pp.80-4.
Schweitzer, A. *Geschichte der Leben-Jesu-Forschung*. 2nd edn.
   Tübingen: J.C.B. Mohr, 1913.
Schweizer, E. *The Good News according to Mark*. Transl. D.H.
   Madvig. London: SPCK, 1971.
   "Anmerkungen zur Theologie des Markus" in *Neotestamentica et
   Patristica* (NovTSup, VI), Fs. O. Cullmann, pp.35-46. Leiden:
   E.J. Brill, 1962.
Simon, D.W. "Faith as a grain of mustard seed", *Exp*, 9 (1879),
   pp.307-16.
Smith, C.W.F. "No Time for Figs", *JBL*, 79 (1960), pp.315-27.

284

Smith, W. Robertson. *The Old Testament in the Jewish Church*. Edinburgh: Adam and Charles Black, 1881.
Lectures on the Religion of the Semites. Edinburgh: Adam and Charles Black, 1889.

Solms-Laubach, H. Graf zu. *Die Herkunft, Domestication und Verbreitung des gewöhnlichen Feigenbaums (Ficus Carica L.) (AKGW, 28)*. Göttingen: Dieterichsche Univ.-Buchdruckerei (W. Fr. Kaestner), 1882.

Stendahl, K. *The School of St. Matthew* (ASNU, XX). Uppsala: C.W.K. Gleerup, 1954.

Strack, H.L./Billerbeck, P. *Kommentar zum Neuen Testament aus Talmud und Midrasch*. München: C.H. Beck, 1922-28. 4 Vols. and 2 later Index Vols. (ed. J. Jeremias, 1956, 1961).

Strecker, G. *Der Weg der Gerechtigkeit* (FRLANT, 82). Göttingen: Vandenhoeck & Ruprecht, 1962.
"The Concept of History in Matthew", *JAAR*, 35 (1967), pp.219-30.

Streeter, B.H. *The Four Gospels. A Study of Origins*. London: Macmillan and Co., Ltd., 1936.

Sundwall, J. *Die Zusammensetzung des Markusevangeliums* (AAA, Humaniora IX:2). Åbo: Åbo Akademi, 1934.

Swete, H.B. *The Gospel according to St. Mark*. 2nd edn. London: Macmillan and Co., Ltd., 1902.

Taylor, V. *The Gospel according to St. Mark*. 2nd edn. London: Macmillan, 1966.

Thiel, R. *Drei Markus-Evangelien* (AKG, 26). Berlin: Walter de Gruyter & Co., 1938.

Tonkin, S. "The Withered Fig-Tree", *ET*, 34 (1922-3), pp.323-6.

Traub, H. *Theological Dictionary of the New Testament* (ed. G. Friedrich, transl. ed. G.W. Bromiley), Vol.5, οὐρανός ad loc. Grand Rapids, Mich.: W.B. Eerdmans, 1967.

Trench, R.C. *Notes on the Miracles of Our Lord*. Repr. 1st edn., 1846. London: Pickering & Inglis Ltd., 1958.

Trilling, W. *The Gospel according to St. Matthew* (NTSR). Transl. K. Smyth. London: Burns & Oates, 1962. 2 Vols.

Trocmé, E. *La Formation de l'Évangile selon Marc* (EHPR, 57). Paris: Presses Universitaires de France, 1963.

Turner, C.H. "The Gospel according to St. Mark" in *A New Commentary on Holy Scripture* (ed. C. Gore, H.L. Goudge, A. Guillaume). London: SPCK, 1929.
"Marcan Usage", *JTS*, 25 (1923-4), pp.377-86; 26 (1924-5), pp.12-20, 145-56, 225-40; 27 (1925-6), pp.58-62; 28 (1926-7), pp.9-30, 349-62; 29 (1927-8), pp.275-89, 346-61.

Tyson, J.B. "The Blindness of the Disciples in Mark", *JBL*, 80 (1961), pp.261-8.

Violet, B.   "Die „Verfluchung" des Feigenbaums" in ΕΥΧΑΡΙΣΤΗΡΙΟΝ
    (FRLANT, 19), Fs. H. Gunkel, ed. H. Schmidt, pp.135-40.
    Göttingen: Vandenhoeck & Ruprecht, 1923.
Weeden, T.J.   *Mark - Traditions in Conflict*. Philadelphia:
    Fortress Press, 1971.
Weiss, B.   *Das Marcusevangelium und seine synoptischen Parallelen*.
    Berlin: Wilhelm Hertz, 1872.
    Das Matthäusevangelium und seine Lucas-Parallelen. Halle: Verl-
    ag der Buchhandlung des Waisenhauses, 1876.
Weiss, J.   *Das älteste Evangelium*.   Göttingen: Vandenhoeck &
    Ruprecht, 1903.
    Die Schriften des Neuen Testaments (ed. W. Bousset, W.
    Heitmüller). Vol. I. 3rd edn. Göttingen: Vandenhoeck &
    Ruprecht, 1917-20. 4 Vols.
Wellhausen, J.   *Das Evangelium Marci*. Berlin: Georg Reimer, 1903
    (1st edn.), 1909 (2nd edn.).
    Das Evangelium Matthaei. Berlin: Georg Reimer, 1904.
    Das Evangelium Lucae. Berlin: Georg Reimer, 1904.
Wendling, E.   *Ur-Marcus*. Tübingen: J.C.B. Mohr, 1905.
    Die Entstehung des Marcus-Evangeliums. Tübingen: J.C.B. Mohr,
    1908.
Wenham, J.W.   *The Goodness of God*. London: Inter-Varsity Press,
    1974.
    "The Fig Tree in the Old Testament", *JTS*(NS), 5 (1954),
    pp.206-7.
Wensinck, A.J.   *Tree and Bird as cosmological symbols in Western
    Asia* (VAA, XXII). Amsterdam: Johannes Müller, 1921.
Werblowsky, R.J.Z./Wigoder, G.(eds.).   *The Encyclopedia of the
    Jewish Religion*. London: Phoenix House, 1967.
Williams, C.S.C.   *Alterations to the Text of the Synoptic Gospels
    and Acts*. Oxford: Blackwell, 1951.
Winer, G.B.   *Biblisches Realwoerterbuch*, Vol. I, 'Feigenbaum' ad
    loc. 3rd edn. Leipzig: C.H. Reclam sen., 1847.
Wohlenberg, G.   *Das Evangelium des Markus* (KNT). Leipzig:
    A. Deichert, 1910.
Wolff, H.W.   *Dodekapropheton. 1. Hosea* (BK, XIV.1). Neukirchen:
    Verlag der Buchhandlung des Erziehungsvereins, 1961.
Wood, H.G.   "Mark" in Peake's *Commentary on the Bible* (ed. A.S.
    Peake, A.J. Grieve). London: T.C. & E.C. Jack, Ltd., 1919.
Wrede, W.   *Das Messiasgeheimnis in den Evangelien*. Göttingen:
    Vandenhoeck & Ruprecht, 1901.
    The Messianic Secret (LTT). Transl. J.C.G. Greig. Cambridge/
    London: James Clarke & Co., Ltd., 1971.
Zahn, T.   *Einleitung in das Neue Testament*. 2nd edn. Leipzig:
    A. Deichert, 1900. 2 Vols.

286

Introduction to the New Testament. Transl. J.M. Trout et al.
(fr. 3rd edn.). Ed. M.W. Jacobus. Edinburgh: T. & T. Clark,
1909. 3 Vols.
Das Evangelium des Matthäus (KNT, 1). Leipzig: A. Deichert,
1903.
Zerwick, M. *Untersuchungen zum Markus-Stil*. Rome: Pontifical
Bible Institute, 1937.

A. INDEX OF ANCIENT AUTHORS AND SOURCES

The figures in brackets indicate notes.

I. OLD TESTAMENT

288

I. OLD TESTAMENT

I. OLD TESTAMENT

I. OLD TESTAMENT

I. OLD TESTAMENT

I. OLD TESTAMENT

II. OLD TESTAMENT APOCRYPHA AND PSEUDEPIGRAPHA

II. APOCRYPHA & PSEUDEPIGRAPHA

4 Ezra		Psalms of Solomon		Apocalypse of Moses (Book/ Life of Adam and Eve)	
7.123	203(71)	11.4	116		
8.52	19,203(71)	11.5,7	170(66)	20	190,202(70)
		14.1-3	137	22	190
		17.33	268(55)	28.2-4	203(71)

III. NEW TESTAMENT

Matthew		Matthew		Matthew	
1.1	265(17)	6.14	53,54	9.18	88(50,51)
2.6	173(118)	6.15	50,53,54	9.21	89(58)
2.15	172(109)	6.25	67(94)	9.22	87(33,38)
3.7-10	83	6.30	123(39)	9.27-31	88(41)
3.7	93(107)	7.7,8	50,54,56	9.27	265(17)
3.9	210	7.11	65(79)	9.29	88(41).
3.10	209-10,225,	7.16	212	9.34	93(107)
	241(18)	7.19	241(18)	9.35	87(39)
4.5	62(24)	7.21	65(78)	10.5-6	93(104)
4.23	87(39)	7.29	93(107)	10.19	65(65)
5.13	89(54,56)	8-9	72	10.32,33	65(79)
5.16	65(78)	8.3	91(81)	10.42	89(58)
5.17-18	93(104)	8.10	87(36)	11.2ff.	116
5.17	83	8.11	240(9)	11.5	92(101),171
5.20	93(107)	8.12	93(105)		(85,91),206,215
5.23-24	53,54,62	8.13	87(33,38)	11.27	89(54,56)
	(24),83,86	8.16	87(39)	11.29	171(75,91)
	(16)	8.19	88(50,51)	12.2	93(107)
5.28	68(120)	8.25	91(81)	12.3	85(15)
5.45	65(79)	8.26	92(94),123	12.4	77,89(54)
5.47	89(58)		(39)	12.5	85(15)
6.1	65(78)	8.27	87(36)	12.6	62(24),83
6.5,7	53,54	8.28-34	88(41)	12.7	172(104)
6.9	52,53,54,	8.33	77	12.14	93(107)
	65(79)	9.11	93(107)	12.15	87(39)
6.12	54	9.13	172(104)	12.23	265(17)
6.14-15	51,65(74)	9.14	91(81),93	12.24	89(54,55),93
			(107)		(107)

294

III. NEW TESTAMENT

295

III. NEW TESTAMENT

Matthew		Matthew		Mark	
21.19	74-8,86(24, 25),88(45), 178	23	93(105, 107)	1.11	256-7
21.20	74-5,78,86 (25)	23.3	93(104)	1.15	19,67(95), 211-2
21.21	54,chaps.3 & 4 *passim*, but esp.72, 76-9,81,86 (17,21,24, 25),95-104	23.16ff.	62(24)	1.16-17	159
		23.37-39	83	1.16,19, 20	62(36)
		24.1-2	83	1.21-28	88(41)
		24.29	173(125)	1.21-27	63(47,49)
		24.31	171(85), 172(94)	1.22	63(44,46), 124(45)
21.22	55,56,68 (117),74, 79-80,86(17, 24)	24.32-36	212,213, 214	1.24	264(14),267 (35)
		24.36	77	1.27	63(46), 124(45)
		24.42-51	224	1.28	63(46)
21.23	63(43),84(6), 91(81)	24.44	67(94)	1.29	122(37), 265(25)
		26.36	87(30)		
21.24	86(17)	26.61	83	1.31	62(36)
21.25	86(19,21)	26.67-68	91(81)	1.32	62(30), 124(45)
21.26	86(17),90 (72)	26.69	88(50,51)		
		26.71	87(30)	1.34	263(4), 267(35)
21.28-32	90(72)	27.14	87(36)		
21.34	211	27.25	83	1.35	7,55,62 (29,30, 36)
21.40-43	93(105)	27.47	87(30)		
21.41	90(72)	27.51	83	1.39,40	62(29)
21.42	85(15)	27.62	93(107)	1.44	263(4)
21.43	55,67(94), 72,83,241 (25)			1.45	62(35),68 (119),124 (45),255,265 (26)
		Mark			
21.45-46	93(107)	1.1	262		
21.45	86(19)	1.2	163,264 (15)	2.1	62(29,36,37), 122(37),265 (25)
21.46	72,86(19), 91(81)	1.3	264(15), 265(22)		
22.1-10	93(105)	1.6	174(143)	2.4	62(36),124 (45)
22.15	93(107)	1.7-8	267(32)		
22.22	87(36)	1.9-11	267(32)	2.5	67(96,107)
22.34-40	85(16)	1.9	264(14)	2.6	68(120)
22.46	84(5)				

III. NEW TESTAMENT

Mark		Mark		Mark	
2.8	67(107)		(106),124		(35),268
2.9ff.	92(101)		(45)		(49)
2.11	122(37),265	3.34	62(33),67	4.35-41	206
	(25)		(106)	4.35	62(30)
2.12	63(46),124	3.35	120(12)	4.36	124(45)
	(45)	4.1	62(35,37),	4.39-41	92(100)
2.13	62(29,37),		124(45)	4.40-41	92(93),267
	124(45)	4.3	67(106),268		(36,39)
2.14	62(36)		(53)	4.40	67(96),267
2.15	122(37),265	4.6	211		(40)
	(25)	4.8	206,211	4.41	63(46)
2.17	67(107)	4.9	92(100),268	5.1-20	88(41)
2.18ff.	106		(53)	5.1	62(29)
2.23ff.	198-9(31)	4.10-12	256,263(5,6),	5.7	267(35)
2.24	67(106)		268(49)	5.15	63(46)
2.25	198-9(31)	4.10	62(28)	5.17	124(45)
2.28	254,255	4.11	267(35)	5.19,20	254,255
3.1	62(29,37)	4.12-13	143-4	5.20	62(35),63
3.5	62(33),67	4.12	92(100),		(46),124(45)
	(107),144		146,268(53)	5.21-43	63(47,49)
3.6	63(46)	4.13	92(93,98),	5.21	62(37),124
3.8	62(24)		267(36)		(45)
3.9	124(45)	4.15ff.	268(53)	5.22	62(29)
3.11-12	263(4)	4.15,16	65(70)	5.24	124(45)
3.11	51,60(5),	4.17,22	68(119)	5.25-34	257
	267(35)	4.23,24	268(53)	5.27,30,	
3.16	67(104)	4.25	120(12)	31	124(45)
3.18	219	4.29	65(70),154,	5.32	62(33)
3.20	62(29,37),122		173(125),	5.33	63(46)
	(37),124(45)		211	5.34	67(96)
3.21-35	63(47,49)	4.30-32	101,102,	5.36	63(46),67
3.24	52		168(52),		(96)
3.25	52,120(3)		207	5.37	67(104),89
3.26	52,68(119)	4.31	65(70),99,		(56),90(74)
3.28	65(76),121		120(10)	5.38	122(37)
	(13)	4.32	65(70),140,	5.39,41	67(107)
3.29	65(76),68		157	5.42	63(46)
	(119),120(12)	4.33-34	256,263(5)	5.43	263(2,4)
3.31	65(73)	4.33	260(53)	6.1	62(29)
3.32	65(73),67	4.34	263(6),267	6.2ff.	124(45)

III. NEW TESTAMENT

Mark		Mark		Mark	
6.2	62(35),63 (46)	7.17	122(37),124 (45)	8.18	56,260,268 (53)
6.3-4	85(14)	7.18	92(98,100),	8.21	92(100)
6.4	122(37)		267(36)	8.22-26	75,84,88(41),
6.5	89(56)	7.19	68(119)		264(11)
6.6-31	63(47)	7.24	122(37),255,	8.22	62(29)
6.7	62(35)		265(24)	8.26	122(37),263
6.8-9	68(119)	7.28	254		(4),265(24)
6.8	89(56)	7.30	122(37)	8.27-28	85(14)
6.10	122(37)	7.31-		8.27	62(29),258,
6.11	268(53)	37	75,84		264(15)
6.13	206	7.31	62(37)	8.28	266(28)
6.14-16	85(14)	7.33	124(45)	8.29ff.	67(104)
6.14	55	7.36	255,263(4)	8.30	263(4)
6.20	63(44)	7.37	63(46),171	8.31ff.	267(35)
6.30-44	206,207		(91)	8.31-33	267(46)
6.34	62(35),124 (45),159,174 (143)	8.1- 10	206,207	8.31	62(35),63 (46),267(44)
6.35	62(30)	8.1	62(37),124 (45)	8.32	62(35)
6.45-52	206,257	8.2	124(45)	8.33	68(119),267 (36)
6.45	124(45)	8.3	122(37),264 (15)	8.34-9.1	267(42)
6.46	7			8.34	124(45)
6.47	62(30)	8.5	266(28)	8.35	120(12)
6.50-51	267(39)	8.6	124(45)	8.38	52,120(12)
6.50	63(44,46)	8.11	62(29)	9.1	19,53,90(68),
6.51-52	92(98)	8.12	19,120(4),		121(13),206
6.51	63(46)		121(13)	9.2ff.	67(104),263
6.52	68(119),92 (93,100),143, 267(36)	8.13	62(37)		(6),268(49)
		8.14ff.	259,263(6), 267(36),268 (49)	9.2-8	41,257
6.55	62(35)			9.2	62(30),89 (58)
7.5	68(119)	8.14	89(56)		
7.6-7	146,171(85)	8.17-		9.5	67(105,107),
7.14	62(37),92 (100),124(45) 268(53)	21	92(98),259		88(42),258
		8.17- 18	92(93),143, 144,147,159 171(75)	9.6	63(44,46), 92(93,98), 267(39)
7.15	68(119)			9.7	257,267(35), 268(53)
7.17ff.	259,263(5,6), 265(24),268 (49)	8.17	67(107),92 (100)	9.8	62(33),89 (58)

III. NEW TESTAMENT

III. NEW TESTAMENT

300

III. NEW TESTAMENT

Mark		Mark		Mark	
11.30	267(32)	12.40	122(37)		185,189,195,
11.31	67(95),267	12.41-44	72,235		200(45),212,
	(32)	12.41	124(45)		213-8
11.32	63(46),124	13.1-37	149,150,	13.28,29	65(70)
	(45),260		159,213-8	13.30	90(68),206
12.1-12	21,137,144,		*passim*,	13.31	174(152)
	211,227,		257	13.32	52,77
	256-7,262	13.1-2	39,83,217	13.33-37	224
12.1	62(35)	13.1	67(106)	13.33	212
12.2	171(83),	13.2	59,90(68),	13.34,35	122(37)
	211-2,233		119,152,233,	14.1-11	63(47)
12.6	266(31)		261,266(30),	14.1-2	63(46)
12.7	266(28)		268(59)	14.1	41,42,150
12.9	227	13.3	67(104)	14.2	63(44),
12.10-11	147,174	13.4	65(70),		124(45)
	(138)		217-8	14.3	122(37)
12.11	265(22)	13.5	62(35)	14.7	65(70)
12.12	63(44,46),	13.7	65(70),	14.10-11	63(46),267
	124(45),		217-8		(42)
	260	13.8	174(152),	14.10	258
12.14	264(15)		217-8	14.12ff.	39,63(39),
12.16	266(28)	13.9	52		266(30)
12.17	63(46)	13.11	65(70),	14.14	122(37),266
12.18	62(29)		217-8		(28)
12.24	55	13.12	152	14.17	62(30)
12.28	62(29)	13.14	52,65(70,	14.18	174(138)
12.29	265(22),		73),217-8	14.19	62(35)
	268(53)	13.15	122(37)	14.20-21	267(42)
12.30	265(22)	13.19	90(68),	14.24	174(143)
12.32-34	72,83		173(127)	14.25	90(68),207
12.33c	150	13.20	254,265	14.26	62(29)
12.34	63(46)		(22)	14.27-31	260,267(42)
12.35-37	254,255,257,	13.21	67(96,106)	14.27	174(143)
	262	13.24-25	147,154	14.28	267(44)
12.35	88(42),174,	13.24	173(125),	14.29ff.	67(104)
	(152)		174(152)	14.31	90(68)
12.36	174(138),	13.26-27	217-8	14.32	62(29)
	265(22)	13.27	147,174	14.33	62(35)
12.37	124(45),		(143,152)	14.36	52,53,174
	260,268(53)	13.28-32	11,12,160,		(152)

III. NEW TESTAMENT

Mark		Mark		Luke	
14.37-50	267(42)	15.29-30	232	6.44	212
14.38	53,55	15.29	39,59,174	7.22	171(85,91),
14.41,42	67(106)		(138)		206,215
14.43	124(45),	15.32	67(96)	9.37-43a	104-9
	258	15.34	174(138)	9.51-	
14.45	67(105),	15.35	52,67(106)	18.14	230
	258	15.36	174(138)	9.52-56	231
14.48	88(42)	15.38	39,83,119,	10.18,19	206
14.49	39,42		145	10.22	89(54)
14.50	174(143),	15.39	52,257	10.29-37	172(109)
	267(39)	15.42	62(30)	11.2	52,53
14.53-72	63(47)	15.43	62(24)	11.9,10	56
14.53	62(29)	15.44	63(46)	11.13	52
14.54	67(104),	16.6	67(106),	11.20	206,215
	267(42)		264(14)	11.29	89(54)
14.56-59	268(59)	16.7	67(104),	12.13-21	224
14.58	39,59,83,		266(28)	12.28	123(39)
	127(81),	16.8	63(44,46),	12.35-48	224
	172(108),		258,266	12.54-56	206,215,224
	232,249		(28)	12.57	214
	(136),269	16.18	206	13.1-9	16
	(59)			13.1-5	224,227-8,
14.62	262				246(90)
14.65	62(35),	Luke		13.6-9	11-14,38
	173(119)				(152),137,
14.66-72	67(104),	1.8ff.	232		166(19),168
	267(42)	1.9,21,22	232		(52),210,212,
14.67	264(14)	1.55	173(118)		224-38
14.69-70	52	2.27,37,		13.6	102,234
14.69,71	62(35)	39	232	13.7,9	241(18)
14.72	56,260	2.41ff.	62(24),	13.28	65(65)
15.4	67(106)		232	13.29	240(9)
15.5	63(46)	2.46	232	13.31-33	227,230
15.7	248(119)	3.8	210	13.32-33	172(108)
15.8	62(35),	3.9	209-10,	13.34-35	227,228,231
	124(45)		225,241(18)	13.35	249(130)
15.10	63(44)	4.9-13,		17.1-2	108,123(42)
15.11,15	124(45)	14ff.	232	17.3-4	108
15.18	62(35)	5.3,4	86(27)	17.5-6	chap.4
15.24	174(138)	6.34	65(67)		passim,230

III. NEW TESTAMENT

III. NEW TESTAMENT

Romans		1 Corinthians		1 Thessalonians	
5.15,16, 17,18,20	65(75)	15.4	150	1.8	68(116)
8.26	67(98)	15.52	171(85), 172(94)	3.8	52,65(67)
9-11	154	15.54-55	149	4.5	171(75)
9.4	245(57)	15.54	171(85),	4.16	171(85),172
9.6-8	210,219, 244(57)	16.13	172(92) 65(72)		(94)
9.20	173(126)				
9.25,26	172(101), 173(126)	2 Corinthians		2 Thessalonians	
9.27	173(126)			2.15	65(72)
9.33	146,171 (85),173 (126)	5.19 9.6ff. 10.17	65(75) 149 171(75)	1 Timothy	
10.11	146,171(85)	11.22	245(57)	5.11	65(65)
10.13	154,173 (125)				
11.1	245(57)	Galatians		Hebrews	
11.8	146,171 (85),173 (126)	1.15 5.1	171(75) 65(72)	6.1 6.7-8	68(116) 209
11.11,12	65(75)	6.1	65(75)	6.8	242(31)
11.16-24	240(13)			10.27	171(85), 172(93)
11.27	171(85), 173(126)	Ephesians		10.37	171(85)
14.8	65(67)			12.12	171(85)
		1.7	65(75)	13.15	172(109)
		2.1,5	65(75)		
1 Corinthians				James	
1.19	146,171 (85)	Philippians		1.5	56
1.31	171(75)	1.27	52	1.6	56,68(120)
3.5-17	209	4.1	65(72)	2.4	68(120)
7.5	122(31)			3.12	212
10.1-5	203(81)			5.16,17	55
13.2	95,96,102, 109,110,118, 124(49)	Colossians			
14.21	171(85)	2.13	65(75)		

III. NEW TESTAMENT

IV. RABBINIC AND OTHER JEWISH SOURCES

1. MISHNAH (ed. H. Danby)

IV. RABBINIC AND OTHER JEWISH SOURCES

2. BABYLONIAN TALMUD (ed. I. Epstein)

IV. RABBINIC AND OTHER JEWISH SOURCES

2. BABYLONIAN TALMUD (cont'd.)

Niddah		Sanhedrin		Shekalim	
47a-47b	183	24a	110-11	VI.3	204(89)
50a	197(22)	55a	170(63)		
		70a-70b	202(70)		
		90b	187	Soṭah	
Mo'ed Ḳaṭan		107a	200(42)		
				9b	112-3
17a	197(26)			47a	199(33)
		Shabbath			
Pe'ah		30b	193	Ta'anith	
		68a	197(22)		
I.4	197(22)	110a	201(55)	7a	203(71)
				24a	187-9,198(26)
				29a-30b	171(73)
Pesaḥim		Shebi'ith			
6b	197(26)	I.3	177	Yoma	
53a	177	IV.7	177		
87b	170(65)			21b	191-2
111b	169(58)			39b	204(85)
119b	203(71)			86b	177

3. PALESTINIAN (JERUSALEM) TALMUD (ed. M. Schwab)

Berakoth		Mo'ed Ḳaṭan		Ta'anith	
II.4	264(12)	III.1	113,114	IV.5	115
II.8	221-2				
IX.3	167(29)				
		Shebi'ith		Yoma	
Demai		IV.7	177	IV.4	204(85)
		V.1	196(5)		
I.1	198(26)				

IV. RABBINIC AND OTHER JEWISH SOURCES

4. MIDRASH RABBAH (ed. H. Freedman, M. Simon)

5. EXTRA-CANONICAL TRACTATES AND OTHER JEWISH SOURCES

IV. RABBINIC AND OTHER JEWISH SOURCES

5. EXTRA-CANONICAL TRACTATES AND OTHER JEWISH SOURCES (Cont'd.)

Sifre on Deuteronomy	Targums	Targums
317 126(74)	On Jb.2.11 204(87)	On Mi.7.1,2 180
	On Ct.2.13 182	On Mi.7.2,6 152

V. RABBIS CITED

Abba Areka (Rab)	126(63)	R. Johanan b. Nappaha	111,125
R. Abbahu	181		(58),181,
R. Abraham b. David	200(54)		184,185
R. Abraham b. Solomon	200(54)	R. Johanan b. Zakkai	125(59)
R. Akiba	115,125	R. Jose	192
	(54,56),	R. Jose b. Abin	201(57)
	199(35)	R. Jose (of Yokereth)	187-9,
R. Ashi	125(53),		201(57)
	201(57)	R. Jose b. Joezer	180,199
R. Assi II	113,126		(33)
	(64)	R. Jose b. Johanan	180,199
Baba b. Buta	112,126		(33)
	(62)	R. Jose b. Judah	198(26)
R. Eliezer b. Hyrcanus	113-4,118,	R. Joseph b. Hiya	
	125(59),	(Raba)	111,125
	187		(55,60)
R. Eliezer b. Jacob	192	R. Joshua b. Hananiah	125(56),
R. Gamaliel	125(59),		192
	169(61),	R. Judan	184
	193	Maimonides	247(109)
R. Hanina	177	Mari b. Mar	180
R. Hisda	180	R. Me'asha	183
R. Hiyya b. Abba	181,184,	R. Meir	95,110,
	187,199		125(54)
	(35)	R. Netanel	200-1
R. Hoshaya (Oshaia)	191,199		(54)
	(35)	R. Phinehas	189
R. Jeremiah b. Abba	168(46)	Raba b. Joseph b. Hama	111,125
			(55)

V. RABBIS CITED

Rabbah b. Nahmani	95,111, 125(55), 126(60, 61)	R. Simeon b. Gamaliel Simon II	111,125 (59), 192 125(59)
Rabina I	110,125 (53)	R. Simon b. Azzai	95,111, 125(56)
Rabina II (b. Huna)	110,125 (53)	R. Simon b. Laḳish	95,110, 111,125
R. Samuel b. Abba	112,126 (63)		(52,58), 197(26)
R. Samuel b. Nahman	113,126 (65)	R. Ulla b. Ishmael	110,125 (51)
Shammai	126(62)	R. Zadok	177

VI. CLASSICAL AND HELLENISTIC AUTHORS

Dioscorides   104

Josephus		Josephus		Josephus	
Antiquitates Judaicae		**Bellum Judaicum**		**Bellum Judaicum**	
VIII.136	204(85)	I.39	93(102)	519	27(8)
XIII.311-13	245(63)	78-80	245(63)	IV.622-9	245(69)
XIV.451	245(65)	328	245(65)	V.562	93(102)
XV.373-9	245(64)	II.60-5,			
XVII.41-3	245(67)	66-71	248(121)	**Contra Apionem**	
166	246(84)	112-3	245(66)		
213-8	248(121)	114-6	246(84)	II.103-9	93(102)
254-64	248(121)	159	245(62)	106	92(102)
345-8	245(66)	175-7	248(119)		
349-53	246(84)	261-3	244(50)	**Vita**	
XVIII.60-62	248(119)	321	93(102)		
85-7	248(119)	441-8	248(121)	87	248(121)
85	93(102)	III.351-4	245(68)		
XX.169-72	244(50)	399-408	245(69)		

VI. CLASSICAL AND HELLENISTIC AUTHORS

VII. CHURCH FATHERS

VIII. EXTRA-CANONICAL CHRISTIAN SOURCES

B. INDEX OF MODERN AUTHORS

The figures in brackets indicate notes.

Dähnhardt, O.   201(60)

Dalman, G.   1,3,17,159,165
(17,18),166(19),167(31),
168(45),169(58),196(12),
197(15),198(28),202(70),219,
241(18,30),242(31),245
(58,61,73)

Daube, D.   87(33,34,35)

Delling, G.   241(27)

Derrett, J.D.M.   23,24,27(10),
29(17),31(55),32(66),34
(93),37(133,134,141),126
(75),132,152,158,166(19),
167(39),171(70),186,196
(11),199(32,40),200(52),
201(63),214,222-3,240(8),
243(42),246(93),247(96,100,
106)

de Wette, W.M.L.   13,26(3)

Deyling, S.   26(4)

Dibelius, M.   1,41,43,61(20),
63(39),81,130

Dobschütz, E. von   15,48

Dodd, C.H.   21,68(121),129-30,
143,146,149,150,154,159,161,
171(79,87),172(107,108,109),
173(126),174(137,149)

Doeve, J.W.   21-22,24,71,132,
143,144

Donahue, J.R.   25,35(103),62
(35,37),67(102),127(79,81),
164(3,10,13),263(10),268-9
(59)

d'Outrein, J.   26(4)

Dowda, R.E.   15,33(86),35(102,
106),37(133,141,145),63(49),
68(121),85(8),91(85),167(35),
168(46),170(68),171(70),175

(161),204(88,89),232,244
(50),260-1,264(16),265(17),
269(59)

Dupont, J.   215-6,242(33,34),
243(36,37,42),244(47)

Edersheim, A.   4,27(7),30(37),
88(48),124(49),196(5,10,11),
197(22),199(38),227,247(105,
109)

Eisler, R.   167(30),248(119)

Enslin, M.S.   87(37)

Farmer, W.R.   68(111),71,85
(7,9),90(74),91(85),93(102),
203(82)

Fawcett, T.   168(44,46,54),169
(57),170(62,67),202-3(71),
204(84),240(13)

Feliks, J.   165(17)

Filson, F.V.   88(41)

Foerster, W.   170(63,67)

Frazer, J.G.   167(31)

Fuller, R.H.   85(15)

Gaston, L.   24,30(37),35(102,
106),63(49),68(121),93(102),
241(17),247(97),269(59)

Gautier, L.   197(16)

Geldenhuys, N.   247(101,102)

Giesen, H.   30(37),35(106),63(49),
144,174(141),212,235,241(22,
23,24)

Ginzberg, L.   126(74),196(7),198
(28),199(37,41),200(45),202

Schniewind, J. 1,11,14,19,
30(37),35(102),62(24),92
(101),159,265(17)

Schrage, W. 120(3),121(22),
127(78)

Schreiber, J. 25,41,259,264
(15)

Schulz, S. 165(15),259,267
(33)

Schürmann, H. 6,240(1,2)

Schwartz, E. 11,12,18,213,
214-5,216,242(34),243(35,
37)

Schweitzer, A. 1,10,18,19,
36(128),263(10)

Schweizer, E. 30(37),35(106),
63(49),101,171(82)

Simon, D.W. 121(15)

Slater, R.L. 200(45)

Smith, C.W.F. 12,14,15,22,24,
27(10),28(13),29(28),30(38),
35(102),235,236

Smith, W. Robertson 166(25),
169(57,60)

Soden, H. Freiherr von 66(89)

Solms-Laubach, H. Graf zu
165(17),166(21),197(25)

Stählin, G. 6

Stendahl, K. 164(11),172(104,
109),173(118,128)

Strack, H.L. *See* Billerbeck, P.

Strauss, D.F. 1,13,26(3)

Strecker, G. 61(12),66(88),
87(30,37),92(88,90)

Streeter, B.H. 101

Suhl, A. 165(15)

Sundwall, J. 43,61(20),67(92)

Swete, H.B. 1,7,9,28(14),29
(22,33),30(37),31(50),60(8),
66(89),67(99),88(42),89(62),
121(13),124(44,48),174(140),
266(27)

Taylor, V. 14,27(10),29(17,22,
28),30(42,43),31(56),33(88),
35(104,106),57,60(5),61(23),
62(25,28),67(92,102,108),68
(110,116,120),89(62),93(102),
101,124(47),266(27,30),268(51)

Thiel, R. 41,48

Tittmann, J.A.H. 26(5)

Tonkin, S. 7,8,9,30(38)

Toup, J. 26(5)

Traub, H. 65(77)

Trench, R.C. 1,4,5,26(4),29
(22,34),31(56),32(69),80,
202(70),241(21)

Trilling, W. 92(101)

Trocmé, E. 60(2),62(38),124
(45),244(49),249(127),269
(59)

Turner, C.H. 3,16,25,29(33),30
(36),32(69),60(5,8),62(35,37),
124(48)

Tyson, J.B. 259

Violet, B. 7-8,9,89(62)

Volz, P. 200(46)

Wassenbergh, E. 26(5)